SCHOOL OF
ORIENTAL AND AFRICAN STUDIES
UNIVERSITY OF LONDON

London Oriental Series
Volume 11

19TH CENTURY MALAYA

SIAM

PERLIS

KEDAH

Georgetown

PENANG

PROVINCE WELLESLEY

LARUT

DINDINGS

P. PANGKOR

Kota Bahru

KELANTAN

TRENGGANU

Kuala Trengganu

PERAK

S. Perak

Kuala Kangsar

S. Kiula

PAHANG

S. Bernam

SELANGOR

S. Pahang

Pahang

Pekan

Kuala Lumpur

S. Klang

Triang

NEGRI SEMBILAN

S. Landat

SUNGAI UJONG

REMBAU

LUKUT

Cape Rachado

MALACCA

Malacca

S. Muar

Muar

JOHORE

S. Endau

STRAIT

OF

MALACCA

Batu Pahat

S. Johore

Johore Bahru

SINGAPORE

RIAU

SUMATRA

ARCHIPELAGO

MILES

0   25   50   75   100

LONDON ORIENTAL SERIES · VOLUME 11

NINETEENTH–CENTURY MALAYA

THE ORIGINS OF BRITISH POLITICAL CONTROL

BY

C. D. COWAN

*Professor of the History of South East Asia
in the University of London*

LONDON
OXFORD UNIVERSITY PRESS
NEW YORK   TORONTO

Oxford University Press, Amen House, London E.C.4

GLASGOW NEW YORK TORONTO MELBOURNE WELLINGTON
BOMBAY CALCUTTA MADRAS KARACHI LAHORE DACCA
CAPE TOWN SALISBURY NAIROBI IBADAN ACCRA
KUALA LUMPUR HONG KONG

First Published 1961
Reprinted 1962

PRINTED IN GREAT BRITAIN

PREFACE

Most of the research upon which this book is based was originally undertaken in the preparation of a thesis presented for the degree of Doctor of Philosophy in the University of London in 1955. The publication has been made possible by a grant from the School of Oriental and African Studies, for which I wish here to express my thanks. I also wish to thank the Earl of Kimberley for permission to use material from the Kimberley Papers at Kimberley, and the Cabinet Office for allowing me to consult Cabinet Minutes in the Gladstone Papers at the British Museum. Like many other scholars I am much indebted to the constant helpfulness of the officials and staff of the Public Record Office, the India Office Library, the British Museum, and the Library of the School of Oriental and African Studies. Lastly I should like to acknowledge the advice, assistance and encouragement I have received at various stages of my studies from Professor G. S. Graham, Professor D. G. E. Hall, Professor C. H. Philips, and Sir R. O. Winstedt.

C. D. C.

School of Oriental and African Studies,   25th March 1960
University of London.

CONTENTS

CONTENTS

PRELUDE: THE BACKGROUND AND
SCOPE OF THE SUBJECT

Concern for the defence of India and of the China trade led the East India Company to establish settlements in the Straits of Malacca. During the first half of the nineteenth century it defeated Dutch and Siamese attempts to gain control over the southern portion of the Malayan Peninsula, and itself became the paramount power in the area. The East India Company refused to accept any responsibility for the internal affairs of the Peninsula, but in the second half of the century economic factors increased the interest of the Straits merchants in the Peninsular states, and their affairs became linked with those of the British settlements. The Colonial Office, which assumed control of the Straits Settlements in 1867, at first continued the Indian Government's policy of non-intervention. But in 1873 it reversed this policy, and several of the Malay States came under British control. This book investigates the circumstances which produced this change of policy, and explains the nature of subsequent events.

(i) The Establishment of the British Connexion with Malaya

Britain's territorial interest in Malaya dates from 1786, when the East India Company secured the island of Penang; off the west coast of the Peninsula. Malacca, taken from the Dutch during the Napoleonic Wars but returned in 1818, became British territory in 1825; and Singapore, the last of the three outposts known collectively as the Straits Settlements, was occupied in 1819. These footholds in Malaya brought Britain into conflict with Dutch and Siamese interests in the area, and in the end drew her into the internal politics of the Malay States. In its origins however the British connexion arose neither from Britain's relations with Holland and Siam, nor from any interest in the Peninsula itself. Before attempting to discuss events in Malaya, therefore, we may glance for a moment at the external factors which stimulated British interest in Malaya and Indonesia at the end of the eighteenth century.

The strategic element in the foundation of Penang is well-known and has been given due notice by most of the historians of Malaya.[2] Successful naval operations in the Bay of Bengal, and

2 See for instance, L. A. Mills, British Malaya 1824-1867, JRASMB, iii, pt 2 (1925) pp 18-21; and H. P. Clodd, Malaya's First British Pioneer, the Life of Francis Light (1948), pp 1-2.

PRELUDE: THE BACKGROUND AND SCOPE OF THE SUBJECT

CONCERN for the defence of India and of the China trade led the East India Company to establish settlements in the Straits of Malacca. During the first half of the nineteenth century it defeated Dutch and Siamese attempts to gain control over the southern portion of the Malayan Peninsula, and itself became the paramount power in the area. The East India Company refused to accept any responsibility for the internal affairs of the Peninsula, but in the second half of the century economic factors increased the interest of the Straits merchants in the Peninsular states, and their affairs became linked with those of the British settlements. The Colonial Office, which assumed control of the Straits Settlements in 1867, at first continued the Indian Government's policy of non-intervention. But in 1873 it reversed this policy, and several of the Malay States came under British control. This book investigates the circumstances which produced this change of policy, and explains the nature of subsequent events.

(i) *The Establishment of the British Connexion with Malaya*

Britain's territorial interest in Malaya dates from 1786, when the East India Company secured the island of Penang, off the west coast of the Peninsula. Malacca, taken from the Dutch during the Napoleonic Wars but returned in 1818, became British territory in 1825, and Singapore, the last of the three outposts known collectively as the Straits Settlements, was occupied in 1819. These footholds in Malaya brought Britain into conflict with Dutch and Siamese interests in the area, and in the end drew her into the internal politics of the Malay States. In its origins however the British connexion arose neither from Britain's relations with Holland and Siam, nor from any interest in the Peninsula itself. Before attempting to discuss events in Malaya, therefore, we may glance for a moment at the external factors which stimulated British interest in Malaya and Indonesia at the end of the eighteenth century.

The strategic element in the foundation of Penang is well-known and has been given due notice by most of the historians of Malaya.[1] Successful naval operations in the Bay of Bengal, and

---

[1] See for instance, L. A. Mills, 'British Malaya, 1824–1867', *JRASMB*, iii, pt. 2 (1925), pp. 18–21, and H. P. Clodd, *Malaya's First British Pioneer, the Life of Francis Light* (1948), pp. 1–2.

the safety of the East India Company's factories there, demanded
that a harbour on the eastern side of the Bay should be permanently available to the English fleet. From October to May,
whilst the monsoon blew from the north-east, conditions were too
hazardous for sailing ships to remain on the Coromandel coast.
The nearest English port to which the fleet could run was Bombay,
and any hostile squadron which sheltered during the monsoon to
the eastward, at Atjeh or Mergui, could rely on appearing before
Madras when the monsoon changed long before the English ships
could get back into the Bay. In 1763 therefore the Directors of the
East India Company gave orders for the acquisition of a suitable
base to the eastwards, and in the next twenty years Atjeh, Junk
Ceylon (Ujong Salang), the Nicobars, the Andamans, and Penang
itself, were all investigated without result. Suffren's campaigns of
1782 and 1783 however produced a new sense of urgency, which
was probably an important element in the decision to accept
Penang when in 1786 it was offered to the East India Company
by the Sultan of Kedah.

The part played by the Anglo-French maritime conflict in
stimulating British interest in what had till then been a Dutch
sphere of interest did not end with the acquisition of Penang. The
safety of the British possessions in India was not again threatened
from the sea after 1783, though the appearance of a strong French
force in the Indian Ocean was always possible before the victory
of Trafalgar. But serious damage was done by French frigates and
privateers to British trade. This *guerre de course*, in which the
individual brilliance and dash of captains like the Surcouf brothers
was allowed full scope, inflicted heavy losses on British merchants,
and threatened to develop into a full-scale attack on the East
India Company's China trade. Efforts to counter this threat, and
to protect the route to China led on the one hand to the blockade
and capture of Île de France and Bourbon, the main French bases
(1810), and on the other to the occupation of Dutch ports in the
Indies to deny them to the enemy.[2] To this anxiety for the China
trade was mainly due the British occupation of Java itself (1811),
and the retention of Singapore, which after 1819 secured the route
through the Straits of Malacca.

The second important factor in the stimulation of British
interest in the area was the growth in the size of the East India

[2] See C. N. Parkinson, *War in the Eastern Seas, 1793–1815* (1954).

Company's China trade. The trade to China, especially the export of opium by locally owned or 'country' ships, was of growing importance to India, But it was the export of tea from China to Europe, a monopoly of the Company, which was the vital British interest. Between 1770 and 1779 the Company imported an annual average of five to six million pounds weight of tea into Britain, paying on it very high customs and excise duties, which averaged nearly 100 per cent on its value. The annual consumption of tea in Britain was considerably greater than this. The balance, at least seven million pounds by the most conservative contemporary estimate,[3] was imported into Europe in foreign ships, and then smuggled across the Channel. It paid no duties to the Exchequer, and represented a loss to the Company. This state of affairs ceased with the passing of Pitt's Commutation Act in 1784. By the provisions of this Act the duty on tea was reduced to twelve and a half per cent, and the East India Company's monopoly was confirmed.[4] It was estimated that it would be necessary for the Company to import thirteen million pounds weight of tea a year to save the Exchequer from a loss on the transaction. They did better than this. In 1785 they sold over sixteen million pounds, as against about six million in 1784. Two years later imports from China rose to over twenty millions, and the figure continued to increase until in the last ten years of the Company's monopoly it averaged about thirty million pounds a year. In the long run this increase was no doubt caused by the expansion of the market, but there is no doubt that the initial growth in the Company's imports resulted from the defeat of smuggling, which the lower duty made unprofitable. The duty rose again after 1795, till in 1819 it was again 100 per cent, but the smuggler was never again to be one of the Company's chief troubles.

In fastening on 1785 as a turning point in the development of the East India Company's tea trade we are at once presented with

[3] Raynal, *Histoire Philosophique et Politique des Établissements et du Commerce des Européens dans les Deux Indes* (Geneva, 1780), vol. i, p. 372. For details of imports and duties, see Morse, *Chronicles of the East India Company trading to China* (1926), vol. ii, pp. 116–17; Milburn, *Oriental Commerce*, pp. 459 and 568; Greenberg, *British Trade and the Opening of China* (1951), pp. 3 and 64.

[4] To prevent the Company profiteering, a safeguard clause was inserted whereby if the price rose above a certain figure the ports were to be thrown open to foreign importers. A further safeguard of the Treasury was an increase of the infamous Window Tax, intended to make up any loss caused by the lower rate of duty; any deficit beyond this was to be made up by the East India Company.

a second compelling motive for the British occupation of Penang in the following year. The Company's interest in protecting the route of the China-bound East Indiamen grew with the trade itself, until it formed the most powerful reason for the retention of Raffles's settlement at Singapore in the face of Dutch protests.[5] We should be wrong however in thinking that it was the Company's interest alone which sustained the growth of British outposts along the Straits of Malacca. For the expansion of the tea trade produced a similar growth in the Indian country trade between India and China. The most important branch of this trade was the carriage of opium to China, since this provided the funds which, eked out at first with silver, financed the Company's tea purchases. But at the same time there was a significant growth in trade with the Indonesian islands themselves which yielded silver and local products saleable in China. It was the British and Indian country ships engaged in this trade with the islands, at times a smuggling trade carried on against Dutch opposition, which had most to gain from the establishment of British settlements as trading centres in the area. It was a country trader, Francis Light, who was largely responsible for the acquisition of Penang, and it was this trade which Raffles sought to protect when he founded Singapore as an insurance against the renewal of the Dutch commercial monopoly in the Indies. As the British settlements developed, many private traders made their headquarters in the Straits, especially at Singapore, and built up a permanent trading connexion in the Archipelago which gradually came to form an important interest independent of the China trade. The Straits traders commanded an influential Parliamentary lobby in London, supported by the rising English manufacturing interest, for whom the Eastern Archipelago was an important potential market.

The Malay world into which the East India Company was drawn at the end of the eighteenth century was one in which important changes were taking place. Throughout the seventeenth and eighteenth centuries Dutch sea-power had dominated the essentially maritime civilizations of Malaya and Indonesia. But when the English Company acquired Penang the Dutch East India Company and the Johore Empire, suzerain of the Malay

---

[5] See pp. 7–8 below. In insisting on the British claim to Singapore the British Government was perhaps also influenced by the fact that import duties on China tea provided about one-tenth of the total revenue of the British Exchequer (Greenberg, op. cit., p. 3).

States, were both losing their position as the arbiters of Malay
politics. The Johore Empire, as successor of the Malay Empire of
Malacca, inherited the nominal overlordship of all the Malay states
south of the Siamese frontier. In the eighteenth century the Johore
capital at Riau was dominated by the Bugis, adventurers from the
Celebes famous in Malay lore for their fierce courage and commercial acumen. From their settlements in the Selangor area the
Bugis came to control native politics in the west-coast states too,
so that to the rule of the puppet Sultans of Johore and their Malay
nobility were left only the less wealthy and remote east-coast
states of Trengganu and Pahang. The Malay rulers at Riau,
powerless in their own capital, tried by playing off the Dutch
against the Bugis to secure their independence. But the weapon
turned in their hands, and by 1787 both Malays and Bugis had
lost power to the Dutch.

The paramount Malay power in the Peninsula thus lost its
position to the Dutch at the same time as the Dutch Company
itself was declining into impotence. A gradual decline in the
solidity of the Company throughout the eighteenth century had
been masked by an outward appearance of strength; constant
dividends at home, largely provided by borrowed money, and
lucrative personal rewards for the Company's servants in the East,
supported the illusion. But the Fourth English War (1780–4)
severely shook the apparently sound fabric, and the Revolutionary
War of 1795, which again cut off Holland from the East, completed
the ruin of the Company. It was formally wound up in 1799.

The Revolutionary and Napoleonic Wars gave Britain the opportunity to seize Dutch Malacca (1795), and in 1811 forces from
India occupied Java and most of the Dutch posts in the other
islands. During the period of the British occupation the whole of
this area became a British trading preserve. This was the heyday of
the country traders, who had the whole of the islands open to
them, and private trade between India, the Archipelago and China
prospered. This happy state of affairs threatened to cease at the
close of the Napoleonic Wars, when the British occupation of
Java came to an end. The East India Company, for whom the
occupation of Java had entailed a large financial loss, was deaf to
arguments that the retention of the island would in the long run
be a source of commercial profit to Britain; and the British Government were guided purely by European considerations, chief

of which was their desire to build up a strong Kingdom of the Netherlands able to withstand future attacks from France. The Convention of London (13 August 1814) therefore returned to the Dutch all their eastern colonies except Ceylon and the Cape, which were retained for strategic reasons. In the execution of this settlement however many differences of opinion arose between the British and Dutch representatives on the spot. Though Java itself was returned to Dutch control in 1816 the transfer of many of the outer possessions had not been effected when Sir T. S. Raffles, who had governed Java for the Company from 1811 to 1815, reappeared on the scene as Lieutenant-Governor of Benkulen, the Company's factory on the west coast of Sumatra.

Raffles had bitterly opposed the surrender of Java. He had spent his life in Malaya and Indonesia, and dedicated himself to the forwarding of British interests there. In his mind anxiety to secure for Britain the trade of the Eastern Islands and the moral tutelage of their peoples was accompanied by a hatred of the Dutch and Dutch institutions which blighted everything he did. He now set himself, on his own initiative, to salvage what he could of the British position in the Archipelago. At the same time Colonel James Bannerman, Governor of Penang, was taking steps in the same direction. Both men feared that the Dutch, once in possession of their former posts in the outer islands, would renew the Dutch Company's old monopoly treaties with the local chiefs, and shut out the British and Indian country traders. The years 1818 and 1819 thus saw a local diplomatic struggle between British and Dutch officials. The Dutch won the first round against Bannerman without much difficulty. In West Borneo, at the ports of Pontianak and Sambas, the returning Dutch officials established themselves before Bannerman could conclude treaties of his own with the local chiefs. In Malaya he negotiated treaties with Selangor and the Johore Empire which secured most-favoured-nation status for British trade, and forbade the granting of monopolies.[6] But these were only paper defences, and when the Dutch reoccupied Malacca and sent a Resident and a garrison to Riau in September and November 1818, they easily reasserted their control over these states, and secured the renewal of the old monopoly treaties.

[6] See, Maxwell and Gibson, *Treaties and Engagements affecting the Malay States and Borneo* (1924), pp. 30-32 and 115-16.

Raffles from Benkulen employed direct methods. On various pretexts he refused to surrender Padang or the island of Billiton, and attempted to establish British posts in Palembang and the Lampongs area of Sumatra. There was a good deal of support for this independent action amongst British trading circles in India, and for that matter in Britain itself. The Indian Government, aware that good relations with Holland were necessary to British policy in Europe, refused to be stampeded into extending their commitments in Sumatra. But they appreciated the value of a place like Billiton, which lay on the route to China, and when Raffles visited Calcutta at the end of 1818 he was able to persuade the Governor-General to authorize the foundation of a British post at the southern end of the Straits of Malacca.

The result was Raffles's foundation of Singapore—a British trading centre, and a free-trading centre, in the heart of the Archipelago. As the legal basis of his occupation of the island Raffles secured a grant from Husain, elder brother of the reigning Sultan of the Johore Empire. The British title to Singapore was derived from treaties signed in 1819 and 1824 with Husain, styled by Raffles 'Sultan of Johore', and with the Temenggong, the local ruler of Singapore Island and the present state of Johore.[7] Raffles rested the validity of the title thus gained principally on the proposition that Husain was the legal Sultan of the Johore Empire, and that the installation of his younger brother Abdu'r-Rahman was invalid. The ground on which Raffles stood was not strong, and there followed a heated diplomatic controversy in which he and the Dutch authorities advanced opposed interpretations of the history of the Johore Empire since 1795. Into this controversy it is not proposed to enter here. The issues raised merely cloaked the real struggle between Raffles and the Dutch to convince the British Government and the East India Company of the expediency—or the inexpediency—of retaining the new settlement.

When their initial protests brought no result the Dutch began to think of striking a bargain. It must have seemed to them that a rival empire was in the process of formation in the Archipelago. The British post in the Lampongs challenged their own position on Sunda Strait, and in April 1819 Raffles concluded a treaty with Atjeh, in North Sumatra, which provided for the establishment of a British Resident and prohibited the residence of other

[7] Text in Maxwell and Gibson, op. cit., pp. 116–25.

Europeans.[8] The Dutch therefore decided to abandon their factories in India, which were now of little use to them, if they could at the same time recover their position in the Archipelago. Negotiations between the two governments began in London in July 1820. But neither side was prepared to concede enough to make agreement possible, and the discussions were broken off and not resumed until 1823. This interval was very important, for it gave time for the immediate commercial success of Singapore to become generally known in England.[9] The East India Company were not inclined to part with Singapore in 1820, though the British Government might have done so to remain on good terms with Holland. But by 1823 opinion in the country had hardened in favour of its retention, and it was politically impossible for them to give it up. The Dutch too had time to reconsider the position, and it was seen in Holland that the claim to Singapore would have to be abandoned. With the main source of tension thus removed agreement was soon reached, and a treaty acceptable to both sides was signed on 17 March 1824.[10]

The chief result of the Anglo-Dutch Treaty of 1824 from the Dutch point of view is indicated by the name often given it by Dutch historians—*het Sumatratractaat*. It eliminated British influence from Sumatra and the islands around it, and left the Dutch free to develop their political interests in the Archipelago without a European competitor. They took over the British settlement of Benkulen and received an undertaking from Great Britain to abstain from all political interference in Sumatra and the islands south of Singapore. In return they gave a similar undertaking not to interfere in the Malay Peninsula, abandoned their claim to Singapore, and ceded to Britain Malacca and the Dutch settlements in India.

On the British side it is probably fair to say that the ideas of those who negotiated the treaty in London were essentially

[8] *Treaties and Engagements with Native Princes and States in India, concluded for the most part in 1817 and 1818* (1824), p. cxi.
[9] In the first year of its existence the total trade of Singapore amounted to about Spanish $4,000,000. In 1822 it was $8,568,151, and in 1823 $13,268,397. Its population grew from nothing to 5,000 in the first three months, and by Aug. 1820 was between 10,000 and 12,000. Most important of all so far as the East India Company was concerned, by the latter date the cost of administration was already covered by its revenue, whereas Penang and Benkulen continued to run heavy deficits, nearly £100,000 in the case of the Sumatran settlement (cf. Mills, op. cit., p. 62).
[10] Maxwell and Gibson, op. cit., pp. 8–17.

negative. They were concerned not so much to advance British interests in the East as to make 'territorial changes which have been thought expedient for avoiding a collision of interests'.[11] It is not surprising to find therefore that whilst the territorial provisions of the treaty served their purpose and stopped a nascent colonial conflict, the commercial clauses were unsatisfactory and a source of future trouble. They accepted the principle of discriminatory tariffs; at the same time they contained vague and general phrases—'the most perfect freedom of Trade', 'mutual understanding as to principles between the Governments', 'free communication with Ports belonging to Native Powers'—which were in contradiction to the detailed terms of the treaty, and which were not defined. These commercial clauses, and the accompanying protocols which formed part of the settlement, offered so many loop-holes for evasion and so many opportunities for differing interpretations that they led in time to further Anglo-Dutch conflict.

So far as it concerned the British position in Malaya, however, the terms of the treaty were clear, and its results decisive. The withdrawal of Holland from the Malay Peninsula left Britain as the only European power with a footing there, so that slowly but inevitably she became the paramount power in the area. At the same time the treaty secured British control of the Straits of Malacca, and thus of the route to China, and made it certain that Singapore, and to a lesser degree the other two settlements, would grow into important trading centres from which British influence could spread into the neighbouring states.

(ii) *The East India Company's Relations with the Malay States, and the Nature of its Position in Malaya*

From the moment that it occupied Penang the East India Company regarded its settlements in Malaya purely as ports of call and trading stations on the route to China, and tried to keep clear of commitments in the Peninsula itself. By and large the Indian Government maintained this policy successfully. When the responsibility for the Straits Settlements was transferred from the India Office to the Colonial Office in 1867 they still retained the territorial limits which they had had in 1824, and their government,

[11] 'Note addressed by the British Plenipotentiaries to the Plenipotentiaries of the Netherlands, 17 March. 1824', ibid.

B

unlike that of the Gold Coast settlements in the same period, had not acquired judicial or administrative functions in the neighbouring states. The Indian Government found however that it was not possible to keep entirely clear of political commitments in the Peninsula. From time to time the policy of non-interference had to be relaxed, and it was necessary to compose disputes between the Settlements' neighbours to prevent disorder stopping trade and spreading to British territory.

The problem of keeping such intervention to a minimum was complicated by the position of Siam in the Peninsula. The Company's arrival in Malaya coincided with a revival of Siamese attempts to absorb the northern Malay states which had been a familiar feature of Malayan politics even in the days of the Malay Empire of Malacca. During the eighteenth century Siamese influence lapsed for a time as a result of her wars with Burma, and in 1767 she was prostrated and her capital destroyed by a Burmese invasion. But she recovered quickly, and, though another Burmese war caused a brief check in the early years of the nineteenth century, after 1812 the Chao P'aya of Ligor, the semi-independent Governor of the Siamese states in the Peninsula, began an intensive campaign to assert effective control over the Malay states to the south. The Indian Government was thus threatened with what it regarded as a powerful continental empire as its neighbour in Malaya, and this eventually led it to adopt a policy of supporting the threatened states so as to keep them in existence as a buffer between itself and Siam.

The circumstances under which it acquired Penang ought to have given the Indian Government warning of the trouble they were to have as a result of this Siamese threat. They were offered Penang by the Sultan of Kedah on the clearly stated condition that in return they would protect him from Siam. They took the island but gave no clear promise of support. This left the Sultan exposed to the vengeance of the Siamese, and his chances of placating them were not improved when in 1800, after an unsuccessful attempt to recover Penang by force, he made over to the Company a strip of the coast-line opposite the island, subsequently known as 'Province Wellesley'. He appeased the Siamese for a time by undertaking the subjugation of Perak on their behalf, but the completion of his conquest of Perak was the signal for his own downfall. In 1821 the Siamese overran Kedah, and both that state and Perak became a Siamese province controlled from Ligor. These events caused a great deal of trouble in Penang. Exports of food-stuffs from Kedah were stopped, and Siamese obstructiveness placed Penang in much the same position as Hongkong now occupies in relation to China. The East India Company gave the Sultan asylum in Penang on condition that he did not use British territory as a base for attacks on the Siamese. But they could not prevent his followers and sympathizers, including most of the European merchants and some of the officials, from working covertly for his restoration. An incessant guerrilla war waged by small parties of Malays against the Siamese encouraged piracy, and the frontiers of Province Wellesley suffered continual alarms and incursions.

The able and energetic Robert Fullerton, who succeeded to the Governorship of Penang in 1824, was soon convinced that the Siamese claim to suzerainty over the Malay States had no basis in fact, and was merely the cloak for aggression which would not stop at Perak, but ultimately engulf all the states on the west coast. Events in Perak and Selangor tended to confirm this view of the position. When Selangor helped Perak to expel the Siamese officials from her territory the Chao P'aya of Ligor got together a fleet and an army to conquer both of them, and went so far as to ask for permission to take his armada through Penang harbour on its way. This was an injudicious step which frightened the Penang officials into the idea that the island itself was the object of attack, and the Indian Government was persuaded that it was necessary to come to some sort of understanding with the Siamese in Bangkok. The First Anglo-Burmese War, which had begun in 1824, was not going too well, and it was hoped that in addition to coming to terms in Malaya the Siamese might be persuaded to make diversionary attacks on Burma from the east.

As a result a treaty was concluded in Bangkok in June 1826 by Major Burney, the Siamese-speaking Military Secretary at Penang, which was the basis of the British position in the northern states of the Peninsula for the next fifty years. It fixed the southern boundary of Kedah as the limit of legitimate Siamese control, and secured the independence of Perak and Selangor so long as the British authorities carried out an undertaking to defend Perak from Selangor, and so long as the Sultan of Perak did not exercise the option given him by the treaty to send the *bunga mas* (golden flower), the formal token of vassalage, to Bangkok. This he was not likely to do so long as he was a free agent.

At first the clauses of Burney's treaty relating to Perak were not honoured by the Chao P'aya, who seems not to have been under the complete control of the central government in Bangkok. In October 1826 Fullerton was driven to send an expedition under Lieutenant James Low to enforce the treaty, to advise the Sultan not to send the *bunga mas*, and to give him a vague general assurance of British support. It found that the Sultan was unwilling to stand out against Siam unless given a definite guarantee of protection. Low, a prominent member of the anti-Siamese faction at Penang, gave him the guarantee on his own authority. It took the form of a treaty which provided that so long as the Sultan did not send the *bunga mas*, and held no political communication with Siam or any other state, then the British Government would help him to expel from Perak any Siamese or foreign Malays who entered it to interfere with its internal affairs.[12]

Low's treaty and Fullerton's firmness sufficed to maintain the independence of Perak, and after 1827 Siamese influence on the west coast was confined to Kedah and the states to the north. The Perak treaty was never ratified, but it remained on record, and was acted upon by the Indian Government in the years 1843–8, when they stood by Perak against the Sultan of Kedah, who was attempting to filch a tract of land in the Krian area. The trouble arising from the Siamese occupation of Kedah continued for another sixteen years. In Burney's treaty of 1826 the Company had agreed to prevent the Sultan-in-exile from interfering in his lost kingdom. In return the Siamese undertook to levy only reasonable duties on trade, and to allow the free export of foodstuffs to Penang.[13] Neither undertaking was kept. The Penang Government was unable to prevent the Sultan's followers making a series of futile attempts to recover his throne by force, and the

---

[12] Treaty with Perak, No. 2, 18 Oct. 1826, in Maxwell and Gibson, op. cit., pp. 24–26. By another treaty of the same date (ibid., p. 23) the Sultan ceded to the East India Company 'Pulo Dindings and the Islands of Pangkor', off the Dinding River. The islands were never occupied, and the treaty slept until revived by Sir Harry Ord in 1868 (cf. p. 54, below).

[13] Cowan, 'Early Penang and the Rise of Singapore', *JRASMB*, xxiii, pt. 2 (1950), p. 168. The text of this article in Maxwell and Gibson, op. cit., p. 80, is mutilated. The best account of the implementation of the Burney treaty is in Mills, op. cit., pp. 128–64.

Bangkok Government unable (or unwilling) to prevent the Chao P'aya of Ligor stopping the food-stuffs and levying what duties he pleased. In the end the death of the Chao P'aya enabled a compromise to be reached. The Sultan made his submission to Siam, and was restored to his throne as a vassal of that state in 1842.

The external affairs of Malacca, after 1825 a quiet backwater in British hands, can be dealt with shortly. Its hinterland was inhabited largely by Menangkabau Malay immigrants from Sumatra. They were divided politically into a number of small independent states, loosely grouped into a Confederacy later known as Negri Sembilan (the Nine States). In the eighteenth century these states had begun the practice of bringing over a Menangkabau prince as their head (Yang di-pertuan), but in 1825 they had no generally acknowledged head, and their confederacy existed in name only. In 1831 the East India Company was involved in the Naning War. This was a ludicrous campaign fought with extreme caution by two battalions of the Company's troops against a few score Malays to uphold a claim to jurisdiction over a small settlement on the Malacca border. The Naning Malays were at first supported by the neighbouring state of Rembau. To dissolve this hostile alliance the Company concluded treaties with Rembau freeing her from obligations of vassalage inherited from the Dutch, and recognizing her as a sovereign state. This achieved the desired result. The Rembau chief, Raja 'Ali, changed sides, and Naning was subdued and embodied in Malacca territory. But Raja 'Ali, emboldened by this recognition, attempted to assert himself as Yang di-pertuan, and there began a series of wars between the jealous little states which kept the area in ferment for the next forty years, and prevented the Malacca merchants from exploiting their hinterland.[14]

We have already noted Raffles's foundation of Singapore. One unexpected result of the treaties of 1819 and 1824 was the creation of a Malay state, Johore, which was in many respects a British dependency. Raffles's recognition of Husain as Sultan meant that henceforth the former Johore Empire was split into two parts.

[14] On the Naning War and the Menangkabau States at this time, see Winstedt, 'Negri Sembilan', *JRASMB*, pt. 3 (1934), pp. 59–65, and 91; Mills, op. cit., pp. 126–7; De Jong, *Minangkabau and Negri Sembilan* (1950), pp. 9–10 and 13. The Rembau treaties are printed in Maxwell and Gibson, op. cit., pp. 43–48.

Sultan 'Abdu'r-Rahman under Dutch control reigned from Riau over the islands south of Singapore, whilst Sultan Husain from Singapore exercised the nominal overlordship of Johore and Pahang on the mainland. In fact Husain had no authority in either of these places. Pahang was the holding of the Bendahara of the old Empire, who now went his way as an independent ruler. In the same way the Temenggong controlled Johore, which being almost uninhabited in 1824 was of no use to him. In the early years of the new British settlement both he and Husain lived in Singapore, and were content to draw the pensions given to them by the East India Company in consideration of their cession of the island. Both died in these circumstances, the Temenggong in 1827, Sultan Husain in 1835. Husain's son 'Ali remained, like his father, a pensioner with a modest income and large debts. But the young Temenggong, Daing Ibrahim, succeeded to a far better inheritance. As Singapore grew from a few fishermen's huts to a great seaport town, so Johore also developed from a waste of virgin jungle into a prosperous state. Chinese gambier and pepper planters moved over from Singapore, and the Temenggong's Malay subjects developed for him a valuable *gutta percha* monopoly. By the 1850's the Temenggong had become a rich man, but he remained a British pensioner living in Singapore, and shaped his policy to suit the ideas of the British officials there.

The result of this close connexion between Singapore and Johore was that more and more the British authorities in Singapore were drawn into the affairs of the Peninsula from the south, as they had already been drawn into them from Penang. Two affairs in particular caused them trouble—a dispute between Sultan and Temenggong for control of Johore, and a civil war in Pahang in which the Temenggong and the Siamese were involved.

The Johore dispute, though it split Singapore society into two parties, and dragged on for several years, was essentially a straightforward affair. Sultan 'Ali, supported by a group of Singapore merchants who hoped to profit thereby, and some sympathetic officials, claimed the right to share in the revenue of a country of which he was the titular ruler, and attempted to secure from the Company recognition of his claims to Johore. The merchants already drawing profit from the Temenggong's régime, and the rest of the officials, supported him in opposing this claim. The Indian Government at first refused to sanction any interference, holding that the dispute was a domestic affair with which the treaty of 1824 forbade them to interfere. In 1855 however they lent their authority to a compromise settlement by which 'Ali recognized the Temenggong as sovereign in Johore in return for a fixed monthly pension and a small area between the Kesang and Muar Rivers in western Johore.[15]

The Pahang civil war was a more complicated affair. It began in 1857, when on the death of Bendahara Tun 'Ali the succession to the throne was disputed between his sons Tun Mutahir, the eldest, and Wan Ahmad. Wan Ahmad was helped by the Sultan of Trengganu, Pahang's neighbour to the north, by the Siamese, and by the ex-Sultan of Lingga. Mahmud of Lingga, who had been Sultan of the Riau Empire before being deposed by the Dutch in favour of a more pliant relative, attached himself to Wan Ahmad with the idea of reasserting his family's control over the east-coast portion of the old Johore Empire. He was thus making a parallel claim to that of his cousin 'Ali in Johore, and on the same grounds. Both he and Wan Ahmad secured the backing of Siam, whose position on the east coast had not been limited, as it had on the west coast, by Burney's treaty of 1826. This treaty made no reference to Pahang, and though providing that Siam should not 'go and obstruct or interrupt commerce' in Kelantan and Trengganu, it left the precise status of these states unsettled. The Siamese saw in the Pahang war an opportunity of securing control of the area, and adopted Wan Ahmad and Mahmud as their protégés with the idea of setting up one or both of them as puppet rulers once the other claimant, Tun Mutahir, had been defeated. Tun Mutahir on his side found a champion in the Temenggong of Johore. The Temenggong's support arose partly from family connexions, but was mainly prompted by self-interest. It was only two years since he had secured an acknowledgement from 'Ali of the legality of his position in Johore. He did not yet feel secure on his throne, and he could hardly allow Mahmud of Lingga, the head of the old Johore royal family, to make good a claim to Pahang which applied with equal force to her neighbour Johore. So for six years Pahang was the scene of a war in which for much of the time outside interests decided the course of events.

[15] 'Arrangement between the Sultan and Tumungong', 1855, in Maxwell and Gibson, op. cit., pp. 127–9.

For some time the policy of the Straits Government was directed towards securing an accommodation between Tun Mutahir
and Wan Ahmad, and discouraging third parties from interfering. It was particularly worried that the Temenggong, who still
lived in Singapore, would convert the British colony into a base of
operations against another Malay State, and did its utmost to
prevent him sending men and supplies to Tun Mutahir, but
without much success. In 1862, however, its policy changed.
This was largely the result of an overt act of interference on the
part of Siam. In 1861 Mahmud of Lingga, who was making no
headway in either Pahang or Trengganu, visited Siam, and his
sister married King Mongkut. He was provided with a steamship
and a small force of Siamese soldiers and sent back to Trengganu
in 1862, with three Siamese warships in support. The arrival of a
British gunboat caused the Siamese warships to make off, but
Mahmud and his soldiers remained there.

Colonel Orfeur Cavenagh, who became Governor of the Straits
Settlements in 1859, was an energetic and forceful character, who
saw in these developments another Siamese threat to the independence of the Malay States. To stop this he attempted through the
British Consul-General in Bangkok to get the Siamese Government to remove Wan Ahmad and Mahmud from Trengganu. At
the same time he gave his backing to a treaty of alliance between
the Temenggong and Tun Mutahir, in order to stiffen the anti-
Siamese faction in Pahang.[16] The Siamese temporized, and in
November it became obvious that they were merely waiting for
the approach of the north-east monsoon which would make a
landing on the east coast impracticable, and enable them to put
off action until the monsoon changed again in April 1863. This
would have given Mahmud nearly six months in which to establish himself. So Cavenagh took the law into his own hands, and
despatched two warships to Trengganu to present an ultimatum—
unless within twenty-four hours the Sultan of Trengganu handed
over Mahmud for conveyance back to Bangkok, and promised
not to give any further help to Wan Ahmad, the place would be
bombarded. Mahmud did not appear and the place was bombarded
—without apparent result. The Sultan and Mahmud remained in-

---

[16] Treaty of 17 June 1862, in Maxwell and Gibson, op. cit., pp. 209-11. One
clause of this treaty bound both parties not to enter into alliances or conduct
correspondence with foreign states without the knowledge and consent of the
British Government.

land out of reach of the ships, and Wan Ahmad was not prevented
from prosecuting the Pahang war, which he brought to a victorious
conclusion in 1863, despite the efforts of the Temenggong of
Johore to bolster up his opponents. In the long run however the
bombardment secured Cavenagh's main objective. There were no
further overt attempts by the Siamese to interfere in the area, and
Mahmud died in Pahang in 1864, so that although Wan Ahmad
became ruler of Pahang he was an independent ruler.[17]

The first half of the nineteenth century thus saw the East India
Company established as the paramount power in Malaya. The
nature of this paramountcy is difficult to define. In the north it was
shadowy and based on day-to-day practice rather than on legal
settlements. Kedah was expressly recognized by the treaty of
1826 as a Siamese vassal, and Kelantan and Trengganu were regarded usually as within the Siamese orbit. But in the years
following 1842 Kedah's everyday connexion was with Penang, to
whom she was bound by treaty and by trade, and whose Governor
paid her Sultan an annuity in consideration of his cession of
Penang itself and of Province Wellesley. In the east-coast states,
where English trade and the Company's influence were at first
very small, the vague provisions of Burney's treaty covered
Cavenagh's action in Trengganu, and enabled him to maintain
that 'the districts of Tringanu and Kelantan are protected by
the British Government under the Treaty of Bangkok.'[18] South of
Kedah the removal of Siamese pressure after 1826, and the withdrawal of the Dutch from Malacca under the Anglo-Dutch treaty
of 1824, left the British settlements as the only outside power in
the Peninsula. The Malay States looked to 'the Bengal Company',
which had ousted the Siamese and the Dutch, as the arbiter of
local politics. To it they reported the accession of new rulers, and
from it they asked help when in trouble. Though the Company
was unwilling to assume this role of paramount power, and tried
to keep clear of any official connexion with the Peninsular states,
her links with them tended to grow.

[17] For a fuller account of the Pahang war and the Trengganu incident, cf.
Linehan, 'History of Pahang', *JRASMB*, xiv, pt. 2 (1936), pp. 66–89; Sheppard,
'Short History of Trengganu', *JRASMB*, xxii, pt. 3 (1949), pp. 31–34; Winstedt,
'History of Johore', *JRASMB*, x, pt. 3 (1932), pp. 94–96 and 100–5; and Mills,
op. cit., pp. 164–9.
[18] In 'Report on the Treaties and Engagements with the Native States of the
Malayan Peninsula', Maxwell and Gibson, op. cit., p. 1.

But beyond this gradual and almost accidental growth of influence British paramountcy rested on a definite treaty basis. Burney's treaty of 1826, and Low's treaty with Perak, guaranteed Perak and Selangor against attack from Siam and other Malay states, and treaties concluded in 1825 more particularly protected the two states from attack by each other.[19] Both states were therefore what Cavenagh called 'under British protection'. There was no pledge of protection against outside interference in respect of any other state, but the Anglo-Dutch treaty of 1824 ensured that there would be no such interference from the only other European power in a position to attempt it. There were however two other states, in addition to Perak, over whose foreign relations the East India Company had a treaty right of control. These were Johore and Pahang. Both these states and Perak had undertaken not to sign treaties or conduct correspondence with other states without British consent. Out of the five states south of Kedah (counting the Negri Sembilan area as one) there were thus by 1862 two whom the East India Company were pledged to protect, and three over whose external relations they had a right of control. In no case was there any right of interference in the internal affairs of any state.

On a purely legalistic interpretation Johore and Perak would no doubt have been regarded by some later nineteenth and twentieth-century authorities as protectorates. Sir H. Jenkyns defined a protectorate as first and foremost

. . . a country which is not within the British dominions, but as regards its foreign relations is under the exclusive control of the King, so that its government cannot hold direct communications with any foreign power nor a foreign power with that government.[20]

Lord Justice Kennedy in 1910 began his definition in the same way, saying 'the one common element in protectorates is the prohibition of all foreign relations except those permitted by the protecting state'.[21] But the term 'protectorate' did not assume an inter-

[19] Treaty with Selangor, 20 Aug. 1825, ibid., pp. 32–34; Treaty with Perak, 6 Sept. 1825, ibid., pp. 22–23.

[20] Jenkyns, *British Rule and Jurisdiction beyond the Seas* (1902), p. 165. This passage is of special interest because the book was posthumous, and was edited by Sir Courtney Ilbert, of Indian fame, and presumably commanded his agreement.

[21] Quoted in *Encyclopaedia Britannica* (1929), *sub* 'Protectorate'. Later authorities are however not so sure of the definition. Lauterpracht, in the 8th (1955) ed. of L. Oppenheim, *International Law*, vol. i, p. 192, speaks of it as '. . . a conception which, like suzerainty, lacks exact legal precision, and its real meaning depends very much upon the special case'.

national status until the Berlin Conference of 1884-5 recognized the West African protectorates.[22] Before the 1880's such 'protectorates' as existed were practically ignored by international lawyers. Twiss in 1861 distinguished between 'Protected Independent States' (such as the Ionian Islands) and 'Protected Dependent States' (such as the Princely States of India). But he made no mention of the then much publicized Gold Coast Protectorate, nor of any of the Malay States.[23] Discussing the possibility of a protectorate in Fiji Sir Frederick Rogers, then Permanent Under-Secretary at the Colonial Office, wrote in 1870:

A protectorate is sometimes proposed. I do not quite know what this means. I suppose this is an intimation to the world that nobody must then assume sovereignty over the islands or make war on them—but if they have a grievance against them they must apply to us . . .[24]

However silent international law might have been on the subject at the time, this did not prevent M.P.s, officials and naval officers from using the word freely in the 1860's and 1870's. The term was applied on the Gold Coast to an undefined area extending about 300 miles along the coast, and stretching inland for about fifty miles, where extra-territorial jurisdiction over British subjects, and also jurisdiction over Africans, was exercised. Agitators for the annexation of Fiji, without providing a definition, always said that failing this the alternative should be the assumption of a British protectorate over the islands.[25]

Most of this, however, is theory. In the middle of the nineteenth century the most important factor in the situation in Malaya was not the letter of the treaties, but the spirit of the Indian Government's policy. Though, as in the case of external relations, there were sometimes points in common, the position of the Malay States was in no sense analogous to that of an Indian protected state in a subsidiary treaty relationship with the Indian Government. Even if officials in the Straits Settlements felt a responsibility for affairs in the Peninsula, and even if Governors

[22] 'General Act of the Berlin Conference, 26 Feb. 1885', *A. & P.*, xlvii (1886), pp. 107–17.
[23] Twiss, *The Law of Nations* (1861), pp. 26–35.
[24] Rogers minute, 19 Oct. 1870, on Canterbury to Granville, 12 Aug. 1870, in CO 309/94. I am indebted for this reference to Dr. W. D. McIntyre, whose Ph.D. thesis (University of London, 1959) contains a careful study of the materials referring to Fiji and the Gold Coast.
[25] See Brookes, J. I., *International Rivalry in the Pacific Islands* (1941).

occasionally acted up to and beyond the letter of the treaties, and spoke of states being 'under British protection', it is clear that the Company and the Indian Government did not regard them as being so. It is indeed doubtful whether the East India Company's Directors or the members of the Indian Government knew of or cared about the extent of their treaty commitments in Malaya. Certainly they had no interest in the area outside the British settlements, and no intention of playing a decisive part in Malayan politics. Nevertheless, the treaty basis of the British position was such as to give an ambitious and independent Governor like Cavenagh the opportunity of playing such a part, and to prompt him to write after 1860:

> With the exception of the territories of one or two petty Independent States, the possession of the Malayan Peninsula is divided between the British and the Siamese.[26]

(iii) *The Development of the Malayan Problem*

The undefined character of the British position in Malaya produced no major problems for the Indian Government so long as British interests in the Peninsula remained peripheral. The East India Company's interest was always such; indeed after it lost its China trade in 1833 the Straits Settlements brought the Company itself no direct benefit, and it grudged the money spent on their administration. Even the private merchants of the Straits Settlements had for many years only a marginal interest in the Peninsular states. The commercial role of the settlements, of which Singapore was by far the most important, was that of a gigantic funnel and sorting house combined. Manufactured goods from England and India were distributed throughout South-East Asia, the produce of that area was collected and re-directed to India, Europe and China, and a large amount of goods from China were transhipped before being sent to Europe. This transhipment was made necessary by the Company's China monopoly, which debarred any English private trader from shipping goods direct from China to Europe. Singapore's trade in the period between the Anglo-Dutch treaty of 1824 and the end of the Company's China monopoly in 1833 was apportioned in the following way:

---

[26] Maxwell and Gibson, op. cit., p. 1.

Total Trade (about $14,500,000)	Trade with Malaya	With rest of South-East Asia	Trade with China	With Europe and India
= 100	4	22	23	49

The trade of Penang, which was only a quarter that of Singapore, presented a similar picture. She sold Indian piece-goods to South-East Asia, her best customers being the North Sumatran ports, and shipped produce collected from the Islands to India, Europe and above all to China. Trade with the Peninsula made up at most five per cent of her imports and exports.[27]

Though their commercial connexion with the Peninsula remained relatively unimportant, the distribution of the Settlements' trade began to change gradually after 1833. The end of the Company's China monopoly practically wiped out the practice of transhipment, which had brought the Singapore agency houses a steady one per cent on all cargoes they handled. More important was the British acquisition of Hongkong in 1842, which provided a base for the China merchants close to the treaty ports which the 'Opium War' had forced open. Singapore remained important as a port of call on the route to China, but a good deal of the transit trade between China and South-East Asia which she had handled now passed to Hongkong. The value and volume of Singapore's trade continued to grow, and it remained an entrepôt trade, but it relied far more on the markets and the products of South-East Asia. By 1860 its outlines were as follows:

Total Trade (about $58,000,000)	Trade with Malaya	With rest of South-East Asia	Trade with China	With Europe and India
= 100	3	42	17	36

The dependence of Penang on South-East Asia was even more marked. Its most important trading area was still North and East

[27] The table is based on the return of the trade of the Straits Settlements for the year 1828–9, printed in Cowan, 'Early Penang and the Rise of Singapore', *JRASMB*, xxiii, pt. 2 (1950), pp. 193–203.

Sumatra, but its trade with the Peninsula was increasing, a change associated with the development of Chinese tin-mining in the west-coast states after about 1850.[28]

Singapore had attained the commercial domination of South-East Asia partly because of its position and because as a free-trade centre local merchants preferred to come to it rather than to the customs restricted ports of the Dutch East Indies and the Philippines. In the main however its success was owing to the fact that it was on the receiving end of a great stream of British manufactures, and its mercantile houses were but the last link in an organization engaged in their production and distribution. This, and the increased dependence of their trade on South-East Asian markets, made the Straits merchants particularly sensitive to the attempts of other European powers with interests in the area to shelter their own trade from British competition by the use of various protective devices. At first the Dutch were the main offenders. Having neither the capital, the shipping nor the manufactures to enable them to compete on equal terms with the Indian and Straits merchants, the Dutch Government when they re-occupied Java sought to protect their trade and to encourage the development of Dutch industry with a differential tariff system. The Anglo-Dutch treaty of 1824 accepted the principle of discriminatory tariffs, so long as the duties levied on British trade were not more than twice those which the Dutch imposed on their own nationals. This limitation was successfully evaded by a variety of expedients. The trade of the Dutch National Trading Corporation (Nederlandsche Handelmaatschapij) was given a specially privileged position in the produce export market, and until 1855 duties paid by it in Java were refunded to the Corporation in Holland. Even so the tariff and the Nederlandsche Handelmaatschapij up till 1850 were more an irritant than a serious threat to the prosperity of the Straits merchants. They still, in the heyday of the Culture System, retained at least a sixth of the trade of Java.[29] The other islands, outside a few Dutch-held ports, were open to trade on equal terms, and the treaty of 1824 forbade the conclusion of treaties with their rulers which tended

[28] See Tabular Statements of the Commerce and Shipping of Prince of Wales Island, Singapore and Malacca, 1855–8 (Calcutta, 1858–60); Annual Reports, Straits Settlements, 1859–63. The table is based on the figures for 1862–3.

[29] See figures quoted by Furnivall, *Netherlands India* (1944), pp. 129–30 and 171, and Annual Reports, Straits Settlements, cited above.

'either expressly or by the imposition of unequal Duties, to exclude the Trade of the other Party'.[30] Elsewhere in South-East Asia it was only in the Spanish-held Philippines that duties were imposed which put British merchants at a disadvantage compared to their competitors.

In the second half of the nineteenth century the Dutch began to extend their control to the outer islands of Indonesia, and other European powers began to stake out claims in South-East Asia. For the most part Dutch activity was not directed towards occupation and development, but stopped short with the conclusion of treaties in which the local chiefs declared their territories to be part of Netherlands India, and undertook to submit their external relations to Dutch control. It was thus possible to bring these areas within the scope of the Dutch tariff, and of the regulations which debarred foreign ships from the coasting trade of Netherlands India, without infringing the letter of the 1824 treaty. Between 1843 and 1863 fifty-two such treaties were concluded with states in Borneo, the Celebes and the islands to the Eastwards. The treaties which caused the greatest concern in Singapore however were those made in the same period with Jambi, Siak and Indragiri, on the east coast of Sumatra. Not only did these treaties seem to threaten the trade of an area with which the Straits Settlements had always had very close links, but they were followed by effective control and occupation, so that by 1865 the Dutch had pushed their grip on Sumatra to the southern borders of Atjeh, and had begun to threaten the independence of that state.[31]

A similar narrowing of the area open to free trade resulted from the Spanish Government's drive to bring the southern islands of the Philippines within its jurisdiction. The destruction of the capital of Sulu in 1851, and the insistence in Madrid on the fact of Spanish sovereignty there, prevented the ratification of a treaty concluded with the muslim Sultan of Sulu in 1849 by Sir James Brooke. This treaty had given British trade most-favoured-nation status in the Sulu Archipelago. Now, not only were traders there subjected to the Philippines tariff, which discriminated against foreign shipping, but they were forbidden to call at ports in the area, and trade under non-Spanish flags was confined to Manila

---

[30] Art. III, in Maxwell and Gibson, op. cit., p. 9.
[31] See *Correspondence respecting Dutch Aggressions in the Eastern Seas*, (FO Print 9306), 17 Sept. 1867; *Treaties and Conventions between the Dutch and Native Princes in the Eastern Seas*, 1843–66, a series of unnumbered FO Prints.

and three other ports in the Spanish-held islands.[32] In the same way the French move into Annam and Cambodia after 1858 restricted trade with that area. Foreign shipping was confined by the French authorities to their settlement at Saigon, and the coast of Cochin China between 103° and 106° E. was subjected to a blockade which was extended to the whole of Cochin China and Cambodia in 1867.[33]

Though local dislocation caused by these Dutch, French and Spanish activities undoubtedly injured trade, the effects of their tariffs and general controls does not seem to have been of major importance, and the ups and downs of Singapore's trade may be more reliably attributed to wider economic causes into which we cannot enter here.[34] At the time however the Straits traders did not see this. They were hard hit by a general recession which affected the trade of the East in 1867 and 1868, and they inevitably attributed poor trade, falling profits and increasing competition to the machinations of foreign governments and the weakness of their own. Their apprehension for the future was increased by several new factors which began to operate at about this time, but whose effects could not be predicted. Amongst these we may list the opening of the Suez Canal (1869), the extension of the European telegraph from India to Singapore (1870), the appearance of the steam-ship as an economical freight-carrier (1865), and one might also add as economic factors, the unification of Germany, and the end of the American civil war. All these developments interacted. The new compound engine enabled the steam-ship to operate economically and regularly over long distances. The Suez Canal, which increased the costs of the conventional steam-auxiliary sailing ship beyond all proportion to the advantage gained from quicker passage, was ideally suited to the new ships, since their fuel consumption was directly affected by the time spent on passage. The telegraph enabled the London and European business houses to keep in touch with the state of Asian markets, and to send out large shipments in steamers scheduled to arrive at particular ports on predictable dates. The Canal and the

<hr />

[32] FO 71 (Sulu Papers), vols. i–ii.
[33] Proclamations of the Governor of Cochin China, June 1860 and 25 June 1867, in CO 273/4 and 273/11.
[34] For a brief account of the London financial crisis of 1866 and its effects on trade, see Clapham, *Economic History of Modern Britain*, vol. ii (1932), pp. 374–7.

telegraph made it easier for the European shippers to by-pass the old-established London export agencies, and to ship directly to the East, and the economic development of Germany and the United States in particular added to the commercial competition there.[35]

The Straits trading houses, observing the decrease in the business of the London export agencies, feared that the same causes would operate to undermine their own position as distributors and collectors of goods for European shippers. The Chinese traders complained that they were being squeezed out of the trade to Sumatra, Borneo and Bali by the Dutch, and that the Spaniards were keeping them out of Sulu. They said that the increasing number of European firms engaged in the trade to China and the ports to the eastward meant that the profits were no longer large enough for them to risk their individual capital in it. The European firms complained of the increasing competition in Singapore itself, and Dr. Little, an unofficial member of the Singapore Legislative Council, pointed by way of example to the great increase in the number of German merchants in the port; they almost outnumbered the British, yet he could remember the first German trader coming to the place.

All shades of Singapore opinion were agreed upon the remedy —to open up fresh fields for trade and investment in their own hinterland, Malaya, where they would be safe from the tariff restrictions of other European colonies. Throughout the fifties and sixties the operations of Chinese planters in Johore and of Chinese tin-miners in the west-coast states of the Peninsula made these areas increasingly attractive to speculative investment, and the interest of the Straits merchants in them grew. Chinese and European capital from Singapore and Penang financed tin-mining, and links developed between Straits merchants and Malay rulers. But there the process stopped. Large-scale trade did not develop, and the investors failed to secure steady returns on their capital. This was largely due to the political instability of the area.

[35] There is an admirable chapter on these developments in *Cambridge History of the British Empire* (vol. ii), but though the importance of the compound engine in the development of sea transport was appreciated by contemporary writers (Lindsay, *History of Merchant Shipping* (1876), vol. iv, pp. 434–7, 577–80) and later students of the mercantile marine (Thornton, *British Shipping* (1945), p. 66), its significance in the general economic history of Asia has been noticed only in G. S. Graham, 'The Ascendancy of the Sailing Ship, 1850–85', *EHR*. ix, no. 1, pp. 74–88.

C

Outside Johore and Kedah none of the states possessed a government able to offer stable conditions to the speculator, or even safety of life and limb to his agents. Their titular rulers were weak, and in each state power was divided among a number of chiefs, all more or less independent and at odds with each other. Piracy and brigandage were rife, and traffic on the rivers—the only means of transport—was at the mercy of individual chiefs each of whom looked on it as a source of profit. In these circumstances the presence of large numbers of Chinese miners who brought their own feuds with them often only increased the instability and disorder.

Faced with these problems in the Archipelago and in the Peninsula, the merchants of Penang and Singapore turned to their government for political support. The Indian Government was unable to secure any satisfaction from either Holland or Spain on tariff questions, and unwilling to intervene in the affairs of the Peninsular states. After the severance of its connexion with China the East India Company tended to regard the Straits Settlements as an unimportant Residency in an isolated quarter of its Empire. The Indian Government, immersed in Indian affairs, had neither the time nor the knowledge to cope with the totally dissimilar problems of the Straits, and its unfortunate attempts to foist Indian currency and port dues on them evoked resentment and, after 1855, a demand for the ending of the Indian connexion. The upheaval of the Mutiny and the transfer of the government of India from the Company to the Crown made no difference to the position in the Straits, but by 1859 both the Indian Government and the India Office were prepared to admit that the Straits Settlements would be better administered by the Colonial Office, as Hongkong was. After a long period of haggling between various departments of state over the financial details, the Settlements therefore became a separate Crown Colony in April 1867.

In taking over the Straits Settlements the Colonial Office inherited external problems very similar to those with which they were already grappling in the Gold Coast, where trade and an unsettled frontier combined to involve them in the affairs of the Fante tribes and the Ashanti, and where relations with neighbouring Dutch factories made necessary a diplomatic settlement between England and Holland. From 1867 to 1873 the policies adopted in the Gold Coast and in Malaya followed the same pattern. The British Government shut its eyes to conditions in the hinterlands of its settlements, and sought to solve their problems by the negotiation of a general Anglo-Dutch colonial *détente*. A series of treaties signed in 1870 and 1871 made over the Dutch factories on the Gold Coast to Britain and admitted British trade to Dutch controlled areas of Sumatra on the same terms as those enjoyed by Dutch subjects. In return the Dutch secured an acknowledgement of their right to extend their sovereignty over the whole of Sumatra, and the right to ship Indian emigrant labour to the sugar island of Surinam.[36]

The logical concomitant of the recognition of Dutch sovereignty in Sumatra would have been the extension of British political control to the Malayan Peninsula. But though disorder there increased until it threatened to spread to the British settlements, and the clamour of merchants and investors for government intervention continued, the British Government refused to budge, and continued the non-intervention policy of the Indian Government. Then in September 1873 this same Liberal Government abruptly reversed its policy, and indicated to its representatives in the Straits settlements that it was prepared to accept responsibility for rescuing the Peninsular states from disorder, and for promoting trade with them. As a result three of these states received British Residents and came under British control during 1874.

It is the object of the chapters which follow to detail the circumstances under which British policy in Malaya developed during these years, and to suggest reasons for the change in policy which took place in 1873. They attempt to explain the parodoxical chain of events which led a Liberal and supposedly anti-colonial government to sponsor political intervention in Malaya, and a Conservative and reputedly Imperialist Government to decline the opportunity of annexing the west-coast states in 1876, so that the system of government by Residents, whose effective control was clothed in the forms of 'government by advice', eventually spread to all the states of the Peninsula.

[36] 'Gold Coast Convention, 25 Feb. 1871', in Hertslet, *Map of Africa by Treaty*, vol. iii, pp. 979–80; 'Sumatra Convention, 2 Nov. 1871', in Maxwell and Gibson, op. cit., pp. 17–19; 'Convention regulating Indian Coolie Emigration to Surinam', 8 Sept. 1870', in Hertslet, *Treaties and Conventions*, vol. xiii, pp. 649–54.

I

THE FORMULATION OF A MALAYAN POLICY, AND ITS REJECTION BY THE COLONIAL OFFICE

APRIL 1867–LATE 1868

SIR HARRY ORD, the first Colonial Office Governor of the Straits Settlements, was at first given no instructions regarding the Colony's relations with the Malay States. He was unpopular in the Straits Settlements, but he was an ambitious and energetic man, who was ready to do what he could to restore order and promote trade in the Peninsula. Conditions in Malaya at that time were extremely unsettled. The quarrels of the Malays were intensified by feuds between competing groups of Chinese miners, and the links of the Chinese with the British settlements threatened to involve these too in the trouble. After some experience of negotiating with Malays and Siamese Ord worked out a policy under which he proposed to share the supervision of the Peninsula between Britain and Siam. This policy was disapproved by the Colonial Office, and Sir Harry Ord was directed to abstain from all interference in the affairs of the Malay States.

(i) *The Scene of Action*

To replace the Indian administration in the three Straits Settlements, with their bustling mercantile population, the Colonial Office set up a government on the normal Crown Colony model. This was a good deal more elaborate than the old Indian system had been. The central government in Singapore was now to consist of a Governor and Executive and Legislative Councils. The Governor was in theory and usually in practice all-powerful; the Councils were purely advisory in character. The Executive Council was made up solely by officials—the Colonial Secretary and the heads of the administrative departments—and by what we may term semi-officials—the Officer Commanding the troops in the Colony and the Chief Justice—who usually viewed matters from an official viewpoint, but whose votes were not in the last resort controlled by the Governor, as those of the other officials were. The Legislative Council was more important for it contained four unofficial members appointed by the Secretary of State to represent the mercantile community in the Straits. It was thus the organ through which the opinion of the most influential sections of the local population found expression, and though there was an official majority in the Legislative Council a Governor who acted against the united opposition of the unofficial members, especially in financial matters, would find it difficult to justify his policy to the Secretary of State, who retained an absolute veto on all legislation, and could reverse most of the Governor's administrative decisions.[1]

The first Colonial Office Governor of the Straits Settlements was Colonel (later Major-General) Sir Harry St. George Ord. An officer of the Corps of Royal Engineers, as were his two successors in the Government of the Colony, Sir Harry Ord had been in Colonial Office service since 1855. He had been employed mainly in West Africa and the West Indies, and before coming to the Straits had been Governor of Bermuda.[2] To the task of reorganizing the government of the Straits Settlements and of weaning the Straits officials from the leisurely methods of the Indian administration he brought a strong personality and a close experience of the working of Crown Colony government elsewhere. For guidance he was furnished with a set of instructions drafted by the Permanent Under-Secretary at the Colonial Office, Sir Frederick Rogers.[3] These were voluminous but clear. They set out the principles which were to govern the different departments of government, supplementing the formal *Instructions passed under the Royal Sign Manual*. To some topics they gave special attention. Thus, since the Settlements had always under the Indian Government incurred a budgetary deficit the instructions dwelt on the

---

[1] At first the unofficial members of the Legislative Council in the Strait Settlements were all Europeans, either merchants or land-owners. Later a fifth European member was added, and in 1869 a Chinese member was appointed on the instructions of the Secretary of State. Gov. Straits to Sec. State, 9 Sept. 1869; Sec. State to Gov. Straits, 29 Oct. 1869; in CO 273/31.

[2] Maj.-Gen. Sir Harry St. George Ord, R.E., C.B., G.C.M.G., was educated at the Royal Military Academy at Woolwich, 1835–7, and served in the Royal Engineers, 1837–56, principally in the West Indies, West Africa, and the Anglo-French expedition to the Baltic (1854). Employed as Commissioner to the Gold Coast, 1855–6, and as Commissioner at the Courts of Paris and the Hague, 1856–7 and 1860, for negotiations respecting French and Dutch West African possessions, he became in succession Governor of Dominica (1857), Bermuda (1861) and Special Commissioner to West Africa (1864) before becoming Governor of the Straits Settlement in 1867. After leaving Malaya he was employed as Governor of Western Australia (1877–9), and died in 1885 (CO Lists, various years, *DNB*). Cf. also *One Hundred Years of Singapore* (1819), vol. i, pp. 94–95, for a brief note on his character.

[3] Sec. State to Gov. Ord, 6 Feb. 1867, in CO 273/16.

need for economy in government expenditure. They stressed too 'the assistance which the Governor derives from debates in the Legislative Council', and with the powerful mercantile community in mind urged that he pay great deference to the opinions of the unofficial members of the Council.

But comprehensive as Ord's instructions were they contained no reference to the Colony's relations with the states of the Malay Peninsula. This omission was curious, for the subject had certainly occupied the attention of the Secretary of State and the Colonial Office staff when they were considering the form of government to be adopted in the Settlements. They had decided against any measure of elective government for fear that the inhabitants of the Settlements might interfere in the affairs of the Malay States and become involved in wars from which they would have to be extricated by the Imperial Government.[4] The failure now to give any indication of the lines along which they expected Ord to conduct his dealings with these states, or indeed to authorize him to have any official relations with them at all, was therefore very odd. The subject is however discussed elsewhere in the chapter devoted more especially to events within the Colonial Office itself, so that we need not devote more attention to it here.

Without a lead from London Sir Harry Ord, so far as his dealings with the Malay States were concerned, was thus thrown on his own resources; he was forced to rely on his own judgement, on the guidance of those of his subordinate officers who had been members of the Indian régime, and to a lesser degree on the advice of the unofficial members of the Legislative Council and other prominent citizens of Singapore, Penang and Malacca. Unfortunately his relations with most of these people were not happy. A good deal of the difficulty arose from his own character. He was an able and experienced administrator. But, so far at least as can be judged from the records of his administration, he was overbearing and brusque, confident of his own judgement,

---

[4] Gov. Straits 15 July 1867 and CO Minutes thereon; Hall, *The Colonial Office* (1935), pp. 238–9. Earlier, during the negotiations which preceded the transfer of the Straits Settlements from the control of the India Office several of the Straits merchants had drawn attention to the importance of the Governor's diplomatic relations with neighbouring states, and Sir Hercules Robinson, then Governor of Hongkong, had noticed the subject in his Report on the Straits Settlements made to the Duke of Newcastle in 1864. See *Parl. Pap.* 259 of 1862, 'A. Guthrie and 12 others to the Duke of Newcastle', 30 June 1861'; *Parl. Pap.* (unnumbered) of 4 June 1866, in continuation of *Parl. Pap.* 259 of 1862, contains Robinson's Report.

and unwilling to suffer criticism which, even when it came from the Secretary of State, he took as a personal affront. He was thus a difficult man to serve honestly, and his subordinates must often have kept to themselves criticism or advice which they knew would be unpalatable to him. Occasionally they were provoked into open rebellion or passive opposition, and the records of Ord's government are studded with appeals to the Secretary of State against his decisions. There are many instances in which, though the Colonial Office officials thought it wise to decide in Ord's favour, they obviously cherished a good deal of sympathy for his unfortunate subordinates.

The Governor's early difficulties arose in large measure from the irritations inevitable in the change from one administration to another. The old Indian régime had been despotic. The Government of India need neither consult the interests of the merchant community nor defer to the opinions of the Straits officials. But so long as no additional expenditure was incurred the local government was in fact given a good deal of freedom in the performance of their routine duties. The merchants, though they had no representation in the government, found that their business could be smoothed by social connexions with individual officials and personal notes to old friends. With the coming of a Colonial Office Governor a good deal of the old easy-going ways disappeared. The Straits Settlements officials, with a tradition as a separate civil service dating back to 1805, now had to conform to unfamiliar Colonial Office forms and procedures.[5] Ord's blunt personality did not improve the position, and there was a good deal of friction between him and the old Indian officers on the one hand, and between them and the new appointees with a Colonial Service background on the other.

In the case of the mercantile community this initial period of difficulty was a good deal worse. The Indian officials had naturally

---

[5] The Penang Civil Service was formed in 1805 when the island was created a separate Presidency of India, but it was antedated by the Benkulen Service, which was amalgamated with it in 1824 (Mills, op. cit., p. 85). In 1867 the Straits officials had to accept for the first time the strictures of an Auditor-General's department, and Ibbetson, an ex-Governor living at that time in Penang, expressed to Col. Anson the new Lt.-Gov. there his horror at this unnecessary innovation. He was a unique link with the past, for as a young boy he had seen Raffles, then a junior clerk, kicked away from the fire at East India House by his senior fellows (Anson, *About Others and Myself* (1920), pp. 285–6).

looked forward to the transfer with some apprehension, but the merchants had been loud in demanding the change, and hoped that Crown Colony status would solve all their problems. They were disappointed to find that the new government did not include an elective element, and since 1867 and 1868 were years of trade depression they were not in a mood to condone the shortcomings of their new Governor. They found plenty with which to quarrel. A feud between the Governor and the Chief Justice brought them out in support of the latter, for as in India itself the independence of the judiciary was traditionally regarded as a vital defence against an executive which distance made it difficult for the home government to control. Proposals for lavish expenditure on a new Government House and Government steamers evoked criticism, and in December 1867 an explosion occurred when Ord suggested in the Legislative Council that it might in future be necessary to levy duties on imports and exports in order to balance the colony's budget. Meetings of protest were held in the Straits Settlements, and in London an organisation which later became the Straits Settlements Association was formed by retired Straits merchants to bring pressure on the Colonial Office and Parliament. It was a repetition of the old battle against the Indian Government, but in this case the unfortunate Ord had no defenders and was forced to retreat.[6]

Apart from this *cause célèbre* there was much dissatisfaction with the constitution of the new government and the way it handled day-to-day affairs. The unofficial community in the Straits found that although they had four representatives in the Legislative Council—a luxury they had not enjoyed under the Indian régime—yet the large official majority coupled with the relative impersonality of Crown Colony procedure meant that they had less influence over this government than they had had over individual members of the old order. A local cartoon published in 1870, and entitled 'St. George with the Drag-on', depicted the Governor as St. George riding full pelt towards a chasm marked 'Debt and Despotism', with the five unofficial members of Council hanging desperately to the tail of his horse. Ord himself attributed the unpopularity of his government to the depression of trade, and complained that the mercantile community did not appreciate the increased efficiency of government when it operated

[6] CO 273/18, *passim*; CO 273/21, *passim*.

inconveniently for them in the courts and public offices.[7] However
justified he may have been things were still so bad in April 1869
that when one of the unofficial members of the Legislative Council
resigned because of the lack of freedom allowed in debate Ord was
unable to persuade anyone else to take his place.[8]

Sir Harry Ord was cut off from a great deal of good advice and
information by this bad feeling at the beginning of his term of
office. As an illustration of the extent to which this could affect
his judgement we may cite the case of the Penang riots of 1867.
In July of that year serious fighting broke out in Penang between
two Chinese secret societies. The same societies were also rivals
for the control of the Larut tin mines, and before the disturbances
were quelled both sides were reinforced by Chinese from Kedah,
Province Wellesley, and Larut. But neither in Ord's despatches
to the Secretary of State[9] nor in the Report of the Committee of
Enquiry appointed by him[10] were these riots linked with events
in Larut, though the records of Governor Cavenagh's administration contained ample evidence of the connexion between the
Penang societies and the faction fights in Larut.[11] This connexion must have been known to at least four of the old Indian
officials, and to the older members of the mercantile communities
of Penang and Singapore, but does not seem to have been brought
to Ord's notice till much later.

The factors which prevented him from drawing freely upon
local experience in his relations with the Malay States did not
however stop Sir Harry Ord adopting much the same attitude as
the local merchants and officials to the general problems involved.
He was not on easy personal terms with men like Thomas Braddell,
the Attorney-General, or Colonel Ronald Macpherson, the Colonial Secretary, both old Singapore hands.[12] He tended not to

[7] Gov. Straits to Sec. State, 27 Aug. 1868, in CO 273/21. The cartoon,
which appeared in a periodical named *Straits Produce*, is described in *A Hundred Years of Singapore*, vol ii, p. 293.

[8] Gov. Straits to Sec. State, 26 Apr. 1869, and CO minutes thereon, in CO
273/29.

[9] Gov. Straits to Sec. State, 19 Aug. 1867, in CO 273/11.

[10] *Report of the Commissioners appointed to Enquire into the Penang Riots*
(Penang, 1868).

[11] See p. 49 below.

[12] Thomas Braddell was Straits Attorney-General from 1867 till his retirement in 1882. He was born in Ireland in 1823, and worked in the West Indian
sugar industry until he came to Penang in 1844 to manage an estate there.
After a series of financial set-backs he entered Government service as Deputy
Superintendent of Police, Penang, in 1849. He qualified for the bar whilst on

take their advice in the handling of affairs, nor to employ them on missions to the Malay States. But he did accept their assumption that what went on in these states was naturally the concern of the Straits Government. He assumed from the first that it was his responsibility to use his influence in the Peninsula to protect British trade and to exercise a general surveillance over Malay politics. Similarly, though he was at odds with many of the Singapore merchants on matters of administration within the settlements he became increasingly convinced by the arguments of men like W. H. Read, the senior unofficial member of the Legislative Council and President of the Singapore Chamber of Commerce,[13] that his government ought to do something to secure settled conditions in the Malay States so that trade could prosper. It is significant in this connexion that though at the outset the Colonial Office had given him no official guidance on the subject it was always open to Sir Harry to ask for instructions, and that he did not do so until eight months later, when he had involved himself so deeply with Kedah and Siam that he needed outside help. He was launched on to the difficult sea of Malay politics without guidance, but also without restrictions, and this position he accepted gladly and without demur. He was not ignorant of the type of problems in which he might become involved, for he had seen much service in the Gold Coast, where the position of the English settlements and their relations with the inland peoples were in many ways similar to what he found in Malaya. In 1865, when reporting on the Gold Coast he had written:

leave in England, and in 1862 went into private practice in Singapore in partnership with Andrew Logan. He was employed as Crown Counsel for the Straits Government after 1864. Braddell knew the west coast of Malaya well for he had often sailed native craft up and down it. He published in 1861 *Statistics of the British Possessions in the Straits of Malacca*, an invaluable work of reference (Buckley, *Anecdotal History of Singapore*, pp. 696–7; *100 Years of Singapore*, vol. ii, pp. 423–8). Macpherson had been in official service in the Straits since 1860, and had been Resident Councillor at Malacca and Singapore. At the time of the transfer he seems to have been the only one of the Indian officials who went out of their way to oblige Ord, and the latter secured for him the post of Colonial Secretary in the new régime. But these good relations did not last, and when Macpherson died in 1869 he and Ord were quarrelling bitterly (Buckley, op. cit. vol. ii, *passim*; CO 273/10, *passim*).

[13] W. H. Read was at this time the doyen of the mercantile community in the Straits. He had come out to Singapore as long ago as 1841, and did not return finally to England until 1887. A leading spirit in the agitation for the transfer of 1867, he acted as Dutch Consul-General in the Straits and had long commercial connexions with most of the Malay States (Buckley, op. cit., pp. 367–369; *100 Years of Singapore*, vol. ii, pp. 417–19).

... whenever settlements are brought into contact with warlike and lawless savages such complications as have occurred on the West Coast are by no means infrequent, and are generally productive of financial and other difficulties.[14]

His West African experience however did not deter him from plunging almost at once into disputes and negotiations with several of the Malay States. His previous employment as a negotiator in a subordinate capacity of the West African Agreements with France and Holland (1856–7 and 1860) had whetted his appetite, and he now seized the opportunity to employ his talent in this direction unhampered by any close control.[15] Whatever the reasons the act was entirely typical of the man, sure of his own capacity, and as impatient of restraint from above as he was of criticism from below.

Certainly conditions in the Malay States at the time when Sir Harry Ord arrived in Singapore in April 1867 were as warlike and lawless as those he had studied in West Africa. Nowhere outside Kedah and Johore were there ordered government, or conditions in which trade and economic development could make headway. In most states groups of Malay chiefs fought each other for mastery—the prize either the control of the state itself, or the possession of a river-mouth port. For in these years the rivers provided the key to this wild and roadless country. There were tracks, mainly across water-sheds from river to river, but in the main the rivers provided the only practicable highways for the trader bringing in his wares or for the tin-miner sending his produce out. Along the rivers were found the majority of the population, strung out in small villages, and each local chief ruled over a section of river rather than over an area reckoned in square miles. So the Sultan or Raja established at the river's mouth was able to control the hinterland, and to draw a steady income from tolls on the traffic passing up and down the river. Control of a river and the ability to levy dues on trade and on the inhabitants of the riverside villages represented not only financial affluence but political power and social position. In their struggle to secure

---

[14] Claridge, *History of the Gold Coast and Ashanti* (1915), vol. i, p. 532.

[15] It is perhaps significant here that Ord's employment in 1869 on a mission to the Governor-General of Netherlands India in connexion with the proposed convention to regulate British and Dutch trading rights in Sumatra came as a result of his own suggestions (Gov. Straits to Sec. State, 3 Aug. 1868, in CO 273/21).

control of these assets however the rival chiefs tended to depreciate their value. Ruinous tolls which tended to choke off trade, harsh and arbitrary exactions from the peasantry which crushed all incentive towards industry, a general disregard for all rights of life or property save those of the ruler or the raja class —all these things were part of the normal life of every Malay state. It was the same on the west coast or on the east; the same in a 'Siamese' state like Trengganu or an independent state such as Perak. But in the independent states things were worse, for there civil war led to blockade and bloodshed. In the intermittent struggles between rival Malay chiefs the native traders and the Chinese miners were pawns like the Malay peasants, the *rayat*— to be humoured, squeezed, or plundered as the course of events might dictate. Only in Kedah and Johore was this time-honoured pattern modified to allow a relatively stable way of life.

The better conditions in Kedah and Johore can be ascribed partly to their proximity to British territory, partly to the strong position of their rulers. The Sultan of Kedah was, as we have seen above, a vassal of Siam. He also received a large annual payment from the British Government in consideration of his cession to them of Penang and Province Wellesley. His position was therefore a good deal stronger than that of his fellow Sultans in the independent states to the south, and he had not so strong a motive for plundering the unfortunate traders. This is not to say that conditions in Kedah were perfect. The position of the *rayat* there was much the same as in the other Malay States, there was a good deal of disorder on the borders of Province Wellesley, and duties on trade were high.[16] But regular contact with Penang and the knowledge that indignities offered to British subjects would lead to embarrassing consequences, possibly even to the stopping of the Sultan's annuity, meant that the trader there could usually count at least on the safety of life and limb.

Johore was unique among the Malay States. It owed its existence as a separate state to the British foundation of Singapore in 1819. A close political and economic connexion with Singapore was maintained in the years which followed. In 1855, as we have seen, the British authorities intervened to compose the Johore succession dispute, and as a result the titular Sultan of Johore resigned to the Temenggong sovereignty over Johore state in

[16] Gov. Straits to Sec. State, 31 Dec. 1867, in CO 273/13.

return for the assignment to him of the little district of Muar
and an annual cash payment of $500.[17] Economically Johore was
part of Singapore, and as his state developed the Temenggong's
position grew stronger. In the fifties he was already prosperous
from the proceeds of the gutta percha monopoly.[18] Then as the
soil of Singapore Island became exhausted many Chinese moved
over to Johore and began to plant gambier and pepper there.[19]
This development the Temenggong was strong enough to control
and turn to his own advantage. He granted or leased rivers or
portions of rivers to individual Chinese merchants from Singapore, and left it to them to find the capital and labour to open up
the area.[20] By 1864 there was more than $1 million invested in
gambier and pepper plantations in Johore,[21] and a small port and
saw-milling centre which grew up in the sixties at Tanjong Putri,
on the north shore of the Johore Strait became such a promising
place that in 1866 it was renamed Johore Baharu and became the
capital of the state.[22] Trade flourished and the Temenggong's
revenues increased. But though the ruler of Johore grew more
powerful he was wise enough to see that his ultimate interests
were still linked with those of the British Government of Singapore. Neither the Temenggong Daing Ibrahim nor his son Abu-
Bakar, who succeeded him in 1862, ever pursued their own
inclination or immediate interest on any important subject once
it was intimated to them that British policy favoured another
course. Difficulties arose from the jurisdiction of the Temenggong
over British subjects in Johore and his right to license fishermen
in the Johore Strait.[23] In 1865 a clash was provoked by an attempt

[17] See above, p. 15, and the Treaty between the Sultan and Temenggong
(1855) in Maxwell and Gibson, op. cit., pp. 127–9.
[18] Read, W. H., *Play and Politics, Recollections of Malaya by an Old Resident*
(1901), p. 14.
[19] Buckley, op. cit., vol. ii, pp. 431 and 553. By 1871 there were about 60,000
Chinese in Johore (Acting Gov. Straits to Sec. Straits, 18 Nov. 1871, in CO
273/51).
[20] Cf. Coope, A. E., 'The Kanchu System in Johore', *JRASMB*, xiv, pt. 3
(1936).
[21] Petition from the Chinese traders in Gambier and Pepper to Gov. Cavenagh,
3 Oct. 1864, in CO 273/15.
[22] Gov. Straits to Govt. of India, 26 Aug. 1861, in CO 273/4; Temenggong to
Gov. Straits, 7 Apr. 1865, in CO 273/15; Winstedt, 'History of Johore', *JRASMB*,
x, pt. 3 (1932), p. 108.
[23] The difficulty over jurisdiction arose in 1861 from the arbitrary nature of
justice in Johore, which as in other Malay states depended often on the whim
of the ruler. A situation which in China, Siam and Japan led to the development of extra-territorial jurisdiction was resolved here by the Temenggong
drawing up, with the help of several Singapore lawyers, a regular penal code

of the Temenggong to divert all boats exporting produce from Johore through Tanjong Putri, which the Straits Government regarded as a bid on his part to secure a monopoly of the trade at the expense of Singapore.[24] In every case the Temenggong gave way. As a ruler whose position and prestige were sustained by British influence and the official recognition of a regular treaty[25] the Temenggong was consistently offered and usually acted upon the official advice of the Singapore Government. Temenggong Abu-Bakar had been educated in Singapore and was quite at home in European society there, so that the day-to-day counsel of the Singapore merchants and lawyers, and of the officials in their private capacity was always available to him.[26] There is no doubt that the personal background of its ruler had much to do with the nature of the relations between Johore and Singapore. In 1868 Sir Harry Ord, speaking of Temenggong Abu-Bakar, told the Secretary of State:

In his tastes and habits he is an English gentleman, as a ruler he is anxious to promote in every way the advancement and civilization of

which subsequently received British approval (Cavenagh, op. cit., pp. 312–13; Winstedt, *Johore*, pp. 96–97). The Temenggong's claim to license fishermen in Johore Strait clashed with the British claim to sovereignty over 'the seas straits and islets' within 10 miles of the coast of Singapore Island, which had been ceded by Art. II of the Treaty of 1824 (Maxwell and Gibson, op. cit., p. 123). The British determination to stand upon the letter of their treaty rights was dictated partly by the need to convince the Courts that pirates taken in those waters were subject to their jurisdiction, but also by the fear that any attempt by the Temenggong to bring the crews of foreign ships frequenting Johore Strait under his control might in the existing state of the law in Johore bring about complications with other European Powers (Gov. Straits to Govt. of India, 26 Aug. 1861; Govt. of India to Sec. State for India, 9 Jan. 1862, in CO 273/4).

[24] Here again, in addition to the desire to defend the commercial interests of Singapore, the undesirability of large numbers of foreign ships using the Johore Strait was also advanced as a reason for opposition to the Tanjong Putri scheme (Gov. Straits to Govt. of India, 27 May 1865 and attached papers in CO 273/15).

[25] The Treaty of 1824, supplemented by the Agreement of 1855 with the Sultan of Johore, to which the British Government adhered, recognized the Temenggong as the ruler of Johore, gave him a British pension, and the moral backing of the British Government, in return for which he agreed to submit his external relations to British control (see above, pp. 7 and 14–15). There was however no pledge to give him material support against internal or external opposition, but a definite disclaimer of this in Art. X of the Treaty of 1824 (Maxwell and Gibson, op. cit., p. 125).

[26] In Apr. 1865 the Temenggong's steam yacht the *Johore* blew up as she was preparing to take the Governor and the Singapore notables on a picnic. The description of the incident in Buckley (vol. ii, pp. 719–21) is interesting for it shows the intimate connexion between Singapore society and the Temenggong's relatives and entourage.

his people, and he is the only Rajah in the whole Peninsula, or the adjoining States, who rules in accordance with the practice of civilized nations. He is deeply attached to the British Government and nation, and feeling with their support and encouragement he is most likely to benefit his country he takes no steps of importance in administration without the advice of the local government, whilst he is ready at all times to place the whole resources of his country at our disposal.[27]

If in her relations with the British settlements Johore was a model of what a Malay state should be, her connexions with the other states of the Peninsula, especially Pahang and the east-coast states, were still in 1867 a source of anxiety to the Singapore Government. Pahang at this time was hardly beginning to re-cover from a long civil war. This had broken out in 1857 when on the death of the ruler the succession to the throne was disputed between his sons Tun Mutahir, the eldest, and Wan Ahmad. We have already seen the attitude adopted by the Indian Government of the Straits Settlements towards this conflict, and the steps taken by Governor Cavenagh to prevent the intervention of Siam in the dispute.[28] The war lasted until 1863, when Wan Ahmad was left in possession of the field and became Bendahara. But in 1867 his position on his newly won throne was not yet secure. The Temenggong of Johore, who was related by marriage to the defeated Tun Mutahir and who had given him his active support during the war, was still an opponent to be reckoned with. Tun Mutahir himself died in 1863, but there was still a part for the Temenggong to play in the attempts of Mutahir's three sur-viving sons to regain their inheritance. With his support they at-tempted an unsuccessful invasion of Western Pahang through Rembau and the Triang River area in 1866, and they were to try again through Selangor and Raub two years later.[29] The bad blood thus created between the Temenggong and the new Ben-dahara of Pahang found concrete expression in a dispute over the boundary between their two states. The existing boundary settle-ment was that incorporated in a treaty of alliance between the Temenggong and Tun Mutahir in 1862.[30] This fixed the frontier at the Endau River, and awarded the islands off its mouth to Johore as compensation for the help given to Tun Mutahir in the

[27] Gov. Straits to Sec. State, 10 Feb. 1868, in CO 273/17.
[28] See pp. 15–17 above.
[29] Linehan, 'History of Pahang', *JRASMB*, xiv, pt. 2 (1936), pp. 92–94.
[30] Text in Maxwell and Gibson, op. cit., pp. 209–11. See p. 16 above.

civil war. It was not therefore surprising that this settlement was
not accepted by Wan Ahmad, who claimed the islands for himself
and refused to budge when Governor Cavenagh tried to persuade
him to adhere to the terms made by Tun Mutahir. There was thus
some danger that if the boundary dispute was not resolved it
might be the occasion of a fresh outbreak of violence on the east
coast.[31]

Rembau, through which Mutahir's sons had marched in 1866,
besides being an avenue for attacks on Pahang was also involved
in a quarrel of its own with the other states behind Malacca. This
was a dispute with Sungai Ujong—in which Selangor, because of
its control over the Lukut mines, was also interested—for the
possession of Simpang Linggi, at the junction of the Rembau and
Linggi Rivers. These small states of the Menangkabau Confederacy, as we have seen, had been convulsed by these petty
quarrels for forty years. It is almost impossible to make sense of
the bewildering interplay of personal ambition, family feud and
inter-state rivalry in these years, but the general position in 1867
is clear. The western portion of the Menangkabau Confederacy
was important to the outside world because of the tin deposits
worked by Chinese miners in Sungai Ujong and in Lukut, though
at this time the latter district was inside the boundary of Selangor.
The best route to the mines was up the Linggi River which from
its estuary at the northern boundary of Malacca territory ran
through several small pockets of land claimed by Selangor,
Rembau, the Dato' Klana and the Dato' Bandar of Sungai Ujong,
the little Bugis settlement of Linggi, and several other petty
chiefs each striving to maintain their independence and to wring
some profit from the river. The contending chiefs and many minor
desperadoes and adventurers all erected stockades on the river
and blocked traffic in an attempt to levy tolls and to strike at
their rivals further up and down the river. The result was the
intermittent paralysis of the tin trade in which the interests of the
Malacca merchants were bound up, and the record of the British
Government's relations with these states after about 1845 is little

---

[31] Linehan, op. cit., pp. 90–91. In July 1865, when two British warships
which had been sent to Pulau Tinggi, one of the disputed islands, to hunt down
the murderer of a British subject failed to find him, Cavenagh appealed to Wan
Ahmad for help. Wan Ahmad replied politely that he would be delighted to
look for the murderer since he was a Johore man trespassing on an island which
belonged to Pahang (Winstedt, *Johore*, p. 107).

more than that of a series of fruitless attempts to get the stockades removed and the river cleared for trade. Governor Cavenagh (1859–67) was particularly active in this direction, but his efforts met with only temporary success, and the problem still faced the Colonial Office administration.[32]

We have now outlined the state of affairs in all the Malay states of the Peninsula except Perak and Selangor on the west coast, and a group of three states—Trengganu, Kelantan and Patani—on the east coast. These last need not detain us long. Patani, an old-established centre which in the sixteenth and seventeenth centuries had been a focus for European and native trade with Indo-China and the Far East, had fallen on evil days and was a dependency of Siam. Its people were Malay by race and custom, but it was controlled from Bangkok and since the Straits Settlements Government had little to do with it and recognized the Siamese position there we need not concern ourselves with it further.[33] The position of Kelantan and Trengganu was less clear. Burney's Treaty with Siam (1826) was a model of diplomatic evasion on the subject: it provided that Siam should not 'go and obstruct or interrupt commerce' there, and that 'the English' should 'not go and molest, attack or disturb' them,[34] but it left the question of their status unsettled. In 1862 they were described by the Indian Government as 'Tributary to Siam but protected by Treaty with the British Government',[35] and in general the policy of the Indian Governors of the Straits Settlements seems to have been directed towards belittling the Siamese position there. In fact in the sixties one state only, Kelantan, seems to have been tributary to Siam and to have sent regularly to Bangkok the *bunga mas* (golden flower), the token of vassalage. Its then reigning Sultan, Sultan Senik or Mulut Merah, 'the red-mouthed Sultan'

[32] Winstedt, 'Negri Sembilan', *JRASMB*, xii, pt. 3, (1934), pp. 67–69; Gullick, 'Sungai Ujong', *JRASMB*, xxii, pt. 2 (1949), pp. 18–20; Cavenagh, *op. cit.*, p. 298; Straits Settlements Annual Report, 1860–1, p. 19. The most detailed account of affairs in Sungai Ujong, Rembau and Linggi at this time is in a report by Thomas Braddell, printed in C. 1320 of 1875, pp. 11–36.

[33] In a map produced by the Surveyor-General of the Straits Settlements for the Government of India in 1862, Patani is marked as 'Tributary to Siam' (copy in CO 273/74). We have already discussed the background of the Siamese position in Malaya in the Introductory Chapters of this study; see p. 10 above.

[34] Maxwell and Gibson, *op. cit.*, p. 80.

[35] In the map cited in footnote 33, above. In his 'Report on the Treaties and Engagements with the Native States of the Malayan Pensinsula anterior to 1860' (Maxwell and Gibson, pp. 1–7), Cavenagh describes them as 'protected by the British Government under the Treaty of Bangkok'.

(reigned 1839–77) owed his installation on the throne to Siamese intervention. Trengganu was at this time an independent state with a highly independent ruler, one Baginda Omar (reigned 1839–76), who had conquered his kingdom with the sword. He refused to send the *bunga mas* to Siam, but retained friendly though remote contacts with her as he did with the old suzerains of the Malay world at Riau and with the British in Singapore. He supported the winning side in the Pahang Civil War, though his capital was roughly handled by Cavenagh when that officer suspected that it was being used as a centre of Siamese influence. Both the Kelantan and Trengganu Sultans were strong rulers who kept their states free of internal disorder, the first by a reputation for harshness, the latter by a deliberate policy of centralization; he declined to appoint successors when powerful territorial chiefs died, and instead installed *penghulu* in charge of one or more villages who were directly responsible to him.[36]

Perak and Selangor we have left till last in this review, for in these states Malay politics had attained by 1867 their most advanced stage—here on the west coast conditions were worse than anywhere else. In both states the quarrels of the Malay rajas produced two hostile groups of chiefs. In both large communities of Chinese tin-miners became involved in the quarrels of the Malays, and in both the opposing groups were financed by competing speculators and mercantile syndicates in the neighbouring British settlements. In 1867 both states seemed poised on the edge of civil war which if it came threatened to plunge the whole of the west coast into chaos and to undermine the political safety and economic stability of Penang and Malacca, so far were outside interests entangled in local politics. The position in Perak and Selangor was thus more complex than in any of the other states, and in the next few years events here were to form the crux of Britain's problems in Malaya. The story of the Straits Government's relations with the Malay States will bring us in due course to a closer examination of conditions in Selangor in our next chapter. Here we may more profitably conclude this review of the Peninsular states with some account of the complicated situation in Perak.

In Perak the titular Sultan was weak and the territorial chiefs

[36] Graham, W. A., *Kelantan* (1908), pp. 44–48; Sheppard, M. C. ff., 'Short History of Trengganu', *JRASMB*, xxii, pt. 3 (1949), pp. 27–37.

strong. There was an elaborate and old-established constitution[37] in which the chiefs were grouped into grades—the Four, the Eight, the Sixteen and the Thirty Two—according to their importance. The Sultan was elected by the chiefs, as were the two other most important office-holders, the Raja Muda or heir apparent and the Raja Bendahara, first of the Four, first minister, and head of all the chiefs not of royal blood. It was not however an open election; the choice was confined to those of the royal blood in the male line, and it was usual for a *waris* or heir to the throne to pass in succession through the offices of Bendahara and Raja Muda before becoming Sultan. It was normally therefore not so much a question of electing a Sultan as of assenting to the installation of an obvious candidate. On the death of a Sultan the Raja Muda and the Bendahara moved one rung up the ladder to fill the space at the top, and another princeling, usually the eldest son of the dead ruler, became in his turn Bendahara.[38] Usually the system worked well enough, and most young rajas born in the direct male line and sustained by the influence of their families could reckon that in their maturer years they would come to office. Occasionally however there was trouble and an unpopular candidate would fail to obtain the assent of the chiefs. It is from one such case that we may date the beginning of the internal strife which worried Perak in 1867.

[37] For a full description of the Perak constitution, cf. Winstedt, 'History of Perak', *JRASMB*, xii, pt. 1 (1934), pp. 134–58. For conditions in the west-coast states in general at this time, see also Gullick, J. M., *Indigenous Political Systems of Western Malaya* (1958).

[38] This constitution operated in the nineteenth century within very definite limits. It did not provide the state with an effective executive, for the Sultan though in theory an absolute ruler was powerless without the support of the other chiefs, and this support was rarely forthcoming, for the Sultan was usually at odds with the other leading figures in the state. Nor did the constitution provide a real administrative system. Such a thing was impossible and unwanted in a country where the law was the will of each local chief, and where the writ even of Sultan, Raja Muda or Bendahara did not run outside his own personal bailiwick. What the constitution did do was to act as a rough and ready spoils system, allotting the perquisites and prestige of offices whose functions had now largely atrophied to various branches of the ruling family in turn. By the middle of the century indeed a system of rotation between the different branches of the family seemed to be developing; cf. the genealogical tables in Winstedt, *Perak*, pp. 131–3. It has been customary to use the word 'feudal' as a description of Malay society generally at this time. This is accurate only in the very broadest sense, in so far as all political relationships were personal relationships. So far as Perak is concerned however a very good parallel could be drawn with tenth and eleventh-century France—there was an elected but theoretically all-powerful ruler who in the midst of territorial princes was virtually powerless except in his own domain.

Sultan 'Abdu'llah Muhammad Shah (reigned 1851–7) was for most of his reign in open conflict with the other Perak chiefs, led by Raja Muda Ja'far. Driven from his palace he appealed in vain to the Straits Government for their help, and at the time of his death he was a beaten man, practically without supporters.[39] Under normal conditions Sultan 'Abdu'llah's eldest son Yusuf should on his father's death have succeeded to the office of Bendahara. But his efforts in defence of his father had antagonized the other chiefs, especially Ja'far who now became Sultan, and they united to keep him out. In his place a favourite of Ja'far, one Raja Ismail, was appointed.[40] Ismail was descended on his mother's side from the Perak royal line, but his father was a Sumatran Malay, a Raja 'Abdu'r-Rahman of Siak, so that he was technically a commoner ineligible for succession to the throne. Except for the fact that Yusuf was left as a potential trouble-maker this raised no immediate problem, but it created an awkward situation when Sultan Ja'far died in 1865.[41] The Raja Muda 'Ali succeeded Ja'far as Sultan, as was usual. But Bendahara Ismail because he was not royal could not become Raja Muda in his turn, and some other candidate had to be found. Yusuf had the best claim by birth, but his feud with the other chiefs still rankled, and they were afraid of his harshness and officiousness, or as he said his determination to enforce order and obedience. So they again refused his claim, and the son of the late Sultan Ja'far, Raja 'Abdu'llah, was elected over his head.

From 1865 onwards there were therefore three chiefs, Yusuf, 'Abdu'llah, and Ismail jockeying for influence against the time when Sultan 'Ali should die and the throne again be vacant. This state of affairs was not unusual in a Malay state, and normally would have excited little comment. If the worst came to the worst

---

[39] Winstedt, *Perak*, p. 76; India Office Records, Collection 151.781 to draft 816 of 1854. Britain was bound by Burney's Treaty of 1826 and by Low's Treaty of the same year (see above pp. 11–12) to protect Perak and her rulers against outside attack. But the Indian Government, whilst willing to arbitrate if invited by both sides, refused to intervene in any other way in Perak's internal affairs.

[40] Cowan, 'Sir Frank Swettenham's Perak Journals', *JRASMB*, xxiv, pt. 4 (1951), pp. 13, 54–57.

[41] It was not the first time that a descendant from the distaff side had become Bendahara. The Bendahara was originally prime minister and commander-in-chief, and charged with the control of all chiefs who were not royal. He was thus the first commoner, and it was only towards the end of the eighteenth century that a royal Bendahara was appointed and the office became recognized as in direct line to the throne after the Raja Muda. Ismail's appointment can thus be recognized as a reversion to earlier practice (cf. Winstedt, *Perak*, pp. 137–40).

civil wars were not unknown in Malay states. There was no danger that an outside power would take advantage of these perennial quarrels to intervene as Siam, for instance, had done in Kelantan in 1839. The treaties of 1826 guaranteed British protection against such a disaster, and enabled Perak's nobility to engage in their feuds with impunity. There was however one element in the situation in Perak which was novel, and made the future course of events there of vital importance to the Straits Settlements. This was the development of an area of large-scale Chinese tin-mining, and supported by it a new type of Malay chief.

British treaties protected Perak in these years from the political encroachments of foreign powers, but they could not protect her from the encroachments of the expanding nineteenth-century world economy. The Chinese tin miners came to Perak, and they came after about 1850 in ever increasing numbers to the district of Larut, on the coast almost opposite Penang. There were Chinese miners elsewhere in Perak in these years, in the Kinta valley and on the Batang Padang River, but Larut was the Chinese mining area *par excellence*. There they were more numerous than elsewhere, more strongly organized, and more closely connected with Chinese society in the Straits Settlements.

The representative of Malay authority in Larut when the Chinese invasion began was Che' Long Ja'far, a family connexion of the Panglima Bukit Gantang. This territorial chief was at that time one of the Eight and an important figure in Perak, for he was keeper of the pass between Larut and the rest of Perak, and the defender of its northern frontier. Che' Long Ja'far however was a very lowly individual, employed to collect the tenths on rice and other dues in what was in 1850 sparsely populated swamp country. But as the extent of its tin deposits became known and the Chinese flocked there Long Ja'far throve on the revenue from the mines, and gradually extended his authority from Larut proper to the adjoining areas of Krian, Matang and Selama. By the time of his death in 1857 he had managed to build up for himself a strong position in Larut which bore no relation to his humble origins.[42]

The grant of the Sultan which confirmed Long Ja'far's son Che' Ngah Ibrahim as his successor gave him far wider powers than his father had possessed. It empowered him to make laws,

[42] Wilkinson, R. J., *History of the Peninsular Malays* (1923), pp. 99–100; *Papers on Malay Subjects: History* (1908), pp. 89–90.

and to deal directly with the British authorities in Penang.[43] The affairs of Larut naturally attracted the interest of the Straits Government because of the connexions of the Chinese with their societies and financial backers in the British colony. Many of the miners were British subjects, either in fact or by repute, and looked to the Straits Government for help in times of trouble. Moreover, though the miners in Larut paid dues and customs duties to Ngah Ibrahim they were otherwise left to govern themselves, which they did through their societies with their headquarters in Penang. By 1860 most of the miners and their backers were organized in two large groups. One group, largely of Cantonese origin and connected with the Ghee Hin Society were known locally as the 'Si Kwans' (Four Districts) from their districts of origin in China; the other group, predominantly Hakka (Kheh), owed allegiance to the Hai San Society and were known as the 'Go Kwans' (Five Districts).

Little detailed work has been done on these nineteenth-century societies since the contemporary contributions of Schlegel and Pickering (see Bibliography), and it is dangerous for a non-Chinese reader to venture far beyond this general outline. The famous Triad Society from which the Ghee Hin in Malaya was descended had existed in China for centuries, and had originally been a religious or benevolent association on masonic lines. At the time of the Manchu conquest of China in the seventeenth century the Triad turned itself into a political organization pledged to work for the return of the Ming dynasty, and went underground. It retained its old ritual, with its exhortations to a righteous life, but with the passing of time and the repressive measures of the Chinese Government it gradually degenerated into what Schlegel styled 'a band of rebels and robbers'.[44] In Malaya the Ghee Hin and the other societies had this character from the beginning; a Canadian historian of the Straits Settlements in the first half of the nineteenth century called one of them 'the Pirates and Robbers Co-operative Association'.[45] The Chinese who emigrated to the Straits were mostly men from the lowest classes of society, those with nothing to lose, landless peasants, broken men, paupers and criminals from the southern provinces and the seaport cities

[43] Wilkinson, op. cit., pp. 100–1; Winstedt, *Perak*, p. 79.
[44] Pickering, W., 'Chinese Secret Societies', *JRASSB*, i (1878), pp. 64–65.
[45] Mills, L. A., op. cit., p. 203.

of South China. In the Settlements they were crowded into towns where the few British administrators and police were totally ignorant of their language and customs, and where government made no effort to interfere in their daily life or their relations with each other. The societies seized this opportunity, and for fifty years until the first attempt to register and control them in 1869 they were the only form of authority with which the average Chinese immigrant came into contact. Most immigrants were compelled if necessary by force to join one society or another. The societies kept their members under control by impressive rituals, oath-taking, and a ferocious scale of punishments including the death penalty for transgression against their rules. They decided disputes between their members, and protected them against the law and against outsiders, either by physical force or by financial support. They extorted protection money from brothels, opium dens and shopkeepers, and raised large sums for special occasions by a general levy on their members.[46] Their leaders, usually prosperous merchants and business men of good standing in the community, resembled nothing so much as the Chicago racketeers of our own age as they used the societies to drive a rival out of business or to stage a riot in protest against some Government regulation.[47]

The Penang Ghee Hin Society was almost entirely Cantonese and Tiu Chiu in membership. The members were mainly from the labouring and artisan classes, and included the 'Si Kwans'

[46] In 1850 one society paid a fine of $200 on one individual by a general levy of one cent from each of its 20,000 members (Buckley, op. cit., vol. ii, p. 537).

[47] The best general account of the Chinese Societies in Malaya is in Purcell, *The Chinese in Malaya* (1948), pp. 155–73. An earlier acccount in Mills, op. cit. pp. 203–10, is also useful. A technical distinction may be made here between the *hui* or secret society and the *kongsi* or benevolent association. As a type the *hui* drew its members from all Chinese in Malaya whatever their origin. The *kongsi* on the other hand was generally confined to those coming from the same village or district in China, or having the same surname or clan name, and ideally confined its activities to securing the social and economic welfare of its members—it helped them in sickness and old age, looked after their children when work took them away from home, and so on. In practice however it is difficult to maintain this distinction between the *kongsi* as a harmless institution and the *hui* as a vicious one. In protecting the interests of its members the *kongsi* often became involved in feuds with other *kongsis* just as violent as any secret society war. Many Chinese, loyal members of their clan or district *kongsi*, also belonged to secret societies. On some issues, especially when as in Larut the *huis* were composed largely of Chinese from the same district in China, the interests of the two organisations coincided. In other cases they did not, and fellow members of the same *kongsi* often cut each others' throats cheerfully in a quarrel between rival *huis*.

of Larut; their numbers in 1867 were estimated at twenty-five to twenty-six thousand.[48] The Hai San Society was like the Ghee Hin old-established in Malaya. It had been a Cantonese-dominated society, but between 1845 and 1860 this seems to have changed, and in the 1860's its membership was increasingly Hakka, and its strength was concentrated among the 'Go Kwans' in Larut, where it outnumbered the Ghee Hins.[49] A third society, the Toh Peh Kong, unlike the other two in Penang was of recent formation, dating only from the 1840's. It was much smaller than the Ghee Hin, having only about five to six thousand members in Penang, most of them Hokkiens. But they included nearly all the wealthy merchants and shop-keepers of Penang, particularly the dealers in fire-arms and ammunition. The Toh Peh Kong was also strong amongst the Chinese communities at Junk Ceylon, Rangoon and Moulmein. It was therefore a society of merchants, most of whom would have been longer in the Straits and have a firmer stake in society there than the labourers and artisans who predominated amongst the rank and file of the Ghee Hin, and it had certainly been formed originally as a reaction against the influence of that society.[50]

Though in general the Ghee Hin in Penang was a Cantonese society, the Hai San Hakka, and the Toh Peh Kong Hokkien, society membership often cut across provincial and kongsi lines. So did the economic organization of the tin mining industry in these years. The Toh Peh Kong merchants of Penang were financially far more powerful than the other groups, but had less labour available to them within their own society. They therefore employed both Cantonese and Hakka labour in their own mines, and also financed Go Kwan and Si Kwan mines in return for the

<hr/>

[48] *Report of the Commission of Enquiry into the Penang Riots* (1868). Fourteen to fifteen thousand of these were said to be in Province Wellesley, the total population of all ages and sexes of which was only about 65,000. One of the members of the Commission, in a dissenting report, estimated that 5,000 Ghee Hins a year, including a large number straight from China, emigrated from Penang to recruit the Ghee Hin branches in the Malay States.

[49] Purcell, op. cit., p. 157; Res. Councillor, Penang, to Gov. Straits, 11 Sept. 1861, in CO 273/5.

[50] *Report of Commission on Penang Riots* (1868); 'Proceedings of Straits Settlements Government for 1st Quarter, 1859,' in CO 273/3. The Toh Peh Kong gave its name, in the form Tokong, to the general alignment of societies which grew up in opposition to the Ghee Hin or Triad Society. The other societies in this group were the Hai San in Larut and the Ghee Hok in Singapore, and after 1890 they were known in Malaya as the Sa Tiam Hui or Three Dot Society (cf. Purcell, p. 157).

right to first claim on the tin produced at a price below the current market price.[51] All this made for a very complicated state of affairs which it is almost impossible to unravel in detail from the scanty evidence now available, though the general outlines are clear.[52]

In 1861 the Ghee Hin and the Hai San in Larut quarrelled, and fighting broke out. The Ghee Hin were driven from the mines with considerable loss of life and property and fell back on Penang, and Ngah Ibrahim, seeing the Hai San in control, threw in his lot with them. The beaten Ghee Hin, many of whom were British subjects, appealed to the Governor of the Straits Settlements for redress and he, when he found that Sultan Ja'far of Perak was powerless to pay or to enforce payment of compensation, instituted a blockade of the Larut River. Ngah Ibrahim was the only Malay in Perak able to find the $17,000 demanded and in June 1862, after making his own terms with the Sultan, he handed over the required amount and the blockade was called off. In return for putting up the money to settle this incident Ngah Ibrahim was given by the Sultan full powers in Larut, and it became the practice of the British authorities to deal directly with him rather than to appeal to the Sultan. At the same time the title of Mantri (*Orang Kaya Mantri Sri Paduka Tuan*) was given him. Succession to this old-established office made Ngah Ibrahim one of the Four, and gave him a rank fifth in precedence after the Sultan.[53]

Thus by 1862 Ngah Ibrahim, or the Mantri as we may now call him, had secured for himself a virtually independent position as ruler of Larut. His control of this area gave him a basis of power far more formidable and of a different kind to that possessed by the other chiefs of Perak. Whilst they depended on the modest and unreliable income they derived from the traffic on the rivers of their undeveloped districts and on what they could squeeze from their peasants, he enjoyed a steady revenue which from the

[51] Cf. three Petitions from Oh Wee Kee, trader and mine financier of Penang in 1865 and 1866, in CO 273/15.

[52] Wong Lin Ken, 'The Malayan Tin Industry to 1914, with special reference to the states of Perak, Selangor, Negri Sembilan and Pahang', (1959), an unpublished Ph.D. thesis deposited in the Library of the University of London, contains an exhaustive study of the economic aspects of developments in Larut at this time.

[53] CO 273/5, *passim*; Winstedt, *Perak*, pp. 80–81; Wilkinson, *Papers on Malay Subjects: History*, p. 91, contains a translation of part of this grant.

duty on tin alone cannot have been less than $100,000 a year, and has been estimated as high as $186,000.[54] Whilst they lived in *atap* huts few of which excelled, except in size, the dwellings of their poorest followers, and had almost no contact with the outside world, he lived in a large European-style bungalow in Larut, owned another in Penang together with a steamship, and had at his disposal a regular Police Force. The connexion between the Chinese miners and Penang kept him in contact with the British Government there, and he retained a prominent Penang lawyer to represent him in court cases and other official business. We must not of course exaggerate the difference between Larut and the rest of Perak. The Mantri remained a Malay chief, and his country remained without regular justice or administration, and virtually without roads. But he had an assured and considerable income, he had influential contacts in the Straits Settlements, and (at this time) his credit there was good. So long as he retained control of the situation in Larut he remained by far the most powerful chief in Perak, and in any internal conflict there his influence on one side or the other would probably decide the issue.

After 1865 the Mantri tended more and more to make common cause with Bendahara Ismail as against 'Abdu'llah and Yusuf. Though his *de jure* position in Larut rested on the grants of 1858 and 1862, his peaceful enjoyment of power and independence depended upon each Sultan's indifference to events outside Perak proper.[55] Yusuf was energetic and determined to assert his rights. 'Abdu'llah was the known enemy of the Mantri because of a clash between them over the revenues of Krian, south of Larut, and he lived on the lower reaches of the Perak River near the coast, a position which kept him in touch with the outside world and would if he were Sultan restrict the Mantri's independence. Neither

---

[54] *Parl. Pap.* C. 1111 of 1874, p. 111.

[55] There is some doubt as to whether these grants made over Larut to the Mantri absolutely and in perpetuity, or whether they needed to be confirmed by successive Sultans. Wilkinson, *Papers on Malay Subjects: History*, Parts I and II (1908), pp. 92–93, discusses this, and prints the various grants in translation (ibid., pp. 102–5). There is no doubt that so far as his office of Mantri of Perak was concerned he was a vassal of the Sultan. Basing his argument on the documents however Wilkinson concludes that his position in Larut was not a Governorship tenable for a single life or on good behaviour only, and that it was not revocable by future Sultans. There is also the fact which Wilkinson does not mention that upon the accession of Sultan 'Ali (1865) no fresh grant appears to have been asked or given. Whatever the legal position the Mantri could not be certain of upholding his pretensions against Yusuf or 'Abdu'llah, both of whom had tried to poach on the revenues of Krian.

Yusuf nor 'Abdu'llah therefore were claimants likely to advance the Mantri's fortunes. But Ismail was old and weak, and the fact that he lived in the interior, far up the Kinta River, would leave the Mantri free to deal with the British authorities and the Chinese miners as he thought fit. So the ruler of Larut became more and more friendly with Ismail, and gradually assumed the position of his chief confidant and adviser.

Whilst the Mantri became more powerful in the Malay politics of Perak, there were ominous signs in those years that all was not well in his own district of Larut. The events of 1861 and 1862 which the Mantri had turned to his advantage had long-term effects which were not so fortunate for him. British intervention obtained the restoration of the Si Kwans of the Ghee Hin Society to their mines, but the bad blood which had been created between them and the Go Kwans remained. And since the Mantri had for his own purposes chosen to side with the Go Kwans (and incidentally had taken a large share of the spoils of war) he became involved in the feud. His police force, though it was an unusual asset for a Malay chief, was only about forty strong, and there were between 30,000 and 40,000 Chinese in Larut.[56] Normally therefore the Mantri's control depended on the tractability of his Chinese subjects, and now he had allied himself with the Hai San men his position became to a large extent dependent on them maintaining their superiority over the other side. This in the long run they were unable to do, for in 1867 a new phase of the struggle between the Chinese societies developed.

During 1865 and 1866 the Chinese feud continued sporadically in Larut, and the Hai San with the help of the Mantri managed on the whole to keep the upper hand. The Government of the Straits Settlements, restrained by instructions from the Government of India, were unwilling to intervene again, and made no effective protest.[57] The Ghee Hin, stalemated in Larut, therefore

[56] Winstedt, *Perak*, p. 80; Report of C. I. Irving on Larut, 13 Apr. 1872, in *Perak and Larut Disturbances* (Archive Room, Raffles Museum, Singapore); Memo. by Lt.-Gov. Campbell, 24 Oct. 1872, in CO 273/61.

[57] Govt. of India to Gov. Straits, 15 Feb. 1866 and 4 May 1866, in CO 273/15. The Straits Government were forbidden to interfere except in cases of the murder in Larut of *de jure* British subjects, or of murder and piracy on the high seas. In these cases they were authorized to institute a blockade if all other means failed to produce satisfaction. Most of the Chinese affected were not strictly British subjects, though many of them had lived in Penang for twenty years or more; they never bothered to take out naturalization papers unless for some special cause such as the registration of a merchant ship in their name (cf. Res.

transferred the quarrel to Penang, where they were numerically stronger. They had already on their hands a quarrel with the Toh Peh Kong Society there, for in 1859 they had followed the same tactics with them; being worsted in a contest at Junk Ceylon, where the Toh Peh Kong were stronger, they had set upon the Hokkien shopkeepers in Penang, and these suffered severely before the fighting was stopped.[58] At some time after March 1863 the Toh Peh Kong seem to have made common cause with the Hai San against their common enemy, and at about the same time both sides gained further support from the Malay (more accurately Muslim) Red and White Flag Societies, which allied themselves with the Toh Peh Kong and the Ghee Hin respectively.[59]

In July 1867 the Ghee Hin brought in reinforcements from their members in Kedah, Province Wellesley, Larut and Junk Ceylon and, supported by Malays of the White Flag Society seized upon a trivial incident to set upon the Toh Peh Kong and such of their Hai San friends as were in Penang. The Toh Peh Kong with the Red Flag Malays and what help they could get from Larut and Province Wellesley fought back, but got very much the worst of the argument. For a while the fighting was stopped by the mediation of Colonel Mann, the former Indian Resident Councillor of Penang, who was still in the island awaiting a passage back to India. But in August part of the Penang garrison was sent off on an expedition to the Nicobar Islands, and the Chinese seized the opportunity to begin all over again. For ten days from the 3rd to the 14th August the local government completely lost

Councillor, Penang, to Gov. Straits, 6 July 1866, in CO 273/15). The Indian Government's despatch of 15 Feb. 1866 contained a famous passage to be paraphrased again and again in Colonial Office despatches in the next few years, and beginning—'If British subjects choose to live and trade in an uncivilized country like Perak, they must submit to the local customs and practices . . .'

[58] 'Proceedings of Straits Settlements Government for 1st Quarter, 1859', Collection 10, in CO 273/3.

[59] The Hai San and Toh Peh Kong had a brief clash between themselves in March 1863, and their alliance must have been arranged soon afterwards. The *Report on the Riots of 1867* (1868) places the alliance between the Toh Peh Kong and the Red Flag Society in 1863 and mentions that they had previously fought each other. There were numerous small clashes between the Toh Peh Kong and the Ghee Hin from then on. Gov. Straits to Sec. State, 11 Sept. 1868, in CO 273/21. The Red and White Flag Societies were composed of Malays and Muslim Tamils, and were originally religious societies, founded about ten years before, which had since lost their religious character. Purcell (p. 167) speaks of the Malays and Tamils 'becoming members' of the Chinese societies, and the 'Proceedings . . . 1st Quarter, 1859', mention a rumour that they 'belonged' to them, but the material from 1867 speaks only of the Muslim and Chinese societies co-operating with each other.

control of the situation. In the town of Penang itself some vestige of control was maintained by the erection of barricades which were manned by a motley force of sepoys, police, and hastily sworn European special constables. But in the rest of the island anarchy and lawlessness prevailed. Roving bands of Ghee Hin and Toh Peh Kong set fire to the houses and shops of their opponents, and many of the population not involved in the quarrel suffered injury and financial loss.[60]

In the history of the Straits Settlements themselves the Penang Riots of 1867 are important as the starting point of an attempt by the Government to cope with the problem of the Chinese Secret Societies[61]; they are also important in the history of Perak, since they increased the basic instability of the Mantri's position in Larut. Not only did they weaken the control of the Mantri's allies the Hai San, whose friends and financial backers the Toh Peh Kong merchants of Penang had suffered so severely, but the increased bitterness they caused between the two factions made it certain that there would be no early reconciliation between them. From 1867 onwards the Ghee Hin prepared to turn the tables on their enemies in Larut itself. In Perak proper the potential successors to the now ailing Sultan 'Ali became more and more out of temper with each other. Yusuf and 'Abdu'llah both tried to draw revenue from the Krian area and antagonized each other as well as the Mantri. 'Abdu'llah quarrelled with Sultan 'Ali, and Yusuf in 1869 wrote to the Straits Government claiming the throne for himself when 'Ali should die. Ismail shut himself away up the Kinta River and said nothing.

Such then was the kind of situation which had developed on the west coast of Malaya at the time when Sir Harry Ord began his first term of office in 1867. Perak was perhaps an extreme case, for there trouble in a Malay state not only threatened to dislocate trade, but had disturbed the peace of a British settlement and might do so again. But in Selangor and Sungai Ujong the general outline was the same; the initial rivalries and quarrels of the Malay chiefs provided a background of instability which was intensified by the feuds between competing groups of Chinese miners, and the financial and social links of the latter with a British

---

[60] *Report of Commission of Enquiry* . . . (1868); Gov. Straits to Sec. State, 19 Aug. 1867 in CO 273/11; Report of Col. Anson, 17 Aug. 1867 in CO 273/13; Anson, *About Others and Myself* (1920), pp. 278–9.
[61] Cf. Purcell, op. cit., pp. 168 et seq.

settlement—in this case Malacca and Singapore—threatened to involve British interests.

(ii) *Birth and Death of a Policy*

As we have seen the Colonial Office, so far as their surviving records indicate, began their tenure of office in the Straits Settlements without a Malayan policy. At any rate they furnished to the Governor whom they appointed to their new colony no instructions covering his relations with the neighbouring Malay States. But this officer's character and experience, with which we are now familiar, predisposed him towards an aspect of his duties which gave him a sense of importance and an opportunity for independent action not normally afforded to governors of Crown Colonies. Without asking for instructions from home he began at once to grapple with those questions concerning the Peninsular states which had been left over from the previous administration. Beyond this he took every opportunity to initiate fresh business with these states, and to impress their rulers with British interest in the area. During the first two years of his governorship Sir Harry Ord conducted negotiations with Perak, Kedah, Kelantan, Pahang and Johore, and his dealings with Kedah and Kelantan brought him into contact with Siam. These early years 1867 and 1868 thus stand out clearly as a first phase in the development of British policy towards the Malay States. It is a period occupied by an attempt to work out a positive policy on the spot, and it closes with the rejection of that policy by the Colonial Office.

Ord's early contacts with Perak arose from the long neglected treaty of 1826. By this treaty the island of Pangkor, off the entrance to the Dindings River, had been ceded to the East India Company, though it was never occupied by them and the treaty was never ratified.[62] The territories actually included in this transaction were stated by the treaty to be 'the Pulo Dinding and the Islands of Pangkor, together with all and every one of the Islands which belonged of old and until this period to the Kings of Perak'. The ambiguity which prompted Ord to begin a correspondence with the Sultan of Perak arose from the different constructions placed on the phrase 'Pulo Dindings and the Islands of Pangkor'. The Islands of Pangkor and Little Pangkor stand out to sea and

---

[62] P. 12 above. The text of the Treaty, 'No. 1 with Perak of 18 October 1826', is in Maxwell and Gibson, op. cit., p. 23.

are easily recognizable. The Straits Government therefore maintained that the words 'Pulo Dinding' must mean those portions of the Dinding estuary which though technically islands were embedded in the mangrove swamps of the mainland. The creeks of the estuary were a favourite haunt of pirates, the suppression of which had been the expressed purpose of the treaty. The Malays on the other hand held that 'Pulo Dinding' referred to other nearby islands (though there were none nearer than the Sembilan Islands off the Perak estuary), or alternatively that it was a redundant expression meaning no more than the islands of Pangkor and Little Pangkor.[63]

Ord set out to settle this question, perhaps with a view to the occupation of Pangkor, perhaps merely to stake a claim and impress on the Malays the continuing British interest in the area. Towards the end of 1867 negotiations began between Colonel Anson, the Lieutenant-Governor of Penang, and the Laksamana or Admiral of Perak, a dignitary supposedly in control of the seacoast. But an unexpected and unheralded visit to the Perak River by Ord unsettled the Perak chiefs, who feared that he was about to embark on a policy of annexation, and the negotiations with Anson were broken off,[64] though the correspondence between Ord and the Sultan continued sporadically into 1869.

It was typical of Sir Harry's early adventures in Malaya that these proceedings were not at the time reported to the Colonial Office, and only came to light in 1869 when the Hon. Henry Stanley (later Lord Stanley of Alderley), who had connexions in the Straits Settlements, began asking questions in London.[65] Ord explained his actions by saying that he had only been trying to ascertain the exact position under the Treaty of 1826.[66] He had in fact gone a good deal beyond this in pushing British claims to territory in an area where the Straits Government had shown no interest for nearly fifty years.

[63] Skinner's Précis of Perak Affairs, in CO 809/1, pp. 136–7.
[64] Anson, op. cit., p. 288.
[65] Henry Edwd. John Stanley (1827–93), 3rd Baron Stanley of Alderley (1869). After Eton and Trinity he entered the Foreign Office, where he was Palmerston's précis writer and later held junior posts in the Near East. He travelled widely throughout the East, became a Muslim and was said to have lived as an Arab in Singapore. A frequent speaker on Indian and Eastern topics in the House of Lords, he published several collections of essays and translated and edited six volumes in the Hakluyt series between 1865 and 1881 (DNB and Buckley, op. cit., vol. ii, passim).
[66] Gov. Straits to Sec. State, 14 July 1869, in CO 273/30.

In Kedah Sir Harry Ord continued negotiations begun by his predecessor Governor Cavenagh. These were aimed at amending the Treaty of 1800, which governed conditions of trade and frontier questions, and securing an adjustment of the frontier with Province Wellesley. There were three main points at issue:

1. Article III of the Treaty of 1800[67] stipulated that provisions exported from Kedah for consumption in Penang should be free of duty.[67] This stipulation was not being observed, and as the population of Penang grew the duties levied on these goods came to be an important part of the Sultan's income.

2. The establishment of opium and liquor shops and gambling houses just within the Kedah boundary—which was unsurveyed and had no boundary posts and other markers——led to disturbances within Province Wellesley and reduced the revenues from government opium, gambling and spirit farms in British territory.

3. The Straits Government had found that the existing boundary of Province Wellesley was difficult to police. It had a salient jutting out into Kedah in the south, and there was a similar wedge of Kedah land in British territory in the north. They wished to straighten the frontier to a line running roughly north and south, and thus obtain a shorter boundary which would be easier to control.

Governor Cavenagh had failed to obtain any satisfaction on these points, though he had gone so far as to get the Siamese authorities to bring pressure to bear on their vassal, and had himself suspended payment of the Sultan's annual allowance from the British Government.

Soon after his arrival in Singapore Sir Harry Ord re-opened negotiations. He took advantage of the good offices of the Chinese merchant Tan Kim Ching,[68] who was Siamese Consul-General

[67] Maxwell and Gibson, op. cit., pp. 98–100. This Treaty was not ratified by the Government of India until 1802, and is often referred to as the Treaty of 1802. It was in 1867 obsolete in several other ways. Thus it included Perlis, which he had not controlled since 1821, amongst the Sultan's possessions. It also forbade the residence of all non-British Europeans in the Sultan's territories.

[68] Tan Kim Ching (1829–92) was a perfect example of the cosmopolitan Straits merchant. He was the eldest son of a well-known Straits figure, Tan Tock Seng, founder of the hospital which still bears his name. Taking over his father's business in 1851 he expanded its interests, so that he was soon the owner of rice mills in Saigon and Siam, and of two steamships, and a promoter of the Tanjong Pagar Dock Company. He had great influence in the Malay States, especially in the northern states bordering on Siam, where he owned

in the Straits Settlements and also the trusted adviser of the Sultan of Kedah. Tan persuaded the Sultan to come to Singapore in August 1867. By the 19th September he and Ord had reached agreement.[69] The boundary with Province Wellesley was to be redrawn, a reasonable scale of duties to be levied on provisions exported to Penang, and the clause in the Treaty of 1800 which granted them duty-free status to be annulled. No opium, liquor or gambling shops were to be allowed within two miles of the new boundary, which was substantially the north–south line which the Straits Government desired. These terms were embodied in a 'Memo of Agreement' which was to form the basis of a formal treaty to be submitted for confirmation to the British and Siamese Governments.[70] Meanwhile it was agreed that the terms of the 'Memo of Agreement' should come into force at once, and on the strength of this Ord resumed payment of the Sultan's annuity.

On the 30th December Ord met the Sultan again at Penang, and presented for his signature a draft treaty. This embodied the terms of the 'Memo', but it also included redrafted versions of those parts of the Treaty of 1800 which the 'Memo' had not superseded, and a completely new clause covering the mutual extradition of criminals and accused persons.[71]

The Sultan would have nothing to do with this. He had agreed to the limited settlement embodied in the 'Memo of Agreement' in September. But now he was faced with a long and involved document which he could not properly understand, and his adviser Tan Kim Ching was not there to reassure him. In addition he had his relations with his suzerain, Siam, to consider. He had so far not consulted the Siamese authorities, for the 'Memo of Agreement' was restricted to local issues, and the fact that Tan Kim Ching was the Siamese Consul-General had given him a certain justification. But the conclusion of a full-scale treaty on his own responsibility was another matter, and he refused to sign. He maintained this attitude although Ord again stopped his

many mining concessions, and where his appointment as Consul-General and Special Commissioner for Siam gave him great weight. In the 1870's he became Farmer of the Kuala Perak taxes, and we shall meet him later on in the story as an adviser there of Sultan 'Abdu'llah (cf. Song Ong Siang, *One Hundred Years of the Chinese in Singapore* (1923), pp. 92–93).

[69] Gov. Straits to Sec. State, 31 Dec. 1867, in CO 273/13.
[70] Text of Memo. in CO 273/13, dated 19 Sept. 1867.
[71] Text in CO 273/13, annexed to Gov. Straits, 31 Dec. 1867.

E

annuity and wrote to the British Consul at Bangkok to bring pressure on the unfortunate Sultan from that quarter.

On the 31st December Sir Harry Ord reported the Kedah negotiation to the Secretary of State for the first time. Since he had bungled the matter, mishandling the Sultan, and involving Siam in the affair without result, he found himself at a loss; more-over with the bringing in of Siam he had invaded the sphere of the Foreign Office. In addition to describing the course which nego-tiations had taken and asking for instructions, therefore, he raised the question of his general position in relation to the neigh-bouring states. He admitted that under normal Colonial Office practice the Foreign Office was responsible for the external relations of Crown Colonies. But he asserted that under the Indian régime the power of negotiating and making treaties with Malay states had been vested in the local government of the Straits Settlements, subject of course to the approval and later ratification of the Government of India. The Straits merchants had supported this arrangement in 1861, when they suggested to the Colonial Office that after the transfer to the Colonial Office the Governor of the Straits Settlements should be appointed 'H.M.'s Commissioner and Superintendent of Trade in the Eastern Archipelago', with full powers to deal not only with the states of the Malay Penin-sula and Borneo, but also with other European settlements in the East.[72] Now, whilst pointing out that he had been given no indication of the limits of his authority in this direction and asking for general instructions, Sir Harry Ord drew attention to this earlier suggestion. He warned the Home government that any decrease in the accustomed powers of the Governor of the Straits Settlements would involve a loss of prestige which would be re-flected in an increase of piracy and of disturbances in the Malay States, and a loss of trade.[73]

The Perak and Kedah negotiations arose out of regular treaty relationships between those states and Great Britain, and con-cerned only their external affairs. But there were other occasions during his first year as Governor when Sir Harry Ord seemed to be feeling his way towards a policy of limited interference in the

---

[72] 'W. H. Read and others to the Duke of Newcastle, 30 June 1861', in *Parl. Pap.* 259 of 1862, p. 76.
[73] Gov. Straits to Sec. State, 31 Dec. 1867, in CO 273/13.

internal affairs of some of the Peninsular states. Opportunity for this was not lacking. We have already seen that 1867 and 1868 were years of bad trade in the Straits. In these circumstances obstacles to trade in the Peninsula became more serious, and complaints that the Straits Goverment ought to do something about it more frequent. In October 1867 the Singapore Chamber of Commerce complained that the Sultan of Kelantan was monopolizing the sale of cotton-yarn, opium, tobacco and gambier in his country to their great disadvantage. So Sir Harry wrote to the Sultan asking him to give up his royal monopoly, and reading him a lecture on the merits of free trade. When this produced no result he arranged with the Consul-General at Bangkok for the spur to be applied from that quarter, and a Siamese Commission was sent off to visit Kelantan and afterwards to discuss with the Governor of the Straits Settlements 'matters touching the welfare of the Siamese-Malayan States generally'.[74] When Ord saw them in Singapore in March 1868 they overwhelmed him with good news and fair words. They apologized for the Sultan's disrespect, and his lack of attention to the Governor's wishes, and assured him that the monopoly would be stopped.[75] At the same time they disposed of the Kedah affair, which had been at a standstill since December. Without consulting the unfortunate Sultan, who was present at the ceremony merely as a spectator, they signed Ord's draft treaty on his behalf, thus removing the Governor's biggest immediate worry and leaving him a very happy man.[76]

Sir Harry had been fortunate in his first connexion with the Siamese, and this experience of successful co-operation in the northern states seems to have brought him to regard a policy of sustained intervention in the states of Southern Malaya as a practical idea. He had not as yet received an answer to his despatch of the 31st December, with its proposition that he should act as a British pro-consul in South-East Asia. The Kedah affair was now however, as he thought, satisfactorily disposed of, and he was

[74] Ord to Raja of Kelantan, 22 Oct. 1867; Raja to Ord, 1 Nov. 1867; Ord to Consul Knox, 19 Nov. 1867; Consul Knox to Ord, 3 Dec. 1867, in CO 273/17.
[75] Gov. Straits to Sec. State, 23 Mar. 1868, in CO 273/17.
[76] Gov. Straits to Sec. State, 26 Mar. 1868. There were some slight modifications to Ord's draft. The Siamese reserved their right to navigate the Muda River which provided an outlet to the west coast for the Kroh (Patani) tin mines, and a clause was inserted permitting Kedah to stop the export of rice to Penang if her own crop failed. As a 'penalty' for not signing the Treaty before, the Sultan lost about half the land formerly allotted to him under the boundary rectification clause.

therefore emboldened to propose to the Secretary of State in April an extension of British influence in the Southern states.[77] After describing what he conceived to be the position of Siam as the suzerain of Kedah, Trengganu and Kelantan he wrote:

I may take this opportunity of expressing my opinion that the subjection of the Native States of the Peninsula to Powers stronger and more civilized than themselves is an advantage to themselves and to all who have relations with them. Nothing can be more unsatisfactory than the condition of the Native States which are not dependent on any superior power.

After saying that in all the states except Johore the insecurity of life and property checked the spirit of enterprise 'even of the Chinese' and scared off capital investment he went on:

I feel that it would be greatly to the advantage of the Settlements if our influence could be thus extended over the Peninsula, and I shall not fail to avail myself of any opening that may present itself for doing so.

Developing this intention in practice Sir Harry intervened in August to settle the boundary dispute between Pahang and Johore, the antecedents of which we have discussed earlier in this chapter.[78] The first step was to persuade Bendahara Wan Ahmad of Pahang to accept his arbitration, which he did by using the Sultan of Trengganu as a go-between.[79] Then Ord himself coaxed the Maharaja of Johore, as the Temenggong now styled himself, into agreeing to return to Pahang the disputed islands off the east coast.[80] On the 24th August he took the Maharaja to see Wan Ahmad at Pahang, and secured their approval in principle to an award which fixed the boundary at the Endau River and gave the islands north of its mouth to Pahang and those to the south to Johore. The final text of the settlement was drafted in Singapore and accepted by the two rulers in September 1868.[81]

Thus during Sir Harry Ord's first eighteen months as Governor the first signs of what we may call a forward policy in Malaya emerged. This was associated with closer relations with the

[77] Gov. Straits to Sec. State, 8 Apr. 1868, in CO 273/18.
[78] See above, pp. 39–40.
[79] Linehan, op. cit., p. 91.
[80] Gov. Straits to Sec. State, 24 July 1868, in CO 273/20.
[81] Gov. Straits to Sec. State, 20 Jan. 1869, in CO 273/26. Text in Maxwell and Gibson, op. cit., pp. 211–12.

Siamese Government than had been the rule under the Indian régime in the Straits. The connexion with Siam had rescued Ord from an awkward position so far as the Kedah negotiation was concerned, and had secured better conditions for the Straits traders in Kelantan. Its success was due on the one hand to Ord's recognition of Siam's claim to suzerainty over the northern Malay States, and on the other to the Siamese appreciation of the British attitude to trade. Earlier in the century both these points had caused friction, but during the reign of the enlightened King Mongkut (1851–68) the Siamese viewpoint began to change. The King and his officials came to see that to preserve their independence they needed the goodwill of some of the great powers, and after about 1855, when Sir John Bowring negotiated a 'Treaty of Friendship and Commerce' with Siam, they began to turn to the British Government for advice and support. From the British side the Foreign Office instructions to Sir R. Schomburgk, the first Consul-General in Bangkok, commanded him to abstain from all appearance of dictation, and stressed the fact that Britain had no desire to interfere in the internal affairs of Siam or to make territorial acquisitions at her expense.[82] The Siamese claim to suzerainty in the northern Malay States had always been in the past the main barrier to cordial relations with the Straits Settlements Government, so that once Sir Harry Ord made his gesture and acknowledged the Siamese position in the Peninsula there was nothing to prevent a *rapprochement* between the two governments. This friendship was sealed in August 1868 when Sir Harry, at King Mongkut's invitation, visited him at Whae-Whan near Patani, where the King had gone to observe an eclipse of the sun. He was well received by Mongkut, and after the formal audiences he met the King privately in the royal apartments and had long talks which included a discussion of Siamese relations with the West.[83]

His contacts with the Siamese seem to have convinced Sir Harry that the best solution for the problems of the unsettled Malay States, and the one which would in the end best promote their economic development and assure the safety of foreign investments, was a division of the Peninsula into British and

[82] FO 69/6, 31 Aug. 1857. Cf. Murti, 'Anglo-French Relations with Siam' (London, Ph.D. thesis, 1952), *passim*, especially pp. ii and 41–42.

[83] Gov. Straits to Sec. State, 24 July 1868, in CO 273/20, and 27 Aug. 1868, in CO 273/21.

Siamese spheres of influence. This was in sharp contrast to the policies of his predecessors the Indian Governors, whose aim had been to belittle Siamese claims and to uphold the independence of the Malay States.[84] But it was based on a sound appreciation of British policy, whilst at the same time promoting as far as possible the interests of the Straits Settlements. Ord realized that no Colonial Governor would be supported by the British Government in a quarrel with Siam if it became necessary to press his point to extremes. Experience in Kedah and Kelantan had shown him that Siam would use her influence in the Peninsula in support of the Straits Government. It is possible that during his conversations at Whae-Whan he had been convinced of Siamese good intentions, and their willingness to protect the interests of British traders in the areas under their influence. He preferred therefore to see the northern states of the Peninsula under the control of a power with whom the Straits Government could conduct normal diplomatic relations than that they should be independent and the breeding places of piracy and unrest. For the same reasons he was later to advocate the recognition of Dutch control over the states of Northern Sumatra.[85]

This recognition of Siamese control in the northern states implied acceptance of British responsibility for the maintenance of order in the rest of the Peninsula, and it was this which dictated the tone of Ord's despatch of 8th April 1868. This, as we have described above, frankly stated his intention to accept every opportunity for extending British influence over the states south of Trengganu and Kedah. It is in the light of this declaration of policy that we must view Ord's attempts to reassert British claims in the Dindings area of, Perak, his firm maintenance of British influence over Johore, and his intervention in the Johore–Pahang boundary dispute.

The reaction of the Colonial Office to this trend of thought was sharply hostile. Their attention was first drawn to the subject in February 1868 when they were told about the Kedah negotiations for the first time, and asked for instructions.[86] Ord's despatch

[84] Ord went so far in this that when in 1869 the Sultan of Trengganu sent an envoy with letters to Queen Victoria the Foreign Office, on his advice, refused to send any reply except through the King of Siam (CO 273/32, *passim*; Sheppard, op. cit., p. 34; Murti, op. cit., p. 42).
[85] Cf. Ord to Sec. State, 9 Dec. 1868, in CO 273/22.
[86] Ord's despatch of 31 Dec. 1867 (cf. pp. 72–73 above).

asked for information about his position in relation to all the colony's neighbours, so that it brought the whole subject of the Straits Settlements' external affairs up for review for the first time. The development of policy in London in these years forms the subject of a later chapter in this study, so that we may content ourselves here with saying that during March and April 1868 a set of instructions covering every aspect of the Settlements' external relations was worked out by the Colonial Office officials, in consultation with their Foreign Office colleagues. These instructions divided the colony's neighbours into three categories:

1. The colonies or dependencies of other European states.
2. Malay States under the influence of Siam.
3. Malay States not subject to the influence or control of any other power.

In dealing with other colonial governments the Governor of the Straits Settlements was told to confine himself to routine business of local importance and to the exchange of courtesies. All other questions must be settled by the Foreign Office with the European government concerned. With the Siamese states he might deal direct, so long as he kept the British Consul-General in Bangkok informed of his intentions, and maintained contact through him with the Siamese Government. With the Malay States in the Peninsula not subject 'to any other influence than our own' the Governor was allowed to deal on his own responsibility, under the instructions of the Colonial Office.[87]

In conveying these instructions to Sir Harry Ord the Duke of Buckingham, then Secretary of State for the Colonies, warned him to

. . . remember that the relations of the Settlements with those Powers [the Malay States] are matters which may at any time become of serious importance, and in respect of which Her Majesty's Government are bound to exercise a vigilant and effective control. Although therefore circumstances may not infrequently arise in which you may be called upon to act absolutely on your own judgement, yet it is

[87] CO to FO, 17 Mar. 1868, in CO 273/13. Independent Malay States outside the Peninsula, such as Atjeh in North Sumatra, were not covered by this formula. It was however well known to Ord that the British Government were contemplating a general settlement with the Dutch which would recognize their political supremacy there, and no trouble arose under this head. Britain was in any case precluded by the Anglo Dutch Treaty of 1824 from making treaties with the Sumatran states.

generally undesirable that you should enter into formal negotiations with Native Powers; still less that you should conclude any agreement with them except in pursuance of an object or a policy considered and approved by Her Majesty's Government.[88]

In themselves these instructions were not more restrictive than had been the limitations within which the Indian Governors worked. They were moreover not inconsistent with Sir Harry Ord's general policy of bringing each of the Malay States under the influence of a stronger power, for they directly recognized the position of Siam, and in allowing the Straits Settlements Government to conduct its own relations with these states under the supervision of the Colonial Office rather than going through the normal Foreign Office channels they implied that there was some special link between the Settlements and the Malay States. But they came at a time when Ord had already professed himself committed to a programme far more ambitious than that of any previous Governor, and they were followed by sharp censure of his conduct in the particular case of Kedah. Both Colonial Office and Foreign Office refused to have anything to do with Ord's treaty. They found its substance unobjectionable, but condemned it as irregular in form, since it was negotiated between two non-sovereign authorities. The Colonial Office clerks then proceeded with some relish to draft a reprimand to Sir Harry for acting beyond his authority in negotiating even a provisional treaty without instructions from home, and in stopping the Sultan's annuity.[89]

It was in their reaction to his further proposals for a British forward policy in the Peninsula, however, that the Secretary of State and his officials really showed their teeth. In reply to his despatch of 8th April 1868 Sir Harry was told:

. . . Her Majesty's Government are not disposed to adopt the duty, directly or indirectly, of taking steps for the security of life and property in countries where that security cannot be given by the lawful Rulers, and cannot give countenance to the trend of policy which you appear by the last sentence of your despatch to contemplate. It is clearly of opinion that the true policy of the British Government of the Straits Settlements is not to attempt to control but to keep clear of native disorder.[90]

[88] Sec. State to Gov. Straits, 22 Apr. 1868, in CO 809/1.
[89] CO to FO, 17 Mar. 1868, in CO 273/13. In place of Ord's treaty a nearly identical document between Great Britain and Siam was eventually signed at Bangkok on 6 May 1869. Text in Maxwell and Gibson, op. cit., pp. 82–85.
[90] Sec. State to Gov. Straits, 4 June 1868, in CO 273/18. In addition to Ord's

Then in 1869, when Ord's activities concerning the Dindings came to light, the Secretary of State added the warning: 'I should not be disposed to approve of any proceedings which would extend the responsibilities of Her Majesty's Government in the neighbourhood of the Straits Settlements.'[91]

This prohibition put an abrupt stop to Sir Harry Ord's schemes for extending British influence in the southern Malay States. They had on the whole been the product of his own ambitious brain rather than of any sustained commercial pressure for the protection of threatened British interests; that was to come later. Ord's policy for the gradual extension of British influence, whatever its other merits or demerits, was still in 1868 capable of execution. Its implementation then might easily have saved much trouble for the future. But its rejection was inevitable because it was in every other respect premature—premature in that there had as yet been no strong demand for it in Singapore; premature because the Colonial Office as yet knew little of Malaya, and Ord had done little to show that there was any need for British intervention. The Colonial Office had inherited a well-matured tradition of non-intervention in Malayan politics from the India Office, and in the age if not actually under the administration of Mr. Gladstone they were not likely to reverse it except for good cause shown. The unfortunate result of this was that whilst conditions in the Malay States were becoming increasingly unsettled, and trade with many of them restricted and uncertain, the Straits Government's hands were tied, and they could do nothing to mend matters. From the end of 1868 until Sir Harry Ord went on leave in March 1871, whilst civil war developed in Selangor and threatened to break out in Perak, and whilst the Chinese miners of Larut organized themselves for battle from their base in Penang, those in the British settlements were confined to the role of spectators.

despatch the Colonial Office had also received representations on the subject from W. H. Read, then in London. The Permanent Under-Secretary, Sir F. Rogers, concluded that this was a concerted move by Ord and the Singapore merchants, and minuted 'Settlers and merchants are always ready to call for operations of which they are to reap the profit and Government to bear the cost, in the way of military proceedings, embassies, etc. And Governors are only too apt to fall in with a policy which gives interest and importance to their proceedings' (20 May 1868, in CO 273/18).

[91] Sec. State to Gov. Straits, 10 Sept. 1869, in CO 273/30.

2

THE SELANGOR INCIDENT

1868–1871

AFTER 1868 conditions on the west coast of the Peninsula, where the tin mines in which the Straits merchants were interested were situated, became steadily worse. A civil war raged in Selangor, there was a disputed succession in Perak, and a war between two parties of Chinese tin miners in Larut. Sir Harry Ord was prevented by his instructions from taking any effective steps to improve matters. But while he was on leave in 1871 his deputy, Colonel Anson, made an abortive attempt to intervene in Selangor.

(i) *Selangor and Perak*

After 1868, when Sir Harry Ord's attempt to develop British control in the southern states of the Peninsula came to an end, conditions in the west coast states deteriorated quickly. What were in effect civil wars developed in Selangor and Perak. We have already described the state of affairs in Perak about this time, so that we may turn first to Selangor.

Conditions in Selangor were generally similar to those we have described in Perak, but there were significant differences. There were the same feuds between sets of Malay chiefs and of Chinese tin miners, and the Sultan, as in Perak, made no attempt to control the chiefs. But the position of the Sultan in Selangor was somewhat stronger than in Perak; there was not the same well-developed organization of the other chiefs which obtained in Perak, nor such a complicated system of succession to the throne. So long as he had the approval of the major territorial chiefs a Sultan was succeeded by his eldest legitimate son or his nearest male kin.[1] The appointment of a Sultan might be disputed, as that of Sultan 'Abdu'l-Samad (asc. 1859) was, but his prestige when appointed was high. The territorial chiefs might be independent in their own districts, but they held them from the Sultan, not of right, and they paid

---

[1] In Selangor, as in other Malay states, a Sultan's sons by a royal wife took precedence over his sons by inferior wives and of course by concubines. For purposes of succession only sons by royal wives were fully legitimate, though sons by commoner wives were legitimate in the ordinary sense of the term, and both took the title of 'Raja'.

over to him a fixed percentage of the customs dues and duties they collected.[2] In general the Sultan was thus above and outside the quarrels of the other chiefs. The Selangor civil war, or at least the quarrels between the Malay chiefs which began it, took the form not of a dispute for possession of the throne but a fight between several of the chiefs for control of one or two of the river valleys. The Sultan stood neutral, prepared to recognize whoever was the eventual winner so long as he continued to receive his share of the revenues.

The Selangor chiefs seem on the whole to have been more enterprising and more in touch with the outside world than those in Perak. In part this may have been due to the fact that they were not pure Malays but Bugis, with a long tradition as traders and adventurers in the Indonesian seas.[3] Most of the difference however can be ascribed to geography. The state of Selangor as it existed in the 1860's consisted of five major river valleys, which ran roughly east–west from the mountains of the interior to the coast. Each river was controlled by one major chief, who lived usually at the river mouth. The position of the chiefs gave them more opportunities for trade and contact with other areas than were available to their opposite numbers in Perak, who were mostly shut off in the interior holding different sections of the same river. And since the tin deposits were strung out along the foot-hills of the interior it followed that the Chinese miners were dispersed in several centres served by different rivers, rather than collected together in one district under one Malay chief as in Larut. The threads of Malay and Chinese politics were therefore far more closely interwoven than in Perak. It was of the utmost importance to the miners to be on good terms with the chief who controlled the river, and he in his turn depended on the industry of the miners to make the traffic on the river productive in tolls. Indeed in most cases it was the Selangor chiefs themselves who had taken the initiative in introducing the Chinese.

[2] Middlebrook, S. M., 'Yap Ah Loy', *JRASMB*, xxiv, pt. 2 (1951), later cited as 'Yap Ah Loy', says (p. 23) that up to 1858 80 per cent of these revenues went to the Sultan.

[3] We have already noted the activities of these resourceful sailors from the Celebes in Riau, and seen how they became in the eighteenth century the masters of the weak Sultans of Johore. The Klang area of Selangor with its tin deposits was always a centre of Bugis strength, and its ruler was styled Yamtuan of Selangor until at some time between 1756 and 1770 he became Sultan. He was installed by the Sultan of Perak, as were all later Sultans until 'Abdu'l-Samad, who dispensed with the formality (Winstedt, *Selangor*, pp. 3–7).

The first permanent centre of large-scale Chinese mining in Selangor was the town of Lukut, on the river of the same name. This was the most southerly of Selangor's rivers, and the nearest to the British settlement of Malacca. Chinese miners had come there from Malacca as early as 1824, but its prosperity really dates from the rule there of Raja Juma'at, a raja from Riau who married the eldest daughter of Sultan Muhammad (reigned 1826–57). Early in the 1840's Raja Juma'at invited a large number of Chinese to settle there permanently, and sank his own capital and what he could borrow in Malacca into the venture. By 1850 business in Lukut was booming, tin was being shipped out regularly in Chinese junks and Malay schooners, and the revenue which Raja Juma'at drew from the town averaged $15,000 a year.[4]

Other chiefs soon followed this example. Sultan Muhammad tried on the Klang River in the late 1840's, but met with no success and lost his money. Raja 'Abdu'l-Samad, later to succeed Muhammad as Sultan, was more successful. After his marriage to Muhammad's youngest daughter about 1844 he was given the Selangor River area to administer, and he lost no time in opening up mines up-river in the Kanching Hills district. These mines were successful, the Chinese population grew, and Kanching itself became a thriving town. It was soon followed by new centres on the Klang and Langat Rivers. The Klang district, where Sultan Muhammad had failed so disastrously, he gave to a son by a concubine, Raja Sulaiman. In 1853 however he transferred the grant to Raja 'Abdu'llah, the husband of his second daughter and the brother of Raja Juma'at of Lukut. The two brothers went into partnership together, and with $30,000 raised in Malacca and coolies and stores provided by Juma'at from Lukut they began operations on the upper Klang in 1857. There were initial troubles when the Chinese coolies died like flies of fever, but 'Abdu'llah was always able to get fresh men and supplies from his brother, and in 1859 the mines at a place called Ampang sent down the river the first cargoes of tin. More miners and Chinese traders flocked to the area from Malacca and Lukut, and a new township called Kuala Lumpur grew up a little downstream from Ampang on the confluence of the Klang and Gombak Rivers. The

---

[4] 'Yap Ah Loy', pp. 8 and 14–15; Wilkinson, *Peninsular Malays*, pp. 143–4. Capt. Macpherson, Res. Councillor of Malacca, who visited the town in 1860 was struck by its prosperous and well-ordered condition, and compared it favourably with his own settlement in British territory.

development of the Langat district came later. Sultan Muhammad died in 1857, and was succeeded after two years of wrangling by 'Abdu'l-Samad (for Muhammad's only surviving legitimate son was a young child and unable to assert his rights). When he became Sultan 'Abdu'l-Samad moved from the Selangor to the Langat district, and some time in the 1860's established Chinese miners there too at a place called Bukit Arang.[5]

The development of tin mining in Selangor brought its own problems. It sharpened the contrast between the fortunes of those chiefs who had obtained control of rivers and those who had not. It added a new element to society—the Chinese coolie. Lastly it involved the Chinese and European merchants of the Straits Settlements, who had advanced the necessary capital, in the affairs of the country. Since most of this early development was successful it made other merchants jealous of the fortunate few whose venture had succeeded and eager to follow their example. These, hopeful of future profit, were willing to finance any chiefs who might try to wrest control of the rivers by force from their more fortunate fellows; they put their money into powder and shot in order that they might later receive tin.

Chief of the malcontents who were supported in this way was Raja Mahdi, son of the Raja Sulaiman who had been ejected from Klang in 1853 to make way for Raja 'Abdu'llah. Mahdi had no sort of right to Klang or to any other place, for his father's grant, even before it was terminated, had only been for life. But he was a forceful and assertive character who felt that the state owed him a living. In the 1860's he returned to Klang, ostensibly as a trader. He lived on a small allowance made to him by Raja 'Abdu'llah, and seems to have spent most of his time in quarrelling with his benefactor and demanding more money.

In 1866 Raja Mahdi took advantage of a quarrel between 'Abdu'llah and a group of Sumatran Malays who lived further up the river[6] to seize Klang for himself. The financial backing of a

---

[5] 'Yap Ah Loy', pp. 17–18 and 103 n.; Winstedt, *Selangor*, pp. 18–19; C. J. Irving's Report on Selangor, July 1781, in CO 273/48.

[6] The division between the Bugis and the Sumatran Malays in Selangor was of very old standing. The Bugis, who had seized control in the late seventeenth and eighteenth centuries formed the political governing class, and generally lived in the coastal towns and controlled the mouths of the rivers. The Sumatrans, mainly Mandelings and Rawas, had conducted a bitter but unsuccessful struggle for control of the area in the eighteenth century. They now lived and traded mainly in the interior; those on the Klang River had their own headman,

Malacca Chinese enabled him to form an alliance with the Sumatrans and to lay siege to the town. A relief expedition equipped in Malacca by 'Abdu'llah's son failed, and after five months he and his family returned to Malacca leaving Mahdi in possession of Klang town and the mouth of the river.[7]

There the matter might have ended had not Mahdi needlessly offended the Sultan, and had not Klang been at this time the richest and most desirable prize in Selangor politics.

Sultan 'Abdu'l-Samad was an easy-going man, too fond of his garden and his opium to entangle himself needlessly in the quarrels of others. He had not always been so, for tradition said that in his youth he had killed ninety-nine men with his own hands. Now so long as his share of their revenue came in he listened with equal indulgence to the complaints of his chiefs against each other, and sent them all away happy with a present of gunpowder and lead.[8] So when Ismail, son of the dispossessed 'Abdu'llah came to him asking for justice he was given the usual present and told that as he and Mahdi were both young men they had better fight it out for themselves. But Ismail was without funds, and as the Sultan had betrothed his only daughter 'Arfah to Mahdi the latter's position seemed secure. Mahdi however had not been in possession of Klang for many months when he felt strong enough to discontinue the payment of dues to the Sultan. 'Abdu'l-Samad

the Dato Dagang, who was answerable directly to the Sultan (there is an unflattering pen-portrait of this Selangor worthy in Swettenham, *The Real Malay* (1900), pp. 71–84). There was thus a dual clash of interests, to be found also in the history of Sumatra and Borneo, between two racial groups—a political relationship between dominant and subordinate groups, and an economic relationship between a group which controlled the mouth of the rivers and levied duties on trade and a group further up-river which in order to live was forced to acquiesce. For the eighteenth century background, cf. Wilkinson, *Peninsular Malays, passim.*

[7] 'Yap Ah Loy', pp. 25–26; Winstedt, *Selangor*, pp. 19–20; C. J. Irving, loc. cit.

[8] Swettenham's writings on Malaya contain several passages devoted to 'Abdu'l-Samad, the most accessible of which is that in his *British Malaya*, (1948 ed.), pp. 128–9. Another observer thus described the Sultan in 1874: 'The Sultan has hitherto borne the reputation of being a confirmed opium-eater, but he did not strike our party as being in any way lethargic. On the contrary he seems very sharp and intelligent enough, only showing a certain weakness of character by an indecisive manner of walking up and down when he is required to make up his mind, and fidgeting with his headdress, which he constantly takes off and puts on again. In appearance he is a man of some fifty years, with a quantity of iron-grey hair and plaintive brown eyes, with which he gazes at one appealingly when any decisive action is required of him' (Vetch, *Life of Sir A. Clarke* (1905), p. 159). Cf. also Wilkinson, *Peninsular Malays*, pp. 149–50.

was not amused; when he found that he no longer received the
$500 a month which had been his share of the revenues of Klang
his benevolence for once deserted him. He did not for the moment
do anything more energetic than cancel his daughter's betrothal,
but had he only known it this was the first step from which all his
later troubles followed. It was the disposal of this now unattached
daughter which marked the real beginning of the Selangor civil
war.

Instead of offering his daughter to any of the other territorial
chiefs the Sultan gave her as wife to a foreigner, Tengku Zia'u'd-
din, the younger brother of the Sultan of Kedah. Then came the
difficulty. 'Abdu'l-Samad had no district available to give to his
new son-in-law without dispossessing another chief, which would
have meant fighting or at least a degree of action beyond his inclination. So he provided for him by an expedient which was
typical of the man. Soon after the marriage he gave Zia'u'd-din
an ambiguous document, a *kuasu* or written authority dated 26
June 1868. This purported to make him what the Malays called
'*wakil yam tuan*' in Selangor, a phrase meaning literally the agent
or representative of the sovereign, but later translated by Europeans as 'Viceroy'.[9] In practice Tengku Zia'u'd-din was left to
make what he could of this power, without any help from the
Sultan. It gave him a legal title to anything he was strong enough
to take for himself, without involving the Sultan in the trouble of
getting it for him. As the Tengku's power outside the Sultan's
district of Langat was not recognized by the other chiefs, who
became his enemies as soon as he attempted to meddle in their
districts, the net result of this transaction was to add another
formidable figure to the number of rajas trying to make their
fortunes out of Selangor and her rivers. There was however no
immediate trouble, for at the end of 1868 Zia'u'd-din was recalled

---

[9] The document certainly gave Zia'u'd-din full powers, but there was a
difference of opinion as to whether this was meant to apply to the whole of
Selangor or only to the Sultan's district of Langat. The full text of the *Kuasu*
is given in translation in CO 273/48. The passage in question runs: '. . . we
declare . . . that we give up the country and its dependencies to our son Tunku
Dia Udin to govern and open up so as to bring it into proper order for us and
for our sons . . . and for all the inhabitants of the country also so that they might
receive a course of justice in all matters. And our son Tunku Dia Udin is
empowered to do whatever may be effectual towards fostering our country and
causing profit to us. No person must oppose our son's proceedings. And now
we confirm as to this place Langkat that it is our gift to our son Tunku Dia
Udin to be the place where he should carry out our business as aforesaid.'
There is a slightly different version in Winstedt, *Selangor*, p. 21.

to Kedah by the illness of his mother, and her death and the settlement of her estate kept him there until well into 1869.[10]

Despite his break with the Sultan Mahdi was still potentially
the strongest figure in Selangor, and Klang the most important
town. Lukut had lost its earlier importance, for in 1864 Raja
Juma'at died and under his weak and ineffective sons the town
began to decline—its revenues fell from their former level of
$15,000 a year to a mere $500.[11] Langat was the personal holding
of the Sultan and outside the rivalries of the other chiefs, and the
Bernam River in the far north of the state was so remote and un-
attractive that it served as a sort of no-man's-land between
Selangor and Perak. There were as we have seen important tin
mines up the Selangor River, in the Kanching Hills, but developments among the Chinese miners at this time seemed to be about
to divert a good deal of the traffic from these down the Klang.
Most of the miners in Selangor were Hakkas from the same part
of Kwantung Province, but they belonged to two different clans.
Those at Kanching came mainly from the Kah Yeng Chew clan
and belonged to the Ghee Hin Society, whilst those in Kuala
Lumpur–Ampang area were of the Fei Chew (Fui Chiu) Clan
and members of the Hai San Society. About the time that Raja
Mahdi ousted 'Abdu'llah from Klang the leaders of the Kah Yeng
Chews at Kanching quarrelled amongst themselves. As a result of
this quarrel one of the richest of them sold out his interests in the
mines to a Fei Chew who also had large interests at Kuala Lumpur. Then in 1868 Yap Ah Loy, an able and energetic Hakka
leader, became *Capitan China* or headman of the Fei Chews at
Kuala Lumpur, and it began to look as if the two Hakka clans
would be united under his leadership.[12] This growth in the importance of the Kuala Lumpur area would naturally increase the
amount of traffic on the Klang River, and redound to the greater
benefit of Raja Mahdi.

His fortunate position and the way he had reached it were bound
to make Mahdi the target of other envious chiefs. Despite this he
did nothing to retain the support of those with whose help he had
risen to power. He had already alienated the Sultan. Now he
offended the Sumatran Malays and made an enemy of their leader

[10] 'Yap Ah Loy', p. 41; Winstedt, *Selangor*, p. 21.
[11] Wilkinson, *Peninsular Malays*, p. 144.
[12] 'Yap Ah Loy', pp. 27–28.

the Dato Dagang, who appealed to the Sultan and his new son-in-law to eject the 'usurper', saying that if Tengku Zia'u'd-din would take the lead he would join him.[13]

Before Zia'u'd-din could do anything he was recalled to Kedah, but another enemy of Mahdi now took the first step. Raja Ismail, despite the death of his father, had now succeeded in finding a financial backer in Malacca. One dark night early in August 1869 he descended on the Klang estuary with a scratch force of Malays, Bugis and Ilanun pirates from Riau, and took the forts which covered the mouth of the river. Mahdi was taken completely by surprise and sat in Klang doing nothing whilst Ismail organized a blockade of the town. He did not feel himself strong enough for a direct attack, so a stalemate followed for two months.[14] Then in the middle of October Zia'u'd-din returning from Kedah arrived off the estuary with five hundred of his fellow-countrymen, and joined forces with Ismail.[15] There was still no direct attack on Klang, but Ismail's loose blockade of the town was replaced by a close siege. Zia'u'd-din's European lieutenant De Fontaine, a former midshipman in the French navy, dragged eighteen-pounder carronades through the jungle in sampans and emplaced them on the neighbouring hills, from which he kept Mahdi's stockades under fire. Throughout the rest of 1869 and into 1870 the siege dragged on, with supplies in Klang dwindling and no money coming in from the tin trade with the interior, which had come to a stop.[16]

Among the Chinese miners themselves affairs had taken a turn for the worse. Yap Ah Loy at Kuala Lumpur failed to unite the Hakkas under his leadership, and early in 1869 his representative at Kanching was killed by the Kah Yeng Chews there. A good deal of the trouble between the two Hakka groups was probably due to the fact that both had been reinforced by fellow clansmen from Larut who had brought with them the bitterness which had grown out of the Ghee Hin-Hai San society war there. Whatever the

[13] 'Yap Ah Loy', pp. 29–30.
[14] Winstedt, Selangor, pp. 21–22.
[15] Whether as the result of a previous arrangement dating back to the end of 1868, or because his mediation in the dispute was accepted by Ismail but rejected by Mahdi is not clear. The fact that he brought such a large force back from Kedah seems to support the former view, cf. 'Yap Ah Loy', pp. 42–43, and C. J. Irving, loc. cit.
[16] Report of Com. Bloomfield, R.N., 6 Aug. 1871, printed in Parl. Pap. C.465 of 1872; Winstedt, Selangor, p. 22.

F

reason henceforward the two Hakka clans in the interior were open enemies, and the Kah Yeng Chews took as their leader one Chong Chong, a Fei Chew but a bitter personal enemy of Yap Ah Loy. A Chinese war was now developing in the mining areas as a counterpart to the Malay war on the coast, and in November 1869 Yap Ah Loy came to Langat to seek the Sultan's support.[17] 'Abdu'l-Samad gave the *Capitan China* his blessing, the usual present of gunpowder—twenty-five buckets of it—and in addition half a case of opium and $2,000 cash, and with this Yap Ah Loy returned to Kuala Lumpur. But his visit to Langat was memorable, not so much for the Sultan's assurance of support, as because Tengku Zia'u'd-din was also there. Without making an enemy of him Yap Ah Loy was unable to avoid associating himself with the Tengku as well as with the Sultan.[18]

The meeting at Langat brought together the politics of the Malay and Chinese communities of Selangor, and linked events on the lower rivers with those taking place up-stream in the mining areas. After this the fortunes of Yap Ah Loy's party around Kuala Lumpur were linked with those of Tengku Zia'u'd-din, the 'Viceroy'. The events of 1870 were to bring together the enemies of both into an effective opposition, so that all parties were drawn into the civil war except the Sultan, who continued to give fair words to all. Trouble on the other rivers served to drive trade to Langat, and he was well content.

At some time just before March 1870 Raja Mahdi decided that his position in Klang was hopeless, and leaving the garrison to capitulate on the best terms they could get he fled from the town to the little village of Sungai Buloh, at the mouth of the Jeram River. There he settled down to plan his next move.[19] His hopes were still high. The 'Viceroy's' victory at Klang had only increased the enmity of the other chiefs for him, especially the

[17] Apart from the hostility of the Kanching Chinese Yap Ah Loy was in a difficult position, for he had been installed as *Capitan China* by Raja Mahdi, whose stock had now slumped as result of the blockade of Klang. He needed some other patron, and chose the Sultan because that would insure him against the consequences of Mahdi's fall without committing him to throw in his lot with his opponent, Tengku Zia'u'd-din.

[18] 'Yap Ah Loy', pp. 44–46.

[19] At the same time he found an outlet for his restless energies in helping the two sons of the late Bendahara of Pahang in an attempt to regain their father's kingdom by an abortive invasion of Western Pahang (p. 39 above). Three years later the new Bendahara Wan Ahmad took his revenge for this ill turn and provided the troops which ended Mahdi's hopes in Selangor.

rulers of the northern rivers like Raja Hitam of Bernam and Raja 'Ali of Jeram, who saw in Zia'u'd-din's career a challenge to their own position. Mahdi therefore did not lack allies. With Klang he had lost his source of revenue from the tin trade, but to the north an alternative source was available to him if he could gain control of the Selangor River, down which came all the tin from the Kanching mines. It was the more tempting as a prize since it was held by the least formidable of the Selangor chiefs, the Sultan's weak elder son Raja Musa. From March onwards therefore Mahdi's energies were directed towards collecting forces for a descent on the forts at Kuala Selangor, from which he would be able to control the river.

Meanwhile Tengku Zia'u'd-din and Yap Ah Loy were busy strengthening their own positions. Yap Ah Loy employed himself in recruiting men, holding out as inducements regular wages and pensions for the dependants of casualties, a startling innovation in Malay warfare.[20] At some time between February and June 1870 he felt himself strong enough to make some sort of demonstration towards his opponents in Kanching. The course of events is obscure, but they culminated in a pitched battle in which the Kah Yeng Chews were overwhelmed, and the survivors scattered, some to Langat to tell the tale to the Sultan. Sultan 'Abdu'l-Samad was at first genuinely angry, for it was he who had originally planted the miners at Kanching, but after an apology from Yap Ah Loy his usual *insouciance* prevailed and the incident was forgotten by all except the unfortunate Kah Yeng Chews. Their leader Chong Chong, who had been hidden in the Rawa-Kanching area, escaped southwards to Kuala Langat, and established himself with friends there.[21]

After Zia'u'd-din's capture of Klang it was formally given to him as his personal holding in place of Langat, which reverted to the direct control of the Sultan. The Tengku at once set about consolidating his position on the Klang River and getting the tin traffic moving again. He was also busy raising fresh funds in

---

[20] He raised fighting men in Singapore and even in the Fei Chew district of China, and supplemented these professionals by levies from the miners. He paid $8 per month, offered free medical treatment, and promised pensions of $200–300 for the dependants of men killed in action. By these means he raised about 2,000 men, which were later supplemented by the followers of his Malay allies in the district. In the major engagements of the war there were about 5,000 men engaged on both sides (cf. 'Yap Ah Loy', pp. 44, 55).

[21] 'Yap Ah Loy', pp. 48–52.

Malacca and Singapore, and it was probably at about this time that J. G. Davidson, a wealthy Singapore barrister, became his friend and backer. Zia'u'd-din foresaw that Mahdi's next move would probably be against Selangor. He strengthened its garrison by sending there Sayid Mashor, a noted Malay warrior of reputed Arab descent who proceeded to organize the defence of the Selangor forts under the nominal command of the luckless Raja Musa. But the Sayid was not destined to remain on Zia'u'd-din's side for long. Soon after his arrival at Selangor his brother 'Abdu'llah was murdered at Langat in circumstances which led him to believe that both Zia'u'd-din and the Sultan were responsible. He at once abandoned Selangor to its fate, and from then onwards became Zia'u'd-din's bitterest enemy. He does not however seem to have gone over at once to Mahdi. Instead he made his way to Kuala Langat, where he joined forces with another embittered man, Chong Chong, the erstwhile leader of the Kanching Chinese, who was plotting vengeance against Yap Ah Loy.[22]

Mashor's defection left Selangor exposed to Mahdi's forces concentrating around Jeram. It was probably at the instigation of Tengku Zia'u'd-din and in a desperate effort to counter this threat that 'Abdu'l-Samad in July 1870 wrote to Sir Harry Ord asking for his assistance to prevent supplies reaching his 'enemies' by way of the Selangor, Bernam and Jeram Rivers. Ord had already (21 April 1870) prohibited the export of arms from the Straits Settlements to Selangor, and was prevented by his instructions from more positive action. In any case it was too late. For in July Mahdi and his allies from Jeram and Bernam seized the Selangor forts, and with them control of the Selangor valley. Soon afterwards Sayid Mashor and Chong Chong established themselves in upper Selangor, and in September and October 1870 conducted a campaign against Yap Ah Loy in the area between Kanching and Kuala Lumpur. They were repulsed, but were able to fall back on Selangor, for they had by then made common cause with Mahdi.[23]

[22] Winstedt, *Selangor*, pp. 22–24, tells the story somewhat differently at this point, and makes Mashor desert Zia'u'd-din at the end of 1870 during an attempt to regain Selangor. The text here follows Wilkinson, *Peninsular Malays*, p. 146; 'Yap Ah Loy', pp. 52–53.

[23] Gov. Straits to Sec. State, 9 Apr. 1873, in CO 273/66; Winstedt, *Selangor*, pp. 22–23; 'Yap Ah Loy', pp. 52–58.

By the end of 1870 the feuds of the Selangor chiefs had produced two distinct sides. The 'Viceroy' Tengku Zia'u'd-din held the Klang River, and had as allies the Chinese miners around Kuala Lumpur under Yap Ah Loy. On the other side Raja Mahdi by possession of the forts at Kuala Selangor controlled the Selangor River, from whose headwaters Sayid Mashor and Chong Chong operated against Yap Ah Loy in Kuala Lumpur. Raja Ismail continued the staunch ally of Zia'u'd-din, but most of the other chiefs resented him as a foreigner who had no right on their land, and he had to rely on outsiders as his officers and men. The position of the Sultan was still undefined. After Zia'u'd-din's capture of Klang 'Abdu'l-Samad seems to have been a good deal under his influence, perhaps because of a natural tendency to remain friends with a winning cause, perhaps from relief that Zia'u'd-din had now acquired a place of his own and would no longer administer Langat, which while still nominally under control of the 'Viceroy' was in fact the Sultan's territory and neutral ground. In August 1870 he issued a fiat which called on all to help Zia'u'd-din in his struggle against Mahdi, though it did not specifically recognize his position as 'Viceroy'. But he still retained a good deal of sympathy for those who resented the presence of the interloper from Kedah, and this feeling was to grow stronger when Zia'u'd-din indulged in indiscriminate blockade of the rivers to prevent supplies reaching his enemies. By the middle of 1871, when J. W. Birch the Straits Settlements Colonial Secretary visited the Sultan, he had again moved away from Zia'u'd-din, and there was a strong opposition party in existence within his household.

The year 1871 also saw the chiefs of Perak grouped in two hostile parties. The death of Sultan 'Ali on 25th May brought to a head the latent antagonisms between the Bendahara Ismail, the Raja Muda 'Abdu'llah, Raja Yusuf, and the Mantri, whose origins we have already described in the previous chapter.[24] Ismail, Yusuf and 'Abdu'llah all had a claim to succeed the dead Sultan, and behind them lurked the powerful figure of the Mantri, whose support for any one of them might turn the scales in that person's favour. In normal circumstances 'Abdu'llah as Raja Muda had a perfectly good claim to the Sultanship and would

[24] See pp. 44 et seq. above.

probably have succeeded without dispute. But circumstances were far from normal. Already in 1869 Yusuf had written to the Straits Government claiming the throne as his right when Sultan 'Ali should die,[25] and he showed every intention of backing his claim by force when the moment arrived. Again, in 1870, against the wishes of the Sultan, the needy 'Abdu'llah granted concessions of land and tax farms in the Krian area to a Eurasian named Bacon, a Penang trader and adventurer. This incurred the hostility of the Mantri, who claimed the district as his own. It also alienated the Sultan, and at the time of 'Ali's death 'Abdu'llah was in open rebellion against him.[26] 'Abdu'llah's stock was further lowered at this time by the elopement of his wife with a Raja from Selangor, and his failure to do anything about it beyond declaring her divorced.

Sultan 'Ali died at Sayong, far up the Perak River. His son was at once sent by Bendahara Ismail, who was present, to summon the chiefs for the funeral and for the election of a new Sultan. For some reason 'Abdu'llah did not go. The reasons for this are obscure. To get from his own village at Batak Rabit, on the lower reaches of the river, to Sayong 'Abdu'llah had to pass Raja Yusuf's village. 'Abdu'llah's ex-wife had been Sultan 'Ali's daughter and at the funeral he would have had to meet her brothers. 'Abdu'llah was notoriously timid, and his enemies said that he did not go to Sayong because he was afraid that Yusuf or his wife's brothers would attack him. 'Abdu'llah himself maintained that when he was told of the death of 'Ali he at once wrote to Ismail, who as Bendahara was in charge of the arrangements, saying that he was about to come up the river. Ismail, again according to 'Abdu'llah, replied advising him not to come up to Sayong for the time being. He and the Mantri, who was also at Sayong, sent word that 'Ali's sons were incensed by 'Abdu'llah's treatment of their sister, and that it would not be safe for him to come there. Whatever the reasons for 'Abdu'llah's non-appearance the result was that it was Ismail and not he who was elected Sultan. According to Perak custom a Sultan might only be buried after his successor had been installed. There had been exceptions to this in the past, but the chiefs were not prepared to make an exception in this case. None

[25] Wilkinson, History of the Peninsular Malays, pp. 118–19.
[26] 'Report of Committee on Relations with Native States, 19 May 1871', in CO 273/47.

of them had any enthusiasm for 'Abdu'llah, whose main supporter had stayed with him at the coast, and led by the Mantri they proceeded to install Ismail as Sultan.[27]

The election of Ismail was a vote for anarchy. He was an old man who owed his election to his weakness, and his known disinclination to interfere in the affairs of others. He was a cipher who could neither read nor write, whose installation gave the Mantri the opportunity to do what he liked in Larut, and allowed Ismail's up-country followers to live on the country in the new Sultan's name. Even had 'Abdu'llah acquiesced in the installation of Ismail, therefore, there would have been no effective government in Perak. But 'Abdu'llah did not acquiesce. For some time he took no action, either because he was led to believe that Ismail had been installed as 'acting Sultan', so that 'Ali could be buried, and that when things settled down the regalia and symbols of office would be handed over to him, or because he could not pluck up courage to do anything about it. Then in April 1872, probably at the instigation of the Laksamana, the chief nominally in control of the coast, and the Penang adventurer Bacon, he began calling himself Sultan, and attempted to exercise jurisdiction over the lower stretches of the Perak River and the coastal districts. After naming Yusuf as Raja Muda in his place, so as to secure his support, he transferred his activities to Krian and Larut, and it was on the Larut River on 25 April 1872 that he handed to a British official a letter setting out his claim to the throne of Perak.[28]

By the beginning of 1872 there were thus three *de facto* rulers in Perak. Ismail, the nominal Sultan, lived inland on the headwaters of the Kinta River, and was acknowledged by the up-country chiefs. 'Abdu'llah, also styling himself Sultan, was supported by a number of chiefs on the lower reaches of the Perak River, and on the coast, most of whom were related to him through his mother. In Larut the Mantri, at this date the strongest of the three, controlled the tin mines and dealt with the Penang authorities as an independent chief.

[27] For a discussion of the events leading up to Ismail's installation, cf. Cowan, 'Sir Frank Swettenham's Perak Journals', *JRASMB*, xxiv, pt. 4 (1951), pp. 15–20.
[28] Gov. Straits to Sec. State, 6 Nov. 1872, in CO 273/61; Winstedt, *History of Perak*, loc. cit., p. 94.

(ii) *Colonel Anson and the Selangor Incident*

In 1871 Sir Harry Ord succumbed again to malaria contracted during his services in West Africa. He left the Straits Settlements on sick leave early in March, and handed over control to the Lieutenant-Governor of Penang, Colonel Archibald Anson. Anson had had an undistinguished but blameless career in the Royal Artillery and the Colonial Service. His most outstanding characteristic was a natural self-importance which had been accentuated by his service as Chief of Police in the isolated settlement of Mauritius.[29] This stood him in good stead early in his term as Administrator, when the King of Siam paid a state visit to Singapore (15th–24th March 1871). It was the first occasion on which a reigning monarchy of the dynasty had made such a journey outside his country, and in its way was an important event. The Straits Government and the Singapore Municipal Council spent $10,000 on lavish receptions and entertainments, and the affair—and the Siamese orders and presents which he was offered but not allowed to accept—cannot have done anything to lessen Colonel Anson's self-esteem.[30]

It is a commonplace that Colonial Governors are apt to take delight in reversing the policies of their predecessors, and to this rule Colonel Anson was not an exception. His attempts to strike out a new line, which in the same measure as it brought him credit would reflect discredit on his predecessor, were as we shall see only the first in a long series of such incidents. Between 1870 and 1877 the Straits Settlements had three successive Governors who were all senior officers in the Corps of Royal Engineers. Anson, who was twice Acting-Governor during this time had been the contemporary or near contemporary of all of them at the Royal Military College, Woolwich.[31] Lifelong service rivalries therefore played a part in the attitude which these men took to each other's policies. Add to this the fact that by 1871 Anson had suffered three years of subordination to the domineering Sir Harry Ord, and it appears reasonable to ascribe the excessive zeal with which

---

[29] Anson's career and character may be studied in his memoirs, *About Others and Myself, 1745–1920* (1920), which also contains some excellent photographs of scenes in Penang at this time.

[30] Officer Administering the Government (hereafter 'OAG') to Sec. State, 25 Mar. 1871, in CO 273/45.

[31] The Governors and their approximate dates at Woolwich were—Sir Harry Ord (1835–7), Sir Andrew Clarke (1840–4), Sir William Jervois (1936–9). Anson's time at Woolwich made him a contemporary of Jervois and Clarke.

he set about reforming the Colony's relations with her Malay neighbours to a desire to assert himself and display his own talents now that an opportunity for independent action had arisen.[32] Certainly 'excessive' is not too strong a word for the way in which this caretaker Governor showered suggestions and projects upon the Colonial Office.

Anson's attempts to initiate a policy of his own bear clearly the imprint of his experience in Penang, and his contacts with its commercial community. His first project was a proposal to extend the extra-territorial jurisdiction of the Straits Settlements Courts to the Malay States. The Supreme Court at Singapore had since 1856 had appellate jurisdiction over the decisions of the British Consular Court in Siam.[33] In April 1871 Anson, with the support of Thomas Braddell the Attorney-General, proposed that the powers of the Court should be extended to the trial of British subjects *found in the Colony* for offences against British law committed in the states of the Peninsula, and 'in Islands and places in the Malayan Archipelago not subject to Britain or any other European state.'[34] In the first instance this seems to have been directed against the disturbances in Larut; many of the Chinese struggling with each other for the possession of the tin mines there, especially the leaders of the different factions, were British subjects, and they could if the law were altered in this way be hauled before the Supreme Court to answer for their misdemeanours as soon as they returned to Penang or Province Wellesley.[35]

[32] As the senior official in the Straits Settlements after Sir Harry Ord, Anson was the permanent holder of a dormant commission as Administrator, which automatically came into force upon the death or incapacity of the Governor. He therefore expected to be treated with a certain amount of consideration, which he did not get from Ord, whose snubs and criticisms must have been especially wounding to a man of Anson's character. His dislike of Ord is clear throughout his memoirs, though they were written so long afterwards (op. cit., especially p. 319).

[33] This Court functioned by virtue of an extra-territoriality clause in the British Treaty with Siam of 1855. For a brief account of the Straits Court's Siamese jurisdiction, which was confirmed by the Siam and Straits Settlement Jurisdiction Act of 1870 (33 and 34 Vic., *cap.* 55), but which ceased with the extinction of the Consular Court in 1909 cf. Braddell, *The Law of the Straits Settlements* (1915), p. 36.

[34] OAG to Sec. State, 10 Apr. 1871, in CO 273/47.

[35] The necessity for this extension of the law largely disappeared when the Straits Settlements Penal Code of 1871 came into operation on 16 Sept. 1872. Sections 125 and 126 of this Code made it a crime to wage war against, or commit depredations or make preparations to commit depredations on the territories of, any power in alliance with or at peace with the British Crown. Nevertheless a later Imperial statute, the Straits Settlements Offences Act of 1874 (37 & 38 Vic., *cap.* 38) practically carried out Anson's suggestions in their

In late April or early May Anson made his next move—he appointed a committee to report on the Colony's relations with the Malay States. The antecedents of this committee are not clear. In reporting its proceedings to the Colonial Office Anson explained that he had appointed it because of the adverse effect on trade of the existing conditions in the Malay States. In further explanation he provided only an undated cutting from the *Pinang Gazette* complaining that trade from that place to North Sumatra and the west coast of the Peninsula was being harassed by piracy and brigandage. It made up $7,000,000 (about twenty-five per cent) of Penang's total trade in 1870, and would die off if the Government did not act.[36]

Anson could hardly have chosen a worse time to put forward this argument, for as the accompanying table shows, the Straits Settlements at this time were slowly climbing out of the trade depression which had marked the early years of the Colonial Office régime there.

Total Imports and Exports, in Straits Dollars			
	1869	1870	1871
Singapore	58,944,141	70,789,586	68,768,337
Penang	20,845,163	27,095,871	34,209,019
Malacca	4,780,240	4,552,884	4,846,906
Total	84,569,545	102,439,341	107,825,262

The trade of Penang was in fact developing far faster in proportion than that of Singapore, and in the three years from 1869

entirety. Cf. Braddell, op. cit. pp. 41, 43 and 192–3, where the text is reproduced. As if this suggestion were not sufficient sign of activity from an officer charged with the temporary administration of a Crown Colony, Anson followed it a fortnight later with a proposal that the sum of $10,000 paid annually to the Sultan of Kedah in recognition of his cession of Penang and Province Wellesley be commuted by the payment of a lump sum. (OAG to Sec. State, 25 Apr. 1871, in CO 273/46). There seems to have been no political reason for this proposal, which was merely the result of administrative enthusiasm.

[36] OAG to Sec. State, 3 June 1871, in CO 273/47. As the files of the *Pinang Gazette* held in London only contain one issue for 1871 it has not been possible to trace this cutting.

to 1871 it increased by nearly 66 per cent.[37] The figures for
Penang's trade by value in these years are paralleled by the shipping figures, for the tonnage cleared from the port rose from
303,000 tons in 1870 to 545,000 tons in 1872. The most remarkable
increase was in the number of steamers calling. There were 234
of these in 1870, 346 in 1871, and 482 in 1872. Most of them only
called for a day or two on their way from Europe to the Far East,
but this development and the arrival of the European telegraph
in 1870 stimulated the general trade of the port, so that there was
also a corresponding increase in the numbers of sailing ships and
native craft.

As no particular political problems had arisen since Governor
Ord's departure it seems clear that the 'Committee on Native
States' owed its creation to Anson's connexion with Penang and
its commercial community, and to his readiness to seize on a
few isolated incidents of piracy as an excuse for action. For though
it reported in terms which embraced all the Malay States, the
particular cases which the committee considered were those in
which small Malay or Chinese traders from Penang had been
plundered or ill-treated, and in which requests from the Straits
Government for redress had brought no result. There were only
thirteen cases in all, and all had been on the records of the Straits
Government for some time.[38]

The committee's work came to nothing, but its report is note-
worthy for the introduction of the idea of the Resident into
Malayan politics. It deplored the bad influence of European
adventurers who attached themselves to Eastern chiefs, but made
great play with the flourishing state of Johore, whose ruler was

---

[37] It is true that with the end of the depression prices rose, but tin prices for
instance were stable by 1869 and remained so until the beginning of another rise
in 1871-2, so that in conjunction with the shipping figures these figures can
safely be taken to indicate a real increase in trade. The table and the shipping
figures are compiled from the Straits Settlements Blue Books for 1870, 1871
and 1872, and the Reports of the Governor of the Straits Settlements and the
Lieutenant-Governor of Penang upon them (CO 273/58, 273/59 and 273/70).
[38] Four cases concerned losses arising out of the Chinese troubles in Larut,
and nine covered losses by piracy at the hands of petty chiefs on the coast of
Sumatra (cf. CO 273/47, 'Report of the Committee on Native States, 19 May
1871'). Some of the personnel of the committee, as well as Anson himself, were
interested parties. A N. Birch, the temporary Lieutenant-Governor of Penang,
was noted during his term of office there for his efforts to forward the interests
of the local merchants, and the second member, Cdr. Robinson, was at the
time Senior Naval Officer in the Straits and had a strong professional interest
in the piracy cases. The third member, Maj. Macnair, was an old Malayan
hand with a background of service in the Madras Artillery.

benefited by the advice of British officials acting in their private capacity, but with the approval of the Singapore Government. It wished to extend this system to the other Malay States by the introduction of European 'advisers', who though they were to be selected by the British Government would be accepted by the Malay rulers as their servants. They would act as the channel of communication between the ruler and the Singapore Government, and it was hoped that regular correspondence with the British colony and consistent and sympathetic advice would act as a leaven through which the habits of ordered and responsible government would gradually develop. The flaw in this attractive scheme lay in the initial assumption that the 'advisers' would be accepted and listened to in the Malay States. Macnair, the most experienced of the committee's members was afraid that their presence would merely act as an irritant, and even Anson saw the point. Rejecting the idea on the grounds that neither the Colony nor the Malay States would be ready to find their salaries he observed that their appointment would be premature 'in the barbarous conditions in which the states are'. In their place he suggested the appointment of a 'Political Agent' who would visit each of the states periodically and conduct all the official correspondence with them.[39]

The Colonial Office showed only disapproval and coolness towards all this activity in the Straits Settlements. The minuting on despatches during April and May shows a clear determination not to allow Colonel Anson, as an official in temporary control of the administration, to upset established lines of policy, or to act as a busybody during Sir Harry Ord's absence. All his despatches were forwarded to Sir Harry for his comments, and poor Anson

---

[39] OAG to Sec. State, 3 June 1871, in CO 273/47. This idea came from Macnair who, though he had not been in India since 1853, would be familiar with the use of Residents and Political Agents there. An examination of Indian practice would be out of place here, but we may note that the distinction between 'Adviser' or 'Resident' on the one hand and 'Political Agent' on the other was— with some notable exceptions like the Residency in Burma—a distinction between an officer who exerted some influence on the internal affairs of states in a subordinate relationship to the Indian Government, and one who was a purely diplomatic agent accredited to a state such as Afghanistan, into whose internal affairs Government did not intend to meddle (cf. Lee Warner, *Native States of India* (1910)). Both the Committee and Anson included the states of Northern Sumatra in these proposals, particularly Atjeh. The possibility of extending British influence there was already small because of the Anglo-Dutch Treaty of 1824. It was altogether removed by the conclusion of the Anglo-Dutch Convention of 1871 (cf. p. 27 above).

was told to leave such matters until the return of the Governor, and not initiate business except in case of urgency.[40] The 'Committee on Native States' caused some anxiety amongst the Colonial Office clerks, and provoked a hasty reminder that established policy prohibited any increased responsibilities outside the limits of the Straits Settlements.[41] But the warning came too late. By the time he received it Anson had already allowed himself to be drawn by events into the internal affairs of Selangor.

The Selangor incident of 1871 arose out of a simple case of piracy. The junk *Kim Seng Cheong*, Kong Lee master, sailed on the 14th June from Penang with a mixed cargo of piece goods, provisions and livestock for Larut. On the 22nd June, when she was eight days overdue and rumours of mischief were circulating in the Georgetown bazaars, one of her owners went to Arthur Birch, the Lieutenant-Governor of Penang. The vessel was said to have been taken by pirates who had shipped as passengers and seized her at sea. Nothing was known of the fate of the other passengers and crew, but the story soon became embroidered with tales of wholesale slaughter as it spread round the bazaar. There was little the Lieutenant-Governor could do, for there was no naval force at Penang. So he gave the wretched owner, one Ong Hong Buan, a letter to Colonel Anson in Singapore and shipped him off that evening in the regular passenger steamer *Historian*.[42] Ong reached Singapore on the 24th June. By then his story had grown longer, for on the evening before, when the steamer was near the Torch lightship, a junk had been sighted which he took from the look of the sails to be his. But the captain of the steamer had refused to take any action, and Ong was carried lamenting on, to tell his tale to Colonel Anson.[43]

When he heard the story Anson at once sent off the Government steamer *Pluto* with a police detachment to comb the west coast of the Peninsula, and if necessary the coast of north-east Sumatra too, in search of the junk. On the morning of the 28th

[40] CO 273/46, *passim*.
[41] Minutes on OAG to Sec. State, 3 June 1871; Sec. State to OAG, 26 Aug. 1871, in CO 273/47.
[42] *Pinang Gazette*, 1 July 1871.
[43] OAG to Sec. State, 14 July 1871, in CO 273/48. The despatches and most of the attached papers bearing on the Selangor incident are printed in *Parl. Pap.* C.466 of 1872, 'Papers relating to recent proceedings at Salangore . . .' Where the MS. material in CO 273/48 is thus duplicated only references to the printed sources are given.

June she found her in the Selangor estuary. In the words of the
Pinang Gazette:

At Salangore the police landed on the right bank of the river and
obtained information that a junk of the same name as the one sought
for had discharged her cargo about ten days previously. Crossing to the
opposite bank of the river the party there found the missing junk, with
six Chinese on board, one of whom was identified as Leng Ah Cheok,
her steersman; considerable alterations had been made to her, but the
gong, drum and cymbals found on board still had the junk's name on
them, traces of blood were also on the deck, which had apparently been
recently scraped. On the police going on shore and making search, a
great quantity of her cargo was found. This had been sold, and was
discovered in three shops.[44]

This account, and the reports of Inspector Cox in charge of the
police and Mr. Bradberry, the master of the *Pluto*, make it clear
that the men responsible for the pirating of the junk were Chinese.
It was in the Chinese shops ashore that the loot was found.[45] The
situation was clearly within the terms of a treaty signed with
Selangor in 1825, by which its Sultan agreed not to allow pirates
to resort to his territory, and undertook to hand over to the British
Government any who might be found there.[46] But trouble arose
when Cox and Bradberry tried to obtain the fulfilment of these
terms from Raja Musa, Sultan 'Abdu'l-Samad's eldest son, who
was supposed to be in charge. Musa was friendly and obliging.
But he was not in control of the Selangor River, for it had been
in the hands of the war-like Raja Mahdi and his allies since July
1870. They were no respecters of the English or of the luckless
Musa, so that the efforts of Cox and his police to round up all the
Chinese in the settlement together with a large part of their property soon brought an angry crowd on the scene led by Mahdi's
lieutenant, Raja Mahmud.[47] With him was a character whom we

---

[44] *Pinang Gazette*, 1 July 1871.
[45] *Parl. Pap.* C.466, pp. 2–5.
[46] Treaty with Selangor, Arts. IV and V, in Maxwell and Gibson, op, cit.,
pp. 32–34.
[47] Some of the Chinese seized on the barest evidence may well have been
local shopkeepers. Cf. the following account of the capture of one of them:
'. . . on capturing the fourth—evidently one of the head pirates, he having a
belt round his waist, and, as we supposed full of money—whilst trying to get
him into the boat he laid hold of one of the Malay Chiefs by the leg, at the same
time whispering something into his ear, on which the Chief told us go give him
over to his charge . . .' (Mr. Bradberry's Report, 1 July 1871, C.466, p. 3).
This does not seem the strongest of evidence of piracy, or of being a head
pirate!

have already met, Sayid Mashor, still smarting from his defeat at the hands of the Kuala Lumpur Chinese. Eventually fighting broke out, and Cox was fortunate to extricate his men without loss. They had secured the junk and part of her cargo, and nine Chinese, some of them identified as members of the junk's original crew. They could do no more, so pursued by some random shots from the shore they retired to *Pluto*, and thence with the junk in tow to Penang.[48]

The rest of this affair, so far as it concerned the Selangor River area, can be quickly told. As soon as Anson learnt of Cox's rebuff he sent back *Pluto* with the sloop H.M.S. *Rinaldo*, hoping that together they would make sufficient show of force to secure the remainder of the pirates and their booty. They failed, after an attempt to search the town and come to terms with Mahdi had brought them ten casualties in an inconclusive skirmish. From then on the affair became a punitive expedition. On the next day, 4 July, *Rinaldo* entered the river and remained there for twelve hours, shelling both the Selangor forts and burning part of the town. On 6 July there was more shelling and troops were landed. They found the place deserted. Mahdi and his men had taken shelter in the jungle, and there was nothing for the blue-jackets to do but spike and dismount the guns and demolish as much of the forts as possible before withdrawing.[49]

The bombardment of Selangor was a sharp lesson to 'Malay pirates', and made a great impression on the whole west coast. But it is its aftermath which is of greatest interest from the point of view of this study.

As soon as the result of *Rinaldo*'s expedition was known in Singapore Anson began a diplomatic 'follow-up'. He sent off J. W. Birch, the Colonial Secretary, and C. J. Irving, the Auditor-General, on a mission to the Sultan at Langat.[50] His idea seems to have been to gain as much advantage as possible from the initiative which the bombardment had given him, and at the same time to bring the bombardment as much as possible under cover of the treaty of 1825. For the Sultan had not in fact been

[48] Reports of Mr. Bradberry to Lt.-Gov. Penang (1 July 1871) and of Mr. Cox to same (30 June 1871), in C.466, pp. 2–5. Extracts from *Penang Argus* and *Pinang Gazette*, 1 July 1871, ibid., pp. 14–16.
[49] Reports of Comdr. Robinson, R.N., of *Rinaldo* (6 July, 1871) and Lt.-Col. Shortland, commanding the troops (7 July 1871), ibid., pp. 5–10.
[50] OAG to Sec. State, 28 July 1871, in C.466, p. 18.

summoned to surrender the pirates before force was used, though a letter addressed to him had been handed to Raja Musa. Nor had it been established, though there could be little doubt of the fact, that the pirates were known to be such by the Malay chiefs at Selangor. So in a letter which was now despatched by Birch Anson asked Sultan 'Abdu'l-Samad to comply with the treaty by seizing and surrendering the remainder of the pirates. He also demanded the surrender of Rajas Mahdi and Mahmud 'who caused their followers to fire upon and wound the sailors of Her Majesty the Queen of England, that they may be punished as they deserve'. His letter went on:

I must further ask my friend to give me some guarantee that pirates shall not again be allowed at Salangore, or to occupy the forts there. I therefore ask my friend to place some person in the office of Governor or Chief over the country about the Salangore River, whom this Government can trust to carry out the Treaty between this Government and that of Your Highness.[51]

The demands actually made of the Sultan by Birch went a good deal beyond the terms of Anson's letter, and were backed by a formidable display of force. Indeed this mission is as good an example of 'diplomacy by gunboat' as any to be found in the story of the European penetration of Asia. Birch and Irving travelled to Langat in *Pluto* but they were supported by a man-of-war, H.M.S. *Teazer*, and their journey took on the appearance of a triumphal procession around the state of Selangor. They went first to the Selangor River, where they found that Tengku Zia'u'd-din had taken possession of the forts, and that all was quiet. They then spent a day visiting the Tengku's headquarters at Klang, and expended a large part of *Teazer*'s ammunition allowance in a gunnery exhibition before making their way to the Sultan's *istana* at Langat on 21 July.[52]

At 2 o'clock on the afternoon of their arrival Birch and his companion landed with a large force of marines and seamen from the two ships. The guns of *Teazer* covered them as they marched up to the *istana* to present Anson's letter.[53] There was the usual exchange of courtesies and salutes, and they were then taken into

[51] OAG to Sultan of Selangor, n.d., ibid., pp. 19–20.
[52] Reports of Birch and Irving, C.466, pp. 20–23 and 24–26.
[53] Comdr. Blomfield, R.N., to Vice-Adm. Kellet, 20 Sept. 1871, ibid, pp. 44–46.

the 'Audience Hall', the escort remaining outside, but 'within a few yards'. The letter was read to the Sultan who was, according to Birch, 'highly delighted' with its contents. He at once denied any responsibility for the actions of Mahdi, Mahmud and Sayid Mashor—'bad men and pirates who had long devastated his country'—and said that he had already captured and sent to Malacca the remainder of the Chinese pirates, with the pig-tail of one since dead, as proof of good faith.

Turning to the second part of Anson's letter, which asked that a chief acceptable to the British Government should be placed in charge of the Selangor district, Birch raised the question of the status of Tengku Zia'u'd-din, the 'Viceroy'. The original power given him by the Sultan in 1868 was produced, and acknowledged to be genuine. If properly enforced this would place Zia'u'd-din in control of the Selangor estuary, as of the rest of the country not directly ruled by the Sultan. So Birch pressed the matter, saying that 'without in any way wishing to dictate to the Sultan, he might observe that the renewal of the authority given by that instrument [the power of 1868] to Tunku Dia Oodin, would be very acceptable to the English Government.'[54] The Sultan fenced with this thrust, saying that he could not decide such a matter without consulting his chiefs. Meanwhile they must not waste the valuable time of the Colonial Secretary. If Birch and his party would return to Singapore with their warship he would confer with his Council and inform the Governor by letter of their decision.

This attempt at evasion called forth some very strong language from Birch:

I at once declined, and informed the Sultan that I required an answer in twenty-four hours, and should expect it to be sent to me before 5 p.m. the next day, and that any neglect to comply with this demand, or any unsatisfactory reply would be attended by very serious consequences . . .

Very early the next morning I wrote him a letter,[55] . . . reiterating my demands, and sent it to His Highness by Raja Yacoob [the Sultan's favourite son] requesting him to distinctly say that I still adhered to

[54] Irving's Report, ibid., pp. 24–28.
[55] The text of this letter is printed in C.466, p. 23. It is purely a recapitulation of the demands made of the Sultan the day before, but its most important aspect is the statement in the last sentence: '. . . we promised to assist our friend's Vakeel in case any of our friend's subjects ventured to dispute his authority.'

G

the 5 p.m., for an answer, and that only one hour would be given after that, and that I should then take all the tin in the place and require an indemnity.[56]

This ultimatum, and perhaps the fact that *Teazer*'s guns were trained on the royal palace, produced a reply on the same afternoon (22 July) in the shape of two letters from the Sultan. The first letter, which declared Mahdi, Mahmud and Sayid Mashor outlaws, went as far as could reasonably be expected. Their arrest was probably not within Sultan 'Abdu'l-Samad's power, and the letter gave the British Government leave to arrest them within Selangor, and to call on the assistance of the Sultan's subjects.[57] The effectiveness of this assistance would depend on the energy and goodwill of whoever was appointed to control the country, so that it was the second letter which dealt with this which now became the subject of the negotiations.

The Sultan's second letter was in form a re-appointment of Tengku Zia'u'd-din as Governor of the whole of Selangor. But it contained a proviso that in his executive capacity the Tengku should consult with and secure the assent of the Sultan's nephews, Raja Bot of Lukut and his two brothers.[58] This proviso seems to have been the result of pressure put on the Sultan by Zia'u'd-din's enemies; it is significant that it named as the Tengku's collaborators not the Sultan's sons, as one might have expected, but men who though they would certainly have acted as a check on his activities would have done so in their own interests and not those of the Sultan and the state.[59] It was at once rejected by Zia'u'd-din himself, who pointed out that it threw upon him the responsibility for the administration of the state, but denied him any freedom of action.

Since the Sultan's reply was considered unsatisfactory Birch and the two ship's companies landed again in force within the hour. He demanded the deletion of the clauses referring to Raja Bot and his brothers, and the enactment of a simple grant of full powers to Zia'u'd-din. The Sultan acquiesced, and what was in

[56] Birch, Report, ibid., p. 22.
[57] Sultan to Birch, 22 July 1871, ibid., p. 23.
[58] Reports of Birch and Irving, ibid., pp. 20–23 and 24–28. The text of this second letter has not survived.
[59] Comdr. Blomfield of *Teazer* later asserted that the Sultan wished at the time to appoint as Viceroy one of his sons, the unworldly Raja Musa, whom Raja Mahdi had ousted from control of the Selangor River. Comdr. Blomfield to Vice-Adm. Kellet, 22 Sept. 1871, C.466, pp. 44–46.

fact a re-enactment of the original power given to Zia'u'd-din in 1868 was ceremonially sealed by 'Abdu'l Samad and witnessed by Birch and Commander Blomfield, the captain of *Teazer*.[60] *Wakil yam tuan*, literally 'the Sultan's agent or representative' but rendered by Irving as 'Sultan's Viceroy', was settled upon as Zia'u'd-din's title,[61] and Birch exhorted him to 'maintain good government and to open up his country'.

On the next morning (23 July) with this diplomatic triumph to their credit, Birch and his party left to return to Singapore. As more solid evidence of their success they carried with them a pair of elephant tusks to be presented to Queen Victoria in the name of Sultan 'Abdu'l-Samad and his sons, and $1,000 worth of tin, the property of Raja Mahdi handed over to them by the Sultan presumably as compensation for the Selangor piracy.[62] *Teazer* meanwhile accompanied Zia'u'd-din on a flag-showing trip round Mahdi's old haunts at Kuala Selangor and Sungai Buloh, proclaiming the powers now confirmed to him by the Sultan, and reading to the assembled populations the Sultan's letter calling on them all to assist in the capture and punishment of Mahdi.[63]

The Selangor affair is remarkable in the first instance for the great irresponsibility of the men on the spot. The Colonial officials' actions involved a new departure in the Colony's relations with its neighbours, one quite contrary to the well-established and clearly formulated policy of the home government. The initial action of Colonel Anson in sending *Pluto* to search for the missing junk was part of every maritime government's duty to police the seas and protect the interests of its subjects thereon, and as such was unexceptionable. That he gave no written instructions to his subordinates to govern their actions if—as proved to be the case—they found the junk within the territorial waters of another state certainly indicates some lack of foresight.[64] But

---

[60] Birch, Report, loc. cit. Irving describes an attempt by Zia'u'd-din's opponents to substitute at this point a smaller seal for the great seal of state, so that the validity of the grant could be challenged afterwards.

[61] Irving, Report, ibid., p. 27.

[62] Birch, Report, ibid., p. 22.

[63] Comdr. Blomfield, R.N., to Comdr. Robinson, R.N., 6 Aug. 1871, ibid., pp. 40–44.

[64] Cf. OAG to Sec. State, 19 Oct. 1871, written when Anson was justifying himself against the charge that he had sent an unarmed vessel and a few police to attack a nest of pirates: 'In defence of the action taken by Inspector Cox and Capt. Bradberry, it must be remembered that they were not prepared to find the junk under such circumstances . . .' (ibid., p. 37).

he did provide Cox and Bradberry with letters to the Sultan and Zia'u'd-din which, though they did not call upon them to sur-render pirates of whose existence Anson had then no certain knowledge, asked them to assist *Pluto*'s captain in his search.[65] The letter addressed to the Sultan was handed to Raja Musa at Selangor and he, though he was able to give little practical help, gave his assent to the recapture of the junk and the seizure of the Chinese. That part of the proceedings may therefore be said to have been carried out under cover of the treaty of 1825. It trans-gressed neither against established policy nor the limitations of international law. But no attempt was made to demand satis-faction from the Sultan before *Rinaldo*'s bombardment of the forts, so that this action could not be justified under the treaty. It is true that Sultan 'Abdu'l-Samad could not have enforced reparation from Mahdi if asked. Indeed it was the plea that Mahdi was a rebel against the Sultan's authority, and the admission secured by Birch that Mahdi and his allies were pirates and that 'Abdu'l-Samad was glad that they had been chastised which in part rescued Anson from the accusation that the bombardment had been an attack on a friendly state, and eventually secured Colonial Office approval of it.[66]

The pressure put on the Sultan 'to place some person in the office of Governor or Chief over the country about the Salangore River, whom this Government can trust . . .'[67] was another matter. This was a clear case of intervention in the internal affairs of a Malay state, and a breach of Colonial Office policy. It became more markedly so as result of Birch's handling of the negotiations at Langat. In his hands Anson's request became a demand backed by force to appoint a particular person to a specific office. Instead of 'a Governor over the country about the Salangore River' the Sultan was pressed to appoint Tengku Zia'u'd-din 'to conduct the affairs of the whole country between Malacca and Perak.'[68] Even the form and title of the appointment and the powers of its holder were settled by the British officials and their gunboat. And most important of all, the person appointed was promised the assistance of the British Government against anyone who disputed his authority,[69] and given the services of a British

[65] OAG to Sec. State, 19 Oct. 1871, p. 37.   [66] See below, pp. 95–6.
[67] Anson to Sultan, n.d., ibid., pp. 19–20.
[68] Birch to Sultan, n.d. (written 22 July 1871), ibid., p. 23.
[69] Ibid.

man-of-war to supervise the proclamation of his powers in the areas recently dominated by Raja Mahdi.

How far Birch's conduct was the result of instructions, written or otherwise, from Colonel Anson does not appear from the documents.[70] There is a reference in Birch's report of 26 July (ibid., pp. 20–23) to 'verbal instructions', but their scope is not indicated. But as soon as he learnt of Birch's success Anson was quick to endorse his subordinate's proceedings and to assume his own share of the credit. Praising Birch's diplomacy he described its results as 'very satisfactory'. He did not specifically mention the guarantee to uphold Zia'u'd-din's authority, or the help given to him in establishing himself at Selangor, but he enclosed in his despatch papers from Birch and the naval officers concerned which detailed these facts, and a report from C. J. Irving which looked forward to the development of Selangor under British auspices, with Zia'u'd-din cast as a second Maharaja of Johore.[71] Led on by his officials and sustained by the local Press, which asked for more of this sort of action so that the Malay States might be 'brought under European control',[72] Anson had sponsored that 'extension of our influence' which had already come under the ban of Whitehall in Sir Harry Ord's early years.

No angry Colonial Office thunderbolt descended on his head. Although his despatch reporting the bombardment of the Selangor forts arrived in London on 21 August,[73] when the clerks in Whitehall were engaged in drafting a broadside provoked by the 'Committee on Native States', forbidding in precise terms any new responsibilities outside the British settlements,[74] the news was received with apparent equanimity. Anson was mildly rebuked for using *Pluto* on such dangerous service, and asked to send further details in due course.[75] It is true that Anson's despatch presented the affair as a simple case of piracy covered by

---

[70] In his despatch of 28 July Anson said that he had instructed Birch 'to urge upon the Sultan the appointment of Tunku Dia Udin, or some other person in whom this Government could have confidence, as the responsible officer of his Government' (ibid, p. 18). This went further than his original request in the letter which Birch presented to the Sultan, but it may have been merely an attempt to associate himself with a successful *coup* when it had taken place.

[71] OAG to Sec. State, 28 July 1871, C.466, p. 18; Irving, Report, ibid., pp. 24–28.

[72] *Pinang Gazette*, 12 July 1871.

[73] OAG to Sec. State, 14 July 1871, ibid., pp. 1–2.

[74] Sec. State to OAG, 26 Aug. 1871, in CO 273/47 (cf. p. 85 above).

[75] Sec. State to OAG, 6 Sept. 1871, C.466, pp. 17–18.

the treaty of 1825. But even when his account of the mission to Langat arrived in London on 4 September[76] it was not regarded as raising important issues of policy. It was greeted with great satisfaction as a sharp lesson to pirates and a step likely to lead to 'quiet times'. Doubts among the permanent officials as to the legitimacy of the pledge of support given to Zia'u'd-din were assuaged by Lord Kimberley, who minuted somewhat hopefully:

I conclude that Mr. Birch did not pledge us to give the Sultan's Vakeel material support—the words do not necessarily imply it; I use the word pledge because it might be advisable to give him support, but this is very different from promising it.[77]

We come thus to 13 September 1871, when a decision to approve the action taken in Selangor was already on record in the Colonial Office. So far the matter had received purely departmental consideration, and only the bare account of a bombardment of a pirate fort in the Straits of Malacca had appeared in the Press.[78]

On the morning of 13 September a letter appeared in *The Times* from Sir P. B. Maxwell, late Chief Justice of the Straits Settlements, castigating the British Government for an unprovoked attack on the territory of a small and defenceless state. Maxwell, who had retired earlier in the year after a career on the Straits bench which began in 1856, was a jurist of outstanding talents.[79] He was too outspoken to be a success in mid-Victorian

---

[76] OAG to Sec. State, 28 and 29 July 1871, ibid., pp. 18–24.

[77] Minutes of 7–10 Sept. on OAG to Sec. State, 28 July 1871, in CO 273/48. All the minutes on this despatch suggest that conscious doubts about the pledge of assistance to Zia'u'd-din were consciously suppressed in the hope that no need would arise to face the issue. Cf. the minute of Charles Cox, Head of the Eastern Department: 'I have little doubt that now it is known that prompt measures will be taken to punish pirates and those who encourage or harbour them and that the Sultan and Tunku are upheld by England we may look for quiet times' (7 Sept.).

[78] *The Times*, 5 Sept. 1871.

[79] Peter Benson Maxwell (b. 1816, d. 1893), was an English barrister who made a name for himself when, after serving on a Commission of Enquiry into Crimean hospitals, he published a pamphlet, *Whom shall we hang ?*, which fixed the blame for the Crimean débâcle on the English nation and its niggardly Army Estimates. His was one of the few Colonial appointments to be listed in *Punch*, which in 1856 announced that 'Whom shall we hang has gone to Penang'. In his period on the Straits Bench Maxwell built up a formidable body of case law, most of it reinforced by decisions on appeal to the Privy Council. His judgement in *Regina* v. *Willan* (1858) for instance tackled the whole question of the relative positions of English Law and the Oriental law systems in the Colony. After his retirement in 1871 he published a well-known text-book, *Maxwell on Statutes* (1875) and a polemical work, *Our Malay Conquests* (1878). After 1882 he was employed in Egypt to re-organise the Courts there, but

England but in the Straits Settlements his energy found expression in a vigorous defence of the courts against the local executive, and in an insistence that the benefits of the law were due as much to Asian petitioners as to the European community of the Settlements. His letter, backed by a second which appeared a fortnight later, described the bombardment and Birch's mission as an unjustifiable interference into the internal affairs of Selangor, and an un-English use of force which violated all canons of justice and International usage.

> . . . it would seem that because some inferior officers of Selangore interfered to prevent the extradition of a suspected criminal and the restoration of some stolen property, a Colonial Governor commissioned two vessels to invade the Malay territory and to punish those officers, without even calling on their sovereign to punish them . . . and because the men engaged in carrying out this unlawful order were resisted and fired upon, his towns and forts were . . . destroyed, a number of his subjects were killed, and he himself compelled by threats of further hostilities to appoint to the administration of some province an officer nominated by the English Governor . . .[80]

The tone of this letter, and the second which appeared on 27 September, with their appeal to Englishmen's sense of justice and fair play, and their insinuation that whilst the British Government was eager to claim its own rights under treaties it was slow to admit the application of International Law to petty Malay states, must have been particularly galling to Liberal politicians who were just then sacrificing popularity for the sake of principle over the Alabama Arbitration affair. Its immediate result was Gladstone's intervention, but it was Gladstone the politician, not the Liberal idealist, a man out to prevent trouble, not to stir it up. He was worried by memories of the stir which the Radicals and the Aborigines Protection Society had created over Brooke's bombardment of Borneo pirates in the 1850's, but was soon soothed by assurances that the Sultan's 'apparent approval' of the bombardment covered any flaw in the proceedings.[81]

characteristically resigned on a point of principle. Six of his sons and grandsons served in the Colonial Service, five of them in Malaya and North Borneo. Cf. *One Hundred Years of Singapore* (1921), vol. i, pp. 206–10; vol. ii, pp. 431–4; Braddell, op. cit. *passim*, especially pp. 81–85.

[80] *The Times*, 13 Sept., 1871.

[81] Gladstone to Kimberley, 21 Sept. 1871, in Box Colonial No. 1, Kimberley Papers; Kimberley to Gladstone, 19 and 23 Sept. 1871, Add. MSS. 44224, in Gladstone Papers, British Museum.

The final verdict of the Secretary of State approved generally of Anson's handling of the incident, and complimented Birch on 'conducting a difficult negotiation with ability'. It concluded that the assistance promised to Zia'u'd-din 'referred to general countenance and support, and that no promise of material support was given by Mr. Birch.' Finally the following paragraph represented the criticism of the Prime Minister tempered by the tolerance of Lord Kimberley:

> In any other circumstances the proper course would have been to make formal application to the Sultan for redress for the outrage at Salangore, and not to have resorted to force unless the Sultan failed to execute the Treaty and to make due reparation. But as it appears . . . that the Chiefs in possession of the government at Salangore were in rebellion against the Sultan's authority and that the Sultan has expressed his satisfaction at your proceedings I am not disposed to question the course you pursued. I need scarcely however observe that in dealing with native states care should always be taken that all means of obtaining redress by peaceful means are exhausted before measures of coercion are employed.[82]

With this the question so far as the Colonial Office was concerned was closed. Anson's indignant rebuttal of the charges made by Maxwell in *The Times* produced only a bare acknowledgement of receipt,[83] and a request from Zia'u'd-din for the Straits Settlements Government to settle the boundaries between Selangor and her neighbours when reported to the Secretary of State[84] provoked only laconic instructions to delay action until Sir Harry Ord's return from leave.

Taken at their face value these transactions provoke the reflection that British policy at this time was opposed to the extension of British influence when it threatened to involve liabilities and complications, but condoned it when it did not incur technical responsibility. We need not discuss this general proposition here, but we shall recur to it in our next chapter, which deals with the evolution of policy in London. Before passing on we ought however to look briefly at the effect of Sir P. B. Maxwell's letter in the East.

The issue of *The Times* in which Maxwell's letter appeared

---

[82] Sec. State to OAG, 26 Sept. 1871, *Parl. Pap.* C.466, p. 31. The draft in CO 273/48 is marked—'Seen by Mr. Gladstone'.
[83] Sec. State to OAG, 6 Dec. 1871, ibid., p. 40.
[84] OAG to Sec. State, 24 Oct. 1871, in CO 273/50.

reached Singapore late in October, and at once threw Anson into a great fright. He had as yet no indication of the attitude which the Colonial Office would take, but he had begun to realize that his subordinates had exceeded the limits of Colonial Office policy. Commander Blomfield of H.M.S. *Teazer*, writing to the Commander-in-Chief of the Far Eastern Station, reported on 20 September that as result of his suggestion that Zia'u'd-din should be given further assistance to secure himself in his new position:

His Excellency the Administrator has given me verbally to understand that it is contrary to the policy and instructions of Her Majesty's Government to interfere in any way with the management of the affairs of the various Governments of the Malay Peninsula, and consequently no further steps will be taken.[85]

Now, whilst defending himself against Maxwell's accusation that he had waged war against Selangor and interfered without right in its internal affairs Anson attempted to disassociate himself from the way in which Birch had carried out his mission. The question at issue, he said, had been purely one of piracy, not of politics.

I regretted however to hear from Mr. Birch on his return that he had been so peremptory in his manner to the Sultan when arranging about the appointment of a proper Governor for Salangore, and I expressed to Mr. Birch my disapprobation of this on his return . . . The proverbial dilatoriness and 'shilly shallying' of the Malays, may, however, in a great measure be taken in justification of Mr. Birch's active and vigorous opposition to it; but still it is a pity that . . . an empty threat should have been made when, in all probability, patience and perseverance would have gained the same object.[86]

[85] Comdr. Blomfield to Vice-Adm. Sir H. Kellet, 20 Sept. 1871, C.466, pp. 44–46. Blomfield's suggestion was made in his Report of 6 Aug. (ibid., pp. 40–44). It is not materially different from the proposals of Irving (ibid., p. 28) which had already been forwarded to London, or indeed from the pledge which had actually been given by Birch to assist Zia'u'd-din if his authority was disputed in Selangor.

[86] OAG to Sec. State, 24 Oct. 1871, C.466, pp. 38–39. The naval C.-in-C. seems to have undergone a similar change of heart at about the same time. Writing to the Admiralty in approval of *Rinaldo*'s action at Selangor Sir H. Kellet had said on 2 Aug.: 'My opinion is . . . that no action should be less energetic and decisive to rid the sea of intolerable and merciless Malayan pirates, than that adopted by Commander Robinson' (ibid., p. 36). On 30 Oct. however he wrote: 'With regard to this matter [the proceedings of *Teazer*] and the recent proceedings of H.M.S. *Rinaldo* in suppressing piracy on the seaboard of the territory of the Sultan of Salangore, I have given directions that no such expedition is to be undertaken in future without reference to me, unless immediate action is absolutely necessary, in which latter case care is to be taken that such action is confined to the ordinary duties of the Navy, and that diplomatic and political affairs be carefully avoided' (ibid., p. 44). Perhaps he, too, had read *The Times* of 13 Sept.

He made no reference to the pledge of support. It seems therefore that by the end of October Anson had realized that this pledge was a dangerous breach of policy, and had resolved not to honour it and to allow it to die in silence. Certainly it was not to be referred to again in official correspondence by him or Sir Harry Ord. The fact that this was not at the time made clear to all concerned was to lead to a great deal of trouble in the next few years.

3

DRIFTING WITHOUT A POLICY

1872–1873

AFTER Colonel Anson's intervention in Selangor in 1871 the actions of the Straits Government in the Malay Peninsula were limited to a series of ineffective expedients to keep down piracy, and prevent the disorders from spreading to Penang. So far as he could Sir Harry Ord supported those chiefs whom he thought most capable of restoring order. But in 1873 conditions became so bad that an agitation for British intervention on the part of the Straits merchants spread to London, and it became apparent that some action could not be long delayed.

(i) Drifting

Sir Harry Ord did not return to the Straits Settlements from his leave until the end of March 1872. Troubles in plenty waited for him there. There was a regular civil war in Selangor, a disputed succession in Perak, and a Chinese war in Larut. Since the Selangor affair the Straits Government had lost touch with events in Malaya. Lieutenant-Colonel Anson knew little about events in Selangor except that fighting of some sort was going on in the interior. He knew nothing about the Perak succession dispute, for though Ismail had reported his election to the British government in 1871, nothing had been heard from 'Abdu'llah. But Larut was on Penang's front door-step. Trouble there had immediate effects on the local shipping passing in and out of Penang harbour, and among the Chinese community on the island. A fresh outbreak of fighting amongst the Chinese miners of Larut was therefore a matter of direct concern in the British colony.

War in Larut flared up in February 1872, when the Ghee Hin miners attacked their Hai San rivals. They had been preparing their revenge since 1861. In 1867 they had struck at the Toh Peh Kong, the Hai San's allies in Penang. Now they took the offensive in Larut, and after nearly a month's bloody fighting the Hai San were driven from the mines, the survivors taking refuge in Penang. The Mantri had allied himself with the Hai San in 1861, and at first he appealed to the Lieutenant-Governor of Penang for help, asking him to take action against the Ghee Hin headmen in Penang. But when he saw that his allies were irretrievably beaten he decided to make the best of things for himself. He shipped off the Hai San survivors to Penang at his own expense, and came to terms with the Ghee Hin; Ho Ghi Siu, the head of the Ghee Hin, became the Mantri's Agent and the booty, said to have been worth a million dollars, was divided between them. Thus in Larut the wheel came full cycle. The Chinese group in control of the mines changed and changed about, and the Mantri retained an increasingly precarious balance on their backs.[1]

By the time Ord reached the Settlements it was all over in Larut bar the shouting. This took the form of an appeal from the dispossessed Hai San for Government intervention on their behalf, and a crop of petitions for redress from local traders whose goods and ships had been caught up in the fighting.[2] Ord at once provided a man-of-war to protect Penang's shipping, but since the fighting had died down and the Mantri 'expressed himself as satisfied with the result' he declined for the moment to take any further action. Instead he sent the Straits Auditor-General, Irving, whose reports on Selangor in 1871 seem to have established him as a local authority on the Peninsular states, on a fact-finding mission up the west coast.

Irving's report for the first time revealed to the Straits Government the political situation in Perak outside Larut. Irving visited Klang and Kuala Selangor, then went on to Perak and Larut. There he saw both Raja 'Abdu'llah and the Mantri, and on 25 April 'Abdu'llah handed him a letter setting out the grounds of his claim to be the rightful Sultan of Perak. His talks with 'Abdu'llah, the Mantri and the Laksamana, and the contents of 'Abdu'llah's letter, enabled Irving to present to Ord an account of

---

[1] Lt.-Gov. Campbell, Memo dated 24 Oct. 1872; Capt. Speedy, Report, 23 Oct. 1872; Gov. Straits to Sec. State, 6 Nov. 1872, in CO 273/61. Mantri to Lt.-Gov., 24 Feb. and 26 Mar. 1872; Lt.-Gov. to Colonial Sec., Singapore, 25 Feb.; in Perak and Larut Disturbances, Archive Room, Raffles Museum. Fighting in Singapore between the Ghee Hin and other societies in Nov. 1871 may well have been connected with this outbreak in Larut early in the next year. It is significant that Anson in his report on the Singapore fighting attributes it to the 'influence of some bad lots recently arrived from China'. It is known that both sides were filling up their ranks at this time with professional fighting men from China, and the 'bad lots' may have been recruits en route to Larut (cf. OAG to Sec. State, 25 Nov. 1871, in CO 273/45).

[2] Lt.-Gov. Penang, to Colonial Sec., Singapore, 18 Mar. 1872 (Perak and Larut Disturbances).

Ismail's disputed election, and of the relative strength of the two political camps.[3]

With the facts before him Ord saw at once the need to resolve the schism between the Perak chiefs. The Mantri had shown himself quite unable to control the thirty to forty thousand Chinese in Larut. Some of the Straits officials indeed were afraid that eventually an independent Chinese republic would develop there.[4] In any event the disorders there formed a constant menace to the security of Penang and the trade of the whole west coast. Short of intervention the obvious policy for Ord was to work for the development of a Malay authority which could control the Chinese miners. But the assertion of effective Malay control over Larut was hardly possible whilst there was no effective government in Perak itself. Early in May therefore Ord sent Irving back to Perak to try and arrange an accommodation between Ismail and 'Abdu'llah. He failed. Neither of the two was willing to attend a conference to discuss matters, and their letters convinced Ord that a peaceful solution of the dispute was unlikely. For the moment however there was no fighting, and the Governor resigned himself to watching events take their course.[5]

Concerning Selangor the news brought back by Irving was not very enlightening. He reported that Zia'u'd-din still controlled the mouths of the Klang and the Selangor, but that 'the rebel Rajahs' were active in their headwaters. And since Sultan 'Abdu'l-Samad still showed his favour impartially to both sides Zia'u'd-din's opponents were able to export tin and get in arms and supplies by way of the Langat, which the Sultan controlled. Zia'u'd-din himself had interfered as little as possible with trade, but he

[3] Gov. Straits to Sec. State, 6 Nov. 1872, in CO 273/61; Irving, Memo, CO 809/1, p. 150.

[4] Cf. a minute by Irving, 13 Apr. 1872 (Perak and Larut Disturbances): 'From what Mr. Arthur Birch [then Lt.-Gov. of Penang] has told me I fancy that Larut is a virtually independent state. Its present position is interesting because it is a specimen of what is likely to become a common state of things along the coast. The tin mines have attracted a great number of Chinese to the place . . . They would seem to have evidently outgrown the power of the Malay Government to control them. In the case of the recent disturbances the Chinese were fighting against each other . . . If ever the Chinese chose to combine and turn out the Malays altogether I do not see what is to prevent them. In such a case there would be seen an entirely unprecedented political combination— groups of Chinese republics with Governments of Secret Societies tempered by faction fights.'

[5] Gov. Straits to Sec. State, 6 Nov. 1872, in CO 273/61. True to character Ord only reported these events to London much later in the year, when a newspaper item caused the Colonial Office officials to ask for information.

was compelled to blockade his enemies' traffic coming down the rivers, and this naturally offended the Straits merchants who had advanced money on the tin. There was, reported Irving, fighting of some sort going on in the interior, but matters seemed to have reached a stalemate.[6]

There was little that Ord could do about the fighting in Selangor. His policy between April and October 1872 was directed towards eliminating one aggravating factor—the redoubtable Raja Mahdi, who up to the end of 1871 had been the centre of the opposition to Zia'u'd-din. Shortly after the bombardment of the Selangor forts Mahdi left the state to collect fresh forces. He went to Benkalis in Sumatra, and began to fit out an expedition. At Ord's request the Dutch Resident there agreed to seize him and hand him over to the Straits Government, but Mahdi got wind of this and bolted, abandoning in his flight the ships and arms which he had collected, and his own family. He went first to a village on the west coast of Johore, south of Malacca. The Maharaja of Johore soon discovered his presence, and asked Ord what he should do with him. The Governor was in a dilemma. It was difficult to see how he could be charged in a British Court for his part in the Selangor incident, even if proof of his presence there were forthcoming. But he could not be allowed to return to Selangor. So Ord asked the Maharaja to give Mahdi 'hospitality' in Johore, which he was very pleased to do. Meanwhile the Straits Government would at least know where he was, and Ord seized the opportunity to try and buy him off. He persuaded Zia'u'd-din to offer him a pension of $350 a month so long as he kept out of Selangor politics and abandoned his claim to Klang, and promised him free asylum in Johore. But Mahdi rejected all these blandishments. In June he slipped out of Johore and made his way up the Linggi River and through Sungai Ujong to Selangor. There in July 1872 he joined Sayid Mashor.[7]

    [6] Irving's report, in Gov. Strait's 6 Nov. 1872.
    [7] Gov. Straits to Sec. State, 24 Oct. and 6 Nov., 1872, in CO 273/60 and 273/61; 'Yap Ah Loy', p. 110, n. 29; Winstedt, *History of Selangor*, pp. 26–27. This incident allows us a brief and alas all too rare glimpse of the undercurrents of Singapore politics. The Maharaja of Johore was personally well-disposed towards Mahdi, who had helped the sons of the late Bendahara Tun Mutahir of Pahang in their efforts to regain their father's throne (above, p. 74). Zia'u'd-din was an ally of the Maharaja's enemy, the new Bendahara Wan Ahmad. The Singapore newspapers, who were not absolutely disinterested, therefore accused the Maharaja of protecting Mahdi from punishment at the hands of

Despite the absence of Raja Mahdi affairs in Selangor had not gone well for Zia'u'd-din. As Commander Blomfield had foreseen in 1871 he was unable to maintain his position for long without outside assistance. His alliance with Yap Ah Loy was based on mutual self-interest, but he could not gain the steady support of any of the leading Selangor chiefs. They resented him as an interloper out to curtail their independence. As soon as it was apparent that the Straits Government would do nothing concrete to implement the promise of support given to Zia'u'd-din by Birch he steadily lost ground in the country, and his blockade of the traffic on the rivers set even the Sultan against him.

In August 1871, after *Rinaldo*'s bombardment had given him possession of the Selangor forts, Zia'u'd-din garrisoned both them and Yap Ah Loy's base at Kuala Lumpur with European-led mercenaries raised in Singapore.[8] At the same time he and Yap Ah Loy mounted an expedition from Kuala Lumpur into Ulu Selangor, to destroy Sayid Mashor before he grew strong enough to threaten Kuala Lumpur once more. Mashor was at Kuala Kubu, a place of some strategic importance. It commanded the junction of two important routes: one ran westward down the Selangor River to the sea, and eastward into Pahang by way of 'The Gap' (*Ginting Semanko*); the other reached northward to Tanjong Malim on the Bernam River, and thence into Upper Perak, and southward across the watershed to Ulu Klang and Kuala Lumpur. As well as standing on an important cross-roads

the Singapore Government, and of sending him back deliberately to Selangor. The first part of this accusation was demonstrably unfounded, but when the issues of the paper concerned came to the notice of the Colonial Office they caused a good deal of trouble (pp. 162 et seq. below). The feud spread to the Singapore officials. Braddell, the Attorney-General, to whom the case was referred for a decision as to whether proceedings should be taken against Mahdi in the Courts, was a personal friend of the Maharaja and acted as his legal adviser. His opinion was based closely on the legal technicalities, advising that no proceedings should be taken because of the uncertain nature of the evidence and the doubtful jurisdiction of the Courts, and dwelling on the general inadvisability of interference with 'legitimate warlike operations carried on without prejudice to the interests of neutrals.' Irving on the other hand had been concerned in the Selangor incident and the pledge to support Zia'u'd-din, who was his protégé. He saw Mahdi as 'little better than a treacherous lying savage' who ought to be dealt with at once. For the time Braddell and the Maharaja combined to persuade Ord (Winstedt, op. cit., p. 26; Wilkinson, op. cit., pp. 151–2).

[8] The detachment at Kuala Selangor numbered 140, mainly Sikhs, under the command of a sergeant named Pennyfeather or Pennefather, a man who had been in Zia'u'd-din's service for some time (*Pinang Gazette*, 12 July 1871). There were about 100 sepoys under two European officers, Van Hagen (a Dutchman) and Cavalieri (an Italian), at Kuala Lumpur.

Mashor's position was a strong one, and all the efforts to dislodge him failed. So for some months a stalemate ensued. Mashor's Chinese and Malay assailants, short of supplies, fell back on a stockade on the route to Kuala Lumpur, and sat down there waiting for him to make the next move.[9]

These 'routes' were of course mere jungle tracks, wide enough to allow the passage of a coolie with a bamboo pole across his shoulders, but usually too narrow for a bullock cart. On each side was the jungle. A dense mass of intertwined foliage, trees and sharp thorns, it teemed with animal life including the tiger, and legions of biting insects and leeches. So when each side settled into stockades across the paths the fighting took on the nature of trench warfare. There were minor raids and skirmishes, but as large-scale flank attacks through the jungle were impossible and frontal attacks very expensive the arts of subterfuge and diplomacy came into play. Each side sought to lure the other out of his stockades into prepared ambushes, and at the same time tried to weaken the enemy by detaching his allies and cutting off his supplies. At the same time they busied themselves building up their forces ready for a sudden attack in force on the weakened and dispirited opposition.

In this phase of the operations Zia'u'd-din fared badly. Yap Ah Loy could always recruit Chinese fighting men so long as he had money, but for the Malay chiefs loyalty to the 'Viceroy' had in the long run no future except political subordination and loss of independence. So in April 1872 the stalemate was at length broken by the defection of several of Zia'u'd-din's Malay lieutenants. Supposed to be bringing men and supplies up to Kuala Lumpur they went over to Sayid Mashor instead, and invested the town from the south whilst he threatened it from the north. An attempt by Van Hagen's mercenaries to drive them off failed, and the force watching Sayid Mashor in Ulu Selangor had to be recalled. It fell back on Kuala Lumpur with Mashor's men on its heels. Yap Ah Loy's situation was now critical. A general attack on the town failed, but he was not strong enough to keep his communications open, and in July, after Raja Mahdi had joined Sayid Mashor, the one route still available to the coast through Damansara was cut, and the defenders began to run short of supplies.

[9] 'Yap Ah Loy', pp. 64–68.

In August Van Hagen, the commander of Zia'u'd-din's mercenaries in Kuala Lumpur, decided that the position in the town was hopeless, and leaving Yap Ah Loy and his Chinese to their fate he and his sepoys tried to cut their way out. They set off during the night, making for the coast by way of Petaling and Damansara. In the morning Ah Loy found himself with a depleted garrison; he discovered also that a large part of the besieging forces had gone after Van Hagen, so that the way was open for his own escape. As soon as it was dark he evacuated the town and splitting into small groups his men took to the jungle, to make their way over the hills to the west of Kuala Lumpur. Ah Loy himself emerged after two days and nights in the jungle at Damansara, and managed to get a boat down the river to join Zia'u'd-din at Klang. Most of his men were not so fortunate. One Chinese source puts the number who died in the jungle or were killed in the pursuit at 1,700 out of the total of 2,000. Van Hagen's column fared no better, fewer than forty emaciated survivors drifting into Klang during the next few weeks. Van Hagen and some forty others were captured and taken back to Kuala Lumpur, where their throats were cut.[10]

Soon after the loss of Kuala Lumpur Zia'u'd-din suffered a further disaster when treachery enabled Sayid Mashor to take the forts at Kuala Selangor, killing Pennefather and fifty sepoys. The 'Viceroy' had now lost all his holdings in Selangor except the control of the mouth and the lower reaches of the Klang River. Mahdi and Sayid Mashor were in control of the whole of the interior. They had an outlet to the sea at Kuala Selangor, and were in touch in the south with Sungai Ujong, the route by which Mahdi had returned in July, and in the north with the Bernam River district. The chiefs of both these areas were giving them active help, and most of the other Selangor chiefs were sympathetic to them. As for Zia'u'd-din, short of problematic British support his only hope was help from his friends in Pahang. He had already received a promise of help from Wan Ahmad, the Bendahara, in April, but that help was not in time to save Kuala Lumpur. The

---

[10] This account of the campaign leading up to the capture of Kuala Lumpur is taken in the main from Middlebrook's 'Yap Ah Loy' (the only account to use the Chinese sources), as well as the pioneer work of Sir Richard Winstedt. The throat-cutting incident is taken from R. J. Wilkinson, *A History of the Peninsular Malays*, p. 154, who bases it on a letter written at the time by Syed Mashor. The Colonial Office records, restricted not merely to what Ord knew, but what he chose to write into his despatches, are silent on the subject.

H

Pahang troops crossed the Bentong passes into Selangor in early August, and actually sent a message to Van Hagen telling him to fall back into Ulu Klang and join them. Either Hagen never got the message, or he took it for a ruse of Mashor. At any rate he broke out in the opposite direction, towards the sea, with fatal results for himself. With Kuala Lumpur lost Zia'u'd-din was prevented from establishing contact with his Pahang allies, and they in turn were cut off from their supplies—they were reduced to eating banana stalks and salt—and had to fall back again into Pahang.[11]

The course of the Selangor war created almost as many difficulties for Sir Harry Ord as for Tengku Zia'u'd-din. Birch's pledge of support for his régime after the Selangor affair produced a new wave of investment in the tin mines at Klang, and for a time the Tengku had no difficulty in raising money in Singapore and Malacca. Under his administration 12,000 Chinese miners were said to be employed on the Klang River alone, and the yield of tin doubled.[12] But the victories of Sayid Mashor and Mahdi threw the whole area in chaos and most of this capital was lost or imperilled. Klang itself seemed to be threatened, the Chinese began to desert the mines, and two mines just outside the town were destroyed. The Malacca merchants and the Singapore Chamber of Commerce turned reproachfully on Ord. They were, they said, entitled to support, 'having been induced by the representation of protection and support from the Colonial Government to invest our money in the trade of Selangore. . . .' Since the fighting had been renewed the Government had done nothing to support Zia'u'd-din, nor had it arrested Mahdi, Mashor and Mahmud, the three ringleaders, as it had been authorized to do by the Sultan of Selangor, even though Mahdi himself had been within its power in Singapore and Johore. It was suggested that this was due to British policy having been impro-

---

[11] The fullest account of this aspect of the Selangor War is in Linehan, *History of Pahang*, pp. 94 et seq. The negotiations which led up to the Pahang alliance date from the end of 1871; they were not clinched until Ord and Zia'u'd-din went to Pekan in person, some time between April and August 1872, since Wan Ahmad would not move without British approval. It was through this visit that Zia'u'd-din was absent from Selangor when Raja Mahdi returned there in July, and his enemies put it out that the Tengku had lost the favour of the British Government and was being detained in Singapore. This seems to have had something to do with the defection of his Selangor lieutenants at this time.

[12] Petition of the Malacca Traders, 27 July 1872.

perly influenced by the Maharaja of Johore and his friends in the administration. The merchants urged the Straits Government to live up to its promises, and to intervene in Selangor to get rid of Mahdi and Mashor, and give the support to which it was pledged to Zia'u'd-din.[13]

At the same time Ord also came under fire from the Straits Press. The *Pinang Gazette* in a leading article on the events in Selangor accused the Governor of forfeiting through his supineness the effective influence which his government had acquired, and of jeopardizing the whole of the Settlements' trade with Selangor. Similar comments, if we are to believe the editor of the *Gazette* appeared at the same time in the *Singapore Daily Times*, the predecessor of the *Straits Times*.[14]

The merchants got no change from Ord, but merely what he called 'the usual answer':

If persons, knowing the risks they run, owing to the disturbed state of these countries, choose to hazard their lives and properties for the sake of large profits which accompany successful trading, they must not expect the British Government to be answerable if their speculation proves unsuccessful.[15]

The newspapers he ignored. Their attack was so misdirected that he could afford to. The editors and most of their readers knew

[13] Petition from the Malacca Traders to Singapore Chamber of Commerce, 27 July 1872; Singapore Chamber of Commerce to Colonial Secretary, Singapore, 30 July 1872 (in Gov. Straits to Sec. State, 6 Nov. 1872, CO 273/61, and *Pinang Gazette* 10 Aug. 1872). Though the Petition was signed by 35 Chinese and Muslim traders of Malacca its language makes it clear that it was drafted by an Englishman, probably a lawyer, and the closeness of the dates of the Petition and the letter from the Chamber of Commerce suggest that both had originated in Singapore. Many of the Malacca merchants were in fact the agents of Singapore firms.

[14] *Pinang Gazette*, 10 Aug. 1872. This was editorial opinion, and found no echo in any other section of the paper, indeed not a single letter could be found for publication during this period which called for intervention in the states. A letter printed in the same paper on 5 Oct. from Stuart Herriot, a municipal commissioner of Penang, suggests that the Editor spoke only for himself and interested parties. It attacked the *Gazette*'s views on Selangor as unrealistic and asserted that the actions of Birch and Anson in 1871 had 'always been considered to be wrong and imprudent'. It pointed out that Ord had not the means to manage the internal affairs of the states, and that it would be foolish for him to give orders which he could not enforce. In any case policy was governed by rules laid down by the Colonial Office, similar to those formerly enforced from Calcutta, i.e. insistence on non-interference in the internal affairs of the states, but sanction for the protection of British trade and traders from pirates and the illegal exactions of local chiefs.

[15] Gov. Straits to Singapore Chamber of Commerce, 21 Aug., 1872, enclosed in his 6 Nov. 1872 to Sec. State (CO 273/61).

perfectly well that it was not in the Governor's power to take over the administration of the Peninsular states. They made no constructive suggestions, but fell back on general demands for 'a more vigorous policy' and complaints that Ord and his officials 'threaten much but do nothing'. Accusing Ord of 'supineness' was a particularly unhappy shot. However far he might have been responsible for the troubles of Malaya personal inactivity was the last sin with which to reproach him. Year after year he was attacked in the discussions on the financial estimates for the excessive use he made of the government steamers. He was pictured as dashing ceaselessly to and fro between the three settlements and the different Malay states at a ruinous cost to the colony. This was a true picture of his activities in the second half of 1872, when he was particularly active helping to arrange Zia'u'd-din's Pahang alliance, preventing the Selangor war spreading to Negri Sembilan, and doing what he could to bolster up the Viceroy's stock in Selangor itself.

At some time between May and early August Ord made his visit to the Bendahara of Pahang at Pekan, in order to clinch the arrangements which had been made for the latter to intervene in the Selangor War. There was not much difficulty about this. Zia'u'd-din had offered him the revenues of Klang in payment, and his own political interest was involved, for there was a colony of restless Pahang emigrés just over the border in Selangor whose suppression would secure the Bendahara's grip on his newly won throne. But he would not move without the blessing of the British Governor. No doubt he was nervous that the Maharaja of Johore, who had just been entertaining Raja Mahdi, might interfere. He may also have wanted to be sure that if it became necessary to send troops and supplies round to Selangor by sea they would not be held up by the British Navy. Ord's visit re-assured him, and spurred on by the presence of Zia'u'd-din himself preparations for the invasion of Selangor from the east went forward. As we have seen they were not in time to save Kuala Lumpur from Sayid Mashor. But eventually the men from Pahang tipped the scales in the Viceroy's favour.[16]

[16] Linehan, op. cit., p. 95; Gov. Straits to Sec. State, 6 Nov. 1872, CO 273/61. All Ord's reports to the Colonial Office on these events are uninformative and sent long afterwards, usually as result of a direct request for information. It is difficult to avoid the impression that he himself felt that even the limited part he was playing in the affairs of the Peninsula was in advance of what would be approved in London.

Later in the year Selangor affairs again drew Ord into a sea voyage, this time up the west coast. Apart from the general restlessness in the Straits Settlements and 'the local journals containing charges against me of ignorance, carelessness, and want of consideration for the interests of the people'[17] there were pressing local reasons for all this activity. These centred on the Linggi River area of Negri Sembilan, the only source of Malacca's tin supplies which had not so far been affected by the Selangor war. In July Raja Mahdi had returned to Selangor by this route, going up the Linggi River and being passed through Sungai Ujong into Ulu Langat. Tengku Zia'u'd-din at once intervened, and his efforts to gain control of this route into Selangor threatened to draw the whole area into the war.

In 1870 Zia'u'd-din had concluded an agreement with Sungai Ujong's neighbour-state of Rembau which purported to fix the Rembau–Selangor boundary at Simpang Linggi, on the Linggi River. There were many claimants to some sort of authority over this place, but it was in effective possession of none of them. It was part of a small Bugis settlement which had existed at the mouth of the Linggi River since the end of the eighteenth century.[18] Zia'u'd-din now promised the ruler of Rembau his support in an attempt to secure possession of Simpang, and the latter on his part agreed to hand it over to his backer if he were successful. The point of this manœuvre, as will be seen from the map (at end of book), was that it would give Zia'u'd-din control of the river, the only effective route in and out of the whole area. He would be able to stop any of Mahdi's supplies coming that way, and could at the same time take his revenge on Sungai Ujong by cutting its connexion with the coast. But matters were complicated by the fact that there were not one but two chiefs in control in Sungai Ujong. These were the Dato' Bandar and the Dato' Klana. It was the Dato' Bandar who had helped Mahdi, and at whom Zia'u'd-din's anger was directed. But the Dato' Klana's interests would suffer too. He had already had exchanges with the Straits Government on the subject of keeping the river free for trade, so now he turned naturally to Ord and asked for help, at the same time making what was probably the purely formal gesture of

[17] Gov. Straits to Sec. State, 24 Oct. 1872, in CO 273/60.
[18] Gullick, J. M., 'Sungei Ujong', *JRASMB*, xxii, pt. 2 (1949), pp. 58–60; Winstedt, 'Negri Sembilan, The History, Polity and Beliefs of the Nine States', *JRASMB*, xii, pt. 3 (1934), p. 69.

offering his country to the British Government. This was in
October 1872. A few days later Ord heard that the ruler of Rembau was also willing to leave the settlement of the affair in his
hands. So he prepared to fight one more round in the long struggle
to keep the Linggi open for Malacca's tin trade.[19]

Ord left Singapore for the Linggi River and Selangor at the
end of October. As he told the Permanent Under-Secretary at
the Colonial Office in a bitter little note:

Murders, plundering and burning are the order of the day, and the
bad ones are beginning to believe the popular cry that 'nothing will
induce the Government to interfere'. If you will be content not to
notice the newspaper articles for a little while I shall be able to tell
you exactly what is the state of things, and what should, or *may*, be
done—though it does not follow that you will think it *must* be.[20]

As he set off he was presented with a letter from the Sultan of
Selangor which added to his troubles. 'Abdu'l-Samad had been
won over by the opposition,[21] and he complained that Zia'u'd-din's
blockade was injuring trade; would the Governor force him to
discontinue it! This was a facer for a man who was being asked
on all sides to support the Sultan's Viceroy so as to protect trade.

Despite this inauspicious start Ord's visit to the west coast
was as successful as his voyage to Pahang had been earlier in
the year. Its first stage consisted of a meeting at Kuala Linggi
with Zia'u'd-din and the Dato' Klana of Sungai Ujong to settle
the Simpang Linggi issue. The ruler of Rembau, who failed to
turn up at the meeting, was the nominal claimant, but Zia'u'd-din
—the real prime mover—was satisfied by the Dato' Klana's
assurances, and agreed to let the claim to Simpang drop. The
Dato' Klana, unlike the Dato' Bandar, had no interest in the
fortunes of Mahdi and his allies, but was only concerned to keep
the river open for his own trade. He therefore guaranteed that no
supplies would be allowed to reach Mahdi through his territory,
and with this Zia'u'd-din was content. Since the Dato' Bandar

[19] Gov. Straits to Sec. State, 6 Nov. 1872, in CO 273/61.

[20] Sir Harry Ord to Sir Robert Herbert, 24 Oct. 1872, CO 273/60. The
extent to which Sir Harry's stock had slumped at the Colonial Office can be
judged from Herbert's minute on this letter: 'Most certainly the present
Governor cannot be trusted to interfere wisely.'

[21] Later, on 18 Nov., when troops from Pahang captured Petaling, they found
there a letter from Sultan 'Abdu'l-Samad giving orders for assistance to be
given to Raja Mahdi against his own 'Viceroy' (Winstedt, *Selangor*, p. 29).

lived further upstream than the Dato' Klana he was powerless to interrupt this arrangement. No one seems to have asked him what he thought of it, and for the moment he dropped out of sight of the Straits Government.

Before the second item on his programme—the meeting with the Sultan and chiefs of Selangor—Ord had a heart-to-heart talk with the imperturbable Zia'u'd-din. He warned him that although he was backed by people who were willing to advance money on his chances of success and although the Straits Government would continue to 'give him countenance', yet there were formidable groups opposed to him in Selangor. If he were doubtful about his ability to overcome them he had better give up now, whilst he still could without much loss of face. Zia'u'd-din was well aware of the precarious nature of his position, but he pinned his faith to his new Pahang allies, and though he offered to give up if Ord wished, said that he would prefer to persevere. Ord did not pursue the subject further.[22]

Ord's conference with the Sultan on 1 November was a good deal less spectacular than that of Birch nearly eighteen months earlier. There was the same armed escort of blue-jackets and marines, but it was smaller, and this time the ship herself—H.M.S. *Zebra*—did not ascend the Langat River and the party went up in the ship's boats. There was less argument than before, and no empty threats. Sultan 'Abdu'l-Samad was soon brought to assert that he 'had complete trust in Tunku Kudin as Viceroy' and that he 'was satisfied after some explanation that the blockade was necessary'.[23] Perhaps experience had taught the Selangor chiefs that the best tactic in these encounters was to say 'yes' and think 'no'. The aftermath of Birch's mission had shown them that English words were not followed by English action, and since they would be free to go on as before as soon as Ord departed they no doubt felt that there was no profit in arguing with him.

But this time it did not work out in the same way. There was no British action in the state, but Zia'u'd-din's confidence in his Pahang allies was shown to be justified. From the beginning of 1873 the tide of war began to flow in his favour. Kuala Lumpur was recaptured in March as result of a joint operation between

---

[22] Gov. Straits to Sec. State, 6 Nov. 1872. The meeting at Kuala Linggi took place on 29 Oct., and that with the Selangor chiefs on 1 Nov., so the conversation with Zia'u'd-din can probably be dated 31 Oct.
[23] Ibid.

the Pahang men advancing from the east and a reconstituted Chinese-Malay force from Klang under Yap Ah Loy.[24] From then on most of the work was done by the Pahang troops. There was a brief lull after the capture of Kuala Lumpur whilst Mahdi and Sayid Mashor fell back on Ulu Selangor, and whilst the Pahang forces were regrouped, large reinforcements being sent round by sea to Klang. These attacked and took Kuala Selangor from the sea in November. Meanwhile the overland contingent cleared Ulu Selangor of Mashor's stockades after some bitter fighting. Mahdi and his lieutenant Mahmud fled the country, finding shelter for the moment with the Dato' Bandar of Sungai Ujong, and Sayid Mashor was driven northwards. From the upper reaches of the Bernam River he fell back on Slim; thence he went over the border into Perak, where he took refuge at the court of the self-styled Sultan 'Abdu'llah.[25]

These events secured virtual control of Selangor for Zia'u'd-din, though he was still left with the problem of getting rid of his own allies, who for some time treated parts of the state as a conquered country. But they did not relieve Sir Harry Ord of his troubles. Despite the change of military advantage from one side to the other conditions in Selangor remained disturbed throughout 1873; the tin mines do not seem to have revived very much, there were no returns on invested capital, and Malacca's trade was kept alive only by the traffic up the Linggi River which was liable to be stopped without warning by the local chiefs whose stockades commanded this busy waterway. So Ord continued to receive complaints from the merchants of Malacca, and from interested parties in Singapore. But the worst of his troubles arose from events in Larut, which in 1873 replaced Selangor as the trouble-centre of the Peninsula.

Until December 1872 the disturbances in Larut retained their original character. The Ghee Hin and the Hai San Chinese alternately replaced each other in control of the mining lands, and the Mantri changed sides each time. In February 1872, as we have seen, the Ghee Hin drove out the Hai San. In October the Hai San turned the tables on them. An expedition fitted out

[24] *Pinang Gazette*, 5 Apr. 1873; Linehan, *Pahang*, pp. 96–97; Yap Ah Loy, pp. 79–80.
[25] Linehan, op. cit., pp. 97–99; 'Yap Ah Loy', p. 81.

in Penang and largely composed of well-armed professional fighting men from China drove the Ghee Hin from Larut with great loss. More than 1,000 of them were killed and thousands of wounded and starving Chinese refugees poured into Penang. The Mantri as usual transferred his allegiance to the victors, and though by this time plunder was in short supply he was rewarded with a share of the captured Ghee Hin women.

In December the Ghee Hin struck back. But this time events did not follow their usual pattern. There was no clear change of control in Larut, and the Mantri was thus not able to avoid trouble by a swift change of sides. Indeed his own stronghold at Matang near the mouth of the Larut River was one of the objectives of the attacking Ghee Hin, who marched overland from Krian to cut off the mines from the coast.[26] They took Matang, and pushed up the road to the mines as far as Simpang, where the road from Upper Perak joined it. There they built a stockade. But they were not strong enough to clear the Hai San from the mines inland. So both sides faced each other in Larut in what now became a continuous war. As in Selangor this was a war of stockades, with the Ghee Hin astride the road from the mines to the jetty at Matang, but with the Hai San still in control of the mines. As in Selangor there was the same aversion to frontal attacks on stockades, and once each side had consolidated their main positions their efforts were directed to wearing down the enemy and cutting off his supplies, either by military or diplomatic means.

There was far more scope for this 'cloak and dagger' war in Larut than in Selangor. For in Larut each side was compelled to draw its supplies from the same place, and to use the same operational base—Penang—which was neutral ground. In this sector active operations usually took the form of Secret Society clashes, but this was an unsatisfactory method of proceeding because of the intervention of the Penang Police. Subtler tactics were more effective. Each side kept the Penang Government informed of the other's preparations to ship arms, supplies and reinforcements in the hope that the British officials would interfere

---

[26] *Pinang Gazette*, 14 Dec. 1872. Although several other writers have covered the subject, notably V. Purcell in *The Chinese in Malaya*, pp. 104–8 (1948) and Gullick, J. M., 'Captain Speedy of Larut', *JRASMB*, xxvi, pt. 3 (1953), the best general account of the Larut War remains R. J. Wilkinson's chapter in Winstedt, *History of Perak* (1934).

and prevent the laden junks from sailing.[27] They detained their opponents' ships by initiating proceedings against the owners for a bogus debt, obtaining a writ of sequestration, and hiring a European lawyer to keep the case alive in the courts for as long as possible. If all these political measures failed there was still an opportunity for direct action, for supplies had at some point to be taken across the narrow stretch of sea between Penang and the mainland. So a brisk naval war developed whilst the war of stockades hung fire. Each side operated war junks fitted out at Penang or in one of the many creeks of the mainland, which attempted to run shipments through to their own side and to cut off those of the enemy. In this struggle the Hai San were not so well placed as the Ghee Hin. They had possession of the mines, but they could not get the tin out because the jetty at Matang was held by the Ghee Hin, and they had to smuggle food and supplies in from other points on the coast as best they could. The support of the Mantri, who now that both sides were evenly matched sided with his original favourites, was of some value because of his two steamships, which were good blockade-runners. But it was of little political use, for the Ghee Hin had their own Malay sponsor, the so-called 'Sultan' 'Abdu'llah, so that both sides could claim to be acting on behalf of some sort of legitimate authority.

In truth Malay authority in Larut at the beginning of 1873 was non-existent. 'Abdu'llah's bond with the Ghee Hin was their mutual hostility to the Mantri, who was the foremost supporter of Sultan Ismail and thus one of the men who stood between 'Abdu'llah and the throne of Perak. He promised to pay half of the Ghee Hin's expenses and to give them a monopoly grant to the tin mines if they proved victorious, but he had no money and seems to have given them no effective help, though some of his followers fitted out junks in the Trong River which helped in the blockading of the Hai San supplies.[28] Nor was the Mantri any

---

[27] There was no prohibition on the export of arms from Penang to Larut until 21 Feb. 1873, but under Sections 125 and 126 of the Criminal Code of the Straits Settlements it was an offence to levy war or assist in the levying of war in the territories of states at peace with the British Crown. See below, pp. 115-16. Cases of ships being detained as result of proceedings for debt occur in the Petition of Mahomed Zein and Ho Ghi Siu, the Mantri's Agents in Penang, to the Lt.-Gov. Penang, 16 Oct. 1872 (CO 273/61), and in Skinner's Précis of Perak Affairs, CO 809/1.

[28] Statement of the Master, S.S. *Fair Malacca*, 13 Dec. 1872; Gov. Straits to Sec. State, 24 July 1873 (CO 273/68).

more effective after he had been turned out of Matang. He possessed a second fort at Kota, near Bukit Gantang, which commanded the route into Upper Perak. But when he appealed to Ismail, hoping for reinforcements from this quarter the only help forthcoming was a number of local chiefs sent as 'mediators'. The Chinese of both sides were heartily sick of the Mantri and for the moment had no use for him, so in February 1873 he moved to the Krian-Kurau area, the only Malay part of Larut, where he is said to have lived in a boat so as to be ready for quick getaway.[29] 'Abdu'llah was also living in the area. Common adversity seems to have produced a reconciliation between them, and they were joined by a third unfortunate, Raja Yusuf, whom 'Abdu'llah as 'Sultan' had appointed Raja Muda in order to obtain his services as a fighting man.[30] For the moment therefore it was left to the Chinese in Larut to fight it out without outside interference. Given time the Ghee Hin would probably have starved the Hai San into surrender. But their attempts to maintain their blockade by sea were too blatant, and compelled the Straits Government to act.

The British authorities were naturally eager to stop the Larut fighting or at least damp it down, because of the unrest it caused in Penang. But it was difficult for them to see how to set about it. It was not possible to call on any Malay authority to restore order, for there was no chief whose *de jure* sovereignty in Larut it was politic to recognize, and none of the many claimants to sovereignty had any effective control over events. British military intervention was also out of the question, for Sir Harry Ord had neither the resources nor the authority to attempt it, even had he been willing to face the problem of organizing a government in Larut when he had subdued it. He tried therefore to put an end to the fighting by tackling it from the other end and stopping the use of Penang as a base of operations and a source of supplies.

As the law stood this was extremely difficult to do. Sections 125 and 126 of the Penal Code of the Straits Settlements made it an offence to wage or to abet the waging of war against any power

---

[29] *Pinang Gazette*, 19 Apr. 1873.
[30] In February the Mantri recognized 'Abdu'llah as Sultan, and 'Abdu'llah recognized him as Mantri and as Governor of Larut. A document signed by the 'Sultan' on 14 Apr. ran: 'We acknowledge and confirm the Orang Kaya Mantri, even as before so during our reign, to hold for ever the Government of Larut and its dependencies. This cannot be changed' (Winstedt, *Perak*, p. 86). This is interesting in the light of later disputes over the nature of the Mantri's position in Larut.

at peace with the Queen, or to 'commit depredation or prepare to commit depredation on the territories of any power in alliance or at peace with the Queen' (Section 126).[31] In practice it was almost impossible to enforce this legislation as a preventive measure against anyone who set himself to circumvent its terms. There was no ban as yet on the export of arms and military stores, which had always been one of Penang's normal trades. Nor was it possible to prevent Chinese going as peaceful travellers from Penang to Province Wellesley—both parts of the same British Colony— and there transforming themselves into soldiers and slipping over the unwatched frontier into Larut.[32] In December when the Ghee Hin captured Matang their junks sailed unarmed from Penang, and were fitted out in the Trong River and off Larut with guns and small-arms brought by a trading junk as perfectly legal merchandise, a manœuvre which had already been employed by the Hai San.[33]

Though it was not possible to use these sections of the Penal Code to prevent the prosecution of the Larut War from Penang, it was still open to the British authorities to use them to punish those who actually took part in the fighting if they could catch them red-handed and prove that they had come from British territory. The fighting in Larut itself was outside Ord's reach. But the junks blockading the Larut River and its approaches were within range of the Royal Navy. The Penang authorities, much to Ord's annoyance, had failed to move against the Hai San junks which landed troops and blockaded the Larut River in October 1872. There were several reasons for this.

(1) The actual owners could not be traced—they were said to be in Larut.
(2) The masters of the junks said that they were traders armed for self-protection, and *en route* to Perak (the destination in their Penang port clearances). No independent witnesses had seen them stop or attack another ship, and it would have been difficult to bring a case against them for waging war solely on the evidence of their opponents.

---

[31] This was the new Penal Code, drafted since the Transfer and passed in 1871, which only came into force on 16 Sept. 1872 (cf. Braddell, *Law of the Straits Settlements* (1915), p. 41). The text of Sections 125 and 126 was published in the *Pinang Gazette* of 26 Oct. 1872.

[32] At Christmas 1872 Ord himself saw some of these fighting men passing through Province Wellesley to Larut, but could do nothing about it (Gov. Straits to Sec. State, 24 July 1873, in CO 273/68).

[33] Lt.-Gov. Penang to Colonial Sec., Singapore, 27 Oct. 1872, in CO 273/61.

(3) Most important, the Mantri, as soon as he had transferred his support to the victorious Hai San repudiated his Agent's complaints against the junks and announced that they were acting for and not against him. It was impossible to bring any charge to which this was not a defence.[34]

But in December a better opportunity for action arose when the Ghee Hin in their turn imposed a blockade. A large number of clashes between junks of the two sides, some involving innocent third parties, arose as result of this, but the case seized on by Ord was that of the *Fair Malacca*. She was a British steamer of Straits registry, with a British captain. On 13 December, whilst under charter to the Mantri and carrying food and supplies to Larut, she was fired on by Ghee Hin junks, and in getting clear of them was hit thirty-five times by cannon shot.[35]

Ord was some time deciding how to act, but finally resolved to treat the incident as a case of piracy. On 25 December he sent off Captain Denison, the senior naval officer present, to find out 'whether the junks had acted by any or what lawful authority', and in default of a satisfactory answer to bring as many of them as the master of the *Fair Malacca* could identify back to Penang for an enquiry.[36] Two Ghee Hin junks were picked out as having taken part in the attack, and after some inconclusive parleying with both Chinese factions ashore Denison in H.M.S. *Zebra* took them in tow for Penang. His report makes no mention of their crews, who presumably made themselves scarce. One of the junks sank on the voyage. The other was sold and the proceeds paid into the Admiralty Court, the owner or owners being given a year and a day to appear and show cause why their property

[34] Lt.-Gov. to Colonial Sec., 18, 24, 27 Oct.; Colonial Sec. to Lt.-Gov., 24 Oct. 1872, in CO 273/61. These reasons were those expressed in correspondence. Another potent reason for inactivity seems to have been the uneasiness of the local officials as to their personal liability. The formal evidence was very thin, and it was known that one of the owners had retained a prominent Penang lawyer and would fight out the issue in the courts. The officials concerned had no clear instructions from Ord, and they shrank from an act of seizure which would probably have entailed bloodshed with litigation to follow. The Lt.-Gov. did in fact issue warrants against the absent owners, and one man was eventually charged and released on bail. But the case seems never to have come for trial, and there is no record of any other cases being brought under these sections of the Penal Code (cf. Braddell, op. cit., Appendix IV, Cases arising, etc.).

[35] Master, *Fair Malacca*'s statement of 13 Dec. 1872; Gov. Straits to Sec. State, 24 July 1873 (in CO 273/68).

[36] Gov. Straits to SNO, 25 Dec. 1872, CO 273/68.

should not be condemned. Not being eager to face a charge of piracy they never appeared.[37]

The seizure of two junks did not stop the Penang Chinese from supporting the war in Larut, and there were constant outbreaks between the secret societies in Penang which were only kept within bounds by the prompt action of the police under their Superintendent, Captain Speedy, a colourful personality who had achieved some notoriety in England as result of his part in Napier's Abyssinian campaign.[38] Circumstances urged Ord on to more radical measures, and on 21 February he published an Order in Council prohibiting the export of arms and ammunition to Larut and the whole area between the Krian and Perak Rivers. At the same time he sent the gunboat H.M.S. *Hornet* to cruise between Penang and Larut to enforce the prohibition and protect peaceful traders.[39]

Far from restoring normal conditions in the waters around Penang these measures only served to stimulate piracy. Both the Ghee Hin and the Hai San must by this time have had adequate stocks of arms and munitions. But the Prohibition of 21 February was in practice taken to extend to any items likely to maintain the fighting capacity of the Larut Chinese. Stoppage of supplies of food, opium and tobacco especially affected the Ghee Hin, who could not like the Hai San get emergency supplies up from Upper Perak. They were soon so short of food that they were driven to plundering passing trading vessels in order to secure supplies.[40] British gunboats proved powerless to deal with this piracy. They could catch and deal with junks, but not the vessels which the Ghee Hin now brought into use. These were long, fast, shallow-draught pulling boats, heavily armed with fighting platforms fore and aft and double-banked oars, and manned by about fifty men apiece. The gunboats could not follow them into shallow water, and the ships' boats pulled by blue-jackets

[37] Much to the relief of the Colonial Office, who were very doubtful of the legality of the seizure, since it had taken place within Larut territorial waters. Heavy damages had been recently awarded against Crown agents in a similar case, in the West Indies, that of the *Telegrafo* (cf. SNO to Gov. Straits, 3 Jan. 1873, CO 273/68; Gov. Straits to Sec. State, 4 Oct. 1873; Colonial Office minutes and inter-departmental correspondence Sept.-Dec. 1873, CO 273/70).
[38] *Pinang Gazette*, 8 and 15 Feb., 8 Mar. 1873. For Speedy's career see Gullick, 'Captain Speedy of Larut', *JRASMB*, xxvi, pt. 3 (1953).
[39] *Pinang Gazette*, 21 Feb. 1873; Gov. Straits to Sec. State, 20 Mar. 1873, CO 273/65.
[40] *Pinang Gazette*, 8 Mar. 1873.

were too heavy to catch them in the maze of creeks and inland waterways of the Larut coast, which made an ideal hiding place.

The months from February to July 1873 were thus a time of special anxiety for Ord and Lieutenant-Governor Anson. They were unable to cope with the Larut piracies, and small trading vessels became increasingly unwilling to venture into the area. The inhabitants of the island of Pangkor suffered particularly heavily; they could not get supplies in, and their settlement on the coast was repeatedly pillaged by pirate boats, so that every night they had to send their women and children into the jungle.[41] The same sort of thing was taking place at fishing villages all down the west coast of the peninsula from Kedah to the Dindings. The fighting in Larut came gradually nearer the Province Wellesley frontier. There were continual outbreaks of gang warfare in Penang, and attempts to work up large-scale incidents were only thwarted by the action of the police.[42] Most disturbing of all to British officials who feared the extension of the war to British territory, one of their own number became involved in it. This was Captain Speedy, who till July 1873 was busy earning the plaudits of the Penang Press for the energy with which his police suppressed disorders in the Colony. In July he threw up his post and entered the service of the Mantri, agreeing in return for a large salary and a share in the revenues of the district to reconquer Larut for his new employer. Towards the end of July he left for India to raise a force of sepoys for this service.[43]

Disturbed by all this Colonel Anson, with Ord's support, attempted in August to negotiate a settlement in Larut. On the 10th of the month he managed to get most of the personalities concerned to meet at his office in Georgetown. There were the Mantri and Raja 'Abdu'llah, two Chinese headmen—Ho Ghi Siu the leader of the Ghee Hin and Chang Ah Kwi, a Hai San leader —and for good measure Tengku Zia'u'd-din, who was for some

---

[41] *Pinang Gazette*, 8 Mar. 1873; 'Swettenham's Perak Journals', *JRASMB*, xxiv, pt. 4 (1951), pp. 35–36.

[42] *Pinang Gazette*, Feb.–July, 1873, *passim*.

[43] Gov. Straits to Sec. State, 14 Aug. 1873, CO 273/69; Gullick, *Captain Speedy*, pp. 32–33. According to Sir Harry Ord Speedy was to receive under his agreement with the Mantri $1,000 a month for the services of himself *and his men*. This explains the very large estimates of Speedy's remuneration from the Mantri which Sir William Jervois produced later. To one concerned to represent Speedy's prospects under the Mantri in as favourable a light as possible it was easy to overlook his obligation to provide for 110 men out of his salary (cf. below, pp. 124 and 247).

reason in Penang, and Captain Grant the senior naval officer present.[44]

Both sides agreed to an immediate stoppage of hostilities, and further to accept the arbitration of the Lieutenant-Governor. But it proved impossible to translate this agreement into practice. Under the pressure of food shortage and military stalemate the two sides in Larut had for some time tended to split into bands under individual leaders, mainly intent on plunder whether it were gained ashore or afloat. This was especially true of the Ghee Hin, and it was doubtful how far any one leader possessed sufficient influence to get them all to lay down their arms. If there was such a man it was Ho Ghi Siu. But Ho was not keen to put the matter to the test. He anticipated failure and feared the loss of face and influence which would follow his pressing such unpalatable advice on his nominal followers in Larut. So he went into hiding, and could not be found when the Lieutenant-Governor placed H.M.S. *Midge* at the disposal of the Malay and Chinese leaders and invited them to proceed to Larut to put the agreement into practice.

When it came to the point the only one who was prepared to make the attempt was 'Abdu'llah. He had no influence to lose, and everything to gain from the point of view of Perak politics in acting in Larut in conjunction with the British Government as 'Sultan of Perak'. His activities there were very brief. He arrived off Kuala Larut in *Midge* on 11 August, the day after the Penang meeting, but he refused to go ashore there in case his 'followers' fired on him. Instead he issued a proclamation as 'Sultan' rehearsing the agreement signed in Penang and ordering the Larut Chinese

. . . with your armed junks and boats to come out of the rivers and creeks of Larut with all possible despatch, and come and anchor close to H.M.S. *Midge*. . . . If you fail to obey this order you must take the consequences. Again if you have disputes to settle the headmen and towkays of either faction can go to Penang and refer the disputes to the Lieutenant-Governor. Lastly I order that all your headmen and towkays who are now at Larut will come on board the *Midge* and meet me.

The Ghee Hin refused to be drawn. They would neither lay down their arms nor allow *Midge* up the river, and as 'Abdu'llah would

[44] In a proclamation dated 11 Aug. 1873 'Abdu'llah also lists Sayid Zin (Zia'u'd-din's Agent) and Raja Yusuf amongst those attending this meeting, but their presence is not mentioned by any other source. The text of the proclamation is in Winstedt, *Perak*, p. 87.

not allow Captain Grant to force a passage, nor make any further move, the attempt at a settlement fizzled out.[45]

Everyone concerned had been awaiting the outcome of these abortive peace negotiations, and figuratively holding their breath. The failure of the negotiations was inevitably the signal for a general outburst. Colonel Anson blamed 'Abdu'llah for failing to carry out his part of the agreement, and told him 'that he should never, so far as I had any influence, become Sultan of the Country [Perak]'.[46] 'Abdu'llah relieved his feelings in turn by rounding on the Mantri, and as 'Sultan of Perak' formally deposed him from his position in Larut and deprived him of his rank and titles.[47] The Mantri, anticipating the return of Captain Speedy and his sepoys from India, set out to make sure of his connexion with the Hai San in the interior of Larut. The Ghee Hin had stopped rice being sent to them up the Larut River, so he now landed it at the mouth of the Kurau, some 15 miles to the north, whence it could be taken overland to them. There was a small settlement of Hokkien Chinese at Kuala Kurau. They seem to have been re-garded by the Ghee Hin as neutrals, but were probably members of the Penang Toh Peh Kong society. This settlement was threatened with attack by the Ghee Hin if they allowed the rice to pass, whereupon their kinsmen in Penang let it be known that if the settlement at Kurau were molested they would take im-mediate vengeance on the Ghee Hin in the British colony.[48] These events, and the imminent danger of large-scale fighting

[45] The text of this proclamation is in Winstedt, op. cit., p. 87 (cf. also Precis of Perak Affairs, CO 809/1, and Anson, *About Others and Myself*, pp. 321–2). *Midge* had in company two chartered steamers full of rice for the starving Chinese which were compelled to return to Penang with her on 14 Aug. 'Abdu'l-lah did not dare show his face there, and sent a letter saying that he had been taken ill, and would come when he felt better.

[46] Anson, op. cit., p. 322.

[47] Winstedt, *Perak*, p. 88, prints a letter from 'Abdu'llah to Sir Harry Ord announcing this deposition, which is dated 21 Aug. The date earlier in the text '2 August' seems an obvious misprint, and the reference to a second letter from 'Abdu'llah on the same date protesting against the employment of British sub-jects (i.e. Capt. Speedy) in Larut seems misplaced. This protest came in Sept., after British ships had attacked the Ghee Hin stockades at Larut, and Ord had recognized the Mantri as an independent ruler and given his approval to Speedy's expedition. It is reported in the *Pinang Gazette*, 27 Sept. 1873 (see below, pp. 122–4). There is a similar confusion of dates in Gullick, op. cit., p. 33, where 'Abdu'llah's break with the Mantri is attributed to his arrest by the British Navy. But this did not take place till 20 Sept., after the British attack on the stockades, a month after 'Abdu'llah's first letter.

[48] Capt. Woolcombe, H.M.S. *Thalia* to Admiralty, 6 Sept. 1873, CM 273/72; Straits Settlements Legislative Council Proceedings, 9 Sept. 1873.

in Penang, precipitated a change of policy on the part of the Straits Settlements Government. Anson in Penang at once arrested nine of the leading society headmen and charged them under Sections 125 and 126 of the Penal Code with aiding and abetting disturbances in Larut.[49] A series of urgent telegrams to Ord in Singapore brought him in another warship, H.M.S. *Thalia*, to Penang, where he arrived on 25 August. Hitherto Ord's aim had been to isolate the conflict in Larut, so that it would either die, starved of supplies from Penang, or at least the contending parties there would fight it out without involving the British settlement. Now he decided to throw British influence and material support in the scales on one side in the hope that it would be able to gain control and pacify the country. 'Abdu'llah and the Ghee Hin leader Ho Ghi Siu had been discredited by the failure of the attempted settlement earlier in the month. So on Anson's advice Ord turned to the other side, and recognized the Mantri as the independent ruler of Larut. In a proclamation dated 3 September the prohibition on the export of arms to Larut was lifted so far as they were exported 'for the use of the Mantri or at his request'.[50] At the same time, though he had reason to think that the introduction of Indian troops under a British officer into Larut would be disapproved of by the British Government, and had asked the Secretary of State for instructions on the subject, he made no attempt to stop Captain Speedy, who at the beginning of September left India for Penang with 110 men.[51]

[49] Gov. Straits to Sec. State, 25–26 Aug. 1873, CO 273/69; *Pinang Gazette*, 13 Sept. 1873. Ord's recognition of the Mantri, which followed soon after, made it inexpedient to proceed with the case against the Hai San and Toh Peh Kong headmen, who were his allies. Ho Ghi Siu was committed for trial in Nov. but allowed bail of $15,000. The case against him seems to have died. There is no further record of it in the Colonial Office records, and Ho himself disappears from the story at this point. His name is not among those of the twenty-seven Chinese leaders who signed a bond to keep the peace in Larut at the time of the Pangkor Treaty in Jan. 1874.

[50] *Pinang Gazette*, 13 Sept. 1873; Gov. Straits to Sec. State, 5 Sept., in CO 273/69; Straits Settlements Legislative Council Proceedings, 9 Sept. On the same date Ord issued another proclamation banning the export of arms to Junk Ceylon, whose Siamese Governor was afraid of an outbreak amongst the Chinese there.

[51] Gov. Straits to Sec. State, 14 Aug. 1873, in CO 273/69. As soon as he heard of Speedy's activities in India Lord Kimberley took action through the India Office to prevent him getting his force out of the country. He was too late. The Indian Government had already enquired from Singapore on their own initiative if it were in order for Speedy to raise men in India for the service of a Malay chief, and had been told that the Mantri was a friendly and independent ruler, and that there was no reason to interfere (CO minutes and India Office Correspondence, Sept. 1873, in CO 273/69; Gullick, op. cit., p. 34).

At the same time as he bestowed British backing on the Mantri Ord made another attempt to cope with the Larut pirates. In addition to keeping *Midge* at sea and establishing a marine police station on Pulau Kra to control shipping between Penang and Larut, he formed the boats of *Midge* and *Thalia* into a flotilla which for a week searched the creeks and river-mouths from Krian to the Dindings. Most of the pirate boats evaded them easily, and their bag was very meagre—one small junk and a rowing boat. But the efforts of the sweating seamen, scorched by the tropical sun and drenched by torrential rain, were not entirely wasted, for during the week the pirates thought it prudent to suspend their operations, and the small traders and fishermen of Penang and Province Wellesley were able to resume their activities.[52]

Two startling incidents followed almost at once, both indirectly the result of Sir Harry Ord's assumption of the initiative. First on the night of 16 September the Mantri's house in Penang was blown up by a mine and almost completely wrecked. This was the work of the Ghee Hin, who doubtless hoped to dispose of the Mantri before Speedy and his men arrived from India. So far as they were concerned the attempt was a failure, for the Mantri was not at home and the only casualty was a Malay police constable killed in the affray which followed.[53] On the same day *Midge*'s gig and a Malay schooner were attacked by two Ghee Hin rowing boats in the Larut River. The Malay pilot in the schooner at once abandoned the tiller for a less exposed position, and she went aground. She remained under fire from the two boats and from a stockade for an hour before she could be got off, and during that time two of *Midge*'s officers were seriously wounded. It was not a major disaster (both men subsequently recovered) and it was probably a mistake on the part of the row-boats, who thought they were dealing with an unarmed trader or fisherman. But it was the first time that a naval party had been attacked on that coast since the Selangor affair in 1871, weeks of fruitless rowing

[52] Gov. Straits to Sec. State, 5 Sept. 1873, CO 273/69; for an eye-witness account of pirate-chasing in ships' boats, cf. Swettenham, *British Malaya*, pp. 125–6.

[53] Gov. Straits to Sec. State, 19 Sept. 1873, CO 273/69; Anson, op. cit., pp. 317–18. Ho Ghi Siu's house had been blown up the previous year, and Anson had often been threatened with the same treatment. For most of this period he was always with an armed guard, living under real or imaginary threat of violence.

after pirates whom they rarely saw and never caught had produced rising anger in the naval officers concerned, and they determined to take their revenge. Four days later the boats of *Thalia* and *Midge* and of the Mantri's steamer, ascended the river, and a force of blue-jackets and marines stormed the Ghee Hin stockades. In the town of 'Larut' (i.e. Matang) 4,000 Chinese offered to surrender so long as they were protected from the Mantri, saying that 'they saw they had been very foolish men'.[54] This however was a punitive expedition which had been undertaken without reference to the civil authorities in the Colony, though they were informed that it was taking place. It was not an occupation force, and after destroying the stockades the sailors withdrew. The Ghee Hin forces appear to have withdrawn at the same time some distance inland from the mouth of the river, out of reach of attack from the sea. They were not left in peace for very long.

On 29 September 1873 Captain Speedy with 110 men—mainly Pathans, Punjabis and Sikhs, a very mixed lot—and some Krupp guns sailed from Penang with additional arms, munitions and stores for the Hai San miners in a large convoy of two steamers and fifteen small sailing craft. With this force Speedy quickly gained control of most of the interior of Larut. His first move was to secure the pass at Bukit Gantang, till then held by Raja Yusuf for 'Abdu'llah, and to open communications with Upper Perak. This enabled him to receive reinforcements from the Mantri's friend Sultan Ismail, who is said to have sent five to six hundred Malays. He then turned against the Ghee Hin and captured their main stockade at Simpang. At about the same time the Hai San, now re-equipped, worked their way round the Ghee Hin, got between them and the sea, and occupied the position on the Larut River from which the Ghee Hin had been ousted by the British naval operations of mid-September.[55]

There matters rested for the remainder of the year. The Ghee Hin were penned in by a hostile force at the front and rear, and blockaded by the British Navy. But the Mantri and Speedy made no further move against them. They concentrated on holding the mines and getting the tin trade moving again, so that the

---

[54] Capt. Woolcombe to Gov. Straits, 22 Sept.; Gov. Straits to Sec. State, 27 Sept., in CO 273/69; Capt. Woolcombe to Lt.-Gov. Penang, 26 Sept.; Gov. Straits to Sec. State, 2 Oct. 1873, in CO 273/70.

[55] Winstedt, op. cit., p. 80; Gullick, op. cit., pp. 34–35; *Pinang Gazette*, 29 and 30 Nov., 22 Dec.

Mantri could re-establish his exhausted credit, and Speedy receive some of his promised reward. The Ghee Hin still had 2,700 defiant but hungry men under arms in Larut. In the end they might be starved into surrender, but for the moment their hunger made them desperate, and since they retained possession of several coastal bases the ravages of their pirate boats in the Straits increased rather than diminished. The files of the *Pinang Gazette* record a series of piracies during October, November and December, native trading vessels being plundered and their crews butchered sometimes within sight of British warships.[56] And though conditions in the British colony were a little more settled the unrest under the surface was demonstrated by sporadic incidents, as when an attempt was made in October to blow up the house of Chang Ah Kwi, the Hai San headman. Thus though Ord's support of the Mantri and Captain Speedy's efforts on his behalf brought the end of the Larut war sensibly nearer, they did not mitigate the immediate problems which confronted the British authorities in the Straits Settlements.

We have now taken the story of events in Malaya to December 1873. By this time Sir Harry Ord was no longer responsible for affairs in the Straits. He left for London at the end of his period as Governor on 2 November. His successor was provided with instructions which gave him a wider latitude and greater room for manœuvre in his dealings with the Malay States. So after looking first at the local demand for action we shall turn in our next Chapter from events in Malaya to examine the way in which those events had influenced the authorities in London in framing these instructions.

(ii) *The Local Demand for Action*

The demand for British intervention in the Peninsula states found expression during Sir Harry Ord's term of office mainly in the local Press, and in petitions from interested parties in the Straits Settlements. There were proposals for action from officials, but from the nature of Sir Harry's relations with his subordinates, and because they were aware of the consistent opposition of the Colonial Office to meddling in Malay politics, these

---

[56] *Pinang Gazette*, 23 Oct., 13 Nov.; Gov. Straits to Sec. State, 19 Nov., CO 273/71; Précis of Perak Affairs, CO 809/1.

proposals were infrequent and generally unimportant. The most important attempts to influence policy from below were Colonel Anson's 'Committee on Relations with Native States', whose proceedings in 1871 have been described above,[57] and the proposals of Mr. Campbell, then Lieutenant-Governor of Penang, in 1872.[58] Both suggested the appointment of British Residents or Political Agents in the more important states, and are of some significance in tracing the history of this idea in Malaya. But neither had any immediate impact on events in Malaya, or on the ideas of the Colonial Office officials in London.

Calls for Government intervention in the Malay States had appeared intermittently in the editorial columns of the Singapore newspapers since 1844. Before 1870 they were couched in vague general terms, and bore little relation to the facts of the political situation. Usually they suggested British acquisition of one or more states by purchase or annexation, or the extension of 'wholesome' British influence over them, so that

. . . their soil would be made to yield those rich and abundant crops for which nature intended it, and their mineral wealth . . . be fully developed. A large and wealthy population would cause a large demand for the manufactures of England . . .

These expansive generalities, recalling the language of Raffles, were hardly calculated to appeal to the East India Company. They seem to have represented little but the ideas of individual editors, stimulated by the gossip of the club, and by periods of commercial activity.[59]

---

[57] See above, pp. 82–4.

[58] G. W. R. Campbell was temporarily seconded from Ceylon, where he was Commissioner of Police, to act as Lieutenant-Governor of Penang whilst Col. Anson was on leave. In Sept. 1872, and again in Oct., he pressed on the Singapore Government the necessity for the appointment of a Resident or Political Agent in each of the west-coast states, appealing to Indian experience for support (Lt.-Gov. Penang to Colonial Sec., Singapore, 6 Sept. and 24 Oct. 1872, in CO 273/61 and 'Perak and Larut Disturbances', Archive Room, Raffles Museum). In the second of these letters appears the apocryphal quotation of 'a leading Chinaman', repeated and paraphrased by many subsequent writers —'When the British flag is seen over Perak and Larut every Chinaman will go down on his knees and bless God'.

[59] Files of the early newspapers survive in Singapore, but in London their contents are available only in Buckley, *Anecdotal History of Old Times in Singapore*, 2 vols. (1902), which quotes copiously but uncritically, especially from the *Singapore Free Press*. The extract quoted above dates from 1844 (ibid., p. 421). It is typical of all these early editorials, with their vague references to potential wealth and potential markets. The prize for optimism can be fairly claimed by a passage from the *Free Press* of 1847: 'It only requires

After about 1870 the comments of the Straits Press became more vehement, but at the same time an element of realism began to appear. The basic attitude of the commercial community was well expressed by the *Pinang Gazette*:

... the relations of England to the native states of the Malayan Peninsula require revision. The progress of commerce in this part of the world has been so rapid that treaties entered into 30 or 40 years ago ... are now useless. Then all that was wanted was to keep things quiet. Now more is wanted. The riches of the Peninsula must not and cannot remain longer undeveloped, but must be made to contribute to the wealth of the world. Under the present system of Government obtaining in the Native States this cannot be, and a different one must be inaugurated. In plain words these states must be brought under European control. If England fears to assume the responsibility of doing so then let the Dutch, or any other nation that wishes for the extension of colonial territory, come to the front.[60]

The form of the 'European control' which was demanded varied with the person or interest concerned, but in 1872 and 1873 the idea of annexation dropped out, and appeals for the extension of British 'influence', the establishment of 'protectorates', and the provision of 'support' and 'protection' for British commercial interests, became current.

There are several possible reasons for this change of emphasis. One is that the demand for action was at the same time a personal attack on Sir Harry Ord. His relations with the European population of the Settlements, never good, deteriorated during 1872, and throughout 1873 he was under continuous attack from the local Press—and also from the Straits Settlements Association in London—for his conduct of the Colony's administration.[61] In

that capitalists should deviate a little from the beaten path of buying and selling, and make use of the opportunities which their wealth would give them to find in the Malay Archipelago almost unbounded stores of the most valuable articles of commerce ready to be called forth by an intelligent and prudent search for them' (ibid., pp. 462–3).

[60] *Pinang Gazette*, 12 July 1871.

[61] The particular issues involved, apart from relations with the Peninsular states were the letting of the government revenue farms, the abolition of 'Grand Juries', the alleged restriction of trade as result of the Chinese Immigration Ordinance and other measures to control the Chinese community, and the abolition of the Municipalities. The general accusations made were that all power was concentrated in Ord's hands in Singapore, that public works were neglected, that there was precipitate legislation and neglect of public opinion, and that the quality of administration had fallen as 'the evil spirit of officialdom' had increased (*Singapore Daily Times* and *Pinang Gazette*, 1873, *passim*). The campaign against Ord culminated in an indignation meeting in Singapore Town

this bitter 'cold war' the faults of British policy in Malaya were but another stick with which to beat an unpopular Governor. It was pointless to criticize Ord for not adopting a policy of annexation, which all in the Colony knew was not within his power. The local journals therefore directed their fire at the Governor's 'supineness', and his failure to make proper use of the powers which existing Colonial Office policy did allow him. They sought to show that his actions and attitude were inconsistent with earlier official pronouncements, and that treaties which allowed or required him to use his influence to keep the peace in some of the Peninsular states were being disregarded. The *Pinang Gazette* recalled that in July 1871 it had been publicly announced that the British Government would support Zia'u'd-din as 'Viceroy' of Selangor. As a result traders had been led to invest 'large sums of money' in that state. An editorial in August 1872 lamented that all this capital was being jeopardized by the activities of Raja Mahdi. It called on Ord to end his weak attempts to reach a compromise with this malcontent, and fulfil the Government's promise by driving him out of the state.[62] In 1873, when events in Larut reached a crisis, both the *Pinang Gazette* and the *Singapore Daily Times* asked, not as they had done in 1865, that the British Government should take over the country,[63] but that they should honour their obligations under the treaty of 1826, and intervene to protect Perak against Chinese aggressors, and to insist on rights granted to British traders.[64]

Another reason for the cessation of demand for annexation after 1870 may have been the fact that British interests had grown up in the states which would not necessarily be benefited by British administration. The interests of the political speculators, the backers of Zia'u'd-din and Mahdi, and of 'Abdu'llah and the Mantri, were certainly in this category. The success of their speculations depended on their clients gaining power, and making over to them a large proportion of the economic benefits and

Hall on 15 Sept. 1873, at which resolutions of censure were passed for transmission to the Secretary of State and the Straits Settlements Association in London. Not satisfied with attacking the Governor during his term of office the *Pinang Gazette* in November ran a serial 'Review' of Ord's administration after his departure, which was nothing but a series of scurrilous attacks on his capacity and integrity.

[62] *Pinang Gazette*, 10 Aug. 1872.
[63] Buckley, op. cit., vol. ii, pp. 722–3.
[64] *Pinang Gazette*, 19 Apr. 1873; *Singapore Daily Times*, 12 Sept. 1873.

financial opportunities of office. The last thing they wanted was
a British Government which would insist on the farms and leases
involved being put up for open tender, and which would probably do its best to see that mineral rights and land were not
permanently alienated. Thus none of the petitions presented to the
Straits Government in these years asked for annexation. The
merchants of Malacca who had invested in the Klang tin mines
asked in July 1872 that the Government should help Zia'u'd-din
to drive Mahdi out of Selangor, and consolidate his own control
there.[65] In March 1873 an important petition signed by nearly
250 Chinese merchants of Singapore, Penang and Malacca,[66]
asked that Britain should exert itself to restore order in the
Peninsular states, 'not by expeditions and aggressions, but by a
moral intervention, and a determined attitude in respect of the
affairs of the Territories', 'by the Counsel, advice and enterprise
of Her representative in this Colony'. Again in April 1873 the
traders and speculators with interests in Sungai Ujong, calling for
British intervention, asked not for intervention in the tin fields,
but for action to keep the Linggi River open and free from stockades and tolls.[67]

As events in Larut caused disturbances in Penang, and as piracy
increased during 1873, the calls for any sort of Government
action, so long as it was vigorous action, increased, and there were
few voices to counsel moderation.[68] Bitter criticism of Ord and
his officials, 'who have made so many blunders that any change . . .
is likely to be an advantage'[69] was accompanied by sighs for the
heroes of the past, men like Keppel and Brooke, 'apt to turn a
blind eye to everything but how to get at pirates and murderers;
responsibility, the Gladstone ministry, stakes and chain booms

[65] Petition of traders of Malacca, 27 July 1872, in CO 273/61; *Pinang Gazette*, 10 Aug. 1872.
[66] Translation of a Memorial in Chinese, dated 28 Mar. 1873, enclosed in
Gov. Straits to Sec. State, 10 July 1873, in CO 273/67.
[67] *Singapore Daily Times*, 27 Dec. 1873. This petition does not appear in the
Colonial Office records.
[68] One exception was a series of letters written to the *Pinang Gazette* by
Stuart Herriot, a Penang merchant and a Municipal Commissioner. Defending
Ord against his critics he pointed out in Oct. 1872 that the Governor had not
the means to carry through a policy of managing the internal affairs of the
Malay States, and that in any case he was governed by rules laid down by the
Colonial Office which forbade interference. Again in Oct. 1873 he defended
the Government's policy in Larut. But he was no apologist of Ord or the Liberal
Government in Britain, for he attacked their acquiescence in Dutch action in
Atjeh fiercely.
[69] Ibid., 11 Oct. 1873.

to the contrary notwithstanding.'[70] Even when the uproar was at its height, however, there was no suggestion of any permanent British occupation of the Peninsular states. The *Singapore Daily Times* quoted with approval the recipe of Sir C. Adderley for a similar situation on the Gold Coast:

> A few strong forts; a general understanding that if trade is blocked it will be forcibly opened, whether by river or road, by boats or police, and that this is all we demand; an abstinence from all internal interference, and an encouragement of all local governments impartially; . . .

But in recommending this policy for Malaya the paper's editor specifically excepted the forts from his prescription.[71]

The fact that the campaign for government intervention in Malaya was not directed specifically towards annexation made little difference to the vigour with which it was carried on. It was sustained throughout 1872 and 1873 in the Press, in formal petitions, and by public meetings. During 1873, as we shall see in our next chapter, it was extended to London, and representations were made directly to the Secretary of State by the Straits Settlements Association and other interested parties.

It is extremely difficult to discover the precise economic basis of this agitation, or to assess the motives of the various interests concerned, because of the paucity of the information available. The reasons which made some form of British intervention imperative, as they were stated by the protagonists of a forward movement, can be broadly summarized under three heads:

    (i) The chaotic state of the Peninsula was damaging the trade of the Straits Settlements generally, and had stopped the important trade with the western Peninsular states.

    (ii) It was endangering the capital invested from the Settlements in Malayan tin mining, and in other forms of speculation there.

    (iii) It was preventing the more intensive development of the Peninsula which the Straits merchants wished to undertake to compensate for set-backs which they had suffered (or believed themselves about to suffer) in other areas, and to take advantage of an increasing demand for tin.

The first point was developed at length in the Chinese traders' petition of 28 March 1873.

[70] *Singapore Daily Times*, 9 Sept. 1873.   [71] Ibid., 15 Sept. 1873.

Of late the trade on which we so much depend has very much declined, and from circumstances to which we shall advert seems likely to decline even more, . . . Hitherto there has been a large trade with the Native States of the Malayan Peninsula, but owing to internal dissensions this has in some cases entirely ceased, Laroot, Perak and Salangore have been and are in a state of such disturbance, that all legitimate trade with them is at an end, and unless the British Government interfere to restore order and peace, these rich countries will be impoverished and their inhabitants ruined.

The trade of Sumatra, which forms so large a part of that of Penang is being directed into Dutch channels, the best of the produce being sent to Java. Although by a recent Treaty we enjoy equal commercial privileges with the Dutch, we no longer have such a command of the trade. The trade with Bali, which was at one time so brisk, has now almost ceased.

The trade with Sulu and the Islands in that neighbourhood is now stopped owing to the action of the Spanish Government which refuses to allow goods and merchandise to pass except through their own ports.

Our trade with Labuan, the only British possession on the coast of Borneo, is very small, whilst that with Sarawak is too limited to be of great importance. The trade of the rest of Borneo is pretty much in the hands of the Dutch, and so is that of Celebes and the Islands in that portion of the Archipelago.

The trade with China is no longer so remunerative as heretofore, and the large increase of European firms connected with it has considerably limited the field so far as Your Petitioners are concerned. The trade with Bangkok still remains open, but it does not present very great inducements to a large number of Traders.

Your Excellency will thus see that the above circumstances have so restricted the field for trade around the British settlements in these waters that it becomes necessary for us to seek elsewhere openings for Commerce, and our eyes anxiously turn to the Malayan Peninsula which affords the finest fields for the enterprise of British Subjects and from whence we may hope to reinvigorate that mercantile prosperity which our industry has hitherto secured for us.[72]

It is impossible to check the accuracy of many of these assertions from any information now available. After 1867 the detailed annual analyses of trade by countries prepared by the Indian Government of the Straits Settlements ceased. The Blue Books which replaced them, though in many ways excellent, were compiled on a different basis. They were more interested in commodities than in the direction of trade. Nevertheless a good general picture of the Colony's trade can be obtained from them.

[72] Memorial enclosed in Gov. Straits to Sec. State, 10 July 1873, CO 273/67.

At the same time as the Chinese merchants were preparing their petition Sir Harry Ord, in his report on the Straits Settlements Blue Book for 1872, commented—'the trade of the Colony as a whole is in a very flourishing condition'. At first sight his view, rather than that of his petitioners, is supported by the figures (See Table 'A').

In 1867 and 1868 there had been a slump in the trade of the East, probably as result of the British economic crisis of 1866,

TABLE 'A'

Trade of the Straits Settlements, in Dollars[73]

	Imports	Exports	Total
1865/66	45,590,817	46,645,214	92,236,031
1867	40,086,700	42,717,266	82,803,966*
1868	42,119,708	37,999,856	80,119,564
1869	43,986,222	40,583,323	84,569,545
1870	54,449,388	47,989,953	102,439,341
1871	56,016,661	51,808,601	107,825,262
1872	63,650,222	62,149,329	125,799,551
1873	64,795,135	60,312,143	125,107,278

* Estimate based on figures for period 1 Apr. to 31 Dec. The Indian accounts ran from 1 May to 30 Apr.

the effects of which on British overseas trade did not begin to wear off until 1868.[74] The moral effects of this on the Straits traders were probably more enduring than its direct effect on their trade. By 1869 the trade of the Settlements had already begun to rally, in 1870 and 1871 it was again buoyant, and in 1872 there was a boom which was reasonably sustained in 1873. There can be no possibility therefore that conditions in the Peninsula, which were at their worst during these latter years, had a depressing effect on the trade of the Straits Settlements as a whole. But other possibilities are presented when the figures are broken down to show the trade of the three Settlements separately (See Table 'B').

It then becomes apparent that between 1868 and 1871 the trade

[73] Adapted from Blue Books for the years concerned, and the Reports of Gov. Sir Harry Ord upon them (1 Mexican or Hongkong Dollar = 4s. 3d. sterling).

[74] Clapham, J. H., *Economic History of Modern Britain* (1932) vol. ii, pp. 374–77.

of Penang, 30 per cent of which came from the junk traffic with Sumatra and the Malay Peninsula, recovered far more rapidly than that of Singapore. From this point, however, whilst Singapore's widely based commerce throve, that of Penang almost ceased to increase. In 1873 it declined sharply, as did that of Malacca.

It is possible that the over-all growth of trade shown in the figures for the three Settlements as a whole concealed a process whereby the Chinese and other local traders became relatively worse off than the larger European firms of Singapore. This would

TABLE 'B'

Trade of Singapore, Penang and Malacca, in Dollars[75]

	Singapore	Penang	Malacca	Total
1868	58,250,915	17,888,513	3,974,136	80,119,564
1869	58,944,141	20,845,163	4,780,163	84,569,545
1870	70,789,586	27,095,871	4,552,884	102,439,341
1871	68,768,337	34,209,019	4,846,906	107,825,262
1872	82,435,504	37,215,295	6,148,752	125,799,551
1873	89,632,235	31,717,775	3,655,165	125,107,278

naturally produce a divergence between the trend of the figures for Penang and Malacca, where local trade bulked large, and those for Singapore, which was far more closely tied to world markets, and faithfully reflected world conditions. It would have been strange if political developments in the Peninsula, Sulu, Sumatra and Cochin China had not produced the depressive effects on those trades of which the Chinese traders complained. We know that in the first half of 1873 several brigs and schooners under British colours were detained by a Spanish squadron in the Sulu Sea,[76] and that there were repeated French blockades of the coast of Cochin China.[77] We have seen the way in which the Dutch forward movement in Sumatra was regularized with respect to the

[75] Adapted from Blue Books for years concerned. The Blue Book for 1873 contains a small arithmetical error, so that the figure for total trade obtained by adding the total for each Settlement is slightly smaller than that obtained from the sum of Imports and Exports (Table 'A'). The larger figure has been retained here for the sake of uniformity.

[76] Gov. Straits to Sec. State, 23 Oct. 1873, in CO 273/70.

[77] See above, pp. 23-4.

provisions of the Anglo-Dutch treaty of 1824 by the Convention of 1871[78]; as a result of the outbreak of war between Holland and Atjeh in March 1873 all trade with that state was prohibited, and a strict Dutch blockade maintained.[79] The trades with these areas were essentially 'feeder' trades, carried on by native craft and junks collecting and distributing goods which were imported and exported from the Straits Settlements to the outside world by larger concerns. Set-backs which were of major importance to the Chinese merchants in these trades would have caused scarcely a ripple among the major importers and exporters like Guthries,

TABLE 'C'

Vessels cleared from Penang[80]

	Steam ships	Sailing ships	Tonnage, inc. native craft	Steamer tonnage as percentage of whole
1869	26	533	288,611	21%
1870	234	437	266,165	85%
1871	346	501	370,526	75%
1872	482	461	545,263	82%

Bousteads or Johnstons if other business were increasing. We get some confirmation that some such process was under way from the shipping figures (see Table 'C').

The petition quoted above complains of a 'large increase in European firms', and one of the significant aspects of trade in these years, as the shipping table shows, was the increase of steam ships on the routes between Europe and the Far East. It is reasonable to assume that just as at first these steamers were

[78] See above, p. 27.

[79] In return for the prohibition of the export of arms and ammunition to Atjeh, Gov. Ord secured from the Dutch a promise that what they called 'honest trade' would not be prejudiced. For some months a licence system was operated through W. H. Read, Dutch Consul-General in Singapore, whereby ships in ballast were allowed to ship cargoes in Atjeh for which advances had already been made, and to collect bona fide debts, but in Sept. 1873 this concession was revoked, because it was alleged that the majority of the merchants had not acted in good faith. At the same time the Atjeh war brought some economic benefit to the Straits Settlements, since the Singapore merchants supplied the Dutch expeditionary force through Deli, in East Sumatra, and many Dutch ships, including the blockading squadron, coaled and provisioned at Penang (CO 273/65, 273/66, 273/67, 273/69 and 273/70 *passim*).

[80] Adapted from Blue Books for the years concerned.

mainly confined to the through routes between Suez and China, they were also associated primarily with European business.

If we were writing economic history we should have considerable difficulty in sustaining this argument from the material now available. The detailed trade returns of Singapore and Penang,

TABLE 'D'

Trade of Singapore with Selected Areas, in Dollars

	1871	1872	1873
United Kingdom	15,619,400	18,365,848	19,215,970
India	6,998,393	7,221,222	5,629,604
Hongkong and China	8,567,976	9,848,689	10,975,000
Netherlands India	7,101,705	14,039,087	18,208,543
Bali	353,174	..	..
Borneo*	1,537,361	15,510	..
Cochin China	3,826,363	389,407	587,530
Malay Peninsula	3,521,900	4,443,780	4,765,330
Siam	3,790,462	4,004,739	5,333,017
Sumatra	1,183,893	10,472	..

* 'Dutch' Borneo, i.e. not including Sarawak or Labuan.

TABLE 'E'

Trade of Penang with Selected Areas, in Dollars

	1871	1872	1873
United Kingdom	5,528,074	6,250,758	4,214,494
India	5,713,004	2,862,979	2,605,207
Hongkong and China	2,681,573	3,270,946	3,295,427
Malay Peninsula	3,598,927	4,121,082	1,536,020
Siam	4,176,289	5,669,096	6,254,549
Sumatra	6,582,498	6,541,514	6,506,977

so far as they can be disentangled from the Blue Books, are presented in the next two tables (Tables 'D' and 'E').

At first sight the Singapore Table seems to sustain our hypothesis very satisfactorily. The trade of the port is seen to be supported by the massive and generally increasing through trade between Europe and India on the one hand, and China and

Batavia on the other. There is a valuable but essentially subsidiary trade with Siam and the Malay Peninsula, which, including as it does trade with Johore and the east-coast states, seems unaffected by the disturbances in Selangor and Larut. At the same time there is apparent a spectacular decline in the value of the trades with Cochin China and the outer islands of Indonesia. We should however need to know a good deal more than we do about the way in which these statistics were compiled before we could be sure that this represented a real decline in the trade, at any rate with the Indonesian areas, as a result of the extension of effective Dutch control over them. It is much more probable that trade with Bali and the ports in Borneo and Sumatra has been progressively enumerated under Netherlands India as a result of the proclamation of nominal Dutch sovereignty over these areas. This would partly explain the phenomenal growth of trade under the latter heading between 1871 and 1873.[81] The figures for Penang are even less conclusive. They demonstrate the importance to Penang of the junk trade with Sumatra and the Peninsula, but except for the disastrous effect of the Larut war on trade with the Peninsula they prove little else. The falling off of trade with the United Kingdom and India may be ascribed to the disturbed state of Selangor in 1872 and of Larut in 1873. The failure of the Atjeh war to depress significantly the trade with Sumatra may be explained by the peculiar local conditions of the trade and the operation of the short-lived licence system.[82] The increase of trade with Siam was probably due to an attempt to obtain from that country the tin which could not be got from Larut (see Table 'F').

But most of these explanations are shots in the dark. The overwhelming impression from the figures is that although the events of 1873 reduced Penang's trade, they did not produce anything like a major commercial crisis. Even the tin shortage caused by

[81] These were years in which the final demolition of the remnants of the Culture System, and the opening of Java to private enterprise caused a great increase in private trading. The expansion of trade seems however to date from about 1874 (cf. the figures for cotton imports in Furnivall, *Netherlands India*, p. 215).

[82] It was the custom to export large quantities of goods and specie to Atjeh in the first three months of the year, and to ship back the return cargo later, after the pepper harvest. The outbreak of the war at the end of March caught the Penang merchants at the worst possible moment, and the licence system was designed to allow them to take delivery of the pepper for which they had already paid (cf. Petition of Penang merchants in Gov. Straits 24 Mar. 1873, CO 273/65).

the Larut War was not irremediable, for Larut was not Penang's largest supplier, and the loss was partly made good by increasing the supplies from the Siamese mines further north.

There is much that is obscure in the economic history of Malaya for these years, but since we are here only concerned to supply the background to political developments we may conclude that the demand for political action in Malaya in 1873 was based only to a very limited extent on economic distress—the distress of some Chinese traders engaged in a few trades particularly concerned. These probably formed the hard core of those merchants who produced the petitions of 1872 and 1873. In so far as the wider demand in the Press was motivated by trading interests it would

TABLE 'F'

Penang's Tin Imports. By Weight and Value[83]

	1871		1872		1873	
	cwt.	$	cwt.	$	cwt.	$
Siam	74,310	2,080,432	85,632	2,539,062	99,055	2,753,346
Malay Pen.	48,032	1,276,518	33,048	1,865,285	8,333	124,429

seem to have arisen not from distress but from prosperity, and to have been caused by trading profits seeking new outlets in a period of increasing competition.

We may now turn to the second type of interest involved in the demand for British intervention—capital already invested in the Peninsular states. The nature of this interest is quite clear, but there is no way of gauging its power, or of calculating with any accuracy the amount of outside capital invested in Perak, Selangor and the Sungai Ujong mines before 1873. The capital invested in Larut by the Mantri's creditors ought to be calculable from the Larut records (supposing them to have survived), for they were all repaid from the Larut Treasury after the advent of British control, though there is no record of them in London. But the far larger amounts consumed by the Chinese factions in developing their mines, and in ruining them by war, are unknown.

[83] From Blue Books for years concerned.

K

If we leave aside Larut the sums involved elsewhere cannot have been large by comparison with the trading capital annually employed in the Straits Settlements themselves.

We have no record of any significant investment in Perak proper in these years. The investments in Selangor fall into two categories—advances made in the early years of the tin industry to get mines started, and advances made after 1866 to finance the different parties in the civil war. Most of the early capital seems to have been put up by Malacca Chinese, amongst whom the name of Chi Yam Chuan, the headman of the Hokkiens, is prominent, and by the Malacca firm of Neubronner & Company. In the civil war loans the Singapore merchants also played an important part, and there is reason to believe that some of the Malacca Chinese concerned were merely agents for Singapore houses.[84] We have only occasional statements of the sums involved, but it would seem that the sum needed to start a group of tin mines was of the order of $30,000.[85] An informed guess on this basis would put the initial investment in Selangor's tin mines at about $150,000 not including capital lost in unsuccessful mines, and that in the two groups of mines in Sungai Ujong at about $60,000, an estimate which finds some support in the Malacca petition of 1873, which puts the capital at stake there at $80,000.[86] This would give a total of about $250,000 for the initial investment in the Selangor and Sungai Ujong mines, an estimate with an unknown margin of error. To this must be added unknown amounts for subsequent loans to expand mines and sustain them in bad years. In addition to estimate the amount of capital actually involved at any particular time there must be taken into consideration cash and goods advanced by the Straits merchants at the beginning of each year against tin to be delivered at a later date. It is impossible even to hazard a guess at the total sum involved, but it

[84] 'Yap Ah Loy', pp. 17–18; Song Ong Siang, *100 Years History of the Chinese in Singapore* (1923), p. 406.

[85] In the 1860's, when Sultan 'Abdu'l-Samad established miners on the Langat River he gave the mining concession to one Chin Ah Chan, together with a loan of $20,000 with which to work it. Raja 'Abdu'llah opened up the mines on the Klang River about 1855 with an initial loan of $30,000 from Chi Yam Chuan ('Yap Ah Loy, pp. 18, 28 and 53). The recurrence of figures of this order may however have been an indication of the credit-worthiness of Malay chiefs at this time rather than the amount necessary to start the mines, for $30,000 was also the amount invested in Raja Mahdi's political future in 1870, when he was reorganizing his forces at Sungai Buloh (Winstedt, *Selangor*, p. 23).

[86] *Singapore Daily Times*, 27 Dec. 1873.

was probably of the order of \$500,000–\$1,000,000, and did not run into many millions of dollars.

We cannot even begin to guess at the size of the 'political' capital involved in Selangor, i.e. money advanced to Mahdi and Zia'u'd-din for war purposes. More important than the actual amounts are the people involved. The early loans—those raised by Mahdi to sustain himself after the capture of Klang in 1866, and by his enemy Raja Ismail in 1869—came from Malacca Chinese. Even at that stage however the larger Singapore merchants were involved. When Sultan 'Abdu'l-Samad needed money early in 1866 he farmed his share of the revenues of Klang to a syndicate headed by W. H. Read and Tan Kim Ching[87]—a powerful combination between two merchant princes who were also the Consuls-General for Holland and Siam respectively; we have met both of them before in this narrative.[88] When Mahdi took Klang they were unable to get their money, and after trying unsuccessfully to obtain compensation from the Sultan they threw their weight in the scale on the side of Zia'u'd-din. The Viceroy may also have got some money from Penang, for he spent a good deal of time there on his way to and from his home in Kedah; he was there for instance in 1873, and attended Anson's abortive attempt at peace-making in Larut.[89] But by far the most important of his backers, as we have seen, was J. G. Davidson, the Singapore lawyer. Here again we have no details. We know that Zia'u'd-din was heavily indebted to Davidson because of the horror with which the Colonial Office viewed his later appointment as Resident in Selangor.[90] We shall see the very wide terms of a mining concession granted him by Zia'u'd-din. Whatever the capital involved it is clear that Davidson and Read (who was a member of the Company floated to operate Davidson's concession) had a powerful interest in promoting British intervention in Selangor, and it may have been their influence which underlay much of the agitation in the Singapore Press. Here again we can only speculate, for neither the published materials nor the Colonial Office records available in London give us any clue to the ownership or editorial connexions of the Straits Press at this time. Here, as in Larut, and Penang, is a promising field for local investigation.

Lastly, we may consider for a moment the extent to which the

---

disturbed state of the Peninsula was preventing large-scale development and capital investment there. As we have seen Malaya's most important export—tin—was but a small part of the trade of the Straits Settlements. The capital invested in the tin mines of Selangor and Sungai Ujong, and probably even in those of Larut, was relatively small, and the production of these mines was overshadowed by those of Junk Ceylon and Tongkah, in Siamese territory. Tin mining was almost entirely in the hands of the Chinese, and Europeans had shown no eagerness to enter the industry on a large scale. Nor, for that matter, did they do so after British intervention, and it was not until the close of the nineteenth century that the industry became a highly capitalized and largely European concern.[91] But there was a period before 1874 when appreciable amounts of European capital might have been invested in tin mining.

About 1870 the world demand for tin seems to have increased. There was a general rise in tin prices, which helped the development of tin mining in Australia, and stimulated production in Netherlands India and Cornwall.[92] The initial impulse for this development seems to have come from America, where the canning of cooked meats and fish, condensed and evaporated milk, and vegetables, developed rapidly after the American civil war.[93] Practically the whole of the tin-plate used in the American canning industry was imported from the United Kingdom, and in the 1870's the United States took seventy-five per cent of the output of the South Wales tin-plate industry.[94] As the production

[91] See p. 257 below.

[92] Cf. *Annual Statements of Trade and Navigation*, and Flower, P. W., *History of the Trade in Tin*, pp. 192–202. The development of the Australian industry dates from 1871 and 1872 (cf. Shann, *Economic History of Australia* (1930), p. 229, and *Australasia*; *Oxford Survey of the British Empire*, vol. v, pp. 240, 250–2 and 258).

[93] Literature on this period of the American canning industry is surprisingly scanty, and largely confined to family histories and articles in modern trade journals. Perhaps the most useful of these are May, E. C., *The Canning Clan, a Pageant of Pioneering Americans* (1937), and two articles from *The National Provisioner*, Burt, D. S., 'Men, Meat and the Can' (May 1948), and 'The Significant Sixty: a historical Report on the progress and development of the Meat Packing industry' (Jan. 1952).

[94] Flower, op. cit., p. 219, 'Statement of Tin-plates exported from U.K. to all Ports, 1872–78'. Jones, J. H., *The Tinplate Industry* (1914), dates the modern development of the industry in Britain from 'about 1870', because by the period 1865–70 its methods had become stereotyped, the areas of production more or less settled, and because at about that time its connexion with the American market was consolidated. From then until 1891, when the Mackinley Tariff Act enabled an American tin-plate industry to develop under a protectionist system, the British industry enjoyed a monopoly of this market.

of tin-plate increased the demand for tin grew. The price on the London market rose, and in 1872 reached £7 12s. 9d. per cwt., the highest since 1823 (See Table 'G'). The direct correlation between the expansion of tin-plate production, the rise in price of tin, and the growth of a demand for political action in the tin producing states of Malaya, is not necessarily conclusive. The sharp price rise was not confined to tin, but was apparent in all wholesale prices on the British market in the years 1870 to 1873.[96] And even if the trade in tin did become relatively more profitable than other openings for capital investment it does not necessarily

TABLE 'G'[95]

	London value of Straits tin, per cwt.			Average London price of block tin, after Flower			British tin-plate exports, tons
	£	s.	d.	£	s.	d.	
1865	4	12	0	4	16	3	62,718
1866	4	0	9	4	8	7	70,979
1867	4	8	8	4	11	10	78,906
1868	4	16	7	4	18	0	88,406
1869	6	4	11	6	3	1	96,702
1870	6	6	1	6	7	5	99,851
1871	6	6	2	6	17	6	111,606
1872	7	3	9	7	12	9	118,083
1873	6	16	5	6	13	4	120,638

follow that there would have been a rush to invest in Malayan tin even had conditions in the Peninsula been stable. Investment in the Australian colonies must always have been a more attractive proposition for Englishmen at this time whatever conditions in Malaya. In fact it was partly the increase in the supplies of tin from the Australian mines which met the demand—a demand which seems to have fallen off slightly in 1873. There might however have been some investment in Malaya had conditions been different there. We shall recur in a later chapter to these

[95] Adapted from *Annual Statements of Trade and Navigation* of the United Kingdom; 'Return of the Values of Exports of British . . . Produce since 1854', *Parl. Pap. H.C.*, lxvi (1882); Flower, op. cit., p. 192; Jones, op. cit., Appendix E, pp. 272–3.
[96] Cf. Clapham, op. cit., ii, p. 378.

economic imponderables, when we discuss the aftermath of British political intervention in some of the Peninsular states.

Though there was no sign of a wave of investment in Malayan tin such as that which occurred after 1895, the price rise produced two projects for large-scale tin mining in 1873—the Sungai Ujong Tin Mining Company, and the Selangor Tin Mining Company. The first of these was a Singapore promotion, and the records in London tell us nothing about it. It was formed early in 1873 to mine tin in the area of Sungai Ujong under the control of the Dato' Klana, and its Directors were Ho Ah Kay, better known as Whampoa, a member of the Singapore Legislative Council, a Government contractor, and a powerful figure in Singapore, and a Singapore solicitor, R. C. Woods.[97] Woods's name is interesting in this connexion because he was a partner of J. G. Davidson, and their firm acted as the Company's solicitors. Davidson himself was the moving spirit behind the Selangor Company. A concession granted by Zia'u'd-din to him and his 'sleeping' partner, Count Charles de Seloes of Ngadirodgo, Java, in March 1873, gave them the exclusive right to mine all tin deposits in the Bernam, Selangor and Klang River areas not already worked by others. The original grant was to be good for ten years, at the end of which their company, which was to have a working capital of at least £100,000 sterling, was to be given a further ninety-nine-year lease of all the land which it had actually taken up. The terms of this grant were very broad.[98] They included the right to appropriate any land not already private property, to build and operate roads and railways, to import workmen, and to build houses and shops for their support. Under the terms of this grant the Company must quickly have become the real power in Selangor. It was exempted from all taxes and land-rent, in consideration of the payment to Zia'u'd-din of five per cent of the gross produce of the mines, and of $3 per bahar on all tin exported. If therefore the Company were to exercise its right to take over all mining land not already worked the state would quickly become dependent on it for the bulk of its revenue.

We shall deal in our next chapter with the Selangor concessionaires' attempts to float a company in London, and to secure

[97] *Singapore Daily Times*, 5 Sept. 1873.
[98] The concession is printed in full in CO 809/1, pp. 65–8, and C.1320 of 1875, pp. 64–66.

the backing of the Colonial Office for its activities. What we have been concerned to do here is to indicate the nature of the various private interests concerned in the agitation for political intervention, or for some form of Government action, in Malaya. We must now turn our attention to London, and attempt to trace the effects of this agitation on the development of policy there.

4

THE DEVELOPMENT OF POLICY IN LONDON

In 1867 the Colonial Office itself had no clearly formulated policy covering relations with the Peninsular states, and issued no instructions on the subject to the Straits Settlements Government. But state papers covering the first sixty years of the nineteenth century show that other Departments of State, such as the Admiralty and the Foreign Office, had clearly defined ideas on the nature of British interests in the Malacca Straits/South China Sea area, which resulted in Britain following a consistent policy there. The welfare of the Straits merchants and of British trade in South-East Asia were regarded in London as only a secondary British interest. The country's main interest east of India was felt to be the China trade, and policy in the Malayan area was directed at maintaining control of the sea-route to China and of the Eastern approaches to India. Thus the British Government were reluctant to engage in controversy with Holland and other European governments in order to protect British commercial interests in Indonesia and the Philippines. But they were willing to take action to prevent any other European Power establishing itself in a controlling position in the Straits of Malacca or in North Borneo. The same factors are apparent in the development of British policy in Malaya between 1867 and 1874. Before 1871 the Liberal ministry and the Colonial Office officials were completely unsympathetic to requests for the Straits Settlements Government to intervene in the Peninsula to halt disorder and to protect the traders' interests there. After that date a change of personnel in the Colonial Office and in the Cabinet brought a wider interpretation of Imperial responsibilities in Africa, Oceana and Malaya. But it was fear that some other Power might profit from the situation in the Peninsula to secure a footing there which eventually brought the decision in 1873 to sanction some action in Perak and Selangor.

We have seen that when Sir Harry Ord was appointed Governor of the Straits Settlements in April 1867 he was given no instructions to cover the Colony's relations with the neighbouring Malay States.[1] The Colonial Office received no papers on the subject from the India Office until July 1867, and they did not begin to think seriously about it until March 1868, when Ord's conduct of negotiations with Kedah forced them to consult the Foreign Office.[2] Before we attempt to trace the evolution of ideas on the subject within the Colonial Office we may therefore profitably consider the experience of the other Departments of State, and their view of British interests in the area.

[1] See p. 30 above.   [2] See pp. 62 et seq. above.

Fundamentally there was but one British interest which counted —the safety and freedom of British trade. But in the first half of the nineteenth century there were two interests and two sets of ideas which determined policy. The major interest was always the China trade. There was always a very powerful pressure group concerned with it in London and its preservation and protection was always a cardinal point in British policy. The second, but subsidiary interest, was trade with Malaya and the islands of Indonesia—the Straits trade. It was important, but unlike the China trade not important enough to override the day-to-day considerations of European politics. The petitions and protests of the Straits merchants were almost invariably ignored when re-dress of their grievances would have entailed a breach with Holland or Spain.

We have already noted the principles of the Anglo-Dutch settle-ment of 1824.[3] In the negotiations leading up to this treaty it was the East India Company's interest in the China trade which out-weighed the inclinations of British politicians to appease Holland by surrendering Singapore. The terms of the treaty made ample provision for the safety of the route to China, securing the free-dom of the Malay Peninsula as well as Singapore itself from Dutch influence. But it failed to provide adequately for the freedom of British trade in the Dutch islands, and handed over to the Dutch sphere of influence the states on the east coast of Sumatra, where British trade had till then been protected by treaty.[4] It is signi-ficant that the only Sumatran state whose independence the British Government attempted to secure was Atjeh; this was the only state which possessed a harbour from which the British control of the Straits of Malacca might be challenged. The Treaty of 1824 assured to Britain control of the Malacca Straits route to China, but in the short run the Straits traders lost rather than gained by it. Britain was given an option on the Malay Peninsula which, for the moment, she did not exercise, whilst the Dutch, despite the paper safeguards in the treaty, were able to discri-minate against British trade elsewhere in the Archipelago.

---

[3] See p. 8 above.
[4] The treaties of 1818 and 1823 with Siak (Hertslett, *Treaties and Con-ventions* . . ., vol. viii, pp. 697–8; vol. ix, pp. 921–2), and that of 1823 with Langkat (ibid., vol ix, p. 906). All of these treaties granted British trade most-favoured-nation status, and forbade the granting of monopoly treaties to other powers.

Policy and events in the Straits and the South China Sea for the next forty years followed the same pattern. On the one hand a steady flow of complaints from British merchants against the actions of the Dutch and Spanish governments in restraint of trade brought no effective action from the Foreign Office. On the other hand the danger to China-bound ships from piracy, and the possibility that a foreign power might secure a naval base on the north coast of Borneo from which in time of war they could cut the main trade route, was sufficient to cause the establishment of Labuan (1846) as a coaling station and anti-pirate base.

We have already outlined the nature of the Dutch forward movement in Sumatra, and the complaints of the Straits merchants against the operation of the Dutch tariff.[5] A series of complaints by Britain's diplomatic representative at the Hague between 1834 and 1864 secured little more than vague reassurances and evasions from the Dutch ministers of the day. Dutch political measures were always undertaken 'solely to re-establish peace and security, and protect trade', and Dutch governments were always bent on abolishing monopolies and hindrances to trade gradually, as soon as the political complexion of the Dutch Chamber made this possible.[6] Dutch spokesmen though often yielding the particular point at issue, and promising the release of arrested ships, and the refunding of duties levied contrary to the treaty of 1824, always evaded discussion of the precise status of Indonesian states, and whether or not preferential tariffs and the coasting trade laws were legally applied to them.[7] To avoid diplomatic embarrassment these assurances were usually accepted at their face value. It would, wrote the Chargé d'affaires at the Hague in 1858, be impolitic to challenge the practices and the special privileges of the Nederlandsch Handelmaatschappij, although these contravened the terms of the treaty, because of the vital part which it played in the prosperity of Holland.[8] Even Palmerston, most trenchant of British Foreign Secretaries, followed this line. Though he spoke in despatches of 'the encroachments of the Netherland authorities in the Indian Archipelago',

[5] See pp. 22 et seq. above.
[6] Baron Cremers to Sir J. Milbanke, 7 June 1864, in CO 273/9.
[7] Chargé d'affaires, the Hague, to Lord Clarendon, 25 June 1858, in CO 273/1.
[8] Ibid.

he was careful to have such references deleted before the papers in question were printed for Parliament.[9]

Foreign Office attempts to assert British claims in Sulu were similarly half-hearted. In 1849 Sir James Brooke, then acting as British Commissioner and Consul-General in Brunei, negotiated a commercial treaty with the Sultan of Sulu. In addition to giving British trade most-favoured-nation status, this treaty also bound the Sultan not to cede territory to other states, nor acknowledge their suzerainty, without the consent of the British Government.[10] But before it could be ratified by the British Government the Spaniards stormed and sacked the town of Sulu, drove the Sultan inland, and declared the country a Spanish dependency and an integral part of the Philippines. It thus became subject to the restrictions which confined foreign trade to Manilla and a few ports under Spanish control in the main islands. A diplomatic wrangle ensued between the British and Spanish Governments in Europe as to whether Sulu was or was not independent. On the Spanish side it was claimed that Sulu had from time immemorial been a part of the Philippines, that the attacks on its capital had been merely the subjugation of an internal rebellion, and that in any case the Sultan had since accepted Spanish control and a Spanish pension. On the British side, in addition to eighteenth-century treaties with the East India Company, it was argued that treaties

---

[9] Palmerston to Brooke, 23 Feb. 1848; Parl. Under-Sec., Foreign Office, to Parl. Under-Sec., Colonial Office, 13 Mar. 1850, in CO 144/3. The British Government were not alone in handling negotiations on these matters in the light of European considerations. In 1843 an attempt to reach an understanding on the Netherlands Indian tariff was frustrated 'because H.M.'s Government were not at that time in a position to comply with a demand . . . that H.M. Government should reduce the duties on Dutch butter and cheese on importation into Great Britain' (Aberdeen to Baron Dedel, 4 May 1846). Dutch authorities in the Indies were continually frustrated in their endeavours to 'pacify' Sumatra by orders from the Hague to halt their activities until English protests had died down, and in 1841 their posts in Jambi and Siak were withdrawn, not to be reoccupied again till 1857 and 1858 (De Graaf, *Geschiedenis van Indonesie* (1949), pp. 430 et seq.; Colenbrander, *Koloniale Geschiedenis*, vol. iii, pp. 217, 233).

[10] The text of the treaty, dated 29 May 1849, is in FO 71 (Sulu), vol. i. The British motive in negotiating the treaty was not primarily to benefit trade but to secure the north and east coasts of Borneo from Spanish control. The Sultan of Sulu claimed sovereignty over this area, and his claim had been to some extent recognized by Britain during the Seven Years War, when she accepted the cession of Balambangan Island and parts of Borneo and Palawan at the time of the Manilla Expedition. The danger now was that Spain would take over the Sulu claim to the whole of the east coast of Borneo, and perhaps that over the north coast in the region to the north-east of Labuan (Brooke to Henry Addington, 26 Jan. 1852; FO 71/1 contains a number of papers referring to the eighteenth-century treaties extracted from the records at Madras and Bombay).

signed by Sulu between 1836 and 1849 with the United States, France and Britain, and with Spain herself, as an equal party, proved that in fact she had retained her independent status.[11]

In making this demonstration Lord Malmesbury, then Foreign Secretary, was prompted more by a desire to warn Spain against attempting to take over the Sultan's nominal possessions on the north and east coasts of Borneo, than by a tenderness for the independence of Sulu or the interests of British traders there. Having made his point in Madrid he was not disposed to take the matter further. When he was warned by the British Ambassador that Spanish pride was deeply involved, and that she would probably be supported by France, he minuted 'This question is to sleep'.[12] Frequent appeals from the Sultan for British help, and from the Straits merchants for action to re-open Sulu to direct trade went unheeded by both the India Office and the Foreign Office, so long as the latter were confident that no Spanish base would be established in Borneo.

The points of view of the different Departments of State are well illustrated by their attitude towards Labuan, Sarawak and Brunei. From 1841 onwards Brooke had tried to obtain the countenance and support of the British Government for his position in Sarawak. For various reasons both the Admiralty and the Foreign Office, though not wishing to become involved in the affairs of Sarawak, favoured the acquisition of a port on the north coast of Borneo.

The end of the East India Company's monopoly (1833) and the rise in the volume of the China trade after the opening of the Treaty Ports (1842) had added to the Admiralty's task of protecting British shipping in these waters. Between Singapore and the China coast were 1,500 miles of reef-studded waters without a friendly port. There was no base from which the Navy could operate against pirates, and no harbour of refuge against typhoons. The end of the East India Company's convoy system had multiplied the amount of independent shipping in these waters, and raised new problems of protection. These were complicated by the appearance of the early steam warship, with its crude engine, whose high fuel con-

[11] Lord Malmesbury to Lord Howden (Madrid), 11 May 1852. At the same time letters were produced from the Sultan of Sulu in which he affirmed his independence (Sultan to Sir J. Brooke, 2 Feb. and 25 Aug. 1851, in FO 71/1).
[12] Lord Howden to Malmesbury, 17 June 1852; minutes of 26 Aug. 1852, in FO 71/1.

sumption meant that ships were unable to steam from Singapore to Hongkong against the monsoon without refuelling, and made local bases necessary for naval patrols. An offer to cede Labuan, which Brooke secured from the Sultan of Brunei in 1844, was the more warmly received at the Admiralty because it was known that there were large deposits of good quality coal on the island.[13] Almost as strong as their desire for such a base, however, was the Admiralty's conviction that no other power ought to be allowed to possess a footing so close to this vital trade route.

The latter consideration was prominent in the Foreign Office view of the matter. They were frightened that France, the United States, or above all Holland might establish themselves in the area. They were at the time engaged in a heated controversy with Holland, caused primarily by Brooke's activities in Sarawak, in which the Dutch maintained that under the 1824 Treaty the whole of Borneo was made over to Holland. These considerations were summed up by Aberdeen in 1846:

> The Archives of the Foreign Office are crowded with representations of the injurious effects to British interests arising from the extension of Dutch influence and dominion in the Eastern Seas; and the consequent necessity of preventing the encroachments of that Power, by affording proper countenance and protection to the legitimate trade of Native Tribes with H.M.'s subjects. The demands for protection against the pirate communities of Borneo have been equally numerous. . . . If H.M. Government renounces the intention of occupying such station [Labuan] they will have shortly to be prepared either for the occupation by Holland of the coast in question, and the consequent exclusion of British trade; or for the acquisition by either France or the United States of the very station rejected by them.[14]

The same attitude was taken up by both the Admiralty and the Foreign Office in 1866, when the question arose of admitting Dutch claims in Borneo as part of the price of the abolition of all differential duties in Netherlands India. Throughout all these proceedings the main point in the minds of the officials in these two departments seems to have been the security of the China Sea for British shipping in war-time.[15]

[13] Report by Capt. Bethune, R.N., to Admiralty, 1 Oct. 1845, and memo by Lord Aberdeen, 25 June 1846, outlining the history of the Labuan question, in CO 144/1. See Irwin, G., *Nineteenth-Century Borneo, a study in diplomatic rivalry*, (1955), especially chaps. v and vi.

[14] Aberdeen to Gladstone, 25 June 1846, in CO 144/1.

[15] Foreign Office to India Office and Admiralty, 5 Jan. 1866; Admiralty to Foreign Office, 13 Jan. 1866; in CO 273/9.

The Colonial Office under Gladstone was vehemently opposed to the acquisition of new dependencies which it would have to administer, and Labuan was no exception. They refused to admit that there was need for a naval station there. They were afraid that it would be quite impossible to maintain the distinction between a naval station and a colony, and to prevent settlers and traders coming to the island, and that the colony for these reasons would tend to become entangled in Borneo politics. The real heart of the Colonial Office position however was an aversion to the acquisition of fresh responsibility which under Gladstone became almost a religion.

The multiplication of colonies at the other end of the world must at all times be a matter of serious consideration; but especially at a time when we have already land almost infinite to defend that we cannot occupy, people to reduce to order whom we have not been able to keep in friendly relations, and questions in so many Departments of Government to manage, the discussion of which has been found embarrassing at home, and which appear to be thought fully equal in the demands they make to any energies that the Executive Government is able to apply to them.[16]

After Gladstone's departure from office in July 1846 the attitude of the Colonial Office to Labuan was identical to that of the India Office towards Singapore. It was indeed compared to Singapore, as an island detached from the neighbouring land mass, and it was hoped that it could be treated like Singapore, 'something more than a station and something less than a colony.'[17] Like the Indian Department in Malaya, the Colonial Office firmly refused to have anything to do with the mainland. It regarded British interests in Sarawak and Brunei as the concern of the Foreign Office.[18]

[16] Memo by Gladstone, 18 June 1846, in CO 144/1.
[17] Memo by the Parl. Under-Sec., undated, but written in late 1846, in CO 144/1.
[18] This is well illustrated by the Muka River incident of 1860. Governor Edwards of Labuan, who was also at the time acting as Consul-General at Brunei, interfered in his capacity of Consul in a dispute between Sarawak and Brunei, against Foreign Office instructions. He was therefore superseded as Consul. The Colonial Office took the line that as the actions of one man in two separate functions would not be appreciated by orientals he had better as a matter of expediency be dismissed from the Government of Labuan as well. But they refused to enter into discussion of the merits of the case between Edwards and the Foreign Office, or to take cognizance of the facts of Borneo politics. Sir F. Rogers, the Permanent Under-Secretary, minuted: 'This is not our affair. The Foreign Office (very naturally) direct their Consul (as I understand) on no account whatever to interfere in the quarrels between Sarawak and

At the time of the transfer of the Straits Settlements to its control the Colonial Office seems to have taken exactly the same view of them as of Labuan. The Settlements were a colony occupied in the Imperial interest, and the department's responsibility was confined to their internal administration. It had no knowledge of, or interest in, Malaya itself, though if it had been faced with the question it would probably have agreed that a foreign foothold there, as in North Borneo, would have been against Britain's interest. Its attitude was exactly the same as the Indian Government's had been, and it therefore accepted its predecessor's policy without question. It was never furnished with any reasoned memorandum on Malayan policy by the India Office, but in July 1867 it began to receive from that department in instalments a voluminous collection of papers extracted from India Office files.[19] The hard-worked junior officials, whose time, as one of them subsequently minuted, was fully occupied either in preventing schemes for advances in salaries or in investigating financial defalcations,[20] could do no more than skim through this mass. They fastened with relief on occasional India Office minutes, and on clear-cut instructions such as those given to Cavenagh in February 1866 to abstain from all interference in Larut except for cases of murder and piracy against British subjects.[21] On this one of them commented, 'I should say that these instructions were sound ones', then added with satisfaction, 'These matters do not call for any action at present.'[22] His seniors agreed.

We have already noted an inflexible adherence to this policy of non-intervention during the early years of the Colonial Office period in Malaya. We have seen it applied equally to Ord's negotiations with Kedah and Perak in 1868 and 1869, and to his

Brunai—on the merits of which the Home Government can form no judgement of its own. But Mr. Edwards has interfered; and will without loss of time be superseded by Mr. St. John, who is to start immediately. The only question we have to answer is whether the policy of non-interference will be dangerous to Labuan. And I suppose the answer is that the Secretary of States sees no reason to apprehend that it will be so' (Minute of 25 Oct. 1860, in CO 144/18).

[19] Filed in CO 273/15, and *passim* in CO 273/1–9.

[20] Hall, *The Colonial Office* (1935), p. 124.

[21] ' . . . the Governor-General in Council fears that there may be a tendency among the authorities at Penang to push British interference with the neighbouring native States further than is either necessary or desirable . . . The Governor-General does not see why the British Government should meddle in such matters. If British subjects choose to live and trade in an uncivilized country like Perak, they must submit to the local conditions and practices.' (Gov. of India to Gov. Straits, 15 Feb. 1866).

[22] Minute by Mr. Cox, 1 July 1867, in CO 273/15.

postulation of a policy of 'spheres of influence' in the Peninsula. The references to the Foreign Office which the Kedah negotiations made necessary defined the scope of the Straits Settlements external relations, and the authority by which they were conducted,[23] but they did not alter the most important rule:

The true policy of the British Government of the Straits Settlements is not to attempt to control but to keep clear of native disorder.[24]

Non-intervention indeed seemed in 1868 the only policy which could reconcile Britain's strategic interest in Malaya with the anti-colonial ideas of Liberal and Radical politicians.

But during the years between then and the end of 1873 the tide of political and human life flowed on. There were changes in personnel, in ideas and in political situations, so that by the time the Malayan problem became urgent a new attitude towards distant tropical Crown Colonies had developed in England. Some of the factors involved in this change can only be mentioned briefly here. The swing of the pendulum away from the narrowest forms of 'Little Englandism', and the first signs of an Imperial revival, which occurred in this period, were aspects of a battle of ideas which concerned itself primarily with the colonies of settlement.[25] But it was a battle which was not without importance for

---

[23] See above, pp. 62 et seq.

[24] Sir F. Rogers, 20 May 1868, in CO 273/18.

[25] The Imperialist revival is usually associated with Disraeli's Crystal Palace speech of 24 June 1872, and thought of as a Conservative movement. In fact the movement towards the consolidation of the colonies of settlement seems to date from about 1868, and to have embraced members of both the main political parties. The foundation of the Colonial Society (later the Royal Empire Society), with its motto 'United Empire', dates from June 1868, and its first patrons included Cardwell and Childers as well as Carnarvon and Salisbury. The idea that Free Trade must be coupled with colonial possessions, and that 'by some mysterious process trade has a great tendency to follow the flag', was first expressed in a letter to *The Times* in Nov. 1869. There is a very striking contrast between the ideas of Goldwyn Smith (*The Empire*, 1863) and those of Charles Dilke (*Greater Britain*, 1868). Goldwyn Smith held that the age of commercial monopoly had passed, that it was no longer worthwhile to 'hold colonies in dependence' for the sake of commanding their trade, and that 'there was no other justification for the maintenance of 'this perilous and expensive connexion'. His attention was practically confined to the colonies of white settlement. Dilke, whilst still a separatist so far as the colonies of settlement were concerned, advocated the retention and even the extension of the Crown colonies and of the Indian Empire, because they were a 'nursery of our statesmen and warriors', and because only the British hold over these areas could restrain anarchy and nourish trade. For a detailed study of the Press and public opinion in this period, see Bodelsen, C.A., *Studies in mid-Victorian Imperialism* (Copenhagen, 1924).

the trading posts and strategic outposts of Empire. It developed in the minds of younger politicians and officials, even those in the ranks of the Liberal party, the idea that the British Empire was not necessarily doomed to disintegrate, and that Britain could and should intervene more often to settle the troubles of the Imperial frontier. They began to suspect that when their elders spoke of Government and Empire being over-burdened with cares it was their own rather than the country's energy which was flagging.[26] This was important when troubles on the periphery of the British trading frontier, in Malaya, in the Gold Coast, and in Fiji, raised the question of Imperial intervention in 1873.

The early years of blank refusal to consider any form of interference in Malaya coincided with the time when Granville[27] held the seals of office at the Colonial Office and the department was dominated by the influence of the Permanent Under-Secretary, Sir Frederick Rogers.[28] Both men were close friends of Gladstone. But in 1870 Granville was transferred to the Foreign Office on the death of Clarendon, and in 1871 Rogers resigned.

There was thus an infusion of fresh blood into the department on both the political and administrative levels. The new Secretary of State, Kimberley, was a departmental minister of experience and ability.[29] But he was a poor speaker and an

---

[26] Cf. an exchange between Gladstone and Kimberley, recorded in Drus, Ethel, 'The Colonial Office and the Annexation of Fiji', *TRHS*, 4th Series, vol. xxxii, pp. 102–3, in which Kimberley declared 'I take a more sanguine view . . . of the power and energy of this country than you do'

[27] George Levenson-Gower, 2nd Earl Granville (1815–91); educated at Eton and Christ Church, Oxford; attaché in Paris, 1835; M.P., 1836–46; Foreign Secretary, 1851–2, 1870–4, 1880–5; Colonial Secretary, 1868–70 and 1886; from 1855 leader of the Liberal party in the House of Lords; Chancellor of the University of London, 1856–91.

[28] Sir Frederick Rogers, Bart., later Lord Blatchford (1811–89); educated at Eton, where he was a contemporary of Gladstone and Hallam and at Oriel College, Oxford, where his tutors were Newman and Froude; double first in Classics and Mathematics, then took up Law, and was called to the Bar in 1837. He entered official life in London as Registrar of Joint Stock Companies, 1844; then became Commissioner of Lands and Emigration; 1858 and 1859 sent to Paris to conduct negotiations on introduction of Indian coolie labour into French colonies, 1860–71, Permanent Under-Secretary at the Colonial Office, where he succeeded Herman Merivale. Higinbotham, the Australian statesman noted wryly in 1870, that the Colonies had 'been really governed during the whole of the last nine years by a person named Rogers' (cf. *DNB*; Hall, op. cit., *passim*, Marindin (Ed.), *Lord Blatchford's Letters* (1896)).

[29] Wodehouse, John, created 1st Earl Kimberley 1866 (1826–1902); educated Eton and Christ Church; succeeded to Barony on death of his grandfather in 1846. Under-Secretary for Foreign Affairs under Aberdeen and Palmerston, 1852–6 and 1859–61; Minister at St. Petersburg, 1856–8; Under-Secretary for India; 1864–6 Lord-Lieutenant of Ireland, where he dealt with Fenianism with a

L

indifferent politician, and has therefore received little notice from historians with their eyes fixed on English party politics.[30] An American student of British policy, noting the small part which Gladstone took in Colonial Office business when Granville held the seals, and the considerable correspondence and drafts annotated 'seen by Mr. Gladstone' under Kimberley, has concluded that the latter was something of a cipher.[31] This is far from the truth. Anyone who explores the Kimberley papers cannot fail to agree with Miss Drus that Kimberley was 'a most able and conscientious departmental minister.'[32] But they will also note the independence and long-sightedness of many of his political judgements, and the lack of reverence on the part of the 'young man' of forty-four for the 'middle-aged' leader then in his sixties. Kimberley saw from the beginning the essential weakness of the Liberal Government in foreign policy, which stemmed from Gladstone's idealism, and the damage which this idealism might do in the field of Irish Education and ecclesiastical politics.[33]

Kimberley's views on colonial policy were based on different principles to those of the Prime Minister; 'I take', he wrote to Gladstone, 'a more sanguine view of the power and energy of this country than you do.'[34] This basic optimism and his contact with the realities of overseas problems during his years as Under-Secretary at the Foreign Office and the India Office, made him willing to contemplate firm action in Crown colonies, and averse

strong hand, but noted with regret that 'the heart of the people is against us'; Lord Privy Seal, 1868–70; Colonial Secretary, 1870–4 and 1880–2; Indian Secretary, 1882–5, 1886, 1892–4; Foreign Secretary, 1894–5.

[30] His reputation in this context has suffered especially since, although he was a poor speaker, he was called upon to bear the brunt of debate in the House of Lords, and to justify there the Liberals' handling of the Washington Treaty negotiations and the Alabama Arbitration, Irish Legislation, and Bruce's Licensing Bill, all highly controversial subjects for which he was not responsible.

[31] Knaplund, P., *Gladstone and Britain's Imperial Policy* (1927), pp. 99–100.

[32] Drus, op. cit., pp. 97–98. The best account of Kimberley's background is in the Introduction to the same author's edition of *A Journal of Events during the Gladstone Ministry, 1868–74, by John, First Earl of Kimberley*, Camden Miscellany, vol. xxi, Royal Historical Soc. (1958), pp. vii–xx.

[33] Kimberley Papers, *passim*, especially the 'Journal of events during Gladstone's First Ministry, 1868–74'. In Mar. 1870 he noted (Journal, p. 30), 'Irish Education will probably be the rock on which we shall be wrecked'. The virtues and limitations of his robust, practical approach to most problems are well illustrated by his remark on the opening of the Albert Hall: 'It is a fine building, but of what use it can be unless it is turned into a circus, I can't imagine.'

[34] Drus, op. cit., pp. 102–3. On another occasion, taunted that his main talent was in getting up Blue Books, he wrote: 'I have a heart for the greatness of my country, but I hope a cool head as well.'

to breaking the connexion with the colonies of settlement until this was absolutely necessary.[35] His correspondence with Gladstone, particularly on the subject of ·Fiji, the Gold Coast and Malaya, was, as we shall see, as much a vehicle by which Kimberley persuaded Gladstone to action as it was a means for the Prime Minister to supervise the work of the Colonial Department. In bringing the Liberals to face their colonial fences he was ably seconded by Edward Knatchbull-Hugessen (later Lord Brabourne) who became Parliamentary Under-Secretary at the Colonial Office in 1871.[36] Hugessen had little influence among the elder members of the Party—Gladstone spoke of his 'Imperialistic notions', and he and Granville talked of replacing him with someone more 'reliable'—but he seems to have played an important role in encouraging Kimberley to press his views on the Cabinet when they attempted to evade unpleasant issues.

On the administrative side the retirement of Rogers in 1871 brought to the fore two younger men, Sir Robert Herbert[37] who became Permanent Under-Secretary, and Robert Meade.[38] Both

[35] Cf. his opinion on the future of the Australian colonies: 'Whatever may be said in favour of the independence of the Australian colonies it would be a great calamity that they should separate in anger from us. . . . It is difficult to see in what way their connexion with us can be permanently maintained. But it would be a gain for both us and them if we can keep up the connexion until they become stronger. Separation would then be more natural, and would bring with it less annoyance. Besides, though to me an Imperial Confederacy seems a vain dream, the only chance of its success would be if the colonies approached to some tolerable equality in population and wealth with the home country' (Journal, p. 32, written in May 1870).

[36] Edward Knatchbull-Hugessen, 1st Baron Brabourne (1829–93), was educated at Eton and Magdalen College, Oxford; entered Parliament as a Liberal, 1857, and occupied minor offices, 1859–66; in Gladstone's first Ministry served as Under-Secretary at the Home Office before moving to the Colonial Office in 1871. He was not included in Gladstone's second Ministry in 1880, but received a Barony, presumably as compensation. He had always had 'advanced' views on colonial and foreign affairs, and later in life he changed his political allegiance to the Conservatives. The article on Hugessen in *DNB*, from a Liberal contributor, is written with an envenomed pen, and is singularly uninformative.

[37] Sir Robert George Wyndham Herbert (1831–1905), was a grandson of the 1st Earl of Carnarvon by his youngest son. Educated at Eton and Balliol, he became Gladstone's Private Secretary for a time in 1855, and became a lifelong friend. He went to Queensland as Colonial Secretary in 1859, and was the first Premier of the state, 1860–5. He returned to England in 1867 to become an Assistant Secretary at the Board of Trade, then transferred to a similar post at the Colonial Office before becoming Permanent Secretary there in 1871. He retired in 1892.

[38] Sir Robert Henry Meade (1835–98) was second son of the 3rd Earl of Clanwilliam; his mother was Sidney Herbert's sister. Educated at Eton and Oxford, he joined the Foreign Office in 1859, and served with missions in the Middle East and in Europe before becoming Private Secretary to Granville

were Liberals—they had been Private Secretary to Gladstone and Granville respectively—and both were officials. But they were men of independent mind who had travelled and were acquainted with colonial and Eastern problems at first hand.

We have now to attempt to probe the minds of this small group of ministers and officials, and to interpret their reactions to events in Malaya in the light of contemporary attitudes to the colonial dependencies and the basic British interests in the area which we have sketched in the preceding paragraphs. There are two points to be made here by way of preface.

First, although the Straits Settlements were a small and relatively unimportant colony which claimed a very small part of Colonial Office time, their troubles were part of a wider general problem. This was a problem which arose from the non-coincidence of the Imperial trading frontier and the political frontier in widely separated areas, from West Africa to the Pacific, each with their own peculiar and complicated local circumstances. But in each the essential problem was the same: how far could and ought the flag to follow trade? How far could the policy of restricting Imperial responsibilities within the narrowest possible limits withstand the march of events and the arguments of principle and expediency which were marshalled against it? We have already hinted at the peculiar dilemma with which these questions faced the Liberal party. There was division within its ranks between Radicals and Gladstonian Liberals, who were 'Little Englanders' from a sort of religious conviction, and some of the younger Liberals who tended to argue from an empirical study of particular cases. We cannot enter here into an extended study of British politics and ideologies, or of Imperial history. But it is important to note that this problem of the tropical trading frontier was in the aggregate as important a political issue as the parallel frontier problem of Cape Province and Natal. At the same time as it developed in Malaya various events were also bringing it to a head in West Africa, where the Anglo-Dutch Treaties of 1871 involved Britain in the affairs of the Fante Confederacy and the

in 1864. In 1870, when Granville left the Colonial Office, Meade remained there as an Assistant Under-Secretary. He became Permanent Secretary in 1892, when Herbert retired, and himself retired in 1896. Meade and Herbert, both because of their connexions and their ability, were men of importance, and between them they dominated Colonial Office thought for twenty-five years.

kingdom of Ashanti,[39] and in Fiji, where the activities of traders and labour-recruiters brought chaos which could only be resolvd by the intervention of established authority.[40]

The second point here is the sparseness of the information on which ministers and officials were required to base a policy towards Malaya. Not merely was their view of events there coloured by the progress of affairs in West Africa and Fiji, but it was influenced by the way in which information on Malaya was presented to them. So far in this study we have been concerned by marshalling the facts now known to us to present a balanced picture of developments in Malaya. This will not take us far when we attempt to fathom the development of thought in Whitehall. None of the officials in the Straits Settlements saw the whole of the picture which we have attempted to piece together. They knew little of what went on in the Peninsular states, and understood less, for they were dependent for their information on the reports of traders, and on sporadic communications from Malay chiefs, all with their own interests to serve. Even less did the Colonial Office clerks and the Secretary of State see the whole picture. They were limited for their information to what successive Governors and Administrators chose to tell them, and in the case of Sir Harry Ord, as we have seen, this was very little. In dealing with the metropolitan Government's attitude to the Malay States therefore we need to keep our attention on the official despatches, supplemented occasionally by private communications to officials and ministers. We need to consider events in Malaya, not in chronological order, nor, as has commonly been done,[41] by reviewing events in each state in succession, beginning with Kedah in the north and ending with Johore in the south, but in the order in which they were actually brought to the notice of the Colonial Office.

It is only in the case of Johore that we find concern with the internal affairs of a Malay state forming the subject of Colonial Office business before 1871.[42] Here the papers are voluminous.

---

[39] Cf. pp. 26–7 above, and, for a short account of affairs on the Gold Coast, Ward, *A History of the Gold Coast* (1948), pp. 231 et seq.

[40] See Drus, op. cit., pp. 87 et seq.

[41] For instance in Sir Frank Swettenham's *British Malaya*.

[42] In this connexion we may note that the case of the Kedah Treaty (1867–9), and that of the Dindings dispute with Perak (1869), did not, so far as Whitehall was concerned, involve the internal affairs of these states. See above, pp. 54 et seq.

Some of the earliest Straits Settlements files received from the India Office were those concerning the Tangjong Putri question and the Johore–Pahang boundary dispute.[43] Throughout these papers the intimate relationship between Johore and Singapore stood out. A ruler whose position and prestige were sustained by British influence and treaty engagements[44] was consistently offered, and usually acted upon, the official advice of the Singapore Government and the day-to-day counsel of the Singapore officials in their private capacities. Neither Temenggong Daing Ibrahim, nor his son Abu-Bakar, who succeeded him in 1862, ever, as the papers showed, pursued their own inclination on any important subject once it was intimated to them that British policy favoured another course. In this they knew their own best interest, for they and their state prospered. All this the Colonial Office learned in 1867, and a series of transactions during the next few years drove the lesson home. The conclusion of the Johore–Pahang boundary settlement in 1868[45] and the thwarting of a Prussian attempt to survey Port Blair, on the mouth of the Endau River, as a naval station in 1870[46] showed the desire of Abu-Bakar to co-operate with the British Government. The annual reports demonstrated that the economic penetration and development of Johore raised no political problems and contributed to the prosperity of Singapore as much as they advanced the power of the local ruler. Sir Harry Ord's description of Temenggong Abu-Bakar as a Raja 'who rules in accordance with the practice of civilized nations' and one 'ready at all times to place the whole resources of his country at our disposal'[47] may have been unduly

---

[43] See above, pp. 37–40.

[44] The Treaty of 1824 (Maxwell and Gibson, op. cit., pp. 122–6), as supplemented by the Agreement of 1855 between the Temenggong and the Sultan of Johore (ibid., pp. 127–9), recognized the Temenggong as the ruler of Johore, gave him a British pension and the moral backing of the British Government, in return for which, in addition to ceding Singapore for a cash payment, he agreed to submit his external relations to British control. There was however no question of any pledge to give him material support. Art. X of the Treaty of 1824 ran,—'The contracting parties hereby stipulate and agree, that neither party shall be bound to interfere in the internal concerns of the other's government, or in any political dissensions or wars which may arise within their respective territories, *nor to support each other by force against any third party whatever*' (ibid. p. 125). This was a most one-sided arrangement, for it gave the British Government control over Johore's foreign policy without any obligation to come to her help if war resulted. In practice Britain could not have allowed any other European Power to intervene in Johore.

[45] See above, p. 60.

[46] See below, p. 170.

[47] Gov. Straits to Sec. State, 10 Feb. 1868, in CO 273/17.

eulogistic, and we must remember that Ord, like every Governor after him, was a personal friend of Abu-Bakar. But it is the effect produced by this eulogy in the Colonial Office, and not its literal accuracy, which is important in this context.

Until Anson's 'Committee on Relations with Native States' (1871) the papers on Johore were the only ones concerning the internal affairs of a Malay State which had reached the Colonial Office. They formed the basis for the conclusion that whilst direct intervention could lead to unforeseeable and unwanted complications, the exertion of influence through semi-official channels could have happy results. It seemed to be a question of securing a ruler strong enough to control his own state, and enlightened enough to see that his own best interest lay in following the Government's advice. Anson's Committee, with its suggestions for the introduction of a British Political Agent or Agents to deal with the states, was firmly repressed; partly because the Colonial Office was not yet ready to see the necessity of such a step; largely to discourage meddling in high policy by an officer temporarily administering the government. But it is clear that as early as this the encouraging example of Johore was already leading those who had given the subject any thought to consider such a possibility. On Anson's despatch Cox, the head of the Eastern Department, minuted:

I believe that with judicious and friendly communication with them [the Malay Rulers] we might considerably increase our influence in those quarters in a manner that might bear good fruits in our commerce with them.[48]

It is against this background of almost complete ignorance of the position in the Malay States other than Johore that we must judge the Colonial Office attitude to the Selangor incident of 1871, and its apparent willingness to acquiesce in this intervention into that state's internal affairs.[49] We must bear in mind too that the Selangor incident was from first to last dealt with as a question of piracy. It was so presented by Colonel Anson in his despatches, and dealt with as such by a busy Secretary of State. The intervention of Gladstone gave the subject added importance, but the Prime Minister was, as we have seen, solely concerned with the bombardment of Kuala Selangor, which if badly handled

---

[48] Minute on Anson's 3 June 1871, in CO 273/47.
[49] On the Selangor incident, see Chapter 2, section (ii) above, pp. 85 et seq.

might have become a political issue at home, not with the pledge to support the Viceroy Zia'u'd-din.

So far as Selangor's internal affairs were concerned the Colonial Office officials and the Secretary of State were left with the impression that what had been done was in line with existing practice in Johore. There was already a treaty relationship which though it gave the British Government no control over the Sultan's foreign policy, guaranteed the integrity of Selangor's northern boundary and defined that boundary.[50] In that sense Selangor was already a 'British Protected State'.[51] Its Sultan was not a British pensioner with a European education, like the ruler of Johore, but there was now a 'Viceroy', said by Irving to have 'European ideas about his government' and to have 'always evinced a desire to give the Government every information about his proceedings, and to meet the views of the Government'.[52] He was a chief of 'intelligence and honesty of purpose', with the backing of many of the Straits merchants, and the fact that he was a brother of the Sultan of Kedah, a good friend of the Straits Government, gave him additional standing. In his report on the proceedings of the mission to Langat, which arrived in London at the same time as Anson's despatch on the subject, Irving drew a direct parallel between the situation in Selangor and that in Johore. After expanding on the potential wealth of Selangor, and its readiness to 'burst into exuberant life', and stating that Zia'u'd-din was eager to establish regular systems of justice and revenue, and to employ for this purpose European officers selected by the Straits Government, Irving continued:

Johore, with not a tithe of the resources of Salangore, has become a thriving and opulent state,—and why? Simply because the East Indian Government selected the most intelligent of the Native Chiefs, the present Maharajah, and supported him by their advice and influence.[53]

[50] The Treaties of 1818 and 1825 (Maxwell and Gibson, op. cit., pp. 30–34) (i) established British trade on a most-favoured-nation footing in Selangor, and (ii) defined her boundary with Perak and provided for the prevention of piracy. The pledge to protect the northern boundary as against Siam was contained in Art. 14 of the Treaty of 1826 with Siam (ibid., pp. 77–82) (see above, pp. 11 and 18).

[51] This phrase was in fact used in the Colonial Office at the time of the Selangor incident, when one of the officials in the Eastern Department minuted: 'Salangore is one of the States called 'protected by Treaty with the British Government' (Cox's minute on OAG's 14 July 1871, in CO 273/48).

[52] Memo by C. J. Irving, written early in July 1781, in CO 273/48, and printed in Parl. Pap. C.465 of 1871, pp. 11–13.

[53] Parl. Pap. C.465, p. 28.

In the light of this Memorandum the general but vague pledge given by Birch to support the Viceroy if his authority were disputed seemed merely to place him in the same category as the Maharaja of Johore—a protégé of the Straits Government. It was not regarded as a blank cheque promising the services of a British man-of-war whenever he might call for it. It was thought of rather as an intimation that the British Government approved of his administration, disapproved of those who opposed him, and would always be ready to consider with sympathy any request he might make for help. This was clearly the view taken in the Colonial Office. Cox spoke of Zia'u'd-din and the Sultan being 'upheld by England', and Meade of 'moral support'. Kimberley put the matter exactly when he said 'it might be advisable to give him support, but this is very different from promising it.'[54] The ministers and officials in London approved the course taken because in their view it did not involve the British Government in any additional responsibility. But they gave their approval mainly because they hoped that these steps would prevent piracy and disorder involving British subjects, not because they were primarily concerned with the development of Selangor by the merchants of the Straits Settlements. In Cox's words, they hoped that these measures would bring 'quiet times'.[55]

So far as the Colonial Office was concerned the Selangor affair was an isolated incident. Throughout 1872 the official papers give no hint of any consideration of further action, and whilst fighting raged in Selangor and Larut the British Government remained passive. They had indeed no occasion to contemplate any deviation from the long-established policy of non-intervention. Sir Harry Ord's despatches were most uninformative. From them it could be gathered that the west-coast states were in a very unsatisfactory state and that the war in Selangor was going against Zia'u'd-din. But there was no indication that British interests were seriously involved, and it was not until December that the officials in London learned that the Larut fighting was fomented from Penang, and that the peace of the British settlement was threatened in consequence.[56] Moreover the Colonial

[54] Colonial Office minutes dated 7–10 Sept. 1871, in CO 273/48.
[55] Ibid.
[56] After his return to the Straits Settlements from leave in March 1872 Sir Harry Ord did not address a despatch to the Secretary of State on affairs in Selangor and Perak until 24 Oct. Even then he only reported events in Selangor

Office gravely distrusted the acumen and capacity of its representative on the spot. Sir Harry's inability to get on with the European mercantile community in the Straits, and the unhappy nature of his relations with his own officials had not passed unnoticed in London, and as early as 1870 his removal to another colony had been suggested.[57] At the end of 1872 his failure to keep the Colonial Office informed of developments in Malaya, and his own clumsiness got him into serious trouble over an affair involving the Maharaja of Johore. Abu Bakar wanted rifles for his police force. He enlisted Sir Harry's help, and the rifles were ordered through the Crown Agents. This order came to the notice of the Colonial Office clerks at the same time as a report in the *London and China Telegraph* of 26 August that the Maharaja was shielding Raja Mahdi. They had heard nothing from Singapore on the subject, and therefore stopped the Crown Agents proceeding with the order until the report had been referred to Ord for his comments. Instead of giving the Colonial Office what they should have had from the beginning—a full account of the facts, or merely stating that Mahdi had been kept in Johore at his orders, Ord showed the correspondence to Abu Bakar. The result was a series of indignant denials from the Maharaja (who had been at some pains to conform to British policy against his own inclinations), and a long and belligerent letter from Ord practically censuring the Secretary of State for lack of confidence in him.[58] Abu Bakar's wounded feelings seem to have been healed by the expression of 'Lord Kimberley's great regret'.[59] But the damage

because of Colonial Office enquiries. When the citizens of Penang presented to a retiring Lieutenant-Governor an Address thanking him for his efforts to improve trading conditions in the neighbouring states and 'to bring to bear on them the legitimate influence of the British Government' the Colonial Office officials could only remark that they knew nothing about it (2 Apr. 1872, in CO 273/5)7.

[57] See for instance a minute by Holland, the Legal Adviser: 'I am rather inclined to think that Governor Ord's unfortunate temper and disposition to act harshly and imperiously towards those who do not humbly obey his will has led a party of officials to combine in putting him in the wrong. Any symptoms of this should be repressed. But one cannot help feeling that if he is uncomfortable he made the bed on which he lies. In the interests of the service it seems very desirable to move him to some other Government if practicable' (22 Aug. 1870, in CO 273/38). Again, on an administrative question Herbert commented in Dec. 1870: 'I should be very sorry to see Sir H. O. get his way in this matter because of his generally insubordinate opposition to regulations and instructions' (CO 273/40).

[58] CO 273/60, *passim*, Sept.-Oct. 1872. Herbert minuted: 'This shows that Sir H. Ord hardly understands the rudiments of his duty as a Governor' (Minute of 26 Nov. 1872).

[59] Sec. State to Gov. Straits, 12 Dec. 1872, in CO 273/60.

done to Ord's already doubtful reputation at the Colonial Office was never repaired. When in a private letter he complained that in the Peninsula 'murders, plundering and burning are the order of the day, and the *bad ones* are beginning to believe the popular cry that "nothing will induce the Government to interfere",' Herbert commented 'Most certainly the present Governor cannot be trusted to interfere wisely'. At the same time Kimberley described the politics of Selangor as 'a tangled web which I fear Sir H. Ord is not the man to unravel'.[60] It was clear that whether or not the Colonial Office ever took any action in Malaya they would certainly not do it through Sir Harry Ord.

The Colonial Office records show that during the first half of 1873 the officials and the Secretary of State swung round to the view that some sort of action was in fact necessary in Malaya. At some time in August a decision was taken to make this view known to Sir Andrew Clarke, who was about to take over the government of the Straits Settlements from Sir Harry Ord, and to ask him to consider when he arrived in Malaya what form this action should take. In this the records merely confirm the accepted history of the transaction. What has not hitherto been established is the reason, or reasons, for this change of policy.

The decision to embark on some form of intervention does not seem to have been taken entirely or even principally as result of news of the worsening situation in Malaya. As the nature of the situation in Larut became apparent from Ord's belated despatches the men in the Colonial Office realized that to secure order in Penang it would be necessary to stop the Larut disorders.[61] But Kimberley and his officials recoiled from any suggestion of direct action. Hugessen, whose 'Imperialistic notions' we have noticed, was a somewhat reluctant adherent of this point of view. On 6 January he commented:

> . . . the annexation to British rule of the country in which these disturbances took place . . . would be most beneficial to Penang, and contribute to the tranquillity and prosperity of the settlement in no slight degree. This however is not to be encouraged I suppose just now.[62]

[60] Minute of Herbert on Ord's letter of 24 Oct. in CO 273/60; Minute of Kimberley, 22 Dec. 1872, in CO 273/61.

[61] The most important despatches on the situation in Selangor and Perak were those of 6 Nov. 1872 (received in the Colonial Office Dec. 1872), 11 Nov. (received Jan. 1873), 20 Mar. 1873 (received Apr. 1873). For Ord's policy at this period, see Chapter 3, section (i), above, p. 99.

[62] Minute on Gov. Straits to Sec. State, 11 Nov. 1872, in CO 273/61.

Kimberley's reaction to this was very definite:

> I am unable to agree with Mr. Hughesson that further extension of British territory is the proper remedy for these evils. If we were to annex all the territory in Asia where there is misgovernment we must end by dividing Asia with Russia.[63]

These two comments were the extreme poles of Colonial Office reaction. The considered opinion of the office minutes is more accurately recorded in a minute written by Kimberley after he had read the account of the Larut war in the report from Penang on the Blue Book for 1872.

> I think we must endeavour to put a stop to these disturbances. It is evident that Penang is a base of operations for these contentious Chinese. The difficulty is how to do anything without direct interference with Perak, which is very undesirable.[64]

When this was penned opinion in the Colonial Office was nicely balanced between earnest desire to have an end to trouble and disorder, and fear of action and responsibility.[65] It had been brought to this state by reports from Malaya which dealt only with events up to the end of March 1873. The story of the increasing tempo of the Larut war and of large-scale Chinese piracy, and the petition of the Chinese merchants of the Straits Settlements calling for a change in government policy, did not begin to reach London until the end of August.[66] By then the attitude of the Secretary of State had completely changed. There was no more harping on the difficulty and danger of interference. Cox minuted on the Chinese petition on 28 August:

[63] Minute dated 8 Jan. 1873, in CO 273/61.
[64] Minute dated 7 July 1873, in CO 273/74. The Penang Report was probably written by Campbell, who had been acting as Lt.-Gov. Penang between Mar. 1872 and May 1873. During the summer of 1873 he was on leave in London, and had an interview with Kimberley about the time this minute was written. He had been a constant advocate of the appointment of Residents to the Malay States.
[65] This is most evident in the official minutes, for instance that of Cox on 21 July: 'I can't help thinking that with a judicious Governor we might almost imperceptibly have a considerable moral influence over the various Native Chiefs. But I am aware how dangerous any interference may be' (CO 273/74).
[66] This petition had been presented to Ord in March 1873, and he agreed to bring it to the notice of the Secretary of State when he returned to England, as he was just about to do. But his return was deferred until November, and he therefore forwarded the Petition to the Colonial Office in July. It did not reach London until late Aug. 1873. For the contents of the Petition, see pp. 129-131.

Lord Kimberley is about to consider how far it may be desirable for the British Government . . . to interfere actively in an endeavour to stop the dissensions in the Malay States.[67]

In fact, when the petition reached his desk on 31 August Kimberley had already decided that the British Government must interfere. He began at once to compose a minute which declared that '. . . the interests of the British Settlements require that we shall exert our influence to put an end to the state of anarchy and disorder which prevails in several of the States'.[68] This minute, with a few drafting amendments and one significant deletion, formed the instructions which were later given to Sir Harry Ord's successor as Governor of the Straits Settlements.

The tone and character of Kimberley's minute are in complete contrast to the indecisive minutes of June and July. It was intended from the beginning to be a policy directive to the new Governor:

Refer to Sir A. Clarke . . . Say that the whole subject is one of the greatest importance & requires his immediate and earnest attention: that while H.M.'s Government have I need not say no desire to interfere in the internal affairs of the native States, our long and intimate connection with them . . ., and the interests of the British Settlements, require that we shall exert our influence to put an end to the state of anarchy & disorder which prevails in several of the States, and which if not checked will probably extend through that part of the Peninsula which is independent of Siam, and will ruin these fertile and productive countries.[69]

The last part of the minute will be at once recognized by any reader familiar with the instructions eventually given to Sir Andrew Clarke:

Request him carefully to examine the facts, and to report in the case of each state with reference to the present condition of its affairs and its relations with the British Govt. what mode of proceeding should in his opinion be adopted with a view to restore peace and order, to secure protection to British subjects who may trade with the States, or embark in commercial undertaking in the native territories, and generally to promote the improvement and good Govt. of the native States with which we are connected.

[67] Minute on Gov. Straits to Sec. State, 10 July 1873, in CO 273/67.
[68] Minute of Kimberley, 31 Aug. 1873, in CO 273/67.
[69] Ibid.

Suggest that he should consider whether these ends would be promoted by the appointment of a British agent, of course with the consent of the native rulers & at the expense of the Settlements, to reside at the seat of Govt. of any of the States not under Siam.[70]

The most important part of Kimberley's minute from the point of view of the historian, however, is a passage which does not appear in the final despatch:

. . . we could not see with indifference interference of foreign Powers in the affairs of the Peninsula, on the other hand it is difficult to see how we should be justified in objecting to the native States seeking aid elsewhere if we refuse to take any steps to remedy the evils complained of.[71]

This gives us for the first time a clue to an unstated motive behind the decision to intervene—fear of foreign intervention.

The story behind this part of Kimberley's minute begins on 25 June. On this date a letter was received in the Colonial Office from a firm of London solicitors acting for J. G. Davidson, whom we have already met as the holder of an extensive tin-mining concession in Selangor. Davidson and his associates were hampered in their efforts to promote a company to operate the concession by the disturbed state of Selangor, which was scaring off financial backers. His solicitors therefore put two alternative propositions to the Secretary of State:

1. That the British Government should take 'the territory' (i.e. Selangor) under their protection.
2. Failing this, that they would sanction the proposed Company recruiting its own force of soldiers to protect its property and to maintain order amongst its Chinese workmen.[72]

This approach fell quite flat. The Colonial Office answer employed the usual formula to the effect that British subjects speculated in Selangor at their own risk, and added that the British Government could not sanction the employment of a

[70] Ibid. There is no indication in the minutes of the origin of the idea of British Agent or Resident. It had figured in the report of Anson's Committee on Native States (above, p. 83), and in the suggestions of the Acting Lieutenant-Governor of Penang in 1872 (above, p. 126). There seems no doubt that the example in mind when these suggestions were made was that of the Resident or Political Agent as employed in India, and Kimberley, who had served at the India Office, must have been well aware of Indian practice.

[71] Ibid.

[72] Lambert & Co. to Sec. State, 25 June 1873, in CO 273/74.

private force in a foreign state, with all the risk of complications involved, even though Zia'u'd-din was agreeable to their intro-duction.[73] Davidson's syndicate therefore tried again through their representative in London, a Mr. Seymour Clarke.[74] At some time in the first half of July Seymour Clarke had an interview with Herbert on the subject. There is no record in the Colonial Office files of what took place. But on 18 July he sent a letter to the Permanent Secretary which seems to have been an attempt to blackmail or frighten the British Government into action.[75] After recalling his interview with Herbert, Seymour Clarke went on to say that he had recently heard from 'an old resident of Singapore' who was the intimate of 'many Native Chiefs'. This can only have been W. H. Read. From his channels of information this 'old resident' thought it likely that the smaller states of the Peninsula would put themselves under the protectorate of some European Power, and failing England he had heard Germany mentioned as the most likely. By a curious coincidence the promoters of the Tin Mining scheme had themselves received within the last few days a letter from the 'Viceroy' of Selangor dated 3 June. A passage from this ran:

I would ask you to ascertain if the English, or any other Government, would interfere in any disturbance that might arise in the territory of Selangor from wicked persons, so that merchants desirous of opening up the country may have security for their property and capital in-vested.

As though to make sure that the Colonial Office should not miss the implication of these hints the letter went on to point out the

[73] Colonial Office to Lambert & Co., 5 July 1873, in CO 273/74. Kimberley took the same attitude in September, when he attempted, but too late, to prevent Speedy enlisting troops in India for service in Larut (CO 273/69, *passim*, especially Kimberley's minute of 21 Sept. 1873).

[74] This man had been at one time the General Manager of the Great Northern Railway, and according to the Crown Agents' report had a good reputation in the City. He was the brother-in-law of W. H. Read, one of the concessionaires and a promoter of the Selangor Company, and was already active in pushing a scheme for the construction of a telegraph line through the Malay States to link Bangkok with the new line to Australia. Read held concessions from the rulers of these States for the construction of the line through them, and Seymour Clarke was negotiating on his behalf for the sale of these concessions to the Telegraph Company. The scheme did not mature during the period of this study, and seems to have played no part in influencing British policy, but its development can be followed in the Colonial Office files, particularly CO 273/73 (1873), 273/77 and 273/78 (1874), 273/82 (1875) and 273/89 (1876).

[75] Seymour Clarke to Herbert, 18 July 1873, in CO 273/74.

unprotected state of British commerce through the Straits of Malacca now that the Anglo-Dutch Convention of 1871 had allowed the British guarantee of Atjeh's independence to lapse, and thus eliminated the last vestiges of the British position in Sumatra.[76]

The ostensible purpose of this letter was to enquire whether it would be better for Tengku Zia'u'd-din to place his views directly before the Secretary of State or to make them known through the Governor of the Straits Settlements. In fact however it was an ultimatum, hinting that if the British Government did not act, then the promoters of the Selangor Tin Mining Company would see to it that some other power would be invited to do so.

Seymour Clarke's letter was treated by the junior Colonial Office officials as only another tiresome complaint from merchants who wanted the British Government to help them out of trouble. Its effect on the Permanent Secretary and the Secretary of State was quite different. Herbert, whilst acknowledging that the reply to Seymour Clarke must be that the Government was not prepared to interfere,[77] suggested that it might be as well if Britain could consolidate her position in the Peninsula without incurring any major risks or responsibilities.[78] Kimberley had no doubt about it. When the papers came before him on 22 July he wrote:

It would be impossible for us to consent to any European Power assuming the Protectorate of any State in the Malayan Peninsula. I think we might send this to F.O. and enquire whether they would see any objection to Sir A. Clarke being instructed to endeavour to extend the Treaties with Salangore and the other Malay States by a stipulation that they should not enter into any Treaty ceding territory to a Foreign Power or giving such Power any rights or privileges not accorded to us.[79]

It is clear from the terms of this minute, and from the chronology, that Seymour Clarke's letter was the factor which precipitated a change of policy. The period from 22 July, when Kimberley read the letter, to the end of August was a time of great activity in the Eastern Department of the Colonial Office, when the whole basis of the British connexion with the Peninsular

[76] Ibid. For the Convention of 1871, see above, p. 27. A letter from Capt. Sherrard Osborne, R.N., which appeared in *The Times* of 12 July 1873, had made the same point.
[77] This was the reply actually made (Colonial Office to Seymour Clarke, 5 Aug. 1873, CO 273/74)1.
[78] Minute of 21 July 873, in CO 273/74.
[79] Minute by Kimberley dated 22 July 1873, CO 273/74.

states was reviewed. Thus by 31 August, when the petition of the Chinese traders and Ord's review of conditions in Malaya came before him, Kimberley had already decided on action, and had had ample time to consider what form that action should take. It was probably only coincidence that the formal record of his decision was attached to the Chinese petition.[80]

Reasoning from the Colonial Office papers we therefore reach the conclusion that the decision to take some action in Malaya, and if necessary to intervene in the affairs of the states, was provoked not by conditions in the Peninsula, nor by any consideration of British economic interests there, but by fear of foreign intervention. This is confirmed by the terms in which Kimberley justified his instructions to Sir Andrew Clarke to Gladstone:

The condition of the Malay Peninsula [he wrote] is becoming very serious. It is the old story of misgovernment of Asiatic States. This might go on without any very serious consequences except the stoppage of trade, were it not that European and Chinese capitalists, stimulated by the great riches in tin mines which exist in some of the Malay States are suggesting to the native Princes that they should seek the aid of Europeans to enable them to put down the disorders which prevail. We are the paramount power on the Peninsula up to the limit of the States, tributary to Siam, and looking to the vicinity of India and our whole position in the East I apprehend that it would be a serious matter if any other European Power were to obtain a footing in the Peninsula.[81]

This attitude was consistent with the continuing theme of British policy in Malaya and Indonesia as it has been interpreted in the first part of this chapter. It was in line with the idea that the promotion of British economic interests in the area, however desirable in itself, has in fact always been secondary to the defence of India, the protection of the sea route to China, and the denial of bases along that route to potentially dangerous powers.[82]

[80] This is confirmed by part of a minute compiled by Cox of the Eastern Department in 1874: 'In July last Mr. Seymour Clarke, who was interested in the Selangor Tin Mines, wrote to Lord K. suggesting European protection should be afforded to the Chief of Selangor. This led to a consideration of the General question, & a memo having been prepared for Lord K. showing our Treaties etc. with the different Chiefs, his L'dship wrote his despatch to Sir A. Clarke . . .' (Minute dated 6 Apr. 1874, in CO 273/75).

[81] Kimberley to Gladstone, 10 Sept. 1873, in Gladstone Papers, Add. MSS. 44225, British Museum.

[82] The defence of India was at the end of the eighteenth century a prominent factor in the acquisition of Penang (see above, pp. 1–2), but it did not again figure in British calculations in the Peninsula until the end of the nineteenth

M

Many interesting questions arise from this conclusion, but we can only find space to discuss two of them here. First, what led Kimberley to conclude that the threat of foreign intervention in Malaya was real enough to justify action ? Of the other Colonial Powers Holland was precluded by the Treaty of 1824 from interfering, and a general colonial settlement had been reached with her only two years before with the Sumatra and Gold Coast Treaties of 1871. France was prostrate after her war with Prussia, and her colonial activities were to remain at a stand-still until after the Congress of Berlin in 1878. In the East after the Franco-Siamese Settlement of 1867 secured the recognition of the French protectorate over Cambodia successive French Consuls at Bangkok contented themselves with the administration of their extraterritorial rights in Siam.[83] So little were any other states regarded as potential rivals in London that a large concession in North Borneo granted to the American Consul in Brunei in 1865 passed almost unnoticed in the Foreign Office and Colonial Office records.[84] Even a Prussian attempt to survey Blair Harbour, on the east coast of Johore, and the off-lying islands, for use as a coaling station during the Franco-Prussian War was not taken very seriously in London.[85]

By the middle of 1873 however conditions had changed. A

century, when German sea-power had become a factor to be reckoned with, and when France was threatening the independence of Siam. It was always however a prominent factor in British policy towards Burma.

[83] Cf. an unpublished thesis in the Library of the University of London, Murti, *Anglo-French relations with Siam* (1951), pp. 131–4.

[84] Owen Rutter, *British North Borneo* (1922), p. 117; CO 144/5, *passim*; FO 12/2B *passim*.; Irwin, *Nineteenth-Century Borneo*, p. 195.

[85] When the captain of the Prussian gunboat *Hertha* announced his intentions in Singapore he was warned off by Ord, and the Maharaja of Johore sent one of his own vessels to the area to watch events. A rumour that Prussia had secured the cession of Pulau Tioman, on the east coast, was passed on to the Foreign Office, but they took no action except to refer the matter to the Colonial Office. It was Holland which was the agitated party, and the Foreign Office seem to have been chiefly concerned over the best way to quieten Dutch disquiet. Rogers at the Colonial Office minuted that he did not 'object to European neighbours in the Indian Seas, and if Prussia likes to have an island there I should let her by all means' (Minute of 20 July 1870, in CO 273/42). At about the same time, when Herbert suggested that the problem of Fiji might be settled by inviting the North German Confederation to annex the islands there was general agreement that German occupation would be welcome, since she would not be in a position to challenge British naval supremacy in the Pacific, see Drus, op. cit., p. 94. The Blair Harbour incident illustrated in a striking way the Colonial Office's complete lack of familiarity with the Malayan scene. The Dutch note referred to Johore in the Dutch form—'Djoher'—which for a time nonplussed the Colonial Office officials. Kimberley minuted on 21 July : 'The first step is to ascertain distinctly *where* the Maharajah and his islands are.'

Dutch invasion of Atjeh at the beginning of the year created a focus of unsettlement in the Straits. The Atjehnese leaders, seeking a counter-balance against the Dutch, attempted to obtain the support of some other Power by offering island bases and trading monopolies. Rumours of secret treaties negotiated with the United States and the Italian consuls in Singapore were denied by the countries concerned, but they were taken seriously enough in London to engage the attention of the British Cabinet.[86] Italy and the United States were not the only 'new nations' which had to be considered. Seymour Clarke's letter specifically mentioned Germany, and though a junior Colonial Office official remarked that the prospect of a German protectorate was small[87] the Liberal ministers were not so certain that they might not meet with trouble from this quarter.

There had been a marked change in the British attitude towards Germany during the course of the Franco-Prussian War, which transferred from France to Germany political predominance in Europe. One feature of the uncertainty which followed this disruption of the balance of power was an invasion scare in England, prompted by the publication in 1871 of an anonymous pamphlet, *The Battle of Dorking*. Another was a series of alarming rumours started by the King of the Belgians, who sent warnings to his English friends of an understanding between Russia, Germany, France and the United States to act together in support of Russia against England in Asia.[88] The Liberal ministers were not much impressed by the invasion scare, and Gladstone commented acidly on the warnings from Belgium—'This intelligence rather tends to lower my estimate of the *acumen* of the King of the Belgians.'[89] But they had some basis in fact; the years after 1870 saw a drawing together of Germany and Russia as part of the Bismarckian alliance system, which was consolidated in June 1873 by the creation of the *Dreikaiserbund* between Germany, Russia and Austria. Bismarck's support had already enabled

[86] Gov. Straits to Sec. State, 24 Mar. 1873, in CO 273/65; FO/CO correspondence in CO 273/73, *passim*; Gladstone's Cabinet Minutes, Apr.–May, 1873. Add. MSS. 44641, British Museum.

[87] Minute by Macdonald, 19 July 1873, in CO 273/74.

[88] Granville to Gladstone, 7 Feb. 1873, in PRO 30/29 (Granville Papers), vol. lxii. Bismarck was reported to have said: 'We shall see the eggs we broke at Sedan paid for by England!'

[89] Minute on Granville's letter of 7 Feb., ibid. Gladstone was however concerned about the growth of anti-British feeling in Berlin (cf. Gladstone to Granville, 11 Jan. 1873, in PRO 30/29/62).

Russia in 1870 to denounce with impunity those clauses of the Treaty of Paris (1856) which forbade her to maintain military or naval establishments on the Black Sea. Russia was Britain's most feared rival in Asia, and in the years between 1866 and 1872 her conquest of the Khanates of Central Asia brought her to the boundaries of Afghanistan and enabled her to intensify her pressure on Persia. Both Britain's traditional opposition to any power which aspired to the domination of Europe, and her suspicion of Russia therefore urged her to view with suspicion any hint of the acquisition of territory by Germany.

There is no indication in any of the official papers that in 1873 any minister or official servant of the Crown had knowledge that any other Power actually contemplated the acquisition of territory or influence in Malaya. The consolidation of the British position there seems to have served rather to remove temptation than to forestall a projected movement in that direction. The background to Kimberley's decision is by no means clear, and it remains for some future student of this period to uncover definite evidence of the circumstances which prompted him to take the view he did. It is just possible, in view of events in Fiji and the Gold Coast at this time, that he justified intervention in Malaya in these terms because he thought that no other argument would secure the acquiescence of Gladstone. But until evidence to the contrary is forthcoming the only course is to accept at its face value Kimberley's own declaration that:

Her Majesty's Government could not see with indifference the interference of a foreign Power in the affairs of the Peninsula, and it would be difficult to justify an objection to the Native States applying for aid to other Powers if the British Government refuses to lend its aid.[90].

We come now to the second question for discussion. Granted that some move must be made in Malaya, what should it be, annexation or the proclamation of Protectorates? Again there is little evidence that bears directly on the question. One course of action seems to have been ruled out from the beginning. There was never any prospect of the Liberal Government sanctioning annexation. Two similar problems with which the Liberals were faced in 1873, in the Gold Coast and Fiji, did end in annexation.

[90] Draft despatch composed about 6 Sept. 1873, in 273/67.

But the deed was done not by the Liberals but their Conservative successors. In the Gold Coast the Ashanti War was still in progress when the Liberals quitted office early in 1874, and it was left to their successors to annex the old 'Protectorate'.[91] In Fiji, where the activities of 'black-birders', traders and adventurers kept the islands in turmoil, the Gladstone Government was again faced with the need for action. Both the settlers and the natives pressed for annexation. Kimberley continually urged the reluctant Gladstone to a decision, but in June 1873 the Cabinet fell back on the expedient of a Commission of Enquiry, which staved off responsibility long enough to get the tottering Liberal ministry out of office.[92]

It is tempting to see Kimberley's instructions to Sir Andrew Clarke to 'enquire and report' as an application of Fijian tactics to Malaya. But several circumstances combine to suggest that they were not intended to shelve or delay action, and were not the result of a politically inspired compromise. In the first place the original suggestion came from the Permanent Secretary at the Colonial Office, Herbert, who wrote:

As Sir A. Clarke is believed to be able and cautious in administrative matters it might be well to desire him confidentially to consider after his arrival whether it would be safe & advantageous to extend our influence to some parts of the Malay territories beyond our own Settlements.[93]

In the second place Clarke's instructions were never submitted in draft to any other department of state. Kimberley recorded in his original minute of 22 July his intention of speaking to Granville at the Foreign Office and Argyll at the India Office on the subject, and may have done so. But when detailed memoranda on the situation in Malaya prepared by his officials were presented to him, he realized that under the arrangement reached in 1868 he was entitled to conduct relations with the states not under Siamese influence without reference to the Foreign Office, and

[91] See Chapter 5, below, p. 200.
[92] Drus, op. cit., pp. 102–3. Throughout the Fiji transaction it was always Kimberley who pressed the Cabinet to accept responsibility in the islands, and Gladstone who attempted to substitute unworkable alternatives, and to block action. It is possible that Kimberley used the bogy of foreign intervention in Malaya to avoid fighting the battle of the Gold Coast and Fiji over again. But there is no evidence to support the idea, and in default of evidence it must be regarded as improbable.
[93] Minute of 21 July 1873, in CO 273/74.

insisted on doing so.[94] Lastly, neither Clarke's instructions nor the general situation in Malaya appear ever to have formed the subject of discussion in Cabinet. There is no reference to Malaya in Gladstone's Cabinet minutes. The Liberal Cabinet during 1873 were distracted by continual domestic crises,[95] and what time they had for colonial affairs was occupied by Fiji and Ashanti. Clarke's instructions were therefore entirely the work of Kimberley and his officials, and it was not until 10 September that the draft despatch embodying these instructions was submitted to Gladstone.[96] He returned it without comment.

The instructions in their final and now widely known form were somewhat weaker than the draft. But this seems to have been the result of purely accidental circumstances. From the beginning, as a result of Herbert's suggestion and the departmental memoranda on existing treaties with the Malay States, Kimberley had had in mind an extension of these treaties so as to allow of increased British influence in the affairs of the states, and to exclude the possibility that any other Power might establish itself there. This followed naturally from the nature of the existing treaties. When these were subjected to detailed scrutiny in the Colonial Office it was realized for the first time that Perak, for instance, was almost a British Protectorate already, as result of the 1826 treaties.[97] Thus the draft instructions called on Clarke to report 'what mode of proceeding should in his opinion be adopted', making it quite clear that some form of action was in any case going to be taken, since 'the interests of the British Settlements require that we shall exert our influence to put an end to the state of anarchy and disorder which prevails.'[98] These instructions were originally drawn up in the form of a confidential letter to be given to Clarke before he sailed for Malaya. But probably owing to the time the papers were kept by Gladstone the letter was not ready when Clarke sailed, and it had to be turned into a despatch.[99] It seems to have been this that resulted in the instructions

[94] Memo by Macdonald, 15 Aug. 1873, and Kimberley's minutes thereon. CO 273/74.
[95] See Chapter 5 below, pp. 198 et seq.
[96] Kimberley to Gladstone, 10 Sept. 1873, quoted at p. 169 above.
[97] See the discussion in the Prelude above, pp. 17 et seq.
[98] Kimberley's minute of 10 July 1873, and draft composed about 6 Sept., loc. cit.
[99] Departmental memo of 17 Sept. 1873, Blake to Kimberley; Kimberley minute, 18 Sept., in CO 273/67.

being toned down, and in the passage which dealt with 'the interference of a foreign Power in the affairs of the Peninsula' being
cut out. The operative part of the instructions then read:

> I have to request you will carefully ascertain as far as you are able the
> actual condition of affairs in each state, and that you will report to me
> whether there are, in your opinion, any steps which can properly be
> taken by the Colonial Government to promote the restoration of peace
> and order, and to secure protection to trade and commerce with the
> Native Territories.
> I would wish you especially to consider whether it would be ad-
> visable to appoint a British officer to reside in any of the States. Such
> an appointment could of course only be made with the full consent of
> the Native Government and the expenses connected with it would have
> to be defrayed by the Government of the Straits Settlements.[100]

To sum up, the decision to depart from the policy of rigid non-
interference in Malaya was prompted by fear that if the disordered
conditions in some of the states were not ended some other Power
might be invited to intervene. This decision was taken by the
Secretary of State on his own initiative. He and his officials had
in mind an extension of the existing treaties with Perak and
Selangor which would eliminate the possibility of foreign interference. They also envisaged the possibility that British Agents
might be stationed in these states, but they did not elaborate this
suggestion. Instead they decided that as a first step the new
Governor of the Straits Settlements should be asked to report on
the practicability of these proposals.

This was the state of affairs in London when Sir Andrew Clarke
sailed for Malaya on 18 September 1873. He had been in London
whilst these proposals were being worked out, and was almost
certainly aware of Kimberley's views. He knew that the necessity
for action had been recognized, and that his own views would
probably be decisive in determining its form. But there is no
indication whatsoever in any of the papers that he was encouraged
to take the decision into his own hands, or given verbal instructions
in excess of those contained in the Colonial Office despatch. When
he did take immediate action contemporary opinion in the Straits
Settlements ascribed his policy to confidential instructions from
the Secretary of State. We however can explain it only in the light
of his own character and of conditions in Malaya.

[100] Sec. State to Gov. Straits, 20 Sept. 1873, in CO 273/67.

5

SIR ANDREW CLARKE AND THE INTRODUCTION OF RESIDENTS

1874

SIR ANDREW CLARKE, who succeeded Sir Harry Ord as Governor of the Straits Settlements at the end of 1873, was a man of action, impatient of procedure by enquiry and report. After making some preliminary enquiries he took it upon himself to initiate a form of intervention in the affairs of some of the Malay States without first consulting the Colonial Office. In January 1874 he called a meeting of some of the Perak chiefs and of the Chinese leaders from Penang and Larut, at Pulau Pangkor. There he arranged a settlement of the Larut War, and concluded a treaty with the Perak chiefs by which 'Abdu'llah became Sultan and a British Resident was placed in Perak with an Assistant Resident in Larut. By the end of 1874 he had also placed Residents in Selangor and Sungai Ujong.

Sir Andrew Clarke assumed the government of the Straits Settlements on 4 November 1873. A younger man than Sir Harry Ord, Clarke like him was an officer in the Corps of Royal Engineers. But unlike his predecessor Clarke's mind had not been constricted by routine duties in the lower ranks of the Corps, nor his self-importance inflated by long and uneventful periods as the Governor of isolated Crown Colonies. During his early years in Australia and New Zealand and his later service in the higher ranks of the Royal Engineers and at the Admiralty he had been always in contact with men more eminent and more experienced than himself.[1] His service as Director of Works at the Admiralty in parti-

[1] Lt.-Gen. Sir Andrew Clarke, G.C.M.G., C.B., C.I.E. (1824–1902), was commissioned in the Royal Engineers in 1844 and served in Australia, where he was A.D.C. and Private Secretary to Sir William Denison, and New Zealand. In 1853 he was appointed Surveyor-General of Victoria, and when responsible government was introduced there he was elected to the Legislative Assembly and became a member of the Cabinet as Minister for Public Lands. He returned to England in 1857, and commanded the R.E.'s in the Eastern and Midland Districts until 1864, when he was appointed Director of Public Works at the Admiralty. After serving as Governor of the Straits Settlements he went to India in 1875 as Public Works member of the Viceroy's Council. From 1882 till his retirement in 1892 he held the highest appointments in his profession, Commandant of the School of Military Engineering, and Inspector-General of Fortifications and Director of Works at the War Office. Even in retirement he remained active, being Agent-General for Victoria (1892–4 and 1897) and for Tasmania (1901).

cular had given him an insight into the working of the administrative machinery of Victorian England, and his personal contacts
with both of the English parties gave him a stronger position than
Ord ever had, and at the same time made him aware of what was
and what was not politically possible in the field of Colonial
policy. Hugh Childers, the Liberal First Lord of the Admiralty
and Chancellor of the Duchy of Lancaster, had been his friend
since his Australian days. Another personal connexion was Mon-
tague Corry, Disraeli's Private Secretary. In 1874 when the
Conservative Government came into office, Corry wrote to
Clarke:

> If you ever wish anything brought privately to his [Disraeli's] notice,
> perhaps writing to me will prove the best means, and I shall be delighted
> to do anything I can for you in this or any other respect.[2]

In 1873 Clarke was marked as an able and rising man, with
talents beyond his professional merits as a military engineer. His
work in 1870 on two reports, one on the Suez Canal and one on a
scheme for the manning of the Navy, though they did not lead
to action at the time, did not pass unnoticed. The Colonial Office
was pleased to employ him when he asked for a Colonial Governorship, and intended a compliment when they told him, apolo-
gizing for not employing him on the Gold Coast, that 'in Malaya
matters were much more critical and the situation more difficult
than on the African coast'.[3] Primarily however they thought of
him as a sound administrator who was 'able and cautious'.[4]
The real nature of the man was quite different. There were two
subjects in particular on which his ideas, had they been known
to them, might have caused some concern to Kimberley and
the Colonial Office officials. In the first place he was known
amongst those who came into close contact with him as 'a strong
Imperialist'.[5] His 'Imperialism' was not that of the 'jingo' school.
He had however a marked sense of the importance of the bonds of
Empire, originating no doubt in his early years in Australia and
New Zealand, which shows itself here and there in the otherwise

---

[2] Corry to Clarke, 8 Apr. 1874, quoted in Vetch, R. H., *Life of Lieut-General
Sir Andrew Clarke* (1905), p. 128. This book, with its Introduction by Col.
G. S. Clarke, is the main source for Clarke's life and character.
[3] Op. cit., pp. 114–15.
[4] Minute by Herbert, 21 July 1873, in CO 273/74.
[5] Vetch, op. cit., Preface, p. xii.

objective and purely factual report on the Suez Canal.[6] His years in the Antipodes gave him too a sympathy with the pioneer and the frontier trader, and a natural conviction that it was the Government's duty to smooth their path and provide them with the essentials of public order and administration. Of even greater importance as far as events in Malaya were concerned was his abhorrence of Civil Service procedure by enquiry and report. In 1870 his scheme for the manning of the Navy and the creation of a more adequate naval reserve was sat upon by a departmental committee. The committee reported favourably, but their report was pigeonholed. 'Long afterwards', says Vetch, 'Sir Andrew Clarke used to cite the treatment accorded to the work of this committee as a typical illustration of the bureaucratic ideal : "Inquire, collect information, hear evidence, formulate opinions, then bottle it all up so that no one shall be any the wiser".'[7] His own methods were summed up by one of his juniors :

One lesson he impressed on us young officers by example and precept. We learned to take responsibility, to act first and always to act, to write about it afterwards.[8]

Clarke's instructions from the Colonial Office called on him to 'enquire and report', and as we have seen there is no evidence that he was expected to go beyond the letter of this brief without further instructions. But opinion in Singapore was convinced that his course of action had already been decided on, and that it would take the form of direct intervention in the Peninsular states. In part this opinion was based on the knowledge that the Straits Settlements lobby in London was pressing for intervention, and it was thought that the vigorous policy adopted towards the Ashanti in West Africa was a sign of similar developments impending in Malaya.[9] In part it followed from hints dropped by Clarke himself. At a reception given by 'old Singapore well-wishers' in London in July the new Governor-designate, after referring to possibilities for

    [6] 'Report on the Maritime Canal . . . at Suez', by Capt. Richards, R.N., and Lt.-Col. Clarke, R.E., Hydrographer of the Admiralty and Director of Works, Admiralty, Feb., 1870 (FO 78/2256, *Turkey: Suez Papers*, vol. xviii). The report's comment on the importance of the Canal for English sea-power and the development of the Eastern and Australian trade routes is in striking contrast to the very cool attitude of the Admiralty and the Foreign Office, but is far outdone by the memoranda of the Board of Trade, which deploy all the modern arguments for British control of the Canal.
    [7] Vetch, op. cit., p. 103.
    [8] Op. cit., Preface, p. xii.
    [9] *Singapore Daily Times*, 2 Dec. and 9 Oct.; *Pinang Gazette*, 13 Nov.

development in Malaya, had said of the British Government's attitude 'it is its duty to foster and protect the interests of the Pioneers of Commerce and see that every facility is given them'. In November, after his arrival in Singapore, Sir Andrew and Lady Clarke were entertained at dinner by the Maharaja of Johore. In the course of his speech on this occasion Sir Andrew is said to have outlined a policy for intervention in Malaya 'in unmistakable terms', terms which unfortunately the journalist concerned did not think it worth reporting in greater detail.[10]

In fact Clarke's early weeks in Singapore seem to have been spent in considering what he should do in Larut and Perak.[11] Colonel Anson from Penang strongly advised direct British intervention. This he said was necessary not merely to secure the safety of Penang and to provide stable conditions for trade and development, but in the interests of the Perak Malays themselves. For he was afraid that the Chinese would eventually outnumber the Malays and take over control of the whole state. Already, according to his estimate, the Chinese in Larut—all of them adult males—were equal in numbers to the entire Malay population of the whole of Perak, which he put at about 30,000.[12] Another plea for intervention came from Malacca, whose merchants were again being pestered by stoppages of the trade on the Linggi River.[13] In

---

[10] *Singapore Daily Times*, 26 Nov. and 12 Jan. 1874.

[11] On 10 Nov. a letter was received in Singapore from Selangor announcing that Zia'u'd-din had succeeded in retaking the forts at Kuala Selangor, and now held undisputed possession of the 'entire territory' (*Singapore Daily Times*, 11 Nov. 1873) so that for the moment Clarke was not seriously worried by the position there. In Larut however Capt. Speedy appeared to be making little progress now that he had recaptured the mines for the Mantri, and the Chinese piracies were continually mounting. In the first week after his arrival two Penang junks were plundered in sight of H.M.S. *Avon* and their crews killed without her being able to catch the pirates, and Clarke was compelled to acknowledge that the present naval forces were incapable of dealing with the pirates, and to ask for fast steam-launches to be sent out (*Pinang Gazette*, 13 Nov.; Gov. Straits to Sec. States, 19 Nov. and 29 Dec. 1873, in CO 273/71).

[12] Anson to Colonial Sec., Singapore, 4 Dec. 1873, in CO 809/1, pp. 165–6. According to the estimates of Speedy and Birch in 1875 there were then in Perak and Larut together a total of 29,300 Chinese and 93,000 Malays. (Report on Larut for 1874, C.1320, pp. 68–81; Report on Perak, 2 Apr. 1875, C.1320, pp. 85–93). Larut was then just recovering from the war, so that Anson's figure for the earlier period is probably about right. His estimate of the Malay population of Perak is probably low, and that of Birch high. In 1879 the total population of Perak was estimated at 81,000 (Swettenham, *British Malaya*, p. 224).

[13] *Singapore Daily Times*, 22 and 27 Dec. 1873. It was the same old trouble. The Malacca merchants complained in a petition dated 19 Dec. that Malays from Rembau were erecting stockades on the Linggi River and levying tolls which added to those charged already elsewhere on the river were killing trade (see below, pp. 192 et seq.).

addition to Anson the new Governor is known to have consulted Commander Grant of H.M.S. *Midge* and Thomas Braddell, the Attorney-General, about the situation in Malaya, but what advice they gave him and what other suggestions were pressed upon him in these weeks it is impossible to tell from the Colonial Office records and other available sources. We can only conjecture from the background and known opinions of these officials that they all advised energetic action or intervention in some form.

We know only that by 13 December Clarke had decided on action, and that he made that decision without any form of consultation with the Colonial Office. On the evening of 13 December W. H. Read, who as we have seen had his finger in a good many Malayan pies, dined at Government House. After dinner Clarke asked him to stay for a talk, and in the course of conversation Read asked whether the Governor intended to take any early action in Perak. Clarke replied: 'I am ready at a moment's notice if I can get the key of the door.' 'Give me a fortnight,' said Read, 'and I will get it for you.' The 'key of the door', a letter signed by 'Abdu'llah inviting the British Government to intervene in Perak, was duly produced on 9 January.[14] By 20 January Clarke at a meeting at Pangkor had dictated a treaty providing for the installation of a British Resident in Perak, and settling the sultanship on 'Abdu'-llah. On the same day the headmen of the Chinese factions in Larut signed an agreement to keep the peace and to accept British arbitration in the allocation of the disputed mining land.

Read's account of the 'key to the door' episode is important because it shows that by 13 December Clarke had decided on some form of intervention in Perak. But it is not as evidence strong enough to support the further assumptions which Wilkinson[15] seems to make from it:

1. That Clarke's decision to recognize 'Abdu'llah as Sultan was taken almost 'accidentally', because Read happened to have connexions with him, rather than on the merits of the situation in Perak.

[14] Cf. Read's memoirs, *Play and Politics, Recollections of Malaya by an Old Resident* (1901), published anonymously, pp. 25–26; Vetch, op. cit., p. 149. In Sept. 1873 'Abdu'llah had come to Singapore to seek support from the Straits Government, and amongst others had consulted Read, who advised him to wait for the arrival of Ord's successor. So it was that Read was able to get 'Abdu'llah's signature to a letter drafted by himself, in a relatively short time.
[15] In Winstedt, *History of Perak*, p. 98.

2. That the organization of the Pangkor meeting, at which 'Abdu'llah was 'elected' was made possible only by virtue of 'Abdu'llah's invitation to the British Government to arbitrate in the Perak dispute.

3. That Clarke came to the meeting at Pangkor already determined to secure 'Abdu'llah's election.

The messenger sent off to secure 'Abdu'llah's signature to Read's draft letter did not return with it to Singapore until 9 January.[16] By then Clarke's preparations for a meeting at Pangkor were already far advanced. On 2 or 3 January W. A. Pickering, the Straits Government's adviser on Chinese affairs, arrived in Penang to see if a basis for negotiation between the Larut Chinese could be found.[17] Pickering later did outstanding work as Singapore's first Protector of Chinese, but his remarkable personal gifts were never employed to such effect as in these few days in Larut. Though an outsider and a foreigner he succeeded in convincing the suspicious and desperate Ghee Hin that after years of hatred and fear they could rely on the good intentions and fairness of a foreign official whose government they had till now regarded as hostile, or at best obstructive. By 4 January Pickering had obtained the consent of both sides to a temporary agreement which he summarized tersely as follows:

Sinhengs [Ghee Hin] gladly sign agreement [to cease hostilities and refer the dispute to Clarke's arbitration]; give boats, every thing to your disposal in seven days, meantime beg orders; Speedy to hold his hand. Boats being given up they cannot escape death; agreement being broken then let Speedy do his worst.[18]

This telegram from Pickering set in motion Clarke's preparations for the meeting at Pangkor. First he dealt with the Larut Chinese. He arranged to take delivery of their boats and arms himself at Pangkor on 14 January. He also promised to provide food for the starving Ghee Hin, and to transport those who wished to Penang and Singapore, where work could be found for them until they were able to return to the mines.[19] Then he turned to the Perak

[16] Read, op. cit., p. 26.

[17] *Pinang Gazette*, 8 Jan. 1874. Pickering was described in the establishment lists as 'Chinese Interpreter', but even in 1874 he was more important than that, for the simple reason that the Straits Settlements contained thousands of Chinese and Pickering was the only official competent to deal with them. Later, when the Chinese Protectorate developed, he became a very important official indeed.

[18] Telegram, Pickering to Gov. Straits, 4 Jan. 1874; C.1111, p. 74.

[19] Colonial Sec., Singapore, to Pickering, 5 Jan., C.1111, p. 74.

Malays. On 7 January, i.e. two days before 'Abdu'llah's letter was in his hands, he sent off Major Macnair, the Colonial Engineer, and Captain Dunlop, Inspector-General of Police, to arrange that the Perak chiefs too should be present at Pangkor on the 14th, so that the succession dispute could be settled. The orders given to Macnair and Dunlop[20] include an account of the background to the succession dispute which sheds a good deal of light on the extent of Clarke's knowledge at this point, and on his intentions. The main points in the account are as follows:

1. It states that the succession dispute is at the root of all the disturbances in Perak, because it deprives the state's traditional government of the power to act.
2. It recognizes only two contenders for the throne of Perak— 'Abdu'llah, the heir *de jure*, and Ismail, the successor *de facto*.
3. It points out that whilst Ismail has the support of the Mantri and the Laksamana,[21] 'Abdu'llah has no important supporters, and it goes on to instruct Macnair and Dunlop to sound 'Abdu'llah and find out whether he would be willing to abandon his claim in return for a pension.
4. It admits reluctantly that in any settlement the Mantri will have to remain in control of Larut, though paying tribute to the future Sultan and providing assurance that 'good government' will be maintained.
5. It insists that in any settlement Pangkor and the Dindings must be ceded to the British Government.

The thing to notice about this document is that, apart from the absence of any reference to a Resident, its subject matter follows the same lines as the treaty eventually concluded at Pangkor. The main difference between the treaty and the ideas set out in these earlier instructions lies in their attitude to 'Abdu'llah and Ismail. In the instructions Clarke clearly has in mind the recognition of Ismail as the stronger candidate, and the pensioning of 'Abdu'llah. In the Pangkor Treaty 'Abdu'llah is recognized as Sultan and Ismail is pensioned. In other respects Clarke seems to have had clear in his mind early in January the nature of the settlement which he hoped to put into effect in Perak, and which was in fact imposed on the Perak chiefs.

Only at this point does 'Abdu'llah's letter enter the picture.

[20] Colonial Sec., Singapore, to Macnair and Dunlop, 7 Jan., C. 1111, pp. 75-77.
[21] A bad mistake, the Laksamana was the Mantri's father-in-law, but he was also closely related to 'Abdu'llah's mother, and his consistent supporter (cf. Winstedt, op. cit., p. 99).

Received on 9 January, two days after Macnair's instructions were issued and two weeks after Pickering had been sent to Larut, the letter had no part in initiating the Pangkor meeting. But it might, from the dates, have been responsible for changing Clarke's mind, as it obviously was changed at some point between 7 and 20 January, and deciding him to support 'Abdu'llah rather than Ismail. The letter asked Clarke to act as arbitrator in the succession dispute. It also asked for the conclusion of a new treaty so that Perak might 'settle under the sheltering protection of the English flag', and suggested the appointment of a Resident to 'assist and advise . . . the Government of the country.'[22] It was therefore undoubtedly useful to Clarke. It enabled him to represent the intervention upon which he had already decided as having been undertaken at the request of 'certain Chiefs for the time being of the said Kingdom of Perak'.[23] But if anything it weakened 'Abdu'llah's bargaining position, for it did not make the invitation to conclude a treaty and install a Resident dependent on him becoming Sultan, but only on the succession dispute being settled, one way or the other. It did not in any way change 'Abdu'llah's position in Perak, nor alter Clarke's judgement of him as the weaker candidate—a judgement based on the belief that he had no following in the country, and on stories that he was an opium-smoker and a degenerate of low moral and mental fibre.[24] One is therefore inclined to doubt that the letter could by itself have been responsible for Clarke's decision to support 'Abdu'llah rather than Ismail, and

[22] 'Abdu'llah to Gov. Straits, 30 Dec. 1873, C. 1111, p. 85; Read, op. cit., pp. 25–26. Read prepared his draft of this letter in English, translated it into Malay and sent it off for 'Abdu'llah's signature. When it arrived back in Singapore it was translated back into English by a Government translator. There are therefore two different versions of what 'Abdu'llah signed—Read's account, based on his original draft, and the Government translation. The language of the final English text is much less precise than the original draft, but the differences do not in retrospect appear important except in the case of the request for a Resident. Read's account records that 'to show their desire to act in conformity with the wishes of the British Government' the Sultan *and Chiefs* would request 'a Resident' to 'assist & advise them to carry out the Government of the Country in such a way as to develop its resources, secure the administration of justice, & the peace & happiness of the people'. The final text, to which only 'Abdu'llah's signature is attached, merely asks for 'a man' to 'show us a good system of government'. The Malay text does not seem to have survived.

[23] Preamble to the Pangkor Treaty, 20 Jan. 1874, Maxwell and Gibson, op. cit., p. 28.

[24] Gov. Straits to Sec. State, 26 Jan. 1874, in CO 809/1, pp. 92–95. To the critical reader the fact that 'Abdu'llah had not had the letter signed by any other chiefs was itself evidence of weakness.

these doubts are reinforced by later evidence, which we shall come to in due course, which suggests that he did not so decide until some time in the first two or three days of the Pangkor meeting.

Clarke and his party, most important of whom was Thomas Braddell, the Attorney-General, left Singapore for Pangkor in the Government steamer *Pluto* on 11 January. With them went H.M.S. *Avon* and the steamer *Luzon,* under charter to the Straits Government and laden with rice for the Larut miners. Whilst they were at sea Macnair, Dunlop and Pickering were busy at Penang, supervising the shipment of food to Larut and arranging for the attendance of the Perak chiefs at the coming meeting. On 13 January they were at Pangkor to meet Clarke and to report that letters of invitation had been sent to the Mantri and Ismail, but that they had no means of reaching 'Abdu'llah and the others, and would have to fetch them themselves. Discussion of the Perak succession question therefore had to be postponed till the 15th, when Dunlop and his companion returned in the steamer *Johore* with 'Abdu'llah and eight other chiefs. In the meantime Clarke applied himself to settling the quarrel between the Ghee Hin and Hai San. The Chinese headmen had been taken to Pangkor in the steamer *Fair Malacca* by Frank Swettenham, then a young man in the Land Office in Province Wellesley, on 13 January.[25] No account seems to have been kept of the negotiations with the Chinese, but the result was the conclusion on 15 January of a short and straightforward agreement in which twenty-six Chinese headmen and mine owners agreed:

1. That both sides should disarm and destroy their stockades.
2. That a Commission of British officials, with two Chinese representatives, should settle all claims to the mines, and that future arrangements in Larut should be controlled by a British Resident.
3. That they should enter into a bond for $50,000 to keep the peace and abide by the provisions of the agreement.[26]

Then came three days of parleying with the Perak chiefs. As late as 7 January Clarke had viewed Ismail as the stronger candidate and had tried to get 'Abdu'llah pensioned off. Now his ideas under-

[25] Report of Macnair and Dunlop, 14 Jan. 1874, C.1111, p. 77–78.
[26] Engagement entered into by the Headmen of the Chinese, 20 Jan. 1874, C.1111, pp. 83–84. Although this engagement was settled on 15 Jan. it was not signed until 20 Jan., partly because few of the pirate row-boats had given themselves up and a warship had to be sent in search of them, and partly because the Sultan of Perak was a party to the engagement, and its signing had to wait until it was decided who that dignitary should be.

went a complete change. He was surprised to find that 'Abdu'llah was an alert and rational being, who was described by Braddell on first meeting as 'more than ordinarily sharp and intelligent'.[27] He discovered also that all the chiefs present except the Mantri seemed prepared to recognize him as Sultan. But although these chiefs included three of the Four—the Bendahara,[28] the Temenggong and the Mantri—and three of the Eight—the Laksamana, the Shahbandar, and the Dato' Sagor—they were not representative of more than part of Perak. Apart from the Mantri they were all chiefs who lived on the lower reaches of the Perak River or near the coast, and who were in some way related to 'Abdu'llah. Neither Ismail nor any of the up-country chiefs who supported him came to the meeting; nor did Yusuf, who was not even invited.[29] Ismail's friend the Mantri was alone in his opposition to 'Abdu'llah, and he was so anxious about his own position in Larut that his efforts on Ismail's behalf were very half-hearted. In September 1873 he had been recognized by Sir Harry Ord as an independent ruler. Clarke completely refused to accept this position.[30] He was

[27] Braddell, 'Report of Proceedings at Pangkor and Larut', CO 809/1, pp. 42–47; Gov. Straits to Sec. State, 26 Jan. 1874, loc. cit., pp. 92–95. A passage in Winstedt, op. cit., p. 98, seems at first reading to assert that Clarke had already met 'Abdu'llah in Singapore. It runs: 'Mr. W. H. Read . . . took 'Abdu'llah to the Governor & induced him to write a letter . . . asking for a Resident . . . This was the opening Sir Andrew had desired.' There are many references in despatches which make it quite clear that Clarke had never met 'Abdu'llah before the Pangkor meeting, and the Governor referred to can only have been Sir Harry Ord.

[28] This was Raja Usman, who had been appointed Bendahara by Ismail at the time of his own election as Sultan. The office of Orang Kaya Besar, the last of the Four, was vacant, so that in effect all the highest ranking commoner chiefs were present at Pangkor.

[29] The letter inviting Ismail to the meeting probably did not reach him in time (Report of Macnair and Dunlop, 14 Jan., C.1111, pp. 77–80), but it is doubtful whether he would have come in any case. The failure to consider Yusuf's claims or to invite him to Pangkor, and Clarke's apparent ignorance of his very existence at this time is one of the most puzzling features of this period. In February 1869 Yusuf wrote to Singapore stating his claim to the throne (Winstedt, op. cit., p. 97), but Gov. Ord always kept the conduct of affairs very much in his own hands and it is possible that when Clarke became Governor none of the surviving officials knew enough to bring the incident to his notice. It is still remarkable that no other Straits official seems to have discovered Yusuf's existence in three years of dealing with Perak Malays. See Cowan, *Swettenham's Perak Journals*, p. 57, n. 65.

[30] Wilkinson (Winstedt, op. cit., p. 98) concludes that since the papers dealing with Ord's recognition of the Mantri were not forwarded to Singapore from Penang till 23 Jan. Clarke was not aware of Ord's action until after the Pangkor meeting. Though he may not have known the details nor the grounds for Ord's decision it is incredible that he should have been ignorant of the fact that some form of recognition had been made, since he had been studying the Larut question and taking every available opinion on the subject since November.

determined to establish in Perak an effective government under the control of a British Resident, and to secure lasting peace and stability it was essential that the authority of that government should extend to Larut.

Clarke's attitude was made clear to the Mantri at a meeting on board *Pluto* on 16 January, when he was given a very uncomfortable time by the Governor and Braddell. The Mantri was told that his incompetence and weakness had been responsible for the trouble in Larut, that he had completely lost the confidence of all the parties involved, and that the British Government was determined to intervene. He was brought to agree to Clarke arbitrating between the Chinese factions, to his allies the Hai San being disarmed, and—after strenuous objections on his part—to the appointment in Larut of a British officer to 'assist and advise' him. He even agreed to 'give his allegiance' to the Sultan who might be preferred by the British Government, but only so long as it was recognized that he held the territory of Larut independently of the Sultan. On this point the Mantri refused to budge, and a ding-dong argument followed in which Braddell took the lead from the British side. The Mantri referred to the ruler of Johore as a precedent for a dependent Malay chief becoming sovereign, and offered to agree to a reduction in the territory he claimed so long as he was recognized as an independent ruler. These claims were declared by Braddell to be 'quite inadmissible'. He counter-attacked with the weapons of the lawyer, saying that 'no Sultan had a right to give away territory in this way, which would amount to actual sovereignty and the founding of a new state'. He added insult to injury by pointing out that though the Mantri was spoken to by his followers as *Tuanku* he was really too lowly a man to be entitled to this title, which rightly belonged only to members of royal families, and the Mantri was forced to admit that he had indeed no right to it, and did not use it on his chop or seal.[31] But

Moreover, Ord's announcement of the act of recognition was in the records of the Legislative Council at Singapore (Legislative Council Proceedings, 9 Sept. 1873) and the Proclamation giving effect to it had been published in the Government Gazette. Braddell's account of the proceedings at Pangkor reads as if Clarke knew of the recognition, but disagreed with it after reading the Mantri's grants from previous Sultans and taking Braddell's advice. The same conclusion can be drawn from Clarke's speech to the Legislative Council in September (Legislative Council Proceedings, 15 Sept. 1874).

[31] In Perak *tuanku* is used for the Sultan, the Raja Muda and the Raja Bendahara. The other *waris negeri* or heirs to the throne are styled *engku*. The Mantri, a commoner chief but one of the Four, should properly have been

he persisted in his claims to sovereignty to the end of the interview, which was closed by Braddell accusing him of wishing to become Sultan of Perak, an ambition which he denied.[32]

On the next afternoon, 17 January, a full meeting of the chiefs was held to settle the question of the succession. The Mantri was by then thoroughly cowed. He had been prevented from bringing his lawyer on board, and when he tried to sit on a chair like 'Abdu'llah he was pushed down on the deck among the commoner chiefs by Macnair. When it came to the point his objections to 'Abdu'llah's appointment were easily brushed aside. None of the others present had any objections, and it was agreed that 'Abdu'l-lah should become Sultan and that Ismail should be pensioned off with the courtesy title Sultan Muda. Then 'Abdu'llah, the Mantri, and the four other senior chiefs were appointed to settle with Clarke and his advisers the form of a treaty embodying these de-cisions, and carrying out the request in 'Abdu'llah's letter for a British Resident to reorganize the government of Perak.

The result of their deliberations was the so-called Pangkor Treaty, signed on 20 January 1874.[33] The provisions of this treaty can for convenience be divided into three sections:

1. A section settling the succession dispute and the status of the various Perak chiefs.
2. A section dealing with the various issues outstanding between Perak and the Straits Settlements Government.
3. Most important, a section providing for the appointment of a British Resident, and ensuring, on paper at least, that the effective control of the country should be in his hands.

The first two sections of the treaty need not detain us long. Those

---

styled *tengku* as his predecessors in office had been. Wilkinson (Winstedt, op. cit., pp. 98–99) seems either to have mis-read Braddell's account, or to have assumed that he was using *tuanku* as a synonym for *tengku*, a fairly frequent practice amongst Europeans at the time. He thought therefore that what Braddell asserted and the Mantri admitted was that he had no right to his proper style of *tengku*. To explain this he was driven to suggest that Braddell knew only Singapore and not Perak Malay (though he had been an official in Penang for many years and managed a sugar estate in Province Wellesley), and that the Mantri meant that he was not a *tengku* in its Singapore meaning, 'the son of a prince' (though this would not prevent him using it on his chop in its Perak sense, and for him its true sense). Where Braddell was wrong was in describing the Mantri as 'the son of a Malay trader', with the implication of low social origin. His father was one of the Sixteen, and a member of the family of the Panglimas of Bukit Gantang (cf. the genealogy in Winstedt, p. 145).

[32] 'Report by Mr. Braddell . . . of the Proceedings at Pangkor', loc. cit.
[33] The text of the treaty is in Maxwell and Gibson, op. cit., pp. 28–30.

articles dealing with the Perak chiefs provided that 'Abdu'llah should be Sultan, that Ismail, 'now acting Sultan', should be pensioned as Sultan Muda, that all the other chiefs should retain their offices, and that the grant given to the Mantri by Sultan Ja'far in 1862 should be confirmed by 'Abdu'llah, thus acknowledging the latter's claim to suzerainty over Larut. There were two articles settling outstanding issues with the Straits Government. One confirmed the cession of the Dindings (the two islands of Greater and Lesser Pangkor) to Britain by the Treaty of 1826, and defined the boundary of this territory to include a strip of land on the mainland. The other extended the southern boundary of Province Wellesley, which had previously been marked by the Krian River, to include the land draining into that River from the south.

The treaty gave the Resident no executive powers, but it stipulated that his advice 'must be asked and acted upon on all questions other than those touching Malay Religion and Custom'. Since it was laid down that all revenues were to be collected and all appointments made only in the name of the Sultan, all the chiefs being provided for by a civil list and ceasing to collect their own taxes, and since it was expressly provided that 'the collection and control of all Revenues and the general administration of the country be regulated under the advice of these Residents', the treaty as it stood gave the Resident effective control of the country. At the same time an Assistant Resident was attached to the Mantri, now styled 'Governor of Larut', with the same right of giving advice and insisting that it was acted upon. This Assistant Resident was however subordinate to the Resident and under his general control. Whilst therefore the treaty in form confirmed to the Mantri the status which he had enjoyed since 1862 it in fact ensured that Larut would be administered as part of Perak.[34] At the same time the presence of the Assistant Resident guaranteed that the special problems of Larut and its Chinese mining population would receive special treatment. The treaty itself provided for the appointment of a special commission of British officers to

[34] The Mantri's income was now to be fixed by the Perak civil list, so that he could no longer appropriate the whole of the revenues of Larut to his own personal ends, and any surplus over and above the needs of the government established there could be applied to the administration of the rest of Perak. The Mantri undertook in the treaty to meet the expenses incurred by the Straits Government in settling Larut, and the cost of the Pangkor conference arrangements.

settle questions of compensation and to arbitrate on all disputes.[35] As soon as it was signed Clarke appointed Captain Speedy, who was already on the spot and known to the Mantri and the Chinese, as Assistant Resident, so that there would be no relapse into lawlessness and no unnecessary delay in getting the mines working again.

This ended the proceedings at Pangkor, and stopping only to write to Ismail asking him to surrender the Perak regalia to 'Abdu'llah Sir Andrew Clarke departed for Singapore. He arrived there on 23 January, to compose a series of despatches defending his actions to the Secretary of State, and to enjoy the plaudits of the Singapore merchants and the local Press. There were one or two critics of the deposition of Ismail and the appointment of a permanent Resident, both among the officials and the merchants, but for the moment these warning voices were drowned in the general acclamation. The *Pinang Gazette* praised the Governor for rescuing Perak from 'one vast blood bath', and the Singapore Chamber of Commerce, after expressing its entire approval, called for him to 'continue to pursue the just, firm and conciliatory policy thus inaugurated, until the whole of the so-called independent States of the Peninsula shall be brought under similar control'.[36]

Clarke needed no urging: before he had received this request he had already transferred his attention to Selangor. Tengku Zia'u'd-din had with the help of his Pahang allies brought the war there to a successful conclusion, and driven his main enemies out of the state. But though he and Yap Ah Loy had by the beginning of 1874 begun to restore the prosperity of the Klang River and its tin mines, so that trade was reviving, the area was not yet at rest. The Sultan's territory around Langat was still outside Zia'u'd-din's jurisdiction, and many bad characters who lived by piracy and free-booting found shelter there. Piracy off Selangor began to reach ugly proportions. There was an attack on Cape Rachado lighthouse in January, and it became difficult to relieve the light-vessel on the North Sands. Zia'u'd-din could do little about all this, for the leaders concerned were sheltered by the Sultan, and many of the piracies were generally understood to be organized by the Sultan's sons.

---

[35] Dunlop, Swettenham and Pickering were appointed Commissioners on 20 Jan. and together with one Hai San and one Ghee Hin Chinese began the work of settling Larut at once (Clarke to Dunlop and others, 20 Jan. 1874, C.1111, p. 84).

[36] *Pinang Gazette,* 29 Jan. 1874; C.1111, p. 108.

Early in February Clarke determined to take advantage of the presence in the Straits of a large naval squadron led by the Admiral in command of the China station to make a demonstration. An opportunity lay ready to his hand. On the night of 16 November the previous year a Malacca trading boat returning from Langat had been pirated off the Jugra River, a tidal creek which joined the Langat River near the spot where the Sultan was then living. The vessel was looted and most of the crew and the three Chinese passengers were killed. But one man lived to tell the tale; in the dark he managed to slip over the side unnoticed, and to hang on to the rudder till all was over. Then he swam ashore and made his way to Malacca. Later nine Selangor Malays were identified by him there as having taken part in the piracy, and arrested. It was Clarke's intention to take these men to Langat for trial. He hoped with the backing of the Admiral's squadron to force the Sultan to order their execution, and to consent to the imprisonment of those chiefs who could be shown to be implicated, and to the destruction of the stockades on the Langat River from which the pirates came.[37]

Clarke left Singapore in *Pluto* on 5 February, and on the next day joined forces with the Admiral and six warships at the North Sands light-vessel. On the 7th he went up-river to the Sultan's village, taking three of the small warships with him and picking up Tengku Zia'u'd-din on the way. Sultan 'Abdu'l-Samad was not at first very happy to see them. He had been told by Zia'u'd-din's enemies that if he went aboard *Pluto* he would be seized and carried off to Singapore, and the sight of the three warships did nothing to allay his fears. So Clarke's first meeting with the Sultan was devoted to reassuring him and effecting a reconciliation between him and his Viceroy. After this the negotiations went forward smoothly. 'Abdu'l-Samad readily agreed to the destruction of the offending stockades. He appointed Zia'u'd-din and three other chiefs to try those accused of piracy in his name, and listened respectfully to a lecture on the enormity of the crime of dislocating the light-house system in the Straits.[38] As soon as he had reached

[37] *Singapore Daily Times*, 20 Jan. 1874; Clarke to Vice-Adm. Shadwell, and attached papers, 1 Feb. 1874, C.1111, pp. 92–105, CO 809/1, pp. 114–28.
[38] It was perhaps at this point that the old Sultan made his celebrated interjection, 'Piracy is the affair of the boys, my sons. I have nothing to do with it' (Braddell, 'Continuation of Report . . .'). There are many renderings of this *bon mot*, but all have the sense of piracy as 'boys' play', a trivial affair which 'Abdu'l-Samad only dealt with to humour the Governor.

agreement on these points Clarke himself left to return to Singapore. Before his departure he appointed Macnair and J. G. Davidson, the Singapore lawyer and old supporter of Zia'u'd-din, to serve as British representatives at the trial. The case turned almost entirely on the evidence of the sole survivor of the piracy, but on his identification the court found the unlucky nine guilty and condemned them to death.[39] As formal acknowledgement of his responsibility for the trial the Sultan supplied the *keris* for their execution, and as a more concrete expression of his regret that his sons, 'the boys', had in their games offended the British Government he provided $5,000 in tin to compensate the owners of the plundered vessel and the dependents of the victims.[40]

A recent paper which discusses this incident asserts that during the negotiations 'Abdu'l-Samad 'agreed to sign a treaty similar to the Pangkor Treaty recently signed by the Sultan of Perak', and greeted with pleasure a proposal to install a British Resident in Selangor.[41] There is no confirmation of this in any of the official papers, and no such treaty was ever signed, but it is quite possible that Clarke discussed the appointment of a Resident with the Sultan in general terms. A little later, in a despatch dated 27 June, he spoke of:

... that more active supervision which, sooner or later, must be exercised over them [the Sultan and Chiefs of Selangor], being not alone requisite to secure and consolidate what has been already accomplished, but also imperatively necessary to guard against a relapse into old customs and practices.[42]

But in June he was still confining British activity in Selangor to the cultivation of personal friendship with 'Abdu'l-Samad and

---

[39] Months later, when he came to live at Langat, Swettenham discovered that the accused men, though they had undoubtedly indulged in piracy and deserved their punishment on general grounds, were quite innocent of the particular offence for which they were tried. The survivor's evidence of identification was unshakable but from the rudder on a dark night he can hardly have had a very clear view of what was happening in the boat (Swettenham, op. cit. 184).

[40] Braddell, 'Continuation of Report . . ., Salangore, 18 Feb. 1874'; Gov. Straits to Sec. State, 24 Feb.; Report of Commissioners Macnair and Davidson; all printed in C.1111, pp. 181–99.

[41] Gullick, J. M., 'A Careless, Heathen Philosopher?', *JRASMB*, xxvi, pt. 1, (1953), p. 94. Middlebrooke's 'Yap Ah Loy' (loc. cit.) deals briefly and inaccurately with the subject, saying that Sir Andrew Clarke 'sent two Commissioners with a naval contingent to Langat to enquire into the case' (*JRASMB* xxiv, pt. 2 (1951), p. 84).

[42] Gov. Straits to Sec. State, 27 June 1874, C.1111, p. 240.

Zia'u'ddin, in the hope that this would lead to a spontaneous request from them for the appointment of a Resident.

To the maliciously inclined observer of British policy it must be a source of suspicion that, as soon as a decision to embark on some form of political intervention in Malaya had been taken in Singapore, opportunities and pretexts for that intervention came so quickly and conveniently to hand. First 'Abdu'llah's letter of 30 December enabled the proceedings at Pangkor to be represented as the response to a plea for help. Then just at the moment when a large naval force was available Selangor men chose to attack the lighthouse on Cape Rachado, and nine Selangor Malays got themselves arrested as pirates in Malacca. Now this pattern of events was repeated again. Sir Andrew Clarke had hardly had time to return to Singapore and make good some of the administrative arrears which had accumulated in his absence when a situation arose in Sungai Ujong which led to his intervention there, and brought a pledge of British support for another Malay chief engaged in a local dispute.

The main trouble in the area behind Malacca was as always the stoppage of traffic on the Linggi River. Basically this arose from the undefined nature of the boundaries between the states through which the Linggi and its tributaries ran, and the unsettled state of their politics. The Linggi River formed (and still forms) the western boundary of the settlement of Malacca. In the 1870's the river was navigable for large boats for some six miles from the sea to Simpang Linggi, and its western bank belonged to Lukut, then part of Selangor. At Simpang Linggi the river forks, one branch running down to the main stream from Rembau in the east, the other coming from Sungai Ujong in the north. Sungai Rembau, the eastern branch, was too shallow for any but very small boats, but the northern branch, which retained the name Linggi, remained navigable for larger craft for another seven miles, after which smaller boats were needed to reach the mining centre of Rasah in Sungai Ujong.[43]

[43] The best source for conditions in the area at this time is 'Second Continuation of Report on Proceedings of Government relating to the Native States . . . Rumbowe and Sungie Ujong', C.1320, pp. 11–36, which contains all the available material in the Straits Records, collected and arranged by Thomas Braddell. Gullick, J. M., 'Sungei Ujong', *JRASMB*, xxii, pt. 2 (1949), is also of use.

This twenty miles of the lower Linggi was all things to all men. To the Chinese tin miners, the merchants of Malacca, and the Straits Government it was a public highway, and their interest was to keep it free. To the Malay chiefs of Sungai Ujong, of Rembau and of Linggi, a small Bugis enclave under the Dato' Muda of Linggi who lived at Pengkalan Durian, the spot where the river became too shallow for large craft, it was a source of revenue. To Tengku Zia'u'd-din and the Selangor chiefs it was important as a back-door into Selangor by way of Labu or the headwaters of the Langat River—this way Raja Mahdi had slipped back into the state from his exile in Johore. Rembau sought always to push its territory right up to the Linggi so as to obtain a share of the revenue from tolls and dues levied on passing traffic. Sungai Ujong and the Dato' Muda of Linggi, who generally managed to share the profits between them without serious friction, attempted to defeat these pretensions. Tengku Zia'u'd-din, and from the other side Raja Mahdi and his allies, tried by standing in with one party or the other to exert what control they could over the area.[44]

This complex situation was further complicated during Sir Andrew Clarke's period as Governor by internal disunity and strife in both Sungai Ujong and Rembau. We have already mentioned the Dato' Klana and the Dato' Bandar of Sungai Ujong, the 'Land Lord' and the 'Water Lord', two rivals who, though the Dato' Klana was supposed to be 'head of state', were in fact both independent rulers within the same state. Since Sir Harry Ord had managed to bring Zia'u'd-din and the old Dato' Klana to a compromise settlement of the Simpang affair the old man had died. His successor, Dato' Klana Sayid Rahman ('Abdu'r-Rahman) was a young man, the son of an Arab from Atjeh who had married the sister of a previous Dato' Klana. He was worldly-wise and ambitious, a good diplomatist but a poor fighter, who had lived long in Malacca, where he had considerable landed property and was on good terms with the British authorities. Shortly before he became Dato' Klana he had ordered a large consignment of arms, including two field-guns, from England, with the idea of getting control of the whole area. He also entered into a friendly understanding with Zia'u'd-din. So he was not likely to get on

[44] As recently as 1872 Zia'u'd-din had tried to secure control of the lower course of the Linggi at Simpang Linggi through his protégé the Dato' Perba of Rembau, and since this threatened to close the river to free trade Sir Harry Ord had been forced to intervene (see p. 109 above).

smoothly with the irascible Dato' Bandar, who supported Mahdi in the Selangor war and was prepared to oppose with force any attempt on the part of the Klana to assert his supremacy in Sungai Ujong.

At first however trouble came not from Sungai Ujong but from Rembau, where a disputed succession followed the death of the Penghulu of Rembau at the end of 1872. The claimants, Haji Mustapha and Haji Sahil, styled Dato' Perba, were each declared elected by their own supporters. Fighting broke out between them, in the course of which both sides seized positions on the lower Linggi and interfered with trade. Zia'u'd-din supported the Dato' Perba, and no doubt largely because of this the Singapore Government also looked on his candidature with some favour. The Klana at first inclined towards Haji Mustapha, since he feared that if he were successful the Dato' Perba in concert with Zia'u'd-din would again try to get possession of Simpang. But he had his own relations with Zia'u'd-din and the British Government to consider. The friendship of both was for geographical reasons essential to him, for both controlled the coast, and the Singapore authorities had not yet released his shipments of arms from London. So after a visit to Singapore early in July 1873 he agreed to transfer his support to the Dato' Perba on condition that an understanding was reached between Zia'u'd-din, the Dato' Perba and himself, if necessary through the good offices of the Straits Government, as to their respective rights on the river.

Affairs remained substantially in this state until after the Pangkor agreement, though it is clear from the correspondence that the Lieutenant-Governor of Malacca, Captain E. M. Shaw, R.N., did not share the Singapore Government's warmth for the Dato' Perba, whose Sumatran supporters were continually stopping trade on the river when the traders refused to pay their demands for tolls. On 17 December 1873 Captain Shaw forwarded to Singapore a letter from the Dato' Perba and seventeen minor chiefs of Rembau announcing the final defeat and flight of Haji Mustapha, and calling on the Governor to fulfil his promise to arbitrate between them and Sungai Ujong as to their claim to Simpang and many other stockades on the Linggi. If he did not, they said, there would be disturbances which would inevitably affect Malacca.[45] By February the news of the Government's intervention in Perak

[45] 'Second Continuation of Report . . .', loc. cit., p. 34.

and Selangor seems to have brought the Linggi chiefs to an amenable frame of mind, and the Lieutenant-Governor of Malacca and
some of the more important merchants of the town were able to
get the Klana, the Dato' Muda of Linggi and Dato' Perba to come
to a conference there. At about the same time Clarke sent letters
to these three and to the Dato' Bandar and Haji Mustapha inviting them to come to Singapore and put their cases to him. A
provisional settlement involving the removal of all stockades and
the amicable collection and distribution of all revenue from the
river was reached at Malacca, and Clarke began to envisage the
recognition of the Dato' Perba as the ruler of Rembau in return
for a general agreement guaranteeing the freedom of trade on the
river.[46] But only the Dato' Muda and the Klana came to Singapore, the other chiefs merely sending agents. Whilst they were in
Singapore news arrived on 14 April that despite the provisional
agreement reached at Malacca Rembau men were again stopping
boats on the Linggi at a stockade at Bukit Tiga.[47] The result of
this news was a strong letter from Clarke calling on Dato' Perba
to clear the river, and a perceptible softening of the Governor's
attitude towards the Klana, who up till then had been regarded
with some suspicion in Singapore.

On 21 April an agreement was concluded with the Dato' Klana
to which the Dato' Muda of Linggi was also a party.[48] This agreement combined features of both the Pangkor engagement and the
agreement with the Larut Chinese. On the one hand the British
Government was committed by it to support the authority of the
Dato' Klana, both in Sungai Ujong and on the Linggi River. On
the other the Klana entered into a bond for $50,000 to use the
arms and ammunition which were now delivered to him only for
legitimate purposes. This in the context of the agreement meant
to keep the river open to traders, to levy only reasonable tolls, to
maintain order and prevent illegal toll-collecting, and generally to
act as the policeman of the area to the satisfaction of the Straits
Government. There was no provision for the appointment of a

---

[46] Gov. Straits to Sec. State, 8 May 1874, in CO 273/75.
[47] It was alleged by the protagonists of Dato' Perba that the occupants of
this stockade were Sumatrans whom he had enlisted during his war with Haji
Mustapha, and who now refused to obey him. When the stockade was later
searched by the Klana and the Malacca police however letters were found which
seemed to show that Dato' Perba was still in control of the occupants. Gov.
Straits to Sec. State, 8 May, 1874, CO 273/75; below, p. 197.
[48] Text in Maxwell and Gibson, op. cit., pp. 37-8.

Resident, but it was agreed that the disputed part of the river, from the fork at Simpang to Permatang Pasir just below the Dato' Muda's residence, should be 'placed under the control, order and direction of the British Government'. The significant passage of the treaty was that which promised that

> . . . so long as the conditions of this obligation are faithfully kept by the said Chief [the Klana] and his officers, the moral *and material* guarantee and protection of the British Government will be accorded to them to secure the independence, peace and prosperity of the territory of Sungei Ujong.[49]

The Klana thus gained everything and gave up almost nothing in return. 'Fair and reasonable duties' on the river would give him an ample revenue if he prevented others from drawing off their share by representing them as 'illegal toll collectors'. In this connexion his surrender of the lower part of the river to British control was no sacrifice at all, for he could collect his own revenue just as well further upstream, and the British authorities would themselves prevent interlopers from establishing stockades on the disputed stretch and save him the trouble.

Clarke from his point of view was supporting the Klana as the legitimate authority in the area, in the hope that he would be able to assert his control and establish order. In a sense his view of the Klana's position was correct, for in addition to being the nominal head of Sungai Ujong the Klana was also the senior of the four Undang or law-givers of the Menankabau Confederacy. But as such he was only the spokesman of a body whose decisions needed by custom to be unanimous, and who were (again in theory) inferior to a non-existent Yang di-Pertuan Besar—elected head of a Confederation which had long ago fallen apart.[50] In fact the Dato' Klana was only one of several independent chiefs each of whom had established their own political and territorial rights on the Linggi. The treaty now made the Klana judge of these rights, and ensured that when the Dato' Bandar protested against this by force, as he would, then unless the Klana was unusually maladroit in presenting his case, the Straits Government would intervene to suppress him. And in the course of time so they did.

On 30 April Clarke followed the Klana back to Linggi, sending

---

[49] Ibid. Author's italics.
[50] See Winstedt, 'Negri Sembilan', *JRASMB*, xii, pt. 3 (1934), pp. 89 et seq.; Gullick, op. cit., *passim*, especially pp. 30–31.

ahead of him letters calling on the Dato' Perba and Haji Musta-pha to meet him at Simpang Linggi on 2 May. He travelled in H.M.S. *Charybdis*, and was joined at Malacca by H.M.S. *Avon*. At the meeting place neither of the Rembau chiefs appeared, but letters were received from the Dato' Perba pleading illness for his absence and disclaiming responsibility for the stoppage of trade on the river. This was variously attributed to Sumatrans whom he had employed against Haji Mustapha and who now refused to obey him, to followers of Mustapha, and to a son of the Dato' Bandar. At the same time a report came in that a party of Malacca police on their way up-river with a letter to the Dato' Bandar had been attacked and robbed at a stockade near Perma-tang Pasir. The Klana accepted responsibility for keeping the river open, but he asked for help in destroying the stockades at Bukit Tiga. So on 4 May the boats of *Avon* and *Charybdis* went up-river, and the stockades, which were empty, were burnt down, but not before letters were discovered in one of them from the Dato' Perba which indicated that the occupants had in fact been under his orders. Two days later seven cargo boats laden with tin valued at $50,000 and bound for Malacca came down the river.[51]

After the destruction of the Linggi stockades Clarke returned to Singapore, leaving the Klana to cope with affairs on the river, and if possible to flush Rajas Mahdi and Mahmud from Sungai Ujong, where they were said to be hiding with the Dato' Bandar. A lull now ensued in Malaya, whilst the various chiefs of the west coast digested the news of the events of the preceding weeks and decided on their course of action, and Clarke waited to see what reaction his despatches would bring from the Colonial Office. This is therefore a convenient place to observe the way in which the news of the Pangkor engagement and the events in Selangor and Sungai Ujong were received in London.

Clarke's telegram announcing the conclusion of the Pangkor engagement was answered within three days by one from London telling him not to proceed with the appointment of Residents in Perak until the arrival of more detailed information had given the Colonial Office an opportunity of passing judgement.[52] Then there

[51] Gov. Straits to Sec. State, 8 May 1874, CO 273/75; 'Second Continuation of Report . . .', loc. cit., pp. 35–36.
[52] Gov. Straits to Sec. State, 23 Jan. 1874; Sec. State to Gov. Straits, 27 Jan. 1874; in CO 273/75.

was silence for nearly four months. A series of despatches from Singapore in January and February, one of them a small book filling with its enclosures some ninety foolscap pages of print,[53] produced in answer only a short despatch again postponing any expression of opinion and warning the Governor that Captain Speedy must expect no compensation if it was decided to cancel his appointment.[54] In the meantime news reached the Colony of a general election and a change of government in Britain.

The Liberal Government had been in low water since the rejection of its Irish University Bill in March 1873. We have already mentioned Gladstone's resignation and his resumption of office when Disraeli refused to form a minority government. The reconstruction of his cabinet in August sustained Gladstone for a time, but by-elections continued to go against the government, and early in 1874, as Disraeli observed in the speech in which he likened the Ministers to exhausted volcanoes, 'their paroxysms ended in prostration'. On 24 January, during the Christmas recess, the Prime Minister dissolved Parliament and went to the country. On the same day that Clarke's telegram announcing the Pangkor settlement arrived at the Colonial Office Disraeli, taken by surprise by the dissolution, in two 'miserable' hotel rooms, without secretary, paper or books, was drafting his election manifesto.[55] In the form in which it appeared on 26 January it was a call to defend civil liberty and religious freedom in Britain, not by the 'incessant and harassing legislation' of the Liberals, which caused only dissension and weakness, but by expending 'a little more energy in our foreign policy, and a little less in our domestic legislation', and upholding 'the strength and stability of England'. It ended with a plea to the electors to return him to power 'to resist every proposal which may impair that strength and to support by every means her Imperial sway'.[56] Despite a programme which included a proposal to abolish income tax the Liberals were defeated at the polls, and in February Disraeli took office at the head of a Con-

[53] Gov. Straits to Sec. State, 26 Jan. (CO 809/1, pp. 92–95; C.1111, pp. 85–86); 24 Feb. (re Perak) (C.1111, pp. 108–94); 24 Feb. (re Selangor) (C.1111, p. 181).
[54] Sec. State to Gov. Straits, 6 Mar. 1874, C.1111, p. 88.
[55] Moneypenny and Buckle, Life of Disraeli, vol. v, pp. 272–3.
[56] 'Address to the electors of the County of Buckingham', The Times, 26 Jan. 1874.

servative Government. The Earl of Carnarvon,[57] who had been Colonial Secretary in the previous Conservative administration, returned to the Colonial Office, with J. Lowther[58] as his Parliamentary Under-Secretary.

The Conservative victory ushered into power an administration now associated by most Englishmen with the acquisition of the Suez Canal shares, the Empress of India Act, 'jingoism', and a strong Imperialist policy, just as its Liberal predecessor has become known as a government of 'Little Englanders'. The antithesis was a real one, especially in the field of foreign affairs. But where the Empire was concerned it was not so sharp as ideological prejudices have represented. On the one hand there were few prominent Liberals who desired the dismemberment of the Empire, and some like W. E. Forster who associated themselves with those schemes of confederation with the colonies of settlement of which Carnarvon was the leading Conservative apostle. On the other even Disraeli himself was far from advocating a general acquisition of territory for its own sake, and many Conservatives like Lowther were less inclined to accept annexation as a remedy for trouble on the Imperial frontiers than Knatchbull-Hugessen, Lowther's predecessor at the Colonial Office, had been.

It would be wrong therefore to imagine that the new Conservative Government was eager to reverse the policy of its predecessors on the colonial issues which it inherited from them. In the case of the Gold Coast there was small incentive for it to do so.

[57] Henry Howard Molyneux Herbert (1831–1890), 4th Earl of Carnarvon, was a widely read man of able and independent mind, who took a First at Oxford. He had travelled widely, and from the beginning of his political career (1854) was interested in foreign and imperial affairs. He was concerned to preserve and tighten the bond with the colonies, but at the same time to hold the balance between the colonists and the native races of the Empire. He was successful in securing the Confederation of Canada (1867), but failed to achieve the same result in South Africa, and had no success as Lord Lieutenant of Ireland (1885). He was keenly interested in problems of Imperial defence, and was Chairman of the Committee on Colonial Defence, 1879–82. Ensor (*England, 1870–1914*, p. 32) characterizes Carnarvon as 'Brilliant but erratic'. He was often at issue with his fellow ministers, and did not hesitate to vote against his party in the House of Lords on occasion. As result of these differences he twice resigned from office, in 1867 and 1878. See *DNB*, and Hardinge, Sir A., *Life of the 4th Earl of Carnarvon*, 3 vols., (1925).

[58] James Lowther (1840–1904) was a political nonentity who owed his place to Disraeli's fear that if left unfettered he would combine with other backwoodsmen to make 'a Tory cave' (Disraeli to Lady Bradford, 27 Feb. 1874 quoted Moneypenny and Buckle, op. cit., vol v, pp. 295–6). He lost his seat in 1880 and did not regain it till 1886. In this second period in Parliament he made a reputation as 'a rare survival of old toryism'. He was a great racing man and a steward of the Jockey Club (*DNB*, 2nd Supplement, pp. 482–4).

Under Sir Garnet Wolseley the Ashanti campaign was a success purchased at a very moderate cost, and Disraeli was able to announce the capture of Kumasi at the end of February at the same time as the names of his government, so that the one gained some reflected glory from the other. The settlement which followed the war was on Gladstonian lines. A moderate treaty, the draft of which had been prepared for Wolseley by the Liberal Government, was accepted by Carnarvon; the Ashanti military confederacy was left untouched, and no attempt was made to press home the temporary advantage and to retain political control at Kumasi. The ill-defined area under British influence around the coastal forts was indeed annexed as the Gold Coast Colony, but with great reluctance and in default of any acceptable alternative.[59]

The same caution may been seen in Carnarvon's attitude to Fiji. Almost his first official action as Secretary of State was to despatch a telegram to the Commissioners appointed by the Gladstone ministry forbidding any precipitate attempt at intervention or the declaration of a Protectorate.[60] The Fijian chiefs' offer of unconditional cession was in the end accepted, and the islands were proclaimed a British colony in October 1874. But it is clear that Carnarvon's decision was taken not because of the strategic importance of the islands, nor because of the eagerness of the Australian colonies, but as a result of a feeling of moral responsibility. The troubles of the islands were caused largely by their British traders and settlers, and Carnarvon thought it as much the duty of the British Government to protect the Fijians against the excesses of the settlers as to respond to the demands of the latter for organized government.

English settlers—English capital—English crime—wanted an English Government.[61]

These were political decisions, taken in the case of Fiji at least, in opposition to the views of Herbert, the Permanent Under-Secretary at the Colonial Office, who opposed them on financial

[59] See Lowther's minute, 20 Apr. 1874: 'Complete annexation or total abandonment are I fear the only alternatives. The former is too ghastly a scheme to contemplate, the latter too charming to be capable of execution.' CO 96/114, quoted Ward, *History of the Gold Coast*, p. 257.
[60] Drus, E., 'The Colonial Office and the annexation of Fiji', *TRHS*, 4th Series, vol. xxxii (1950), p. 105.
[61] Memo. by Carnarvon, quoted Drus, op. cit., p. 107.

grounds. But they were not part of any general scheme for colonial aggrandizement, and would probably have been forced on the Liberals themselves had they remained in office.

Disraeli undoubtedly approved of these decisions, but his hand is not particularly obvious in the making of them. His election manifesto had contained an attack on the Anglo-Dutch convention of 1871 as a surrender of British influence in North Sumatra which prejudiced the freedom of the route through the Straits of Malacca. It seems to have been an electoral squib which fizzled out when the Conservatives were exposed to the sobering influence of office. Disraeli himself did nothing to raise the subject again. As soon as the task of forming his government was over the physically exhausted Prime Minister was involved in the popular ferment over the Bishops' Public Worship Regulation Bill, aimed at the Ritualist element in the Anglican Church. This seemed at one time likely to split the Government, and Disraeli was fully occupied by it until the end of August.[62] He had neither time or energy to intervene in the business of the Colonial Office, so that Carnarvon was left to deal with Clarke's despatches as the advice of his permanent staff and his own inclinations suggested. Carnarvon's own brand of 'Imperialism' was directed more to the retention and consolidation of the colonies of settlement than to the extension of what a later generation has styled 'the dependent Empire'. He seems to have had none of Dilke's early enthusiasm for India and the eastern colonies as 'a nursery of our statesmen and warriors'.[63] He had taken the lead in the Confederation of Canada, and was soon to come to grief attempting to force a similar measure on South Africa. But in Malaya, as in Fiji and West Africa, he was prepared to be cautious, to listen to his departmental staff, and to give due weight to the opinions of the men on the spot, before making up his own mind.

When Clarke's first reports on the Pangkor settlement began to come in Carnarvon, like Herbert and his officials, was encouraging but non-committal. Official minutes opined that Sir Andrew had met with success in his bid to deal with 'anarchy and piracy', but sounded a note of warning on the subject of the proposed Residents. 'The questions raised are very important and it is essential

[62] Moneypenny and Buckle, op. cit., vol. v, pp. 313–31.
[63] Dilke, Charles, *Greater Britain* (1st ed., 1868), *passim*.

that we should not make a false move at starting.'[64] Until more information arrived they could take no decisions, and they confined themselves in answer to expressing a hope 'that without unduly compromising H.M.'s Government in the internal affairs of these states they [Clarke's measures] may have the effect of allaying disorders and promoting peaceful trade'.[65]

On 30 March Clarke's ninety-page explanation of his policy was received in London.[66] Ostensibly this was the result of his instructions to enquire and report on affairs in the Malay States. In fact it was a justification of actions which exceeded those instructions, and was confined solely to events in Perak. The main lines of the Pangkor settlement and of the events which led up to it have already been discussed, so that we need do no more here than indicate briefly the extent to which these actions contravened Clarke's instructions. The main tenor of these, it will be remembered, was to direct the Government to ascertain 'the actual state of affairs in each state', and to report on steps which might be taken to restore order and encourage trade, including the appointment of Residents.[67] Of course any action at all was technically a breach of instructions which asked merely for enquiry and report. But in fact there were two counts on which Sir Andrew had laid himself open to reprimand and disavowal:

1. He had initiated negotiations and signed a treaty with a Malay State without asking for or receiving instructions. This was not merely exceeding his orders, but was a breach of standing instructions laid down at the time of Ord's abortive Kedah Treaty (1868).

2. He had appointed an Assistant Resident (Speedy) and installed him in Larut without instructions.

Clarke's justification was briefly this. He had been forced to arbitrate in the dispute between the Larut Chinese to preserve the security of British territory and to stop piracy. Such arbitration was not 'intervention', and had always been approved of in the case of former Governors. Since Larut was part of Perak arbitration

[64] Minute by Cox dated 3 Mar. 1874, in CO 273/75. Herbert agreed.
[65] Sec. State to Gov. Straits, 6 Mar. 1874, C.1111, p. 88. A phrase expressing the opinion that Clarke's measures had been 'in the right direction' was cut out of the draft by Carnarvon (Minute of 6 Mar.).
[66] Gov. Straits to Sec. State, 24 Feb. 1874, and enclosures, C.1111, pp. 108–194.
[67] Sec. State to Gov. Straits, 20 Sept. 1873, in CO 273/67. See above, p. 175

in Larut was useless without a settlement of the dispute among the Perak Malays at the same time. So he had settled this too, and this again was merely a matter of arbitration. But neither settlement was of the slightest use without a guarantee that there would be no relapse as soon as his influence was withdrawn. It had therefore been necessary to embody them in formal documents such as the Chinese bond and the Pangkor engagement, and to provide for the residence of British officers to supervise their execution. In the case of Larut, where both sides faced each other with arms in their hands, the immediate appointment of Speedy was necessary to prevent a fresh outbreak of fighting, enforce general disarmament, and provide visible evidence that after so many false starts the Straits Government was at last in earnest.[68] In conclusion Clarke excused himself by saying that what he had done had not irretrievably committed the British Government, at the same time making it clear that in his view it was not morally possible for them to repudiate him:

I trust Your Lordship will understand that in so giving my assent I have in no way bound Her Majesty's Government to any particular course, and that it is perfectly possible now to withdraw from the position I have temporarily assumed. But . . . the time has arrived when as a nation, we shall be neglecting a great and paramount duty if we any longer delay that intervention which the causes of civilization and good order now so loudly demand.[69]

This was the sort of *fait accompli* with which the Colonial Office officials were familiar in the days before the telegraph. But it caused them no dismay now, partly because Clarke had merely put into practice what they had been turning over in their own

[68] Gov. Straits to Sec. State, 26 Jan. 1874, loc. cit., and 24 Feb. 1874, loc. cit. A private letter, Clarke to Childers, Jan. 1874, quoted Vetch, op. cit., p. 154, comes nearer the truth. After admitting that he had gone beyond his instructions Clarke wrote: 'The C.O. may say that I might have submitted my scheme to them for their approval before putting it into force, but the only chance of success I had was to do what I did rapidly, so that not a soul knew my plans until I had almost pulled them through. The Chinese were moving and had no idea who was moving them. I had got hold of the heads of both parties and neither knew that I knew the other. I sent a steamer for the Malay chiefs telling them to come and see me at the Dindings, giving them no time to hesitate, nor telling them what I wanted them for, nor affording them time to send for their lawyers . . . I was assured I could not get them together under six weeks or two months. I collected them in a week, & they were without their lawyers. Only one, the Mantri of Larut, had one; but as none of the others had, I would not assent to his putting in an appearance.'

[69] Gov. Straits, 24 Feb., loc. cit.

minds for some time, partly because they had already forbidden the appointment of Residents until further orders. They now looked forward to a long period of departmental discussion, intending no doubt to watch how things went in Larut before they came to a decision. Among themselves they had nothing but praise for Clarke's achievements, and even looked forward to the appointment of a British Resident in Selangor.[70] But they knew from much sad experience elsewhere that all might not go as well as Clarke hoped. 'I do not see', wrote Cox, 'why it is not to work well. At the same time we must not keep out of sight that for some unforeseen cause we may possibly be called upon to take steps to prevent some attempted violation of the Agreement, or to enforce an adherence to some of its provisions.'[71] So they refused to take a decision on the general question of Residents, or to express their approval officially, and asked again for more information, especially on developments in Selangor.[72] Carnarvon did not interfere.

In the middle of May however the Secretary of State was compelled to take a definite stand when a motion calling for correspondence, which was in effect a motion of censure, was moved in the House of Lords. Lord Stanley of Alderley, whose Malayan connexions we have already mentioned, introduced the motion, and called on the Government not to approve Clarke's policy in Malaya. The result of his arbitration in Perak had been to impose two British officials as the virtual rulers of the country. If persisted in this policy must inevitably lead to the invasion and conquest of the whole Peninsula—it would turn out to be another Ashanti. He deplored the morality of the Straits Press and the local government, which advocated such a policy for Britain at the same time as it condemned the Dutch for adopting similar measures in Atjeh. Instead of Residents with wide but undefined powers he suggested the appointment of Consuls with if necessary some magisterial functions; they should be selected not from the ranks of the local officials but from the Consular Service, and be responsible to the

---

[70] Minutes by Cox (6 Apr.) and Herbert (2 May) in CO 273/75.
[71] Ibid.
[72] On 4 May, in answer to a private member's question, Lowther announced in the House of Commons that the Government 'were awaiting further information' (*Hansard*, 3rd Series, vol. ccxviii, p. 1588). Kimberley was more generous. In April he wrote to Clarke: ' . . . as far as I was able to judge from your telegraphic despatches, which I received before I left office, I anticipated that I should have approved generally the course you had taken' (quoted Vetch, op. cit., pp. 155-6).

Foreign Office. This part of Stanley's speech might have come from the radical wing of the Liberal party rather than from a peer with Conservative inclinations who sat on the cross-benches of the House of Lords. It was sensible, restrained and in many ways far-sighted. But it was spoilt by an irresponsible attack on the character and competence of some of the Straits officials, and by accusations of corruption and misgovernment dating back to 1867. This made it easy for Carnarvon to avoid any detailed discussion of policy, and supported by Kimberley, who had been the responsible minister, he devoted himself chiefly to a rebuttal of criticisms of the Straits Settlements administration under Sir Harry Ord. Both men however felt it necessary to express their entire confidence in Clarke, and their belief that some form of intervention was necessary.[73]

After this debate it was not possible to procrastinate any longer, and a despatch expressing formal approval of the Larut and Pangkor settlement was sent off on 29 May.[74] Writing privately to Clarke Carnarvon warned him against going too fast or too far in the west-coast states:

> I feel that I may count upon you, for the great interests which are at stake in the matter, and which would be easily jeopardized by pre-cipitancy or immature ambition, to exercise now as much caution and forbearance as you have shown energy and decision . . . Much must depend upon the personal character and ability of the Resident in each place and this I doubt not you will watch carefully.[75]

This call for caution seemed to have done its work, if anything, too well, for by the beginning of September proposals for Residential appointments in addition to that of Speedy had still not been received in London.

The Colonial Office therefore took the initiative. A despatch dated 4 September reminded the Governor that though he had

[73] *Hansard*, 3rd Series, vol. ccxix, pp. 467–77.

[74] Sec. State to Gov. Straits, 29 May 1874, C.1111, p. 231. At the same time Clarke was authorized by telegram (1 June) to proceed at once with the appointment of Residents if he thought it necessary. This telegram was not acted on, and has not survived in the Colonial Office records. The only reference to it seems to be in Sec. State to Gov. Straits, 4 Sept. 1874, C.1111, pp. 241–2. The formal decision to approve the action taken in Selangor was not taken until 7 Aug.—the Colonial Office had asked for more information on which to act, and in order not to appear inconsistent they thought it necessary to wait until another despatch on Selangor (Gov. Straits, 27 June 1874) arrived. Cf. Minutes of 4–7 Aug. in CO 273/75.

[75] Carnarvon to Clarke, Private and Confidential, 27 May 1874, in PRO 30/6-40.

been given conditional authority to appoint Residents by telegram on 1 June he had taken no action and made no reply. It called for an early expression of his views on the appointment of Residents, and for details of the men he had in mind for these 'unusually difficult positions'. At the same time it repeated the Government's general approval of the Pangkor engagement, and in asking Clarke to convey to the chiefs who had signed it the Secretary of State's satisfaction it concluded:

> You will at the same time inform them that Her Majesty's Government will look to the exact fulfilment of the pledges which have now been voluntarily given, and will hold responsible those who violate the engagement which has been solemnly agreed upon.[76]

So far as the Home Government was concerned, then, all was set fair by September for a trial of Clarke's policy. Residents and 'government by advice' on the lines of the Pangkor engagement could now be let loose on the west-coast states as soon as the Governor cared to set the wheels in motion.

It was not an excess of caution but local difficulties which were holding Clarke up, and he did not make formal proposals for the appointment of Residents in Perak, Sungai Ujong and Selangor until the end of December. There was no trouble about Perak. J. W. W. Birch, the Straits Settlements' Colonial Secretary, had of his own initiative applied for the post, and had written to Cox at the Colonial Office to press his claim.[77] Birch toured Perak in April, and seems by mid-October to have been acting as Resident there pending his official appointment.[78] Clarke had not as yet brought the Sultan of Selangor to ask for a Resident there, but there was not much difficulty about that either. In August, when formal approval of the Pangkor settlement reached Singapore, Sir Andrew sent F. A. Swettenham, who had recently returned from a journey through Perak with Birch, to live with the old Sultan at Langat.[79] The main idea of this was to prevent the Selangor malcontents re-establishing their influence over him, but Swettenham

---

[76] Sec. State to Gov. Straits, 4 Sept. 1874, C.1111, pp. 241–2.

[77] Minute of 7 Apr. 1874, in CO 273/75. Cox commented, 'I think he would make a good one'.

[78] During his stay in Perak, with Swettenham as his companion, Birch tried unsuccessfully to get Ismail to surrender the Regalia to 'Abdu'llah. See 'Swettenham's Perak Journals', *JRASMB*, xxiv, pt. 4 (1951), pp. 59–69. That he was in fact acting as Resident by October appears from Clarke's letter of instructions to him, dated 16 Oct. 1874. See below, p. 224.

[79] C.1320, p. 7.

managed the old man so well that by 1 October he was prepared
to make over the management of the state to the Governor's
nominees and to pay their salaries.[80] Then the trouble began.
Clarke wished to appoint as Resident J. G. Davidson, who as an
old friend would be able to co-operate amicably with Zia'u'd-din
in the administration of the state.[81] But Davidson was already
heavily committed in Selangor. He had been a financial backer of
Zia'u'd-din from the beginning, and was a leading member of the
syndicate which had secured a large mining concession from
Zia'u'd-din and were trying to float the Selangor Tin Mining
Company in London.[82] Birch was also involved in financial difficulties, and whilst these were being cleared up and Davidson was
arranging to transfer his interests in Selangor into other hands,
Clarke was unable to put forward the name of either as a satisfactory Resident.[83]

In addition to these minor embarrassments, and the necessity of
intervening in September to smooth out a dispute between Johore
and Pahang, Clarke was also held up by a recurrence of trouble in
Sungai Ujong. After his adoption as a British protégé in April
the Dato' Klana set out to exploit his connexion with the Straits
Government as a weapon against his rival the Dato' Bandar. He
asked Clarke to send a British officer to support him, and made preparations to hoist a British flag over his house at Ampangan 'so
as to be under the protection of the Great Governor'.[84] Clarke

[80] Sultan to Gov. Straits, 1 Oct., Maxwell and Gibson, op. cit., pp. 35–36.
[81] The use of Davidson as a Commissioner to watch the piracy trial in
February may have been a move towards this appointment. Clarke's intention
to appoint Davidson as the first British Resident in Selangor was known un-
officially in London as early as May (Lord Stanley to Carnarvon, 10 May 1874,
PRO 30/6-21).
[82] See above, pp. 142 and 166–7.
[83] Davidson's financial claims on Zia'u'd-din were transferred to a commercial house in the Straits, but the arrangement was regarded with suspicion by
the Colonial Office, and he was still employed in Selangor 'on sufferance' when
events in Perak made it necessary to transfer him to that state in 1876 (see
p. 245 below). Birch, together with Braddell, was involved in allegations of
corruption in Singapore. The Attorney-General had always been allowed to
undertake a certain amount of private practice in addition to his official duties,
and he had received retaining fees from the Maharaja of Johore, Zia'u'd-din,
and the Dato' Klana. Birch was heavily in debt, and he had unwisely accepted
loans from the Chinese holders of the government opium farm at a time when
tenders for its renewal were under consideration. The Court of Enquiry found
that there was no evidence that either man had allowed these considerations to
influence the course of official business, but its report was not completed until
Nov. 1874, and the episode caused Clarke considerable anxiety (Report of
Court of Enquiry, 20 Nov. 1874, in CO 273/76).
[84] Klana to Lt.-Gov. Malacca, 24 Sept. 1874, C.1320, p. 40.

declined as yet to commit himself, and took no action beyond flushing a band of pirates out of the Labu district, on the borders of Selangor and Sungai Ujong. As result of this Raja Mahdi, who had been hiding in the area, came to Singapore and gave himself up. But this did not help the Klana, and in September he was asking again for British assistance against the Bandar. In November an armed conflict between them began. The immediate responsibility for this is difficult to assess. The Bandar was undoubtedly an aggressive character who had ruled the roost in this part of the world for many years, and, as he told Pickering in November,[85] he saw no reason why he should take orders from his younger rival or tolerate the interference of British officials. He was the strongest man in the area, and the presence of that great fighter Raja Mahmud of Selangor at his side struck fear into his opponents. The Klana was described by all who saw him at this time as a physical coward. But he was politically very shrewd, and he probably calculated that provided he could count on British support under the agreement of 21 April it would be in his interest to provoke the Bandar into attacking him. He certainly gave him a good deal of provocation, persistently treating him as a minor chief, and attempting to make him surrender Mahmud. Finally, in September, matters came to a head when the Bandar prevented the Dato' Klana hoisting the British flag over his house.[86] This provided the Klana with the opportunity he wanted, and he called on the Straits Government to honour its promise in the agreement to protect him against attack. He asked that Clarke should provide him with sufficient help to destroy the Dato' Bandar before the latter could attack him.[87]

Clarke was placed in a difficult position. He could hardly fail to support his own protégé or allow the control of the country to pass to the Dato' Bandar. At the same time he did not want to involve the government in a war, and he was afraid that if war did come the 10,000 Chinese miners in the country would take sides, and that he would have another Larut on his hands. So he sent Pickering, whose mediation had been so successful in Larut, on a series of visits to Sungai Ujong to try and bring the Bandar to terms, and to persuade the Chinese to keep clear of the dis-

---

[85] Gov. Straits to Sec. State, 29 Dec. 1874, C.1320, p. 9.
[86] Klana to Lt.-Gov. Malacca, 24 Sept. 1874, C.1320, p. 40.
[87] Ibid.

pute.[88] Though he succeeded in keeping the Chinese out of trouble Pickering failed to stop the Klana and the Bandar from coming to blows. The Bandar refused to sign the agreement of 21 April or to have anything to do with it. He would not meet the Governor or the Dato' Klana, and though he disclaimed any intention of attacking his rival he proceeded to throw up stockades and to collect his forces.

But it was the Klana who struck the first blow. With a motley force of 300 Malays and about forty Arabs recruited from ships' firemen in Singapore, all lavishly provided with arms, he set out to deal with the Bandar himself. He took the Bandar's stockades at Rasah and Rahang on 16 November with little opposition, and on the next day attacked his headquarters at Kapayang. Here he met the Bandar's main force under Raja Mahmud. As soon as they realized the nature of the opposition all the Klana's Malays abandoned their breach-loading rifles and the Krupp gun which had been brought with so much trouble from England, and bolted almost without firing a shot. Only the intervention of Pickering with his small escort of Malacca police enabled the Klana himself to get back in safety to Ampangan. There he and Pickering, deserted by all except the police and the Arabs, were surrounded by Mahmud and the Bandar's men.[89]

Clarke was now forced to intervene, and he despatched a mixed force of seamen, marines, soldiers and police, amounting altogether to about 200 men, to Pickering's rescue. They found that Pickering and the Arabs had already taken the offensive, driving off their assailants and retaking Rahang and Rasah from Mahmud. The combined force soon dealt with the Bandar and Mahmud, who abandoned their stronghold at Kapayang before it could be subjected to a full-scale assault, and fled into Selangor.[90] This left the Dato' Klana as the undisputed ruler of Sungai Ujong. He had

[88] At the same time, since Clarke was a little doubtful of the constitutional position of the Klana and the Bandar he sent Swettenham into Sungai Ujong from Selangor to make enquiries from both sides, and to lend his weight to Pickering's efforts to persuade the Bandar to compromise (C.1320, p. 8; Swettenham, *British Malaya*, pp. 186–7).

[89] Pickering to Gov. Straits, 23 Dec. 1874, C.1320, pp. 44–45.

[90] Early in December, being refused shelter by Sultan 'Abdu'l-Samad, they gave themselves up to Swettenham at Langat, and were taken by him to surrender themselves to Clarke in Singapore (*British Malaya*, p. 191). There they signed bonds acknowledging their war-guilt, and undertaking not to leave Singapore without the Governor's permission. They were provided with quarters and a small allowance, and the Bandar ended his life in retirement there (C.1320, pp. 53–54 and 61–62).

received such a fright that he was only too willing to do whatever was required of him, and since the Chinese miners, who had stood neutral during the fighting, constituted the majority of the population and were eager to get the mines working again, order was soon restored. It was not considered necessary to keep a large British force in the country, but a small detachment some fifty strong was retained as a guard for Captain Tatham, R.A., who remained with the Klana as an unofficial Resident.

With Sungai Ujong pacified Clarke was at last able to submit to the Colonial Office his list of Residents. These were:

Perak: J. W. Birch to act as Resident with the Sultan.
                Captain Speedy to continue to advise the Mantri in Larut as Assistant Resident.
Selangor: J. G. Davidson to act as Resident attached to Zia'u'd-din.
                F. A. Swettenham to continue to advise the Sultan as Assistant Resident.
Sungai Ujong: Captain Tatham to act as Assistant Resident with the Dato' Klana.

All these appointments were of course temporary pending the approval of the Secretary of State.[91]

These appointments were not received with very much enthusiasm in the Colonial Office. Considering Davidson's financial connexions with Zia'u'd-din they regarded his appointment as 'very questionable'. But since they were about to replace Clarke by a new Governor, Sir William Jervois, they decided that it would be courting trouble to intervene. Clarke's nominees were therefore allowed to act temporarily until Jervois had had time to make his own assessment of the position on the spot.[92]

So by the end of 1874 each of the west-coast states which had caused the Straits Government and the Colonial Office so much

---

[91] Gov. Straits to Sec. State, 30 Dec. 1874, CO 273/76, C.1320, p. 55.
[92] CO minutes dated 2 and 16 Feb. 1875; Sec. State to OAG, 5 Mar. 1875, in 273/76. Jervois's appointment was made necessary by Clarke's promotion to a position on the Council of India. Before he left England Carnarvon wrote to Jervois: 'I am clearly of opinion that this [Davidson's] employment at the Residency to which he has been provisionally appointed would be undesirable'. He was not satisfied that the transfer of Davidson's financial claims to other hands was sufficient guarantee of his future disinterestedness as a public servant, and he urged Jervois to try and employ him in another position where his Malay connexions would be useful (Carnarvon to Jervois, 8 Apr. 1875, endorsed 'Given to Sir W. Jervois the day he left England', in CO 273/76).

trouble in the preceding years had British Residents installed in them, and the experiment of administration by advice had begun. Writing privately to Carnarvon on 31 December Sir Andrew Clarke said:

. . . I hope I can now assure Your Lordship that I have every reason to believe that an appeal to force is not likely to occur again for many a long day to come, either in Sungei Ujong or in any of the States where we have intervened in their affairs.[93]

Time was to prove him a poor prophet.

[93] Clarke to Carnarvon, 31 Dec. 1874, PRO 30/6-50.

6

GOVERNMENT BY ADVICE AND
THE REACTION TO IT
1875–1876

THE British Residents placed in Perak, Selangor and Sungai Ujong during 1874 were supposed to improve conditions there by giving influential advice which the Malay rulers pledged themselves to accept. The Resident system worked fairly well in Selangor, in Sungai Ujong, and in Larut, though the Residents did not in fact confine themselves to giving advice. But in Perak conditions were less favourable to the extension of the Resident's control, and friction developed between him and the chiefs. Sir Andrew Clarke sought to avoid trouble by moderation, but after the arrival of Sir William Jervois as his successor in 1875 mounting irritation on both sides led to ill-considered action, and an explosion took place. The Resident, J. W. Birch, was murdered. Trouble also broke out in Sungai Ujong, and punitive expeditions had to be undertaken to pacify these two states.

The year 1874 ended so far as Malaya was concerned in a blaze of optimism, with the appointment of British Residents in the states of Perak, Selangor, and Sungai Ujong. During 1875 however a reaction set in. Selangor and Sungai Ujong were fairly quiet. But in Perak both Malays and British officials soon began to have second thoughts about the régime introduced by the Pangkor Treaty, and before the end of the year dissatisfaction on both sides produced hasty, ill-considered action and an explosion.

There is little information on conditions in Sungai Ujong in this period.[1] Captain Tatham, the first Assistant Resident, began the

---

[1] On the whole however there is a wealth of printed material for the years 1875 and 1876. Practically all the relevant despatches and attached papers have been published as Command Papers (see Bibliography); these are supplemented by a number of Confidential Prints in the Series CO 809. In addition a great deal of the material collected by the Commission of Enquiry into the complicity of the Perak chiefs in Birch's murder were printed verbatim or summarized in the *Précis of Evidence* published by the Straits Settlements Government in 1876. The MSS. sources, on the other hand, are astonishingly meagre, apart from the three volumes of evidence taken by the Commission of Enquiry (CO 273/86–88). Many of the papers were destroyed after being printed, and a good deal of the business was transacted by telegrams, the originals of which have disappeared. By the time many despatches arrived in London the business to which they referred had already been dealt with by telegram, and they were sent off at once to the printers before being dealt with in the Colonial Office. In consequence minutes in this period are also very scrappy and disappointing. In the pages which follow references are normally to the most easily available printed source.

construction of a road from Rasah to the Linggi River, built a police station there, and established gambling, opium and pawn-broking farms. He also granted twenty-year leases for all existing tin mines so as to encourage the Chinese miners, and fixed a permanent tariff for the export duties on tin.[2] The Resident's relations with both the Dato' Klana and Dato' Muda Linggi were good, and they appear to have been perfectly satisfied with the new order of things.[3]

In Selangor there was the same concern with the reopening of the tin mines and the reorganization of administration, and the same easy relationship between British officials and the chiefs. Davidson, the Resident, lived with the 'Viceroy', Zia'u'd-din, at Klang, and busied himself with the putting in order of Zia'u'd-din's shaken finances, the collection of revenue from import and export duties, and the consolidation of the state's credit. Zia'u'd-din had incurred extensive debts in the course of the civil war, and the gradual repayment of these by the state had to be provided for from revenue. Local officials had to be appointed and supervised, and law and order enforced. The main task of the Resident how-ever was to travel throughout the state and to re-establish confidence and security in areas like Kuala Selangor which had become largely depopulated during the civil war. These areas had seen Zia'u'd-din, Raja Musa and Raja Mahdi replace each other as their nominal rulers, only to be driven out again, and only the constant presence of the Resident could provide assurance that the present régime would be permanent, and lure the coastal Malays back to their coconut and sago plantations. In this work Davidson was ably seconded by the Assistant Resident, Swetten-ham, who lived with the Sultan at Langat, and travelled widely in the interior. Much of their work was advisory in the true sense, for the Sultan and Zia'u'd-din were both eager disciples, and fell in readily with any suggestions made to them by Residents with whom they lived on terms of personal friendship. Indeed so far was Sultan 'Abdu'l-Samad fired with enthusiasm for the

---

[2] Tatham to Colonial Sec., Singapore, 18 Dec. 1874, in *Parl. Pap.* C.1320 (1875), p. 54. There were then about 100 mines in Sungai Ujong, but many of them were very small, employing only eight to ten men each. The larger ones employed up to 140.
[3] Report on a visit to the Malay States, 22 Mar. 1875, in C.1320, pp. 105-11. Tatham was removed from the scene by ill-health in Apr. 1875 and replaced by Cdr. Murray, a retired naval officer (loc. cit., p. 104).

development of his country that one amused visitor observed him felling timber for a new road with his own hands.[4]

But administrative reform and roads were only the framework of development, and it was the return of the Chinese miners to the once abandoned mines in the interior which provided the real guarantee of Selangor's economic recovery. The driving force here was the 'Capitan China' of Kuala Lumpur, Yap Ah Loy. He had seen the town destroyed three times by war, and he now set to work to rebuild it again, and to reopen the mines. He built roads, stimulated the development of the Kanching mines further to the north in Ulu Selangor, and prevailed on his countrymen to return to the area. By the middle of 1875 more than 2,000 had come in through Klang, and intending immigrants were being left behind on the jetty at Malacca because there was no room on the steamer for them.[5]

The one difficulty of a potentially serious character which arose in Selangor at this time was an aftermath of the help which Zia'u'd-din had received from Pahang during the civil war. When Zia'u'd-din visited Pahang in 1872 he seems to have made a verbal bargain with the Bendahara to make over to him the revenues of Klang in return for the services of Pahang troops.[6] In part fulfilment of this bargain, one of the leaders of the Pahang levies, the Orang Kaya Pahlawan of Semantan, was left in charge of Ulu Klang (the area beyond Kuala Lumpur adjoining the Pahang frontier) to collect the revenues of that district on behalf of the Bendahara. This worthy however kept whatever he collected for his own use, and neither the Bendahara nor Zia'u'd-din saw any part of it. So in April 1875 the Bendahara wrote to Zia'u'd-din

[4] Reports from the Resident and Assistant Resident, Selangor, 27 Apr. 1875, loc. cit., pp. 94–104; Report on a visit to the Malay States, loc. cit.; Sultan 'Abdu'l-Samad said of Swettenham at this time: 'He is very clever; he is also very clever in the customs of Malay government and he is very clever at gaining the hearts of Rajas with soft words, delicate and sweet, so that all men rejoice in him as in the perfume of an opened flower' (Winstedt, 'History of Selangor', *JRASMB*, vol. xii, pt 3, p. 32).

[5] 'Yap Ah Loy', loc. cit., pp. 89 et seq.; C.1320, pp. 99–100. At this date the Capitan China was still unfettered by any administrative control, and it was not until 1879, by which time Kuala Lumpur had become by far the most important town in Selangor, that a British official was stationed there.

[6] The bargain was not put into writing, and there is some disagreement on what Zia'u'd-din did promise. The Bendahara claimed the revenues of both Klang and Selangor, meaning presumably Ulu Klang and Ulu Selangor, and this may have been so, for Linehan ('History of Pagang', *JRASMB*, vol. xiv, pt. 2, pp. 99–100) says that after the war Pahang chiefs were in control of Ulu Selangor as well as Ulu Klang.

asking for a share of the revenues of Klang, and for a lump sum of $20,000. Zia'u'd-din was quite unable to find any such sum. He was being pressed by his own creditors. 'God and his Prophet,' he said, 'alone know my difficulties'. Luckily for him the Straits Government were too concerned with the maintenance of peace in the Peninsula to allow the affair to develop. Mahdi was still sulking in Johore and refusing to abandon his claim to Klang, and they were afraid that he would take advantage of any trouble in Ulu Klang to interfere. So they supported a compromise whereby Zia'u'd-din promised to pay 6 *baharas*[7] of tin (worth about $260) monthly to the Bendahara as interest on his investment in the Selangor civil war, and to find immediately $3,000 worth of tin in repayment of a cash debt incurred since the war. The tin was sent round to Pahang in the Government steamer *Pluto*, in charge of Frank Swettenham. At his insistence the Bendahara agreed to accept these terms, and to agree to the removal of the Orang Kaya from Ulu Klang.[8]

The successful initiation of the Resident system in Sungai Ujong and Selangor was due to a very favourable combination of circumstances. The idea of placing Residents in these states was not forced precipitately on their rulers, but was allowed to develop gradually during 1874. As a result the Sultan of Selangor himself asked for a Resident, and the Dato' Klana was forced to appeal for British intervention in order to maintain his position. In both stat.s the presence of a Resident accorded with the chiefs' own interests. The Dato' Klana knew himself unequal to grappling alone with the task of keeping the Chinese miners under control and defeating the attempts of chiefs in the surrounding states to establish themselves on the Linggi. Sultan 'Abdu'l-Samad had always been in favour of letting others bear the burden of administration so long as his revenues were forthcoming; Zia'u'd-din had incurred a crushing burden of debt, and knew that he could not keep his creditors at bay without the support of the British Government and of a Resident who happened to be himself one

---

[7] The *bahara, bahar,* or *bhar* = 3 *pikuls*, or about 400 lb.

[8] C.1320, pp. 113–16; Linehan, op. cit., pp. 99–100; in July 1875 Gov. Sir William Jervois visited Pahang and tried to persuade the Bendahara to accept British advice in the opening up of his country. The Bendahara however did not take the bait. He affected not to understand what Jervois meant, and when Jervois explained in words of one syllable he excused himself by saying that he would have to consult the chiefs of the interior before he could answer (Gov. Straits to Sec. State, 7 Aug. 1875 in C.1505, p. 9; Linehan, p. 102).

of those creditors. So, quite apart from the fact that Davidson and Swettenham were personal friends of the 'Viceroy' and the Sultan, all three chiefs were predisposed to co-operate with the Residents and accept their advice. Lastly, and perhaps most important of all, all three had obtained effective control over the whole of their states, and were able as well as willing to put the Resident's policy into practice. In Selangor and Sungai Ujong therefore, conditions were as near as possible ideal either for a system whereby the local ruler governed with the advice of the Residents, or for government by the Residents with the acquiescence of the chiefs.

These circumstances were not present in Larut, but there were other factors which made the régime ushered in by the Pangkor settlement a success. It would be an understatement to say that the Mantri did not welcome British intervention, but as we have seen he was too unsure of his position to oppose the conclusion of the Pangor Treaty openly. Nor had he the means to obstruct its performance. Larut had by 1874 become a Chinese-populated province. By December of that year it contained 26,000 Chinese out of a total population of 33,000,[9] and all of them were eager to take advantage of the peace which British intervention had brought, and to push on with the development of the mines. The Mantri's Malay police force had been absorbed into Speedy's Indian troops, and he was without money or credit so that though sullen and resentful he was powerless to influence events.[10] Perhaps the most important factor in the situation in Larut was that Speedy's appointment as Assistant Resident was made as soon as the Pangkor Treaty was signed. At the same time the Commission appointed to settle disputes over mining land and to disarm the country got down to work at once, so that there was no interregnum, and no opportunity for disorderly elements to create confusion. In these circumstances the Mantri was simply brushed aside, and there was no attempt at governing by advice. On the contrary, from the time when the Commissioners completed their work and left Perak in February, until the appointment of Birch as Resident of Perak in November 1874, Speedy ruled Larut

[9] C.1320, p. 70.
[10] Cowan, 'Sir Frank Swettenham's Perak Journals', *JRASMB*, vol. xxiv, pt. 4, p. 44); Gullick, 'Captain Speedy of Larut' (ibid., vol. xxvi, pt. 3, p. 57). He could not go to Penang to get help because his creditors had obtained judgement against him in the High Court there, and he would have been arrested for debt.

himself, without reference to any other authority.[11] From then on he was subject to the intermittent control of the Resident, but at no time does any attempt seem to have been made to associate the Mantri in the work of government. The only local authorities of whom Speedy made use seem to have been the secret society headmen of the Hai San and the Ghee Hin. As the wealthiest and most influential men in Larut, they were used as the main channel of communication with the Chinese miners, even though Speedy and his officials did not comprehend the real basis of their authority.[12] For most purposes however Speedy worked through European subordinate officials. In 1874 and 1875 there were five of these— a Treasurer, who also sat with Speedy as a Magistrate; an Inspector of Mines; an Inspector of Roads; a Harbour Master and Customs Collector; a Medical Officer.[13]

During 1874 Larut became once more a thriving and prosperous state. The Chinese miners flocked back to the mines, and in the second half of the year large quantities of tin were exported, so that Government revenue, which came from duties on tin exports and on opium and other imports assumed respectable proportions. Most of Speedy's limited funds were spent on the upkeep of roads and bridges, the laying out of new towns to house the increasing population, and the construction of Government buildings, including a very fine new Residency. Speedy tended to be extravagant with Government money, and Birch and other visitors to Larut in 1875 found fault with his distribution of expenditure, and with the state of the roads and the drains. Birch's own contributions to administration however were not very successful. He insisted on letting out the collection of opium duty to a farmer instead of having it collected direct by Government. Moreover he gave the farm to the Chinese farmer already operating in Perak, who was a Singapore man. This alienated the Penang financiers and society headmen, who considered that Larut was their preserve, and frightened the miners, who thought that their opium would cost them more. The revival of the Sungai Ujong and Selangor mines

[11] See Report on Larut for 1874, in C.1320, pp. 68–81. Lord Stanley of Alderley and his India Office friends complained to the Colonial Office about Speedy's arbitrary assumption of control in Larut (ibid., pp. 117–19). One of their complaints was that he had too many delinquents flogged. Jail however would have been a very light penalty, for as yet Speedy had not managed to obtain any doors for the new prison.

[12] Gullick, op. cit., p. 43.

[13] Ibid., p. 56.

P

had created a great demand for mining labour, and several of the Larut contractors took their men off to Klang, so that the number of Chinese in Larut dropped by as much as 5,000 during 1875.[14] Despite this, British intervention in Larut during 1874 and 1875 must be counted a success. It restored order and security, got the tin trade moving again, made good much of the material destruction due to the war, and made a contribution to the revenues of the rest of Perak. Whatever Speedy's shortcomings the results achieved in Larut were miraculous compared with the miserable failure of the Resident system in Perak.

In Perak there were none of the saving factors which had allowed the British Residents to dominate the situation in Sungai Ujong, Selangor and Larut. In the first place there was no one authority through whom the Resident's advice and influence could become effective. 'Abdu'llah and the down-river chiefs had signed the Treaty of Pangkor, but their influence did not extend further inland than Pasir Salak, the home of the Maharaja Lela. Beyond that point the Perak and Kinta Rivers were under the control of Ismail, Yusuf, and a host of lesser chiefs, most of whom still recognized Ismail as Sultan. None of them had signed the Pangkor Treaty, and it remained for Birch to persuade them to accept its terms. Attempts made by Birch in 1874 to win Ismail over and to get him to surrender the Perak regalia to 'Abdu'llah failed.[15] But Yusuf, whose existence the Straits Government seem now for the first time to have discovered, was persuaded by Swettenham in June 1874 to go to Penang and see Sir Andrew Clarke.[16] He then realized that the Straits Government now meant business and that resistance would in the end be futile, and saw therein his opportunity to regain power. From that point onwards he was a consistent supporter of British policy in Perak. He had however almost no following outside his own village of Senggang, and was generally unpopular amongst the other chiefs. In November 1874 when Birch took up his post as Resident, the attitude of the majority of the chiefs of Upper Perak was one of passive hostility.[17]

---

[14] Speedy, Report on Larut, loc. cit.; Cowan, op. cit., pp. 44–46 and 74–75; Gullick, op. cit., pp. 40–59.
[15] See Cowan, op. cit., pp. 58 et seq. for Swettenham's account of these negotiations.
[16] Ibid., pp. 78 et seq.
[17] In July 1874 Pickering visited Ismail and got from him a letter in which he said in vague terms that he would always be glad to follow British advice, and that he resigned all his affairs into the hands of the Governor (Précis of

Nor were the Resident's relations with 'Abdu'llah and the down-stream chiefs satisfactory. 'Abdu'llah had agreed to take a Resident in order to get British support for his candidature as Sultan. But he had no real comprehension of what was involved. He had not had to fight for his throne, or to call in British troops to defend him against his rivals. The proceedings at Pangkor had undoubtedly made an impression on him, as upon the other chiefs who were present, but for nearly a year no Resident was appointed, and no step taken to keep the new Sultan under control, and the impression faded. 'Abdu'llah meanwhile was busy using this period between the Pangkor engagement in January and the appointment of Birch in November to raise money. He enjoyed the declared support of the British Government without the embarrassing restraint of a Resident's advice, and he proceeded to farm the Perak estuary customs duties to a Singapore Chinese for ten years at $26,000 a year, taking half a year in advance.[18] Most of this money went on gambling, opium and cock-fighting, or on personal indulgences such as the purchase of an impressive uniform which was ordered from Europe at a cost of $4,000.[19] During this time life in Lower Perak, as on the upper reaches of the river, went on much as it had always done—each chief levied his own taxes on his own stretch of river, kept large numbers of debt-slaves,[20] and

Evidence, p. 4, and Appendix ix). How little this represented Ismail's real attitude was shown in October, when he held a meeting with the Mantri and the other up-river chiefs, and they agreed that they would if necessary fight to keep the regalia from 'Abdu'llah, and that they would pay a Penang lawyer, Mr. Woods, to go to England and challenge the validity of the Pangkor engagement in the Courts (Précis of Evidence, p. 5).

[18] Précis of Evidence, pp. 4–5; Birch's Report on Perak, 2 Apr. 1875, in C.1320, pp. 85–93. Both the Shahbandar and the Temenggong however continued to collect duties themselves, so that goods coming into Perak passed through customs three times.

[19] Précis, p. 8; Winstedt, History of Perak, p. 107. Birch wrote of 'Abdu'llah in his diary four days after his arrival in Perak as Resident: 'He is eminently silly and foolish; opium, too, has become his bane again, and he is good for very little. He has been evidently giving himself up a good deal to indulgence since I saw him in May; he has no house of his own, but is surrounded by his so-called doctor, a blackguard who smokes opium with him, and fights his cocks and gambles, and looks a thorough debauchee, and two or three others, and lots of women all of whom are slaves, and most of them prostitutes' (Précis, p. 5).

[20] Debt-slavery as an institution was common to most of the Malay States at this time, but seems to have been at its worst in Perak. In theory it involved the debtor unable to pay his debt becoming the slave of his creditor until the debt was discharged, In practice the creditor could if he wished refuse to accept the money, and keep the slave indefinitely. He could also enslave the debtor's wife and family. Moreover the practice in Perak was not confined to bona fide debtors. Any chief could make a man his debt-slave simply by imposing on him

treated the local peasantry as he pleased. 'Abdu'llah certainly asked at times for his Resident to be sent to him.[21] But he thought that this Resident would be someone to carry out his orders and add to his prestige. He had no idea that the presence of a Resident would involve unpleasant restrictions on his power to treat his section of the country as his own personal estate, to be mortgaged and re-mortgaged at will.[22]

Thus when Birch was appointed British Resident in Perak, and began to expound schemes for the collection of all revenues by Government officials, for the punishment of 'illegal tax-gatherers', and the suppression of slavery, he incurred at once the hostility of 'Abdu'llah and the other chiefs. Birch arrived in Perak as Resident on 4 November 1874. His first action was to declare the farm of the *kuala* customs illegal, and to tell the Chinese farmer to compete for the farm in the proper way when it was put up for tender. Within a month he had eliminated the private collection of customs at the river-mouth, and established one collection centre under the supervision of a European clerk, who kept the accounts. He then described to the down-river chiefs his scheme for the reorganization of the tax-system. This included the imposition of a tax on paddy, on carrying arms, and on boats, the issuing of permits for the right to cut timber and *atap*, and the establishment of one joint opium, spirit and gambling farm. To prevent illegal taxation, maintain order, and collect the revenue from these new taxes Birch proposed to introduce his own Code of Civil and Criminal Law, to organize a Government Police Force, and to install a principal *Hakim* or Judge and to place Penghulus or Headmen in all the villages who would be chosen by and responsible to the Government, i.e. the Resident, and not to the local Chief.[23]

'Abdu'llah and his chiefs now realized for the first time that Birch meant to take direct control over revenue out of their hands,

an arbitrary fine which the man was unable to pay. For examples, cf. Speedy's Report on Larut (C.1320, p. 76) and Cowan, op. cit., p. 118. Speedy reckoned that seventy-five per cent of the Perak Malays were slave-debtors to the other twenty-five per cent.

[21] Cowan, op. cit., p. 88; Précis, p. 4.

[22] It is doubtful how far any of the Malays appreciated the effect of the phrase in the Pangkor Treaty which required that the Resident's advice must be asked and obeyed on all subjects other than Malay religion and custom, or, since 'custom' could be so elastic a term, how far they were aware of the British attitude to this clause. Anson, the Lt.-Gov. of Penang, asserted afterwards that none of the chiefs present really understood what had taken place at Pangkor (Anson, *About Others and Myself* (1920), pp. 322–3).

[23] Précis, pp. 5–6.

and to strip them of their prerogatives. No doubt he mentioned that in return they would receive fixed allowances and the opportunity of official posts to which salaries would be attached. But ignorant of what the new taxes would bring in he could make no firm promises. He seems to have been more concerned to dwell on the iniquities of the existing system and the steps which ought to be taken to alter it. The Mantri, who was then in Lower Perak with 'Abdu'llah, was able to tell 'Abdu'llah that he had warned him that this would happen at Pangkor:

> Your Majesty will see an example in Captain Speedy: I gave him pay, and he worked under me; and how has he treated me since? I have the same opinion of Mr. Birch. How dare he put Europeans to take charge of Salama? And how can they receive all the taxes from Larut, and keep them for themselves. I think Mr. Birch will by-and-bye keep many more Europeans to take charge of the country, and have Stations and Sepoys and Police. After a few years they will surely drive us out of the country. . . . It is improper for Your Majesty to follow the Resident, for his rank is only that of a Datu. We were all forced to sign the Treaty. It was not with our own consent. Therefore I think, if we go before the law, the Pangkor Treaty will be void.[24]

This expresses very well the depth and violence of the reaction to the unsuspecting Birch's lectures. It was not merely that the chiefs were unused to the idea of a central government, and did not grasp the fact that what they gave up in taxing capacity would be made up to them under a civil list. It was not merely the money. To them the right to levy dues and to keep slaves was an important part of their political and social position, and in proposing to abolish it the Resident struck at the very root of their social organization as well as threatening the only means of livelihood they knew.

'Abdu'llah was so concerned that he even sought to co-operate with his rival Ismail against Birch. In January 1875, when the Resident was taking him up-river for a meeting at which he hoped that Ismail would hand over the regalia so that the Sultan could be formally installed, 'Abdu'llah sent secretly to Ismail, telling him on no account to give up the regalia or to give his adherence to the Pangkor settlement:

> I am now ascending the river, not according to my heart's desire, but that of Mr. Birch. And if Mr. Birch asks for the Regalia, or desires to make me King, do not my royal grandfather give up the Regalia, or

[24] Précis, p. 7.

consent to my being nominated King. And should my royal grand-father consent to my being made King, on that day, of a truth, the country of Perak will be given over to the English, for my words have caused me to be very much indebted to the English.[25]

Ismail of course declined either to give up the regalia or to sign the Pangkor Treaty. In February and March 1875, when Birch asked him to sign proclamations putting into effect his scheme for the collection of revenues and the organisation of government, 'Abdu'llah was aghast to find that they practically took all control of the country and all direct share of the revenues out of his hands. Backed by the Laksamana and the Mantri he twice refused to sign. The Maharaja Lela began to erect a stockade at Pasir Salak, and announced his intention of resisting if the Resident attempted to interfere in his village. The Mantri, expecting trouble, removed his family and dependants to Larut out of danger.[26]

In May a reproof from Sir Andrew Clarke for the obstinacy with which he obstructed Birch's reforms had so little quietened 'Abdu'llah that he sent off a deputation to Singapore to wait on the Governor and to ask that the Resident might be removed or his powers restricted. Clarke refused to reply officially, but sent a letter of mild reproof, telling 'Abdu'llah not to address the Governor except through the Resident, and to listen to the Resident's advice. Nevertheless, in June when Birch again presented the Proclamations to 'Abdu'llah he once more refused to sign them. Birch gave him until 20 July to think it over, saying that if he did not take care he would soon be put off the throne by the British Government. As result of this threat and the failure of his deputation to Singapore 'Abdu'llah called a meeting of down-river and up-river chiefs at Durian Sa-batang on 21 July, at which all the Perak chiefs were present in person or by proxy except Yusuf. At this meeting it was suggested that Birch should be killed (the Maharaja Lela volunteering to do the deed), and that a combined movement of the up-country and downstream chiefs should be organized to drive the British out of the country. Outwardly how-ever 'Abdu'llah maintained his connexion with the Resident. On 24 July he signed proclamations authorizing the Resident and the Shahbandar to control all taxes and to appoint and dismiss

[25] Précis, p. 7.
[26] Ibid., pp. 8–9.

headmen, and appointing the Resident and Raja Dris ('Abdu'llah's cousin) as Judges.[27]

The personal rancour which 'Abdu'llah felt for Birch was sharpened by a number of incidents which involved the Sultan's jurisdiction with regard to individual Malays, over whom he had under the old régime the power of life and death. The main cause of the trouble arose from the institution of debt-slavery. After the signature of the Pangkor Treaty numbers of these slaves escaped from their masters in Perak and took refuge on the island of Pangkor. In February 1875 Birch had established himself at Bandar Bahru, on an island at the confluence of the Kinta and Perak rivers, and about forty-five miles from the sea. The Residency there soon became a place of refuge for escaping slaves, much to the anger of their owners, who regarded Birch as the stealer of their property.[28] The situation was made worse by the fact that most of the slaves were women. At the beginning of August 'Abdu'llah took advantage of the temporary absence of the Resident in Singapore to demand the return of three of these women, and the surrender of a man being held on a charge of shooting at Birch's Malay Inspector of Police. He also asked for the return of a woman who had gone to the Residency to marry Birch's Malay boy, saying that it was against Malay custom for the girl to be married without his consent.[29]

All these incidents came to a head on 17 August, after Birch's return. 'Abdu'llah, with the Laksamana, the Shahbandar and a large following, came to the Residency to ask for money. Birch told him that he had no money for him, and that he would get none until the taxes whose introduction he had himself resisted, had been raised. The Resident then used the occasion to take 'Abdu'llah to task for his conduct in asking for the return of the debt-slaves, and demanded by what right the Sultan sought to prevent the marriage of his servant to a girl whose father was a free man. Far from giving up the man who had fired on the Inspector of Police, he insisted on 'Abdu'llah surrendering for trial another man accused of the same crime, who had taken refuge with the Sultan.

[27] Précis, pp. 10–14; Winstedt, op. cit., pp. 108–10.
[28] By contrast Speedy in Larut was punctilious in respecting the rights of property involved in the debt-slavery problem, so long as the institution remained part of the customary law of Perak. He returned slaves who came to him for sanctuary to their owners, though he often brought pressure to bear upon them to accept repayment of the debt involved (Gullick, op. cit., p. 58).
[29] Précis, pp. 15–16.

On the next day he forced 'Abdu'llah to surrender the man, and put him in the Residency lock-up. At the time the Sultan tried to laugh off Birch's lecture, but he was seething at the insult offered to him in the presence of his followers. He sent to Penang to buy arms, and held *main berhantu* (a spirit séance), at which he attempted to forecast or contrive the death of the Resident by the arts of Malay magic.[30]

Sir Andrew Clarke was of course largely ignorant of the passions which surged below the surface of events in Perak. But he was aware of the dangers inherent in the situation, and attempted to exercise his influence in the direction of moderation. His original instructions to Birch spoke of allowing the immediate system to go on until a new order could be introduced with agreement, 'when not of such an irregular character as to require immediate alteration'.[31] He talked in a private letter at the same time of the need to show 'gentleness and deference' to Ismail, and of dealing 'gently but firmly' with 'Abdu'llah.[32] Birch, as we have seen, was not a man to whom such an approach came easily. He had many virtues—energy, bravery, sympathy for the depressed and downtrodden, loyalty to his superiors. But his view of the minimum standards acceptable for an Eastern administration were drawn from his experience of the Crown Colonies of Ceylon and the Straits Settlements. He had the fixed and rigid moral standards of his age, which did not embrace toleration of slavery. He was not a fluent Malay speaker, and was unable to converse with those around him or to gain any insight into their feelings. And his reputation as a negotiator with Malay chiefs had been gained by the use of firmness and strength at the time of the Selangor incident— gun-boat diplomacy at its most successful. His view of Malay institutions is summed up in his report of 14 December 1874:

> But really it concerns us little what were the old customs of the country, nor do I consider they are worthy of any consideration in dealing with the present taxation of the country.[33]

In his eyes almost everything he met in Perak was 'of such an irregular character as to require immediate alteration'. Clarke seems

---

[30] Précis., pp. 16–17. This séance is described in Winstedt, op. cit., Appendix (i), pp. 172–4.
[31] Ibid., p. 9.
[32] Clarke to Birch, 16 Oct. 1874, in Vetch, *Life of Lieut-General Sir A. Clarke* (1905), pp. 176–7.
[33] Quoted in Précis, p. 6.

to have been aware of some of the Resident's failings as well as his virtues. He wrote to Anson: 'I am very much annoyed with Birch and the head-over-heels way in which he does things; he and I will come to sorrow yet if he does not mind.'[34] And again, at the beginning of 1875, he counselled caution:

Limit all your efforts to the sea-coast and navigable waters, never mind the regalia, now and then have Ismail told quietly that he was losing money by holding back, but do not bother about the upper rivers where there are only Malays. Have patience with them. Debt-slavery is a bad thing, but until we are prepared to compensate in full and to show a better system to secure credit, let it for the present alone.[35]

But in May 1875 Clarke's moderating influence was withdrawn. He went to India to become Public Works member of the Governor-General's Council, and was succeeded as Governor of the Straits Settlements by Major- (later Lieutenant-) General Sir William Jervois, R.E. Jervois was a 'thruster', an ambitious man with a brilliant career behind him and a reputation for getting things done.[36] He was every bit as able as Clarke and like him a strong Imperialist. But he had more than a touch of Sir Harry Ord's masterful imperiousness, and an eye always on his own reputation.[37] In response to a request from the Singapore Chamber

[34] Anson, op. cit., p. 323.
[35] Vetch, op. cit., p. 182.
[36] Lt.-Gen. Sir William Francis Drummond Jervois, R.E., G.C.M.G., C.B., F.R.S., was born in 1821 and educated at the Royal Military Academy, Woolwich. He was commissioned in the Royal Engineers in 1839 and served at the Cape, 1841–8. He was employed on the fortifications of Alderney, 1852–5, and as Assistant (later Deputy) Inspector-General of Fortifications, 1856–75. At the same time he acted as Secretary of the Committee on Empire Defence, and in 1859 of the Royal Commission on National Defence. Between 1863 and 1866 he reported on the defences of Canada, Nova Scotia, Bermuda, Malta and Gibraltar, and in 1871 and 1872 he was employed by the Government of India to report on Aden, Perim, Bombay, the Hooghly, Rangoon and Moulmein. He was regarded as an expert on the strategic outposts of the Empire, and had built up a large number of influential connexions through this work and through his posts on the Defence Committee and the Royal Commission. He was Governor of the Straits Settlements, 1875–7, and after advising on the defences of Australia in 1877 he became Governor of South Australia, 1877–82, and of New Zealand, 1882–9. He retired from active employment in 1889, but four years before his death in 1897 was appointed Colonel-Commandant of the Royal Engineers.
[37] During the Perak War Swettenham drafted a report on the capture of Pasir Salak (below, p. 235), and Maj. Dunlop, the Government Commissioner with the troops, signed it. When it was shown to Jervois aboard the Government steamer *Pluto* he asked Swettenham to change the Report so as to indicate that the attack had been carried out on his (Jervois's) instructions. When Swettenham pointed out that this was not true Jervois (according to Swettenham) said that he could not allow any report to go to the Secretary of

of Commerce and the Straits Settlements Association it was arranged that Clarke should stay in Singapore for a time after Jervois's arrival to brief him on conditions in the Peninsula and on British policy there.[38] This decision was most unfortunate. Clarke naturally tried to ensure that Jervois would continue the policy that he had laid down, in particular counselling patience and urging that the Malay chiefs should be given time to come round to accepting the Residents' advice. But Jervois was senior to Clarke in the Royal Engineers, and declined to be dictated to.[39] Two days after his predecessor sailed from Singapore Jervois wrote privately to Carnarvon describing the unsatisfactory state of affairs in Perak, and suggesting that the chiefs ought to be held to their engagements. He admitted that everything could not be put right at once, but urged the taking of a stronger line with the obstructionist tactics of 'Abdu'llah and his followers:

I cannot however help considering them with reference to para. 8 of Your Lordship's Despatch of September 4th 1874 . . . wherein it is stated that 'H.M. Government will look to the exact fulfilment of the pledges which have now been given, and will hold responsible those who violate the engagement which has been solemnly agreed upon.'[40]

Birch's letters and his diaries, which he transmitted regularly to the Governor, only tended to confirm this line of thought, and Jervois became increasingly sceptical of the eventual success of the Resident system as it was then being applied.

In another private letter to Carnarvon dated 10 July he stated the position as it appeared to him, and suggested a radical change of policy. He noted the little real progress which had been made since the signing of the Pangkor engagement, and the growing

State describing the first success in the Perak War unless it gave him credit for planning the operation. Swettenham extricated himself from this situation by saying that Dunlop had signed the report and Dunlop must alter it, which after an interview with the Governor he did (Swettenham, *Footprints in Malaya* (1942), p. 63).

[38] Boustead and Read to Sec. State, 6 Mar. 1875; Sec. State to Gov.-Gen., 8 Mar. 1875; Sec. State to Boustead, etc., 19 Mar. 1875; in CO 273/82.

[39] Anson, op. cit., p. 323; Vetch, op. cit., pp. 182–3. Jervois landed at Singapore on 8 May and assumed office on the 10th. But Clarke did not leave until the 26th.

[40] Jervois to Carnarvon, 29 May 1875, PRO 30/6–40. It was typical of Jervois, and became a common-place of his dealings with the Colonial Office, for him to justify a policy or a course of action by the use of earlier statements of an adversary or a superior, often out of their context, and to attempt to prove that he was only doing or suggesting what they had themselves proposed. Perhaps his facility in these tactics came from his service on Parliamentary Committees.

financial burdens imposed on the Straits Settlements Government by the Resident system. Fifteen thousand pounds had been advanced in Perak out of the total of £20,000 expended in all the west-coast states. In addition the government had made itself responsible for the debts of the Mantri, to the extent of about £50,000. There was small prospect of recovering any of this money in the foreseeable future. 'Abdu'llah was incapable and impracticable, and not recognized by the majority of the people. Illegal taxation was widespread, and debt-slavery far more extensive than had been supposed. The Chinese would never be adequately ruled under a Malay Government, and preferred British control. The Resident, with power only to advise and not to control, would never, he thought, make any appreciable impact on these problems. Therefore he suggested to Carnarvon that the British Government should 'take possession' of the Malay States, beginning with Perak, pension off the chiefs, and rule through selected rajas who would be virtually British officials.[41]

In September Jervois decided to go to Perak and see conditions for himself. Accompanied by Birch and a party of officials which included Davidson from Selangor and Speedy, he went to Larut, and thence overland to join the Perak River at Kuala Kangsar. He made a progress down the river, having talks with Ismail, Yusuf and 'Abdu'llah on the way. In these interviews, having already been convinced by Birch and the other officials that continuance of the 'government by advice' system was impossible, he proposed to the chiefs that Perak be handed over to the Crown for administration by British officers. At the same time he promised liberal pensions to those chiefs who accepted this new scheme.[42]

Ismail, after consulting his advisers, refused to have anything to do with this, or to acknowledge the validity of the Pangkor Treaty.[43] Yusuf told the Governor that he was quite willing for

---

[41] Jervois to Carnarvon, 10 July 1875, in PRO 30/6–40. In another private letter to the Secretary of State, dated 7 Aug., he wrote: 'Everything seems tending to render it inevitable that Perak must become part of the British Dominions—and that without costing a farthing or firing a shot.'

[42] *Parl. Pap.* C. 1505 (1876), pp. 34–38; *Précis*, pp. 19–20; Swettenham, *British Malaya*, pp. 199–200; Cowan, op. cit., pp. 93–95. 'Abdu'llah, who thought that Jervois might be going to have him arrested and deported because of his opposition to Birch, is said to have arranged with Sayid Mashor, who now formed part of his entourage, to *amok* the Governor's party if they attempted to seize him (Swettenham, p. 200).

[43] He seems at this time have been completely under the control of the Mantri and the other up-country chiefs. At the meeting itself, though the others refused Jervois's scheme outright, Ismail declined to say yea or nay, but said

the British Government to take over the administration of Perak, and that he thought this was the only way to get the country out of its troubles. 'Abdu'llah said that he was unable to accept or reject Jervois's proposals until he had consulted the Chiefs of the blood royal—his normal method of evading a question. He was therefore given fifteen days in which to consult Ismail and the other chiefs and to make his decision, and on 15 September Jervois returned to Singapore, leaving Birch and Swettenham watching events in Perak. During the fifteen days of grace great pressure was put on 'Abdu'llah and some of the other chiefs to get them to agree to the Governor's proposals. Yusuf and Raja Dris were both induced to sign letters asking Britain to take over the government of the country. In return they received from Birch guarantees of government pensions, and a lump sum on account.[44]

Finally on 1 October 'Abdu'llah, who had made no attempt to go up-river and consult the other chiefs, gave way and signed a letter drafted by the Resident in which he accepted in full the Governor's proposal that the country should be handed over to the British Crown. He received the same written promise of a pension as had Yusuf and Dris, and in addition an undertaking that until the whole question of debt-slavery was cleared up the Resident would surrender on demand any debt-slaves taking refuge in the Residency at Bandar Bahru.[45]

On the previous day two letters had arrived from Singapore. The first offered a concession to 'Abdu'llah, proposing that instead of annexation the country should be administered by British officers in the name of the Sultan. The second letter, to be used only if 'Abdu'llah refused to yield, was addressed to Yusuf and offered to make him Sultan in 'Abdu'llah's place. Neither letter was delivered on that day, the first because Birch thought that it would encourage 'Abdu'llah to bargain for further concessions when he was about to acquiesce in the original proposals, the second because it was not necessary. Only on the day after (1 October), when 'Abdu'llah had already signed the letter of agreement, did

---

that he must consult his advisers. His rejection of the scheme was made in a letter subsequently (text in C.1505, p. 46), and since Ismail could neither read nor write this was probably much more the Mantri's composition than his own.

[44] Cowan, op. cit., pp. 95–102; C.1505, pp. 34–37. The text of the letters signed by Yusuf and Dris is in C.1505, p. 47.

[45] Cowan, op. cit., pp. 106–7; C.1505, p. 48; Précis, p. 22.

Birch take the Governor's first letter to him and 'congratulate' him on being allowed to retain the title of Sultan.[46]

'Abdu'llah was now in a happier state of mind than he had been for some time. He had an assured income of $2,000 a month, a promise that his runaway slaves would be given up, and a letter signed by Jervois that the government would be carried on in his name. It is possible that if Birch had been content to let well alone 'Abdu'llah might have given up the plot against the Resident's life and remained quiet for long enough to allow the new system to be inaugurated. But on 2 October Birch put before 'Abdu'llah for signature two proclamations carrying into effect the policy to which he had already in principle agreed. The first invested all British officers appointed to reside in Perak with the power of judges, competent to punish all crimes and to appoint magistrates. The second acknowledged the same officers as the Sultan's representatives to collect and administer all revenues, to appoint all chiefs and headmen (Dato's and Penghulus), and generally to order and administer all the affairs of the country.[47] There was no real need for this. 'Abdu'llah had already signed a letter asking the British Government to take over the government of the country, but Birch seems to have been obsessed with the idea of driving home the moral advantage which he had secured, and of getting signed these two proclamations, which had been a bone of contention between him and the Sultan for so long. 'Abdu'llah, as always, was willing if necessary to make concessions of principle which would only be carried into effect in the comfortably distant future. But he recoiled from putting his hand to these proclamations, which brought him face to face with reality. In the end Birch had to threaten him with the Governor's second letter, that offering to make Yusuf Sultan, to get him to sign. This he did on the night of 2 October, and the next day Swettenham left for Singapore with the proclamations and with the letter in which 'Abdu'llah had earlier accepted Jervois's scheme of British control.[48]

In Singapore, with 'Abdu'llah's letter now in his hands, Jervois worked out his plan for the government of Perak, and committed himself to it by a proclamation dated 15 October 1875. This

[46] Ibid., p. 107. All these letters are printed in Appendices to the Précis of Evidence.

[47] Text in Cowan, op. cit., pp. 146–7, and Précis, Appendix, pp. xxxi-xxxii.

[48] Ibid., pp. 107–10.

declared that H.M. Government 'in compliance with the request of the Sultan and chiefs of Perak' had determined to administer the government of Perak in the name of the Sultan through Commissioners and Assistant Commissioners of the Queen. They would act under the Governor's instructions, but would be advised by a Malay Council, consisting of 'Rajahs of Perak of the highest rank'.[49] On 16 October, the day after signing his Proclamation, and more than a month after his initial proposals to the chiefs in Perak, Jervois for the first time in an official despatch reported his policy to the Colonial Office and asked for their approval.[50] A few hours later came a private letter from Carnarvon, in answer to that which Jervois had sent him in July, rejecting all idea of an immediate extension of British control and saying that the Resident system must be given a further period of trial.[51] Jervois, as Clarke had done in 1874, concluded his justificatory despatch by saying:

> . . . I endeavoured to avoid any step which could in any way embarrass Her Majesty's Government. Should the policy which I have adopted not be approved, it will be possible, without difficulty, either to recede or to advance, according as your Lordship may desire.

Carnarvon's letter was clear warning that his policy would not meet with approval,[52] and he was thus given the opportunity to cry halt if, as he maintained, this was still feasible. But he had in fact already gone too far to draw back, and he could do nothing but present the Colonial Office with a *fait accompli*, hoping that he would be justified by success. So, although the telegraph was available to use had he wished, he pressed on with the implementation of his policy in Perak.[53]

[49] C.1505, pp. 50–51; Précis, Appendix, pp. xxxii-iii. Jervois anticipated that this Council would be composed of 'Abdu'llah, Ismail, and the Bendahara, Yusuf and Dris, but that only the last two would take any active part (C.1505, p. 37).

[50] Gov. Straits to Sec. State, 16 Oct. 1875, in C.1505, pp. 31–38.

[51] Carnarvon to Jervois, 13 Sept. 1875, in PRO 30/6–40.

[52] C.1505, p. 38.

[53] It is clear from a private letter which he wrote to Carnarvon on 18 Oct., justifying his action, that Jervois did this deliberately. Thus he wrote: 'Your Lordship may consider that I should have represented to Your Lordship the circumstances which I have mentioned in my despatch before taking action, and that I should have waited for instructions. . . . In the desire expressed by some of the Perak Chiefs that the British Government should undertake the government of that state I saw an opportunity for dealing with difficulties of no ordinary character . . . Had I shown indecision, or waited until I could have received instructions from Your Lordship . . . the opportunity for action might have passed away . . .' (PRO 30/6–40).

The Colonial Office seems to have been uneasy, from about the middle of 1875, that the trend of events in Malaya was leading the local officials to take affairs too much in their own hands. This had been apparent in Clarke's handling of administrative matters within the British Settlements, as well as in the Peninsular states.[54] The officials took care to see that Sir William Jervois was warned not to allow the Residents to go beyond the giving of advice. They were still thinking in terms of obtaining the virtual control of affairs without having to undertake any of the inevitable responsibility. Thus Herbert insisted on adding to a despatch acknowledging the Residents' reports on Selangor and Perak a paragraph enjoining caution:

> Care is also needed in the character of the advice given by the Acting Residents to the Rulers of the different States; how far it should direct their policy, and how far it should be so framed as to avoid unnecessarily committing you to undefined responsibilities connected with the affairs of those States.[55]

At the end of July, when he had received complaints in London of the extent to which Speedy was assuming the direct government of Larut, Carnarvon was even more explicit. In a despatch communicating the criticisms to Jervois for his comments he observed:

> . . . I desire clearly to impress upon you, that in my opinion, the British Residents should, in all ordinary cases, confine their action to advice tendered by them to the native Rulers, under whose direction the government of the country should be carried on.[56]

Not for the first time the Colonial Office authorities were out of touch with conditions in Malaya; they had sanctioned the introduction of the Resident system largely because they had been led to believe by the men on the spot that it was feasible, and that the Residents' advice would be accepted.

Carnarvon was therefore shocked to receive Jervois's letter of 10 July proposing that Britain should take over the government of the Malay States. He was so impressed by the need to nip such ideas in the bud that he wrote at once from Balmoral, where he was in attendance on the Queen, on 13 September:

---

[54] See Minute by Meade, dated 13 June 1875, in CO 273/80.
[55] Sec. State to Gov. Straits, 15 July 1875, C.1320, p. 112; Herbert's minute of 27 June in 273/80.
[56] Sec. State to Gov. Straits, 27 July 1875, C.1320, p. 117.

I will not say that the time may not be at hand when such a step may not become necessary. I am quite aware that the change would probably be one for the benefit of the peoples; and it is possible that as you say no serious opposition or difficulty would arise on the spot. But I am clearly of opinion that this time, whether it be near or less near—has not yet come. . . . I think there would be fair ground for objection in England that before the system of Residents has really had a trial, and whilst great improvement is taking place under it, a very large change should be forced on without any strong and ostensible reason for it.

After pointing out that it was only within the last few months that British opinion had become aware that the Government was working towards indirect control in Malaya he went on:

We must in all things move in harmony with that public opinion; and as a matter of wise policy I desire to see our present system somewhat more consolidated, and the results of it somewhat more clearly ascertained and understood before we make the next move.[57]

From September till the beginning of November Carnarvon waited in vain for an answer. Jervois's reply to this letter, and his despatch announcing and justifying his embarkation on the policy of direct control in Perak, had not arrived in the Colonial Office on 1 November. Instead, on the 4th, came a bombshell—a telegram announcing the murder of Birch.[58]

On 23 October Swettenham had again left Singapore for Perak taking with him printed copies of the proclamations which were to announce and explain the new administration to the people of Perak—Jervois's proclamation of 15 October, the two proclamations signed by 'Abdu'llah on the night of the 2nd, and six notices outlining the details of British control over taxes and revenue.[59]

Meanwhile in Perak tension was mounting. Notwithstanding Birch's pledge of 1 October runaway slaves continued to be sheltered at the Residency, and the Resident made it plain that with the powers with which he was now armed he intended to make an end of debt-slavery as an institution as soon as possible. 'Abdu'llah by now had got over the fright in which he had signed Birch's proclamations on the 2nd, and remembered only his anger. He determined to rid himself of Birch and effect a *rapprochement*

[57] Carnarvon to Jervois, 13 Sept. 1875, in PRO 30/6–40.
[58] C.1505, p. 17.
[59] Cowan, op. cit., p. 112; Precis, p. 24.

with Ismail before British control was consolidated and his power to act slipped away. In this he was probably pushed on by his followers. Soon after Swettenham's departure for Singapore he was visited by the Maharaja Lela, most belligerent of the downstream chiefs, who declared that rather than allow the Resident to assume control over his village he would kill him, and 'Abdu'llah is said there and then to have given him written authority to do so.[60]

About 9 October, when news reached him of the events lower down the river, Ismail at Blanja summoned a meeting of those who acknowledged him as Sultan to decide whether to submit to British control. On the 12th the Laksamana, acting on behalf of 'Abdu'llah, sent a letter to Ismail saying that the Maharaja had been authorized to kill the Resident. Ismail read out this letter to a large meeting of his chiefs and it was agreed that they should support the Maharaja, and that after *Hari Raya* (the feast marking the end of the fasting month, which fell that year on 1 November) they should combine in an attack on the Residency. In this the chiefs not then present (notably the Mantri, the Bendahara and the Temenggong) whom Ismail counted as his adherents were invited to join. Only Yusuf among the chiefs remained completely uncommitted.[61]

The majority of the Perak chiefs were thus united in their determination not to submit to British control when on the evening of 26 October Swettenham arrived at Bandar Bharu with the proclamations from Singapore. The next day copies were posted in front of the Residency with a salute of twenty-one guns. On the 28th Swettenham left for the upper river to distribute the proclamations and explain the new régime in the inland villages, leaving Birch to carry out the same task in lower Perak. Everywhere Swettenham heard talk of war, and in the Malay camp preparations were going forward to put into execution the plan which would dispose of the Resident once and for all. On 29 October both 'Abdu'llah and Ismail sent supplies and arms to the Maharaja Lela at Pasir Salak, and gave orders for the people

---

[60] Précis, pp. 23–24.
[61] Ibid., p. 26; evidence of Raja Yahyah, Haji Mat Yassim and Haji 'Ali in CO 273/87–88. The Mantri made preparations through the Penghulu at Kurau so that when the general attack was made on the Residency he would go round by sea from Kuala Kurau and attack the customs house at Kota Stia, in the Perak River (Gullick, op. cit., p. 64).

Q

of the neighbouring villages to be ready to rally to his support.
Finally on the 31st 'Abdu'llah sent a *kris* to the Maharaja Lela,
a symbolic command to proceed with the execution of the Sultan's
enemy.[62]

On the evening of 1 November Birch arrived at Pasir Salak by
boat with his Malay clerk, a naval officer Lieutenant Abbot, an
escort of sepoys, and a large supply of printed notices. The Maharaja at once sent out messengers to collect men from the surrounding villages, and when next morning the clerk began to post
the notices he was cut down, and the mob rushed the floating
bath-house in which the Resident was taking his morning bath.
Before the sepoy guard was awake to what was going on Birch had
been stabbed and hacked to death. The sepoys made good their
retreat to the boats, and fell back on the Residency at Bandar
Bharu, as did Abbot, who had been out shooting on the other
side of the river. Luckily for them the projected attack on the
Residency did not materialize. Two days later Swettenham, on
his way back down-river after posting the proclamations upstream,
was stopped at Blanja with the news of Birch's murder. An attempt
was made to get him ashore, but distrusting the good faith of
Ismail's chiefs he determined instead to push on. Though chased
he managed to reach the Residency in safety the next morning.[63]

After Birch's death all was for a time confusion. When the news
reached Penang Colonel Anson sent off sixty men of the garrison
with some police under a Captain Innes as Commissioner in
charge, to take control of the situation at the mouth of the Perak
River. They relieved the Residency, but were repulsed in a too
precipitate attack on the Maharaja Lela's stockade at Pasir Salak,
and Innes was killed. Meanwhile Jervois, after cabling frantically
to London for reinforcements from India and Hongkong, went
himself with 150 men from Singapore to Perak, so that there was
no one left in Singapore with authority to deal with the flood of
cables which poured in from London and India. Jervois, from the
scene of action, sent messages for transmission asking for more
and more troops as news reached him of unrest in Selangor and
Sungai Ujong as well as in Perak. Lord Carnarvon indignantly
declined to supply troops until Jervois had given him some indication by cable of what he was up to, and finally, getting no

---

[62] Cowan, op. cit., pp. 115 et seq.; Précis, pp. 24–26.
[63] C.1505, pp. 83 et seq.; Swettenham, *British Malaya*, pp. 203–6.

reply, decided that he could no longer assume the responsibility of further delay in the despatch of troops. He laid all responsibility on the Governor's shoulders, telling him that in any case annexation was banned. The Indian Government asked whether it should send Indian or English troops, and whether it could send an officer in command who would be senior to the officer in command in the Straits. The Flag Officer at Bombay wished to know whether things were serious enough to justify him interfering in Malaya, which came under the China station. Finally, when the confusion was at its height, the cable broke between Penang and Madras, and all immediate contact with the outside world was lost.[64]

By the end of November troops had arrived from India and Hongkong, a Naval Brigade had been landed, and the situation had sorted itself out. Jervois had at first assumed that he had to deal with a national rising, and the Maharaja Lela's stand at Pasir Salak had confirmed his opinion that a hard campaign lay ahead. But in fact 'Abdu'llah and Ismail had not thought much beyond Birch's death. They had assumed that once he had been killed the British Government would lose interest. When the reverse proved to be the case 'Abdu'llah, the Laksamana and the Shahbandar professed their loyalty to the Governor, and the Maharaja Lela was persuaded to fly up-river to Ismail, every effort being made to conceal 'Abdu'llah's complicity in the murder. On 15 November the troops from Singapore and Penang with naval help captured Pasir Salak. Soon afterwards the occupation of the country and the pursuit of Maharaja Lela and his accomplices began. A column of troops from Hongkong with men of the Naval Bridge went up the Perak River in boats to take Blanja, and Ismail fled into the jungle with the Maharaja Lela at their approach. From Blanja the column marched on Kinta, which after much trouble getting their guns and stores through the jungle they occupied on 17 December. Meanwhile another column of 1,200 men from Calcutta disembarked at the mouth of the Larut River and marched to Kuala Kangsar. From there 200 men went down the river to Blanja and joined the Hongkong troops at Kinta. The rest of the men from India took Kota Lama on 4 January 1876, and subdued the surrounding villages.[65]

[64] C.1505, pp. 17–26, *passim*, pp. 89–92.
[65] Précis, pp. 30–31; C.1505 and C.1512 of 1876 contain a mass of papers detailing the military conduct of the pacification and occupation of Perak. The most important despatches are C.1505, pp. 119–23, 174–5, 224, 243–5 and 268–9.

The trouble in Selangor came to nothing. It had mainly taken the form of freebooting in the interior, and was easily put down by the Resident's police and a force of 200 Chinese raised by Yap Ah Loy at Kuala Lumpur. No doubt the arrest of Mahdi in Johore and his confinement in Singapore jail also helped to restore order; in any event things were quiet again by the end of 1875.[66] There was however some sharp but short-lived fighting in the states behind Malacca, where the events in Perak encouraged opportunist chiefs to try their own luck. But trouble arose not from dissatisfaction amongst the Sungai Ujong people with the Resident system, but from the rivalries of the petty chiefs of the Menangkabau Confederacy. The chiefs of the surrounding states disapproved of the presence of British troops in Sungai Ujong, and were afraid that the Dato' Klana would use British support to extend his power over the rest of the Confederacy. He had already quarrelled with the acknowledged claimant to the office of Yang di-Pertuan, Tengku Antar of Sri Menanti, and given his support to his rival, Tengku Ahmat Tunggal, son of the last Yang di-Pertuan who had died in 1869. The Straits Government also declined to recognize Tengku Antah as Yang di-Pertuan, so that when a British survey party from Sungai Ujong crossed the border into the neighbouring state of Terachi at the end of November 1875 he and his allies took fright and invaded the British protected state. A strong force of Gurkhas and some British troops was at once moved into Sungai Ujong, and by the middle of January they had driven the invaders out of that state and sub-dued Terachi, Sri Menanti, and Ulu Muar. Both contenders for the title of Yang Di-Pertuan, Tengku Antah and Tengku Ahmad Tunggal, had by then fled, so that the Straits Government were left in effective control of the whole area.[67]

In Perak all the fugitives were secured by the middle of 1876, and the Maharaja Lela with three of his followers directly con-cerned in Birch's murder were hanged in Larut in January 1877. Before that enough evidence had been uncovered by a Commission of Enquiry to expose the complicity of 'Abdu'llah and the other chiefs, and he and the Mantri, the Laksamana and the Shahbandar were deported to the Seychelles. Ismail and three of his followers

---

were removed to Johore, and Yusuf, practically the only important chief not implicated, and as Raja Muda the legal successor to the Perak throne, was recognized as Regent and later became Sultan.

By the end of 1876 the British Government were thus in complete control of the west-coast states from Perak in the north to the borders of Malacca. They now had to decide what policy they intended to pursue there.

7

THE AFTERMATH

THE Perak War was paralleled by a bitter controversy between Sir William Jervois and Lord Carnarvon over the degree of responsibility for it which attached to the local government and to the Colonial Office. As a result the Secretary of State was never able to admit that it was necessary for the Residents to exercise power wider than the giving of advice if they were to function successfully in the Malay States. In order to produce results in an area where effective governments did not exist the Residents were forced to take responsibility on their own shoulders, and to act as the chief executive officers of their states in direct opposition to Colonial Office instructions. Thus a form of British control grew up in each of the states under British protection which was at variance with the constitutional theory as set out in the Treaties and in the Colonial Office policy directives. Direct government by the Residents was cloaked in the forms of advice, and the Malay rulers surrendered their actual power into the hands of the British officers and administrative officials.

This system was extended between 1877 and 1895 to the other states of Negri Sembilan in addition to Sungai Ujong, and to Pahang. It was consolidated in 1895 with the formation of a Federation made up of Perak, Selangor, Negri Sembilan and Pahang, which had as its chief executive officer a British Resident-General. In 1909 the northern states of Kedah, Perlis, Trengganu and Kelantan passed from the Siamese to the British sphere of influence, and took British Advisers whose powers were similar to those of the Residents in the other states. Then in 1914 the pattern was completed when Johore, which had always had intimate links with the British Government, formalized the relationship by taking an Adviser in her turn. Thus the process which was begun in Perak in 1874 reached its logical conclusion, and the foreign policy and internal administration of all the states of the Peninsula passed under British control.

(i) *The Resident System after 1876*

Birch's murder and the Perak War discredited Jervois's scheme of direct government for good. Carnarvon had already disapproved of the tentative suggestions which Jervois made in July, and the news of the outbreak in Perak ensured that the full-scale exposition of the new policy contained in the Governor's despatch of 16 October 1875[1] was never given any objective study. The first reaction of Carnarvon and most of the Colonial Office officials was that the new policy had caused the war, and they never saw reason to make any major modification to this view. Jervois naturally resented this, and did not hesitate to indicate in his despatches that he thought their attitude both mistaken and unfair.

[1] C.1505, pp. 31–38.

The fighting in Perak was therefore paralleled by a paper war between the Secretary of State and the Governor, which began in December 1875 and extended throughout the first half of 1876. The character of this correspondence does not reflect much credit on either side. Jervois was primarily concerned to rescue his reputation and his career; the Secretary of State with public opinion and Parliament. As a result each showed more concern for shifting blame and responsibility on to others than for the transaction of public business. Hard words were used, tempers became ruffled, and considerable bitterness was produced.

Carnarvon's first despatch on the subject was written on 10 December 1875.[2] It was ostensibly a reply to Jervois's despatch of 16 October, announcing and justifying his policy, but it was written under the shadow of the telegrams bringing the news of Birch's death and the failure of the first assault on Pasir Salak. To the anger directed against a Governor who exceeded his powers and dictated policy was added the shock of disaster. It was inevitably therefore a strong despatch. Carnarvon condemned Jervois for acting without consultation, and he disapproved of a policy whose introduction had been, in his words, 'the signal for resistance and attack' and 'in opposition to the whole tenor of my directions'. His despatch was an indictment, but also a call to Jervois to defend himself if he could:

> . . . I desire that you should understand that I am not now pronouncing a final decision upon your proceedings, and if I state freely and unreservedly what I conceive to have been grave errors of policy and of action, my present object is to elicit those full explanations which it is on every ground desirable that I should receive, and which, coming from an officer of high reputation in whom great trust has been reposed, are entitled to be very fully weighed by Her Majesty's Government before his conduct is condemned.[3]

Jervois's deliberate refusal to consult the home government before putting his policy into force was, in the circumstances, hardly justifiable. He would have been wise to have acknowledged this, for the policy itself was perfectly defensible, and he could still have argued that it was not the prime cause of Birch's murder. But Jervois was not the man to admit a mistake. Instead he took an entirely different course, denying that what he had done was a departure from existing policy at all.

² Op. cit., pp. 64–67.   ³ Ibid.

In a despatch dated 10 February 1876[4] he sought to show that ever since the Treaty of Pangkor the Residents had in fact ruled, that this was implicit in the treaty itself, which insisted that the Sultans must take the advice offered to them, and that any Governor must have inferred from the despatches and official reports available to him that the Secretary of State knew of and approved of this state of affairs. In these circumstances his own action in placing the administration of Perak in the hands of British Commissioners who would rule in the Sultan's name, merely recognized existing facts. If, as the Secretary of State maintained, this was virtually annexation, then so was the régime ushered in by the Pangkor Treaty. Though this argument was somewhat overdrawn it was not without a basis in fact. The Residents had everywhere gone beyond the mere giving of advice, and Larut had been ruled as if it were a British province. This had been made quite clear in the official reports sent home, so clear that protests against it had been made in London. And though the Secretary of State had warned the Residents to exercise caution, and not to go too far, he had at no time disapproved their proceedings— quite the reverse.

When we have said this in fairness to Jervois, however, we have said all that can be urged in defence of this despatch. It is first and foremost a dishonest document. It is quite clear from all the papers, and from Jervois's private correspondence with Carnarvon before the new system was introduced, that he regarded himself as making a great innovation in Perak. This attitude he maintained as late as 16 October, after his scheme had been launched.[5] The main argument of Jervois's despatch was therefore aimed at obscuring this basic fact. So far as the Secretary of State was concerned it had no hope of succeeding,[6] and Jervois must on any

---

[4] C.1503, pp. 3–19; C.1512, pp. 7–24.

[5] See his remark on the title of 'Queen's Commissioners' which he proposed to give to British officials in Perak: 'I consider it very desirable that the change of policy from one of mere advice to one of control should be marked by a change in the titles of British Officers' (C.1505, p. 37). Again in the same despatch he wrote: 'I am sensible that, in acting without instructions, I have incurred a grave responsibility . . . I trust that when Your Lordship weighs the reasons which I have given for action, and for that action which I have taken, Your Lordship will not fail to appreciate the advantages which may fairly be expected to result from establishing a more direct control over a semi-barbarous State . . . in which so much may be done, with the power that we shall now possess, . . .' (op. cit., p. 38).

[6] Carnarvon wrote on 23 March: 'It is simply impossible,—both from his private correspondence as well as from the official history of the transaction—

sensible calculation have known this. Either he was obsessed by some deep psychological need for self-justification, and prompted by it lost his head, or he calculated that the correspondence would be published, and sought by these specious arguments to exculpate himself and discredit the Colonial Office.

Certainly the form and the language of the despatch are more reminiscent of a polemical pamphlet than of a colonial governor addressing a minister of the Crown. To support his arguments Jervois used fragments from the Secretary of State's despatches, sometimes even single words, shorn of their context and manipulated so as to show that Carnarvon recognized and approved of a system of direct control on the part of the Residents. He told the minister that he had an erroneous idea of the policy to which he had given his approval, and that his views were based upon 'an imperfect acquaintance with facts'. He expressed doubt whether the Colonial Office ever really expected the Residents to confine themselves to advice, and observed that he had taken the line he had because

I did not for a moment imagine that it could ever be contemplated on our part to break the Pangkore Treaty, and to ourselves refuse to carry out engagements which Her Majesty's Government decided should be strictly fulfilled by the Sultan and Chiefs of that State. I conceived that in affairs of this solemn character . . . we were equally bound by our engagements as they, and that there was no withdrawal from the position we had assumed in relation to Perak. . . . I was anxious if possible, not to reverse the policy as approved by Her Majesty's Government . . .[7]

Carnarvon was scandalized by this. He described the despatch as 'one of the least satisfactory I have ever read since I have been connected with this office'. Meade and Herbert sought to make excuses for the Governor, but Carnarvon would have none of it. 'It unquestionably has the merit of cleverness', he conceded, 'but it is unscrupulous in argument, unbecoming in tone, and very disingenuous in character.'[8] His notes abound in exclamation marks and expressions of indignation and horror: 'Monstrous', 'Absurd', 'An outrageous doctrine', 'The insolence of this expression can

that Sir William Jervois can have thought that when he issued the Proclamation in Perak he was only making "a slight modification" in the existing system. I am satisfied that he meant it to be the first immediate step to annexation.' Minute in CO 273/83.

[7] C.1503, p. 12.

[8] Minute of 22 Mar. 1876, in CO 273/83.

hardly be matched in any Colonial Despatch', 'One of the strongest charges ever brought against a Secretary of State by a Colonial Governor'. He was particularly incensed by the use of quotations from a Parliamentary debate against him.[9] But in the course of six pages of notes on Jervois's text he appears for the moment to have relieved his personal feelings enough to come at last to the gravamen of the charge against the Governor:

> . . . one thing I desire to lay down in clearest language that I will not sanction a great measure of State policy being adopted by a Colonial Government without the sanction, and in opposition to the instructions of the Home Government. When annexation has become expedient H.M. Government must have the exclusive responsibility of the measure.[10]

His official reply to Jervois however did not confine itself to this theme, but sought to rebut the Governor's arguments in detail. In this Carnarvon was less than candid. He had no trouble in showing that the passages on which Jervois had relied to support his arguments would not bear their weight when read in their context. The Secretary of State had not given official approval to a régime of direct rule by Residents. He could not have done so, for whatever the actual practice of the Residents in the Malay States the Colonial Office had never been furnished with a coherent account of it.[11] If he had been frank however he would have admitted that he had some idea of what was going on in the Peninsula.[12] Instead he sought to divest himself entirely of responsibility, maintaining that until Jervois's despatch of 16 October he had no idea that the Residents were doing anything except giving advice.

The character of this correspondence was most unfortunate, for each side was so intent on making out its own case that it was never possible to discuss openly the undoubted difficulties of a Resident

---

[9] 'The first time I imagine a Colonial Governor has ever quoted a Parliamentary debate against his official Chief to attack or trip him up. The debate ought to be referred to, the accuracy of the quotation verified & its suitability; and I ought to see the passage to make sure that it was a fair Report of what I said. *Hansard is no authority that can be admitted—still less a newspaper report*' (Carnarvon's marginalia on Jervois's despatch of 10 Feb. 1876, in CO 273/83).

[10] Ibid.

[11] Even Clarke's instructions to the various Residents had never been sent home to the Colonial Office.

[12] He had read and approved of Speedy's Report on Larut for 1874, and the Reports of Swettenham and Davidson on Selangor in 1875; he had also Jervois's private letters, especially that of 10 July 1875, summarized in the preceding chapter, pp. 226-7.

system. The Colonial Office was not able to acknowledge that
'advice' pure and simple was impracticable, so that future Residents, as we shall see below, were left in a most invidious position. On the personal side however these spirited exchanges
seem to have cleared the air and brought both sides to their senses.
Though Carnarvon was forced to insist that Jervois had not been
unjustly censured he treated him henceforwards with great deference.[13] He was left in the Straits Settlements for long enough to
deal with the aftermath of the Perak War, and then employed in
important positions in Australia. In the settlement of Perak and
Negri Sembilan Jervois was highly successful, and he left Malaya
in 1877 with the goodwill of both the Colonial Office and the
Straits merchants.

The formal victory of the Secretary of State was celebrated in a
despatch dated 1 June 1876, in which he laid down future policy.[14]
It is a curious and in many ways ambiguous document, embodying
all the contradictions and hesitations of Colonial Office policy. On
the one hand it stated clearly that there could be no question of
annexation or of government by British officers and that the
Resident system must be given a further trial. On the other it left
the position and powers of the Residents completely undefined.
It talked of the Resident whose position was 'well understood in
the East' giving 'influential advice to the native ruler'. It approved
Jervois's proposal to create a Council of Malay chiefs and British
officers, because it would give the Resident 'an opportunity of
gauging the strength of native feeling on questions of proposed

[13] Cf. the last paragraph of the Secretary of State's despatch of 20 May
1876. 'It is not my object to convey censure, and, indeed, I have already highly
approved the conspicuous ability and determination with which you acted subsequently to the outbreak of these disorders. I am glad to take this opportunity
of repeating my appreciation of your conduct during this period, but I am
confident that your long experience as a distinguished servant of the Crown
will make you fully aware, on reflection, that an officer representing Her Majesty
in a distant dependency must be most careful to assure himself that the Government to which he is responsible not only understands but approves any important
administrative or political changes which he may contemplate; that he is not at
liberty of his own motion to initiate such measures; and that the necessity for
obtaining a distinct assurance of approval is so great as to outweigh any advantage
which might appear to him likely to ensue from more immediate action. I am
equally confident that I can rely as fully upon your cordial and unreserved co-
operation in that policy which will be announced to you as if it had not unfortunately been my duty to disapprove of some of your recent acts and opinions'
(C.1503, p. 31). Soon after this the two men exchanged personal letters of reconciliation (Carnarvon to Jervois, 17 Oct. 1876; Jervois to Carnarvon, 30 Nov.
1876; in PRO 30/6-40).
[14] C.1512, pp. 98–100.

reform; and the knowledge so gained would tend to the exercise of greater discrimination in the nature of the advice given by the Resident to the chief native authority'. But at the same time it spoke of the Resident settling by regulation the nature of the questions that must be brought before this Council, maintaining peace and law, initiating a sound system of taxation, and supervising the collection of revenue. It envisaged the training of chiefs of 'sufficient capacity and enlightenment to appreciate the advantages of a civilized government' so that they might 'render some effectual assistance in the government of the country', in the same way that the proposed Council would associate some of the chiefs with the government. But it assumed throughout the existence of some entity, which it called in one place 'the Executive Government', which was quite apart from the chiefs, from the Council, and from the Resident. The chiefs were to be trained to assist it (at some unspecified stage in the future), the Council was to be a body quite distinct from it, the Resident was to advise it.

The truth was that such a thing as a government did not exist in Perak apart from the acts of British officials there, and the Colonial Office refused to undertake the formal responsibility for providing one. But they wished to have the power to replace one ruler by another, to control the general lines of the country's development, and to have created a police force whose officers were to be appointed by the Secretary of State. The Secretary of State willed the end, but restricted the means available to his local representatives in fulfilling it, and left it to them to find some way out of the *impasse*. After the Perak War, therefore, as before, the initiative still lay with the local government. The shortcomings and dangers inherent in such an incoherent policy were quite clearly stated at the time by the editor of *The Economist*, who wrote:

Lord Carnarvon has . . . taken up a very determined attitude, and though opinions may differ as to the wisdom of his policy, it is at any rate satisfactory that there will be no further ambiguities in the counsels of the Colonial Office on which too zealous local officials may found daring and embarrassing enterprises. Yet this is now an advantage confined within the narrowest limits. We are committed, for good or evil, to responsibilities in Perak and the adjacent regions which we cannot shake off by a despatch from a Minister in Downing Street. The position in which we find ourselves . . . impresses upon the official world a warning,—not without many a parallel it is to be feared,—

against the negligent vagueness of the policy dictated from the mother country, quite as much as against the perilous audacity of colonial governors and their local advisers.[15]

The conditions under which the Resident system operated in Perak after 1876 differed appreciably from those in force in earlier years. There was a clean sweep of almost all the more important chiefs. The evidence collected by the Commission of Enquiry proved that all except Yusuf were guilty to some extent of complicity in Birch's murder. The Maharaja Lela with three of his followers immediately concerned in the deed were hanged at Matang, in Larut, in January 1877. 'Abdu'llah and the others were not brought to trial, since there was no British court competent to try them, and 'Abdu'llah as sovereign ruler of Perak could hardly be 'advised' to constitute a court for the occasion in Perak, nor to execute its judgment on himself. Instead they were all removed from the country as an 'act of state', on grounds of general expediency, after the Executive Council of the Straits Settlements had examined the evidence, and 'Abdu'llah's statements on his own behalf, in order to satisfy themselves that this was necessary. 'Abdu'llah, the Mantri, the Laksamana and the Shahabandar were deported to the Seychelles. Ismail and three of his followers, who had never given their allegiance to the Pangkor Treaty and were guiltless of breaking an engagement which they had not signed, were with the Maharaja's consent, removed to Johore. Yusuf, the only chief not involved and the heir by blood to the throne, was recognized by the British Government as Regent, with the idea that after a satisfactory period of 'probation' he might become Sultan, which he eventually did.[16]

There were also significant changes in the British personnel in Perak. J. G. Davidson was at first transferred from Selangor to take Birch's place as Resident and established himself in the Kuala Kangsar area, where he was in touch by road and by telegraph with Larut and Penang. Davidson's position was a most unhappy one. He had little contact with the people of Perak, for most of their leaders had been removed, and the villagers themselves were frightened and sullen. The country was being held down by troops,

[15] *The Economist*, 24 June 1876, p. 736.
[16] C.1709, *passim*; *Proceedings of the Executive Council and Correspondence upon the Case of Ex-Sultan Abdullah and other Perak Chiefs*. Singapore, 2 Apr. 1877.

over whom he had little control, but who could not be removed until an adequate police force was raised. There was no money, and an adequate revenue system had still to be created. By July 1876 the Straits Settlements had spent nearly $500,000 on account of the various Peninsular states, the great majority of it in Perak, and the local government, in addition to obtaining credits from the Imperial Government, had to borrow on the London money market in order to meet its normal commitments for the second half of 1876. It was not until November 1876 that the Straits Government received permission to appropriate £25,000 of these advances for the organization of local police forces in the states, so that the troops could be withdrawn, and the money did not become available until early in 1877.[17]

Davidson, with his charm and knowledge of the Malays and their language, seems to have had some success in bringing the people of the up-river villages around Kota Lama to a more amenable frame of mind. But he had not the same interest in the state as in Selangor, and he never looked like coping with the difficulties of the situation. In February 1877 he took advantage of a bout of fever to extricate himself from an unpleasant position, and to return to his law practice in Singapore.[18] His successor as Resident in Perak was Hugh Low, who had been for many years Colonial Secretary at Labuan, and who was a Colonial Office nominee.

Soon after Low's arrival he took Larut under his own control from his base at Kuala Kangsar, and Speedy, the Assistant Resident, was moved to Durian Sa-batang, where he directed affairs in Lower Perak. This reorganization was one of the basic reasons for Low's success in Perak. Larut was the wealthiest part of the state, and its revenue surplus was Perak's only current asset. It was logical that it should come under the supervision of the Resident, who was best placed to co-ordinate development there with that in the rest of the state, and under Low's remorseless insistence on economy it provided an increasing amount for the use of the poorer Malay areas of Perak. So far as Speedy was concerned however the move was a change for the worse. Durian Sa-batang and its mud-flats provided a sombre contrast to the bustle and the expansive life in the lordly Residency in Larut, and Mrs. Speedy

[17] Winstedt, *Perak*, pp. 116–17; C.1709, pp. 60–64 and 68–69.
[18] Winstedt, op. cit.,; 'Yap Ah Loy', p. 87; C.1709, p. 131.

complained bitterly. So did Low, when he found that Speedy was spending money in the same lavish way as in Larut, and building himself another Residency on the same scale as the one he had left. He said that Speedy was 'recklessly wasting the resources of the country':

Speedy says 7,000 dollars have been already spent on the site of this new town and the road to the Residency. There is nothing to show for it but a few ditches of a very small size. I went down the road, it was quite impassable for carts . . . He and I could not quite hit it off about the proper sites for public buildings and Chinese houses, every view he says will interfere with the comfort or privacy and outlook of the Residency.[19]

Speedy's position in Malaya was made extremely uncomfortable in December 1876 and May 1877 when the Colonial Office published two further instalments of official papers which contained despatches from Jervois reflecting on his administrative ability and his probity. At the end of 1877 he threw in his hand and resigned.[20] So the last of the adventurers passed from the scene. The future, in Perak and in the other west-coast states, belonged to the professional administrators.

Similar changes in personnel took place in Selangor. Davidson was replaced as Resident in 1876 by Captain Blomfield Douglas, R.N.R., a retired naval officer. A State Council was formed, with Tengku Zia'u'd-din as President, and the collection of revenues on the several rivers was gradually taken out of the hands of the chiefs in return for fixed allowances. At the end of 1877, when the process was completed, these allowances totalled $60,000 a year, or one-third of the state's total revenue. Zia'u'd-din was not happy under the new dispensation. His debts had all been taken over by the state, he received a guaranteed income of $1,000 a month, and his position as Viceroy was recognized by the British Government. But he missed Davidson, and was not on easy terms with Douglas, who seems to have been something of a martinet, with a brusque personality. He was away in Kedah for six months in 1876, and again in 1878. At the end of 1878 he gave up his position as Viceroy, and eventually retired to Penang with a

---

[19] 'Journal of Sir Hugh Low, Perak, 1877', [Ed.] Emily Sadka, *JRASMB*, pt. 4 (1954), p. 88.
[20] Gullick, *Captain Speedy of Larut*, pp. 78–83. Jervois had been hostile to Speedy for some time, and had tried to prevent him from returning to Malaya when he went on leave in 1876.

gratuity of $30,000 and a pension for himself and his family. There is no evidence to support the assumption, but he may well have been bought out at Douglas's instigation. Certainly his going 'regularized' the position in Selangor. It left Sultan 'Abdu'l-Samad, notorious for his easy-going attitude to politics, as the only Malay authority in the state. So instead of having to deal with a Viceroy who took an active part in administration Douglas was left very much alone to direct affairs as he thought fit.[21]

Developments in Negri Sembilan were more complex and far-reaching. The punitive expedition of December 1875, as we have seen, left Sir William Jervois in control not only of Sungai Ujong, but virtually of the neighbouring areas of Terachi, Sri Menanti, and Ulu Muar as well.[22] For the moment he was at a loss what to do with the initiative so gained. Information on conditions in the separate states was very scanty, and the two contenders for the title of Yang di-pertuan, Tengku Ahmat and Tengku Antar, had both decamped into the interior. So he contented himself with establishing police stations in Terachi and Sri Menanti, and at Kuala Pila and Kuala Jempol in Ulu Muar, under the control of a chief named Dato' Sutan, a son of a former Dato' Klana of Sungai Ujong, and under the general supervision of the Assistant Resident of Sungai Ujong. Then in the spring of 1876 two things happened. In February Tengku Ahmat came to Singapore for an interview with the Governor, in which he expressed himself as 'anxious to meet the wishes of the British Government'.[23] In the first week of April a number of Menankabau from Ulu Muar and the neighbourhood attacked the police stations and drove out the Malay policemen stationed there, so that a British force from Sungai Ujong had again to intervene and to occupy the area.[24]

On 20 April Jervois therefore put forward a scheme for extending British control over Sri Menanti and the Ulu Muar region. Those parts of Negri Sembilan which actually formed the boundary with Malacca, the states of Rembau and Johol, presented no problem. Their chiefs were willing to co-operate with the British authorities in maintaining order on the frontier, and Jervois proposed to negotiate general treaties of friendship with them. He

[21] 'Yap Ah Loy', pp. 86–88, p. 94.
[22] See above, p. 236.
[23] Gov. Straits to Sec. State, 20 Apr. 1876, in C.1512, p. 88.
[24] Assistant Resident, Sungai Ujong, to Colonial Sec. Singapore, 5 Apr. 1876, printed C.1512, pp. 93–96.

saw clearly that the revival of the office of Yang di-pertuan would only create discord amongst the states. Apart from the rivalry between Tengku Antar and Tengku Ahmat and their respective followers, the Dato' Klana of Sungai Ujong and the chiefs of the other larger states were opposed to the appointment of any chief to a position of paramountcy in the area. But something had to be done to secure order on the eastern boundary of Sungai Ujong. Jervois therefore proposed to recognize Tengku Ahmat, not as Yang di-pertuan of Negri Sembilan, but as 'Malay Captain' of the Ulu Muar area and of Sri Menanti; at the same time he proposed to take these states under British protection, and to appoint a British Agent to 'assist' Tengku Ahmat.[25] This idea became more practical in June when Tengku Antar came to Singapore, and promised to live peacefully in Johore under the wing of the Maharaja.[26]

The Colonial Office, however, would have nothing to do with this. They were unwilling to allow any extension of the Resident system until it had proved itself in Perak and Selangor. They could not see anything in Jervois's despatches to indicate that Tengku Ahmat would be able to maintain order in Ulu Muar without the help of British troops or police, and they were afraid that further entanglements in these states might follow.[27] So Jervois was told to think again before committing himself:

I trust that you will now be able to make such satisfactory arrangements as will enable the Government to disentangle itself from further complications with these States, beyond what are involved in the case of Sungie Ujong . . . I would impress upon you the necessity of adhering to a line of policy which will . . . avoid a further and especially an undefined and uncertain extension of our political responsibilities in the Malay Peninsula, . . .[28]

In the upshot Jervois attained his ends by an ingenious arrangement which avoided any formal assumption of British responsibility. With the help of the Maharaja of Johore he collected most of the chiefs concerned in Singapore in November. There it was arranged that the 'states' of Sri Menanti, Ulu Muar, Jempol and Johol, and the 'districts' of Terachi, Gunong Pasir and Inas,

[25] Gov. Straits to Sec. State, 20 Apr. 1876 (C.1512, pp. 86 et seq.) and 13 May 1876 (C. 1709, pp. 3–6).
[26] Gov. Straits to Sec. State, 7 June 1876, ibid., pp. 7–8.
[27] Minutes of 28 May and 27 June 1876, in CO 273/84.
[28] Sec. State to Gov. Straits, 19 Aug. 1876, printed C.1709, pp. 41–42.

should form a confederacy. The chiefs were willing to accept Tengku Antar as their suzerain, but not Tengku Ahmat. So Jervois discarded Ahmat, and recognized Tengku Antar as *Yam-tuan* of Sri Menanti, 'having authority over' the other states of the confederacy. This arrangement was embodied in a treaty in which the chiefs agreed also not to interfere with their neighbours, and not to molest traders. Most important, they agreed to refer disputes between themselves to the Maharaja of Johore, and he at the same time undertook to deal with these disputes in concert with the government of the Straits Settlements.[29] The effect of this arrangement was to divide the states behind Malacca into three classes. First, the states of Rembau, Jelebu, Tampin and Kesang (or Lower Muar), which remained independent, and in the case of the first two concluded treaties of friendship with the British Government.[30] Second, Sungai Ujong, which was a British-protected state with a British Resident. Third, the states of the Sri Menanti confederation under Yam-tuan Antar, which came under the nominal influence of the Maharaja of Johore.

The influence of the Maharaja of Johore was further increased in 1877, when Sultan 'Ali of Kesang died. The position of this state, which formed the eastern boundary of Malacca, was a special one. It had been created in 1855 for 'Ali, then styled Sultan of Johore, when he had renounced the sovereignty of Johore in favour of the Temenggong, later known as the Maharaja.[31] The Treaty of 1855 provided that Kesang territory should not be alienated to any third party without first being offered to the East India Company, and then to the Maharaja of Johore.[32] When 'Ali died the British Government refused to recognize any of his sons as his successor; nor were they interested in acquiring the territory for themselves. So after a form of election by the headmen of the area it passed to the Maharaja and became part of Johore.[33]

[29] Gov. Straits to Sec. State, 13 Dec. 1876, printed C.1709, pp. 84–86; 'Agreement entered into by certain Chiefs of the Nine States, 23 November 1876', in Maxwell and Gibson, op. cit., pp. 60–61; Jervois to Maharaja of Johore, 29 Nov. 1876, in C.1709, p. 89.

[30] Treaty with Rembau, 31 Mar. 1877, in Maxwell and Gibson, op. cit., pp. 48–49; Treaty with Jelebu, 26 Apr. 1877, ibid., pp. 52–53. Both these states also agreed to refer disputes with neighbouring states to the Maharaja of Johore.

[31] See p. 15 above.

[32] Maxwell and Gibson, op. cit., p. 128.

[33] Ibid., pp. 137–42; Emerson, *Malaysia*, p. 200; Winstedt, *Johore*, pp. 112 et. seq.

At about the same time the western boundaries of Malacca and Sungai Ujong were also tidied up. First the Klana of Sungai Ujong, then in September 1877 the ruler of Rembau, ceded to the British Government possession of the disputed ground at Simpang Linggi, and it became part of Malacca territory.[34] Then in February 1878 a boundary treaty was signed between Sungai Ujong and Selangor, which as result of various adjustments, the most important of them being the transfer of Lukut from Selangor to Sungai Ujong, created a well-defined frontier between the two states.[35]

By the beginning of 1878 therefore affairs in Perak, Selangor and the states behind Malacca had settled down, and the position had been clarified, so far as the personalities involved and the territorial limits of their jurisdiction were concerned. But the divergence between theory and practice, between the functions of the Residents as defined by the Colonial Office, and the position which they were in fact compelled to take up in order to achieve anything, was never resolved. The Resident's function, as defined by the Secretary of State and the Governor of the Straits Settlements, was confined to the giving of influential and responsible advice to the ruler concerned. The way in which Governors and Residents approached this problem was indicated in a correspondence which took place in May and June 1878. This was prompted by an incident in Selangor, in which the Resident was held by the Governor, at that time Sir William Robinson, to have exceeded his powers. In addition to reprimanding Douglas the Governor addressed a circular letter to all the Residents, reminding them of the Secretary of State's definition of their functions, and warning them that

. . . the Residents have been placed in the Native States as advisers, not as rulers, and if they take upon themselves to disregard this principle they will most assuredly be held responsible if trouble springs out of their neglect of it.[36]

Douglas, already humiliated by having his action reversed with the full knowledge of the Selangor State Council, and Murray in

[34] 'Deed of Cession of land at Sempang by the Datoh Klana of Sungei Ujong, 31 May 1877', Maxwell and Gibson, op. cit., p. 39; 'Deed of Cession of land at Sempang by the Datoh of Rembau, 27 September 1877', ibid., p. 49.

[35] Boundary Agreement between Selangor and Sungei Ujong, 10 Feb. 1878, ibid., pp. 212–13.

[36] Colonial Sec., Singapore, to H.B.M. Residents, 17 May 1878, in CO 809/18.

Sungai Ujong, both promised meekly to do their best to conform to their instructions, and kept their private thoughts on the subject to themselves. But Low in Perak faced the issue squarely, and his letter is worthy of extensive quotation. He began by saying that there was in Perak no government to advise, and no chief who would defer to a Resident confined to the giving of advice:

> When I came into this country it was under military occupation, and there was no native Government in it. . . . When I asked Mr. Meade, 'Who was the Rajah I was sent out to advise ?' he said 'We don't know of one, you must try and ascertain whether there is anyone fit for the position, and then he will be supported.'
> My greatest difficulty in endeavouring to settle the country has always been the Rajah Muda [i.e. Yusuf] . . . he has no idea of government except that the ryots [the peasants] were created to produce revenue for the rajahs, and to be at their entire disposal; if I were only here to advise such a man, and if he did not believe that I had authority to control his caprices when they are most likely to be dangerous to the country, our hope of restoring peace to it would be vain, and the position of the Resident untenable.[37]

Until therefore an effective government had been created the Resident must do far more than give advice.

> . . . I fully understand the wishes of Government and intend to carry them out, but we must first create the Government to be advised, and this is what I have all along been trying to do . . .[38]

The Governor's response to this exposé of the situation facing the Resident dealt with only part of the problem:

> It does not follow [he wrote] because the Resident is only the adviser, that the ruler may reject his advice when the peace and good order of the country are at stake. The advice which the Residents give is authoritative advice, and may not be lightly rejected . . . All the same, the fiction (if such you prefer to call it) that the Residents are merely advisers, must be kept up; and here is just where the adroitness and ability of the officer are so important. To have to say to the ruler, 'I am only here to advise you', and at the same time to make him feel and understand that the advice you give must be taken, is a difficult and delicate task; but that the position is not an impossible one is shown by the success which has attended your efforts to bring about a better state of things in Perak, and in which efforts I need hardly say you may count on my continued support.[39]

[37] Hugh Low to Sir William Robinson, 28 May 1878, CO 809/18.
[38] Ibid.
[39] Sir William Robinson to Low, 9 June 1878, CO 809/18.

This covered the relations between Resident and ruler, but it entirely ignored the fact that in the absence of any other executive government what had been done in Perak had been done by the Resident himself. The giving of advice, however authoritative it was, and however readily it was accepted, would in itself achieve nothing unless the Resident himself also acted as the chief executive officer in the state. This fact the Governor chose not to acknowledge. The Secretary of State, being even further removed from the scene of action, was able to detach himself yet further from reality. After commending the Governor's judicious handling of the situation he added:

I am glad to be able to add that I feel that I can rely on your keeping a watchful eye on the proceedings of the Residents, and taking care that they do not exceed the proper functions.

But he also wrote:

I fully recognize the delicacy of the task imposed on the Residents, and am aware that much must be left to their discretion on occasions when prompt and firm action is called for.[40]

In other words, he was quite ready to allow the Residents to tackle their problems in their own way, and to refrain from asking awkward questions about the way in which results were obtained. But he shelved on to the Governor's shoulders the responsibility for any departure from the policy of advice in case trouble resulted.

There was thus an implied recognition at each level—Secretary of State, Governor, and Resident—that 'government by advice' was only a constitutional fiction. But both Secretary of State and Governor evaded any explicit admission that this was the case, and were quite prepared, in case of trouble, to disavow all knowledge that anything but advice had been practised. Sir William Robinson served clear notice on the Residents to this effect in his letter of 17 May 1878, when he warned them that if they ran into trouble as the result of any action which went beyond the giving of advice 'they will most assuredly be held responsible'. The Residents, in Swettenham's words, 'accepted the responsibility as preferable to a position of impotence'.[41] Hugh Low put the position quite clearly:

⁴⁰ Sec. State to Gov. Straits, 31 Aug. 1878, ibid.
⁴¹ Swettenham, *British Malaya*, p. 221.

I am not in the least afraid of taking the responsibility of the course I am pursuing, and if it fails I must have the blame; it is too early to certainly prophesy success, but I do hope in two years more to have laid a foundation in which a lasting Government may be built up; . . .[42]

(ii) *The Later Development of British Malaya*

The later development of the Resident system has been described fully by Sir Frank Swettenham, and analysed in several other books on Malaya, and need not detain us long here.[43] We have already indicated the ambiguous constitutional position of the Residents in Perak, Selangor and Sungai Ujong, and the practical limitations of their function as advisers. But for a long time communications remained slow and primitive; Singapore was far away, London a remote and unreal world. In practice therefore a Resident who was willing to take the responsibility ruled his state almost as a benevolent despot, without much outside interference. The State Councils, on which sat the ruler, the most important chiefs, and representative Chinese, provided a useful forum for discussion and for the education of opinion, if the Resident wished to use it. In most cases however he ruled through his own officials, and in each state a separate civil service, with Englishmen recruited for the key posts, soon came into being. In the condition in which the west-coast states were in 1877 the form of government did not much matter; it was enough that there was government. Stability and order produced a great increase in trade and revenue, and all the states were soon able to pay off their debts.

Since we cannot here embark on an account of the administrative and economic development of the west-coast states after 1877 we can best close this account of the origin of British political control in Malaya by indicating briefly the way in which it was extended to the remaining Malay states of the Peninsula.

In 1885 a new treaty was negotiated between the British Government and Johore. Its terms indicated the growth of the Maharaja's influence in the Peninsula since 1867, as well as the new position which the British Government had taken up there. The Maharaja and his descendants were now recognized as Sultans of Johore,

---

[42] Low to Robinson, 28 May 1878, loc. cit.

[43] Swettenham, *British Malaya* (1949 ed.), *passim*. See also Emerson, R., *Malaysia, a study in Direct and Indirect Rule* (1937); Lovat, Lady A., *Life of Sir Frederick Weld* (1914); and Thio, E., 'British Policy in the Malay Peninsula, 1880–1909', unpublished thesis, University of London (1956).

and given a formal promise of protection from external attack. At the same time he placed the foreign relations of Johore in British hands (where in theory their control had lain since 1862[44]), undertook not to interfere in the other states, and promised not to grant concessions to foreign Europeans or European-owned companies. The treaty of 1885 also made provision for a British Officer to be appointed to Johore with powers 'similar to those of a Consular officer'.[45]

This treaty merely recognized the existing state of affairs in Johore; no British Agent was ever appointed, and the Sultan continued his traditional policy of close personal collaboration with the Governor of the Straits Settlements. But the treaty itself played an important part in the extension of British control over the neighbouring state of Pahang in 1888. The Bendahara and the Sultan of Johore had by then long made their peace with each other, and become fast friends. In 1887, therefore, when the Bendahara saw that some form of concession to the British Government was inevitable, he was able to enlist the support of the Sultan, and to insist on a treaty modelled on that made with Johore two years before. He thus secured a more favourable position than that occupied by the rulers of the west-coast states. He was recognized as Sultan, and the British official sent to reside in Pahang had his functions confined to those of a Consul-General.[46] In the following year however the murder of a Chinese British subject in the Sultan's Court, in which the ruler himself was implicated, gave the Straits Government an opportunity to exert pressure. The Sultan was induced to write a letter asking for a British officer 'to assist us in matters relating to the Government of our country, on a similar system to that existing in the Malay States under English protection'.[47] From 1888 onwards therefore there was a British Resident in Pahang with exactly the same powers as those in Perak and Selangor.

In the same period there was also an extension of British influence in Negri Sembilan. From 1876 the historian can observe

[44] Under Art. 8 of the treaty signed by Pahang and Johore in that year. See above, p. 16 and Maxwell and Gibson, op. cit., p. 210.
[45] Text in Maxwell and Gibson, op. cit., pp. 132–3. This treaty is unique among Malay treaties in that it was signed in Downing Street by the Sultan and the Secretary of State in person.
[46] Ibid., pp. 66–68.
[47] Ibid., pp. 68–69; Clifford, Sir H., The Further Side of Silence (1920) pp. 280 et seq.

two distinct but connected processes going on there: first, the gradual coalescing of the many small states into larger units and wider confederations, and second, the extension of the Resident system from Sungai Ujong to the other parts of Negri Sembilan, and the gradual increase in the *de jure* element in British influence there. The agreement of 1876[48] had created the Sri Menanti confederation of seven states. Apart from Sungai Ujong this left Jelebu, Rembau and Tampin outside. In 1883 and 1886 agreements were concluded with Jelebu which resulted in a British 'Collector' exercising in that state more or less the same functions as the Residents elsewhere under the general supervision of the Resident of Sungai Ujong.[49] In 1887 another British officer, with somewhat more restricted powers, but with complete control over revenue matters, was installed in Rembau.[50] At the same time supervision over the external affairs of the Sri Menanti confederacy was transferred from the Sultan of Johore to the British Government, and the confederacy promised to make no grants of land to foreign Europeans without British permission.[51] Then in 1889 Tampin and Rembau joined the Sri Menanti confederacy, which now became nine states in fact as well as in name, and to which we can justly apply the historic title of *Negri Sembilan*. Each of the rulers asked for a British Resident to assist in governing the states, and jointly and severally placed themselves under British protection.[52]

The logical conclusion of this development was the Agreement of 1895, whereby all these small states sorted themselves out into six separate units. Two of these were Sungai Ujong and Jelebu. The others were Tampin, Johol, Sri Menanti and Rembau which swallowed up six other smaller states. Thus was formed a Confederation of six states bearing the name of Negri Sembilan (the Nine States). They jointly placed themselves under the protection of the British Government, and asked for a British Resident, whose advice they agreed to follow 'on all matters of administration other than those touching the Mohammedan religion'.[53]

---

[48] See pp. 249–50 above.
[49] Maxwell and Gibson, op. cit., pp. 53–57.
[50] Agreement of 17 Sept. 1887, ibid., pp. 51–52.
[51] Ibid., pp. 61–62.
[52] Ibid., p. 63.
[53] 'Agreement between the Governor of the Straits Settlements . . . and the Rulers of certain Malay States hereinafter called the Negri Sembilan', 8 Aug. 1895, ibid., pp. 64–65.

Up till 1895 the administration of Perak, Selangor, Negri Sembilan and Pahang was conducted separately under the advice and control of their respective Residents. There was as yet no large-scale influx of European capital, and beyond the furnishing of their annual reports and financial estimates to the Governor the Residents were left very much to their own devices. As a result there were fundamental differences in administrative practice, and by the 1890's the states had drifted seriously apart in such matters as the administration of justice, taxation and land settlements. From about 1893 the Secretary of State and the Governor of the Straits Settlements began to consider some idea of federation, so as to ensure uniformity in these matters, and to increase the influence which the Governor could bring to bear on the conduct of administration.

The result was the Treaty of Federation of 1895.[54] This made of Perak, Selangor, Pahang and Negri Sembilan 'a Federation to be known as the Protected Malaya States'. The rulers, including those of each of the states of Negri Sembilan, agreed to accept a British Resident-General, and to accept his advice on the same terms as that of the Residents. The treaty also made provision for the richer states in the Federation to give assistance to the less fortunate by the provision of money or services, and for the Federation to contribute to the defence of the Straits Settlements in time of war.

Though the political entity thus formed was styled a Federation there was no delimitation of Federal and State powers. A clause in the treaty declared that it was:

not intended to curtail any of the powers or authority now held by any of the . . . Rulers in their respective States, nor . . . alter the relations now existing between any of the States named and the British Empire.

But the so-called Federation soon became in effect a union, with the Resident-General as its chief executive officer. The relations of this officer with the Residents meant that most of their control over policy quickly passed into his hands, and the development of large-scale European investment in tin and rubber after 1895 resulted in the proliferation of the specialist departments such as Public Works, Mines, Railways, Posts and Telegraphs, and so on,

[54] Maxwell and Gibson, pp. 70–71.

with their headquarters at the Federal capital of Kuala Lumpur. The Federal heads of these departments quickly took a large share of the responsibility for day-to-day administrative matters too out of the hands of the Resident. In 1909 this situation was to a certain extent recognized and regularized by the creation of a Federal Legislative Council, with power to enact laws for all the Federated Malay States.[55] From that point until 1940, though several attempts were made to loosen the control of the Federal Secretariat and to devolve some of its powers again on to the states, and though the title of Resident-General was changed in 1911 to that of Chief Secretary, his position in the Federated States was not materially altered.

Up to 1909, whilst this constitutional development was proceeding in what became known as the Federated Malay States, the other states of the Peninsula remained outside the sphere of British control. In that year however four of the northern states, Kedah, Perlis, Kelantan and Trengganu, were transferred from the Siamese to the British sphere of influence by agreement between the British and Siamese Governments. The history of this transaction is still obscure,[56] but the main features of British policy at this time can be fairly well discerned. The status of these four states was still determined by the terms of the Treaty of 1826, which since Sir Harry Ord's time had been interpreted as recognizing Siamese suzerainty over Kelantan and Trengganu as well as over the two west-coast states. During the period of Anglo-French rivalry in the Indochinese Peninsula it was a cardinal point of British policy to avoid bringing pressure on Siam, so as to retain her trust as against France, and to avoid weakening her capacity to maintain her independence. The main consideration involved in this calculation was the security of the eastern borders of the Indian Empire, but the British Government was also concerned to avoid any foreign intervention in the Malay Peninsula.

[55] Agreement for the Constitution of a Federal Council, 20 Oct. 1909, ibid., pp. 71–73. It is ironic that one of the motives for the creation of the Federal Council was to improve the positions of the Sultans by giving them a voice in the Federation's affairs at the policy-making stage. But though they were included in the Council, they sat at its meetings, and voted, on the same level as the other members—the High Commissioner, the Resident-General, the four Residents, and four unofficial members—and in the executive sphere the control of affairs remained where it had been before, in the hands of the Resident-General. It was not however until 1927 that the Sultans were removed from a position of some indignity, and ceased to sit in the Council.

[56] See Thio, op. cit., for a detailed discussion of this incident.

The support of colonial officials in Singapore for Malay claims to independence from Siamese control was therefore not sufficient to reverse Foreign Office attitudes to the subject.

After the turn of the century however the Foreign Office officials were less worried about France, with whom Britain had reached an understanding in the Indochinese Peninsula, than the new sea-power of Germany, whose merchants and consular officials became very active in Siam. In agreeing to a formalization of the relations between Siam and the two east-coast states of Kelantan and Trengganu in 1902 Britain secured an assurance that these states would not deal with any foreign Power except through the Siamese Government. They were also precluded from granting concessions to, or employing, anyone except a native of the state concerned without the express consent of Siam, and both states agreed to take a Siamese Adviser to see that these clauses were carried out.[57] The British Government had at this time a secret understanding with Siam dated 1897 on which they felt they could rely to keep out foreign competitors,[58] and in fact the Siamese Advisers when they were appointed in these states and also a year or two later in Kedah and Perlis, were Englishmen in Siamese employment.[59]

The special British position in this area was finally consolidated in the Treaty of 1909.[60] In addition to transferring Kedah, Perlis, Trengganu and Kelantan from Siamese to British control this treaty also pledged the Siamese Government not to allow any other Power to establish itself in that portion of the Malay Peninsula which remained under Siamese control:

. . . the Siamese Government shall not cede or lease, directly or indirectly, to any foreign Government any territory situated in the Malay Peninsula south of the southern boundary of the Monthon or Rajaburi or in any of the islands adjacent to the said territory; also that within the limits above mentioned a right to establish or lease any

[57] Declaration and Draft Agreement with Siam relating to Kelantan and Trengganu, 1902, ibid., pp. 85–88.

[58] This secret treaty was published in 1909, after the signature of the public treaty of that year (*British and Foreign State Papers* (1908–9), cii, 124–5). Under its provisions Siam undertook not to cede or alienate to another Power any part of the Peninsula, nor to grant any special advantage, as regards land or trade to the governments or subjects of any other Power without the written consent of the British Government.

[59] The Siamese Advisers in Kedah and Perlis dated from 1905, when Siam took advantage of the bankruptcy of these states to place advisers there as the condition of a loan (cf. Kedah and Perlis, 'Loan Agreements with Siam, 1905', Maxwell and Gibson, op. cit., pp. 101–2 and 105–6).

[60] Ibid., pp. 88–90.

coaling station, to build or own any construction or repairing docks, or to occupy exclusively any harbours the occupation of which would be likely to be prejudicial to British interests from a strategic point of view, shall not be granted to any foreign Government or Company.[61]

The ultimate result of the transfer of Siamese rights in the northern states to Britain was that British Advisers were established in these states in exactly the same position as the Residents had occupied in the west-coast states before the Treaty of Federation of 1895. The position of the British Adviser in Kelantan was covered by a treaty signed in 1910, by which the Sultan agreed to accept the Adviser's advice in all matters of administration 'other than those touching the Mohammedan religion and Malay custom'.[62] Similar treaties were however not concluded with Trengganu until 1919, and with Kedah until 1923.[63] In Perlis the Adviser's position seems never to have been given a juridical basis until the conclusion of a treaty in 1930 containing the usual formula about the Resident's advice.[64] But whatever the legal position, the British Advisers exercised *de facto* control over policy in all these states after 1909.

Johore, which had been the state longest and most intimately associated with the government of the Straits Settlements, was the last to take a British Adviser and to come formally under British control so far as its internal administration was concerned. The Colonial Office had ruled in 1894 that the relations between Johore and Britain under the treaty of 1885 were those 'of alliance and not of suzerainty and dependence'. They made no move to take advantage of the clause in the treaty which provided for the appointment of a British Consular Agent in Johore, and the excellent relations between that state and the British authorities in Singapore remained, as before, based upon the character and good sense of the Sultan. He continued to avail himself of the services of private European advisers from Singapore, and in 1909

---

[61] Annex III to the Treaty of 1909, ibid., p. 93.
[62] Ibid, pp. 109–11.
[63] Agreement of 1923 with Kedah, ibid., pp. 104–5; Agreement of 1919 with Trengganu, ibid., pp. 113–14. An earlier Agreement concluded with Trengganu in 1910 only provided for an officer of consular status to be stationed in Trengganu.
[64] Except so far as the Adviser's actions were covered by the rights previously held to be exercised by Siam in the state, and transferred to the British Government by the Treaty of 1909. These rights however had never been defined, and only explicit provision for an Adviser was contained in the state's Loan Agreement with Siam of 1905 (cf. Emerson, op. cit., p. 246).

he was actually lent a Colonial Service officer to help in the reorganization of the Johore Government. The political acumen of
the Sultan himself was not, however, enough to ensure reasonably
high standards of administration in circumstances in which the
alien population of the state and the tempo of its economic development were rapidly increasing. In 1914 a scandal over prison
conditions in Johore Bahru was the signal for the British Government to press the Sultan to accept a British Adviser and to increase the number of European officials in the state's service. The
Treaty of 1914 made provision for such an officer, whom in deference to the Sultan it called a 'General Adviser'. His position
none the less was the same as that of the Residents and Advisers in
the other states, in that his advice had to be asked and taken, though
it was agreed that when there was a difference between Sultan and
Adviser the opinion of the State Council should be taken and
communicated to the Governor of the Straits Settlements along
with the Adviser's report.[65]

The placing of an Adviser in Johore in 1914 completed the
process started in 1874 in Perak, and brought the whole of the
Peninsula south of the present Siamese frontier within the sphere
of British control, cloaked in the forms of 'government by advice'.
This brief account has sought to indicate in outline the way in
which British control was extended after 1878 to the remaining
states of the Peninsula in order to give the more detailed analysis
of events prior to the date added meaning and significance. It is not
possible here to enter in any detail into the differences in administrative practice between the Federated Malay States and those
which came under British control at a later date. We may note
merely that British control tended to be most obvious, and to
intrude most directly into the daily life of the people, in the west-
coast states which were 'federated' in 1895, and which were most
affected by economic development. This was especially the case
after 1895, when foreign investment in tin and rubber undertakings
in these states increased rapidly as result of increased demand for
these products on the world market. Apart from the Federated
States it was Kedah and even more Johore which were affected by
this new economic development, especially after the completion

[65] 'Agreement between His Britannic Majesty's Government and the State
of Johore, 1914, as supplemented by an exchange of letters between the Sultan
of Johore and the High Commissioner for the Malay States, May 1914', Maxwell
and Gibson, op. cit., pp. 134–6.

of the north–south railway from Singapore to a point opposite Penang in 1909, and it was this development which was the basic reason for Johore's formal inclusion within the British control system in 1914. So far as the northern states which were acquired from Siam were concerned the primary British motive seems to have been strategic—the desire to deny to a foreign power (and especially a foreign sea-power) a footing in a potentially important area. It was the same motive which had played a part in Kimberley's decision to take action in Selangor and Perak thirty years before, though here British and Chinese economic interests and ambitions were far less prominent.

What does emerge from this brief summary of later developments is the fact that the factors which we have marked as influencing British policy in the 1870's continued to operate in the period 1878–1914. The desire for insurance against hostile intrusion on the main sea route to the East, or on the Bay of Bengal, seems throughout to have been the predominant motive for all extensions of British responsibility, with the local economic motive usually less important. This can be seen in the case of the transference of the northern states from Siam to Britain. It is apparent too outside Malaya in the declaration of British protectorates over Sarawak, Brunei and British North Borneo in 1888. The continuing process of expansion of the area under their control which this desire for security allowed the Government of the Straits Settlements to set in motion and to direct, thus resulted by 1914 in the formation of the administrative framework which Malaya retained until the Second World War. The Straits Settlements, the Federated Malay States, and the Unfederated Malay States, each possessed distinctive features which marked them off from their neighbours. But in all there was one common feature—the fact of British control was a reality everywhere, no matter in what constitutional forms it was clothed.

8

REVIEW

THE initial purpose of this study was to analyse the way in which Britain came to intervene in the affairs of the Malay States in the 1870's, and, in so far as this intervention represented a major change of policy, to determine its cause or causes. The first question which arose was why the traditional policy of non-intervention was abandoned for one of active interference. The answers we obtained were of three sorts. First, there were a number of factors which created conditions favourable to intervention—changes in trade patterns, increased commercial interest in the Malayan Peninsula, the disintegration of local Malay authority, and the need of the British settlements to take steps to protect their own internal security, and that of their trade. Secondly, there were instances where the authorities in Whitehall had taken all or some of these factors under consideration, and had reached definite policy decisions governing action in Malaya. Of these one may mention the arrangements made in 1868 for the Straits Settlements' external relations, the directive given to Sir Andrew Clarke in 1873, and the attitude taken towards Sir William Jervois in 1876 and 1877. Thirdly and lastly, it was possible to explain many of the steps taken in Malaya in these years as the unauthorized actions of Governors and colonial officials which were either subsequently approved by the Imperial Government or which, though they were disapproved, could not be undone. Obvious examples of this are Anson's intervention in Selangor in 1871, Clarke's *fait accompli* at Pangkor in 1874, and Jervois's attempt at disguised annexation which precipitated the Perak War in 1875.

The presence of these different strands, and the broad outline of the pattern formed by them, is clear. What is obscure is their relative importance, the prominence which each ought to be given in the completed picture. In tackling this difficult question we come up against a problem which plagues every historian who attempts to analyse the process of imperial expansion in the nineteenth century. This arises from the many different levels and different locations, at the centre and the periphery, where policy was to some extent shaped and executed. A measure favoured among official circles in the Colonial Office for one reason, or reasons, is approved by the Minister for quite a different one, and then justified by him to the Cabinet or the Prime Minister on other grounds again. By this time events in the colony in question have outrun the power of the central government to control them, largely because of the local officials on the spot. They have probably already become aware of the attitudes of the different authorities at the centre, and have allowed themselves not only to anticipate their decision but to exceed it. In this sort of situation, which is common in the colonial history of other states as well as Britain, it becomes almost impossible to track down the origins of a policy, or to assign reasons or causes to events with any confidence.

The material in the chapter devoted to the evolution of policy in London indicates that probably the most important factor in the development of a forward policy in Malaya was the desire to prevent any other Power from gaining an opening there. In so far as one thinks in terms of the course of events in London, and concentrates on the way in which things happened rather than on their underlaying causes, this is undoubtedly a correct estimate. Though the officials in the Colonial Office came to see that they must do something about 'these contentious Chinese', who kept Penang and the frontiers of Province Wellesley in uproar, they had no enthusiasm on that account for wholesale intervention in Malaya. Even less were they prepared to help merchants and investors who embroiled themselves in the Malay States without their encouragement. It was when some of these investors used blackmail and threatened to call in the help of some other Power, that things moved. The chronological evidence, the dates of the despatches and minutes, and the order of events, make it certain that it was the letter from Seymour Clarke about the Selangor Tin Mining Company, not the despatches from Sir Harry Ord about conditions in Malaya, which prompted Kimberley's change of front in 1873.

The Malacca Straits area was so important to the over-all distribution of British trade, the China trading interests so powerful, and Foreign Office and Admiralty ideas on the subject so precisely formulated, that it was only necessary for a situation to develop which made foreign intervention even a remote possibility for action to be taken. One has to remember in this connection that

events in the Peninsula itself were not the only thing which tended
to draw attention to the area at this time. The Foreign Office and
the Admiralty, as we have seen, had decided that there was no
danger in agreeing to the extension of Dutch control over the
whole of the Sumatran side of the Straits. But the attempts of the
Atjehnese to secure support against the Dutch from some other
European Power, or from the United States, kept the eyes of the
Foreign Office and of the British Cabinet on the area. They also
made the Liberal Government sensitive to accusations from the
Conservative side that they had needlessly surrendered an important British interest in agreeing to the Anglo-Dutch Sumatra
Convention of 1871.[1] It followed also from this background that
the Conservatives, when they came into office in 1874, were not in
a position to take any action which could be represented amongst
their own followers as weakening the British position in the Straits,
though they were not particularly anxious to add to British responsibilities in the Malay States.

   The difficulty is that in evaluating the importance of this strategic element in the Malayan situation one has to consider general
attitudes rather than being able to handle detailed evidence. The
reasoning in the preceding paragraph, though sound enough, is
largely conjecture based on the known attitudes of the departments
of state concerned several years before, when the Sumatra treaty and
the position in North Borneo were under consideration. The concrete
evidence is slender—a few sentences in a minute by Kimberley,
an exchange of letters with Gladstone, and later the minutes and
memoranda of Carnarvon on Malaya and Fiji, and some of Disraeli's speeches, all of which have been noted in the course of
this study. Some British statesmen were already apprehensive of
the effects of German unification on the balance of power in
Europe, but so early as 1873 and 1874 there was no active fear in
London of German colonial aspirations. There is no evidence at
all that there was any likelihood of foreign intervention in Malaya
at that time, though the name of Germany, and even of Siam, was
freely used by Seymour Clarke. Whether the British governments
of the day really thought that the danger of foreign intervention
existed is a question which cannot be answered. Because of the

   [1] Tarling, *British Policy in the Malay Peninsula and Archipelago, 1824–71*,
JRASMB, vol. XXX, pt. 3, 1957 contains a detailed study of British policy in
this area before 1871, but since it did not in fact appear until May 1960 it has
not been available to the author of this book.
   S

nature of Imperial interests in the Eastern colonies discussions of high policy on this topic were conducted usually by ministers in private rather than by civil servants in official minutes, and very few records of these discussions have so far come to light. The bulk of the official material concerns colonial domestic issues, most of which involved questions of finance and were decided in consultation with the Treasury. There, as Herbert himself remarked, the permanent staff were masters in their own house. They made their decisions purely on financial considerations, and worked through the official machine. The papers on these subjects are therefore full and complete. On matters of 'foreign' policy however the reverse seems to have been the case. The affairs of the Eastern colonies raised commercial and strategic issues which invaded the sphere of the Foreign Office, rather than 'colonial' questions as the term was then interpreted. In the Foreign Office the officials occupied in the 1870's a far humbler position than their confrères in the Treasury or the Colonial Office. So discussion on these topics soon moved outside the sphere of official minutes and interdepartmental correspondence, and into that of table conversation between ministers. We find files closed by a ministerial endorsement, 'I will speak to Lord Granville about this', or by instructions to

. . . send this with the papers to which it refers to the F.O. saying I propose to send it with Lord Granville's concurrence. Let them know privately that the despatch *is* concurred in by Ld. Granville and approved by the Cabinet.[2]

So far as the Malayan end of the story is concerned the thing which stands out is the extent to which events were precipitated by the uncontrolled action of successive governors, and this despite the fact that for most of the period the telegraph line from Europe was in operation. The hesitant way in which policy was formulated in London put governors like Sir Andrew Clarke and Sir William Jervois into a position of opportunity. The use which they made of this opportunity was determined in each case by a different mixture of personal ambition, of preoccupation with the needs of the Straits Settlements as against other Imperial interests, and of a disinterested belief in the rightness of extending the *pax Britannica* to the Malay States. In Sir William Jervois the element

[2] Kimberley's minute of 10 May, 1873, in CO 273/66.

of personal ambition was more obvious than in Sir Andrew Clarke. But both were vigorous men of action, on the threshold of the most important period in their careers. Both arrived in Singapore at critical moments in the history of the Peninsula, knowing little of local affairs, and were easily brought to share the opinion of local officials and merchants that action was necessary beyond the limits laid down by official policy. In the event both men were able to commit the metropolitan power to a course of action which the central government was unable to reverse, however many Parliamentary Papers it might produce to demonstrate that its representative had been wrong. Thus, events in Malaya having produced conditions making for intervention, and the way in which the affair was handled in London having produced an opportunity for independent action on the spot, the effective cause of the British forward movement in Malaya was from this point of view the character and ambition of Clarke and Jervois. Sir Harry Ord had quite as much ambition as either of them. But he had not the opportunity for action. Sir Andrew Clarke, through his political connexions in England, and no doubt as result of interviews with Kimberley before he left London, knew how far he could go and still carry the government of the day with him. Jervois, perhaps less well informed, perhaps because of a natural arrogance, went too far. But even he was ultimately able to outface the Imperial government. He was not dismissed, and the essence of his policy was carried out under a face-saving formula.

For the explanation of this one has to look partly to the logic of the situation, which made retreat from the Peninsula impossible and offered no other alternative than that of taking over the control of the affected states, however this might be disguised by the use of the word 'advice'. But behind this logic, which imposed itself alike on Liberal and Conservative governments, was a change in the climate of opinion in Britain itself. Anti-colonialism had worked itself out as an effective force in politics. A desire to preserve the Empire, and a recognition of the Imperial Government's responsibility to protect the traders' frontier in the general interest, was beginning to penetrate the thinking of both political parties and to undermine the earlier predominance of the Manchester school. The full-blooded imperialism of 'jingo' was an extreme manifestation of this, but all sides of opinion in Britain were beginning to be aware that under the threat of foreign competition their country needed to bestir herself to retain her predominant position overseas.

For the most part this study has been concerned to explain the mechanics of the extension of the Imperial frontier in Malaya, to demonstrate step by step how intervention in the Malay States came about, and to examine the events of these years from 1867 to 1877 in detail. In so far as it has broken new ground its result has been to throw some new light on the accounts of the pioneer historians, who were forced to treat this period as part of a much larger story, and to whom a great deal of the Colonial Office material was not available. What it has not been able to do is to establish clear-cut and concrete links of cause and effect on the policy level.

One can however distinguish a number of factors which in one way or other influenced developments in Malaya at this time. The increase in the amount of trade which the Singapore merchants carried on with South-East Asia in proportion to the total trade of the port, the short-term rise in the price of tin between 1869 and 1873, and the debts and concessions which prominent Singapore figures came to hold in the Malay States as a result of the political upheavals there in these years, all combined to build up their interest in the area. This interest was communicated to the colonial officials in the Straits Settlements. Problems of internal security which the disturbances in the Peninsula caused within the British settlements also brought the officials to regard some form of intervention there as a necessity. Lastly, in addition to worrying about the internal security of the Straits Settlements, officials and ministers in Whitehall were disturbed by the apparent growth of other powers' interest in Indonesia and Malaya, and by the more or less remote possibility that one of them might seize the opportunity to intervene in the Peninsula.

The evidence is nowhere strong enough for us to point to one or other of these factors and say *this* or *this* was the reason for the British forward movement in Malaya. As so often in history it is impossible to make all stem from a single cause without distorting some of the facts. Instead we have to accept a more complex picture in which considerations of public policy and private commercial interest are intermixed with personal ambition and individual idiosyncrasy. Commercial interests partly stimulated the

disintegration of Malay politics on the west coast of the Peninsula
since they helped to inject the disturbing element of the Chinese
tin miner into the situation. But at the same time the quarrels
of the Malays provided individual merchants with the opportunity
to acquire claims and to make loans in return either for specific
concessions or the general hope of large returns at some future
date. These economic developments were undoubtedly important
in that they created a bond of financial interest between European
and Chinese circles in the Straits Settlements on the one hand,
and the participants in the struggles in the Malay States on the
other. They do not seem to have excited much interest amongst
the London connexions of the Straits merchants, but they certainly
enlisted for these merchants the sympathies of most of the Straits
Settlements officials. This was partly because these officials identified the welfare of the settlements under their control with the
prosperity of their merchants, but also because it gave to them the
opportunity of activities more interesting and more important
than the normal routine of a small Crown colony. It was this
mixture of economic and political developments which prompted
the Chinese merchants of the Straits Settlements to appeal to the
British Government to protect their interests in Malaya, and which
placed the promoters of the Selangor Tin Mining Company in
a position from which they were able to put pressure on that
Government. But it was not the interests of merchants which
prompted the British Government to contemplate some form of
intervention in the tin states. It was the policy, then some fifty
years old, which saw it as a major interest of Britain to deny to
any other Power a footing on the Malayan Peninsula which might
threaten the free navigation of the Eastern trade route.

The British Government had never been, and were not in 1873,
interested in the Malay States for their own sakes. Their prime
concern was British trade, especially trade with China, and their
interest in the Straits of Malacca and the South China Sea was
strategic, not colonial. They wished to prevent any other power
from becoming established in Malaya or North Borneo, not to become involved in these areas themselves. They therefore gave their
agent, Sir Andrew Clarke, orders which aimed at securing sufficient
stability in the area, and sufficient control over the actions of local
rulers, to deny to any other power an excuse for intervention. And
they hoped that he would achieve this without unduly involving

them in responsibility for the day-to-day conduct of affairs in the states concerned. That they did become so involved, in fact if not in theory, was the result of the ambition and individual initiative of their agents on the spot.

The fact that the Governors of the Straits Settlements after 1873 were able in the long run to impose their will on the government in London was partly the result of the distances involved and the inadequacies of communications. But it was also a direct result of a policy which refused to face facts, or to accept the responsibilities inherent in any sort of intervention. Persistence in advocating a policy of 'government by advice', and refusal to recognize that direct control was in fact being exercised, coupled with an insistence that results which could only be achieved through direct control ought to be forthcoming without it, brought disaster in 1875. Such a policy invited the Governors concerned to withhold unpalatable information, to misrepresent situations, and to refrain from correcting erroneous Colonial Office assessments of the position, in the hope that all would come right in the end, and that their own reputations would be enhanced. The same official viewpoint was maintained in the Colonial Office after the Perak War, but this time there was no major disaster. This was partly because Birch's murder had taught British officials discretion. But a large share in the credit for the success of the Resident system after the war belongs to the restraint of the Malay chiefs, who now offered no resistance to British control. Gradually indeed they came to realize that co-operation in the new régime brought benefits which outweighed its possible humiliations. The Pahang Revolt of 1891–2 was an exception which in many ways illustrates the point. It was started by an up-river chief who had already established a reputation for refusing to submit to the authority of the Sultan before the coming of a British Resident, and it was eventually put down largely by the Sultan and his own men.[3]

Thus the result of Colonial Office policy on the one hand and Malay acquiescence on the other was that an unsanctioned system of direct government by Residents developed which, however successful it may have been, was completely at variance with the *de jure* position. The gulf between practice and theory was only widened by the so-called Federation Agreement of 1895. For what resulted was not a federation of Malay states, but a union with a

---

[3] See Linehan, 'History of Pahang', *JRASMB* (1936), pp. 139 et seq.

British directed central government. This was the system under which the Federated Malay States were administered until the outbreak of the Japanese War. It was only in 1945 that the Colonial Office attempted to bring constitutional theory into line with facts by taking sovereignty in the separate states away from the Malay rulers, and creating a Malayan Union under the Crown. By then however the facts themselves had changed. The Malays were no longer willing to acquiesce in the old system, and they united in opposition to the introduction of the Malayan Union. Fortunately the British Government had by then had enough experience elsewhere to recognize the emergence of a nationalist movement when they saw one. The Union scheme was withdrawn, and in the Federation of Malaya, which has been an independent member of the Commonwealth since 1958, sovereignty and the control of government rest in the hands of the Malay rulers and the people of Malaya.

BIBLIOGRAPHY

I. MANUSCRIPT SOURCES

The main source for the history of Malaya in this period is the series of Colonial Office papers

CO 273.   *Straits Settlements, Original Correspondence, 1838–1919.*

used in conjunction with the series

CO 425.   *Straits Settlements, Entry Books, 1867–73.*
CO 426.   *Straits Settlements, Register of Correspondence, 1867–1919.*

In addition to the Colonial Office correspondence and papers CO 273 contains copies of most of the important documents for the thirty years before 1867 from the files of the India Office (CO 273/1–9, 14 and 15) Many of the originals have since been destroyed.

For British policy in the Malayan area the following series of papers are also important.

CO 144.   *Labuan, Original Correspondence, from 1846.*
FO 71.   *Correspondence relating to Sulu, 1849–1878.*
FO 12.   *Correspondence relating to Borneo, from 1842.*

The following private collections also contain important documents.

PRO 30/6. *Carnarvon Papers, various correspondence, 1872–78.*
PRO 30/29. *Granville Private Correspondence.*

All the above are deposited at the Public Record Office. Further private collections are

Kimberley Papers, at Kimberley, Norfolk, in the possession of the present Earl.
Gladstone Papers, Add. MSS. 44224–44229 and 44641–44648, in the British Museum.

II. OFFICIAL PRINT

CO 809.   *Colonial Office Confidential Prints*

In the main duplicate the published Parliamentary Papers, though there are some documents not to be found therein, especially in later prints such as CO 809/18, *Instructions to Residents and Reports on the State of Protected States* (1878).

Foreign Office Confidential Prints

The most important of these are:

Correspondence respecting the Policy of the Netherlands Government in the Eastern Seas, as affecting British Commerce. 17 Sept. 1867. Confidential Memo on the Sumatra and Gold Coast Treaties with the Netherlands, 1870–71. 29 Jan. 1874.
Treaties, Conventions, etc., between the Dutch and Native Princes in the Eastern Seas: Communicated by the Netherlands Government under the Treaty of 1824, 1843–64. Dec. 1864.
Ditto for years 1865–66. Mar. 1867.

Parliamentary Papers

There are a large number of these which bear to some extent on the subject. The following select list of numbers and abbreviated titles includes all cited in the text of this study. Parliamentary Papers are differently paginated in the single papers and the annual bound volumes. The references to individual pages in the text are to the internal pagination of single papers. The references given here are to the pagination in the annual volumes, so that the paper concerned can be located in the bound set.

Correspondence relating to the transfer of the Straits Settlements to the Colonial Office (July 1858–Dec. 1861), [259] H.C. (1862), xl, 583.
The Trengganu Incident (Nov. 1862), [541] H.C. (1863), xliii, 299.
Further Correspondence relating to the Transfer (Mar. 1863–June 1866), [3672] H.C. & H.L. (1866), lii, 687.
The Selangor Incident (1871), [C.466] H.C. & H.L. (1872), lxx, 661.
Correspondence relating to Native States in the Peninsula (Nov. 1872–Mar. 1874), [C.1111] H.C. & H.L. (1874), xlv, 611.
Further Correspondence relating to Native States . . . (Nov. 1874–July 1875), [C.1320] H.C. & H.L. (1875), liii, 55.
Ditto (July 1875–Feb. 1876), [C.1505] H.C. & H.L. (1876), liv, 287.
Ditto (Feb.–May 1876), [C.1510] H.C. & H.L. (1876), liv., 637 (erroneously numbered [C.1503] in some single papers).
Ditto (Jan. 1876–June 1876), [C.1512] H.C. & H.L. (1876), liv. 669.
Ditto (Apr. 1876–Mar. 1877), [C.1709] H.C. & H.L. (1877), lxi, 395.

Of the publications of the local government of the Straits Settlements the following were used in this study:

Annual Blue Books of the Colony, from 1868.
Report of the Commissioners appointed to enquire into the Penang Riots of 1867. Penang, 1868.
Enquiry as to Complicity of Chiefs in the Perak Outrages. Précis of Evidence. Singapore, 1876.
Proceedings of the Legislative Council of the Straits Settlements. Annual.

T

III. NEWSPAPERS

The Times, London. The Times Quarterly Index is very comprehensive and useful for this period.

Singapore Daily Times (Straits Times). The file in the British Museum newspaper library begins Sept. 1873.

Penang Gazette & Straits Chronicle. Beginning 1871. There are complete files of these newspapers and of the *Singapore Free Press* in Raffles Museum, Singapore.

IV. BOOKS AND PUBLISHED PAPERS

(Published in London unless otherwise noted)

Anderson, J.: *Political and Commercial Relations of Prince of Wales Island with States on the East Coast of Sumatra*. Penang, 1824.

——: *On the Restoration of Banca and Malacca to the Dutch as Affecting the Tin Trade and General Commerce of Pinang*. Penang, 1824.

——: *Political and Commercial Considerations relative to the Malayan Peninsula and the British Settlements in the Straits of Malacca*. Penang, 1824.

Anson, Sir A. E.: *About Others and Myself, 1745–1920*. 1920.

Assey, C.: *On the Trade to China and the Indian Archipelago*, 1819.

Bickmore, A. S.: *Travels in the East Indian Archipelago*. 1868.

Bodelsen, C. A.: *Studies in mid-Victorian Imperialism*. Copenhagen, 1924.

Braddell, R. St. J.: *The Law of the Straits Settlements*. Singapore, 1915 ed.

Braddell: T.: *Statistics of the British Possessions in the Straits of Malacca*. Penang, 1861.

Buckley, C. B.: *An Anecdotal History of Old Times in Singapore, 1819–1867*. 2 vols., Singapore, 1902.

Cameron, J.: *Our Tropical Possessions in Malayan India: Singapore, Penang, Province Wellesley, Malacca*. 1865.

Clapham, Sir J. H.: *Economic History of Modern Britain*, vol. ii. 1932.

Cavenagh, General Sir O.: *Reminiscences of an Indian Official*. 1884.

Clodd, H. P.: *Malaya's First British Pioneer, the Life of Francis Light*. 1948.

Clowes, Sir W. Laird: *The Royal Navy, a History*, vol. vii. 1903.

Colenbrander, H. T.: *Koloniale Geschiedenis*, vol. iii. 's-Gravenhage, 1926.

Coope, A. E.: 'The Kanchu System in Johore', *JRASMB*, vol xiv, pt. 3, 1936.

Cowan, C. D. (Ed.): 'Early Penang and the Rise of Singapore', *JRASMB*, vol. xxiii, pt. 2, 1950.

——: 'Sir Frank Swettenham's Perak Journals', *JRASMB*, vol. xxiv, pt. 4, 1951.

D'Almeida, W. B., 'Geography of Perak and Selangore and the Surrounding States', *Journal Royal Geographical Society*, vi, 46, 1876.

Davidson, G. F.: *Trade and Travel in the Far East.* 1846.

Doyle, P.: *Tin Mining in Larut.* 1879.

Drus, Ethel: 'The Colonial Office and the Annexation of Fiji', *Trans. of the Royal Historical Society*, 4th series, vol. xxxii, 1950.

Dykes, F. J. B.: *Mining in Malaya.* 1912.

Emerson, R.: *Malaysia, a study in direct and indirect rule.* New York, 1937.

Fay, C. R.: *English Economic History*, mainly since 1700. Cambridge, 1948.

Fiddes, Sir G. V.: *The Dominions and Colonial Offices.* 1926.

Fitzmaurice, E. G.: *Life of Earl Granville.* 2 vols. 1905.

Flower. P. W.: *History of the Trade in Tin.* 1875.

Furnivall, J. S.: *Netherlands India.* 1944.

Gammans, L. D.: 'The State of Lukut', *JRASMB*, vol. ii, 1924.

Graham, W. A.: *Kelantan, a State of the Malay Peninsula.* 1908.

Gullick, J. M.: 'Sungei Ujong', *JRASMB*, vol. xxii, pt. 2, 1949.

——: 'Captain Speedy of Larut', *JRASMB*, vol. xxvi, pt. 2, 1953.

——: *Indigenous Political Systems of Western Malaya*, 1958.

Hardinge, Sir A.: *Life of the 4th Earl of Carnarvon.* 3 vols. 1925.

Hertslett, L. and E.: *Treaties and Conventions . . . between Great Britain and Foreign Powers, and Laws, Decrees and Orders in Council concerning the same, so far as they relate to Commerce and Navigation, the Slave Trade, etc.* (*Short title*: 'Treaties and Conventions'). 1820–77.

Irwin, G.: *Nineteenth-Century Borneo, a study in Diplomatic Rivalry.* 1955.

Jenkyns, H.: *British Rule and Jurisdiction beyond the Seas.* 1902.

Jones, J. H.: *The Tinplate Industry.* 1914.

van der Kemp, P. H.: *De Geschiedenis van het Londonsch tractaat van 17 Maart 1824.* Bijdragen van Taal-, Lande-, en Volkenkunde van Nederlandsch Indie, 1904.

De Klerck, E. S.: *History of the Netherlands East Indies.* Rotterdam, 1938.

Knaplund, P.: *Gladstone and Britain's Imperial Policy.* 1927.

Linehan, W.: 'A History of Pahang', *JRASMB*, vol. xiv, pt. 2, 1936.

Makepeace, Brooke and Braddell (Eds.): *One Hundred Years of Singapore.* 2 vols. 1921.

Marindin (Ed.): *Lord Blatchford's Letters.* 1896.

Maxwell and Gibson, (Eds.): *Treaties and Engagements affecting the Malay States and Borneo.* 1924.

May, E. C.: *The Canning Clan, a Pageant of Pioneering Americans.* New York, 1937.

Middlebrook, S. M.: 'Yap Ah Loy', *JRASMB*, vol. xxiv, pt. 2, 1951.

Mills, L. A.: 'British Malaya, 1824–1867', *JRASMB*, Vol. i, pt. 2, 1925.

——: *British Rule in Eastern Asia.* 1942.

Macnair, F.: *Perak and the Malays: Sarong and Kris.* 1878.

Morse, H. B.: *Chronicles of the East India Company trading to China*, vol. ii. 1926.

Newbold, T. J.: *Political and Statistical Account of the British Settle-ments in the Straits of Malacca . . . with a History of the Malay States on the Peninsula of Malacca.* 2 vols. 1839.

Parr and Mackray: 'Rembau', *JRASSB*, no. 56, 1910.

Purcell, V.: *The Chinese in Malaya.* 1948.

Raynal, Abbe P.: *Histoire Philosophique et Politique des Établissements et du Commerce des Européens dans les Deux Indes.* 4 vols. Geneva, 1780.

[Read, W. H.]: *Play and Politics, Recollections of Malaya by an Old Resident.* 1901.

Reinach, de L.: *Recueil des Traités conclus par la France en Extrême-Orient, 1684–1902.* Paris, 1902.

Sadka, Emily [Ed.], 'Journal of Sir Hugh Low, Perak, 1877', *JRASMB*, pt. 4, 1954.

Saleeby, N. M.: *The History of Sulu.* Manilla, 1908.

Schadee, W. H. M.: *Geschiedenis van Sumatra's Oostkust.* 2 vols. Amsterdam, 1918–19.

Sheppard, M. C. ff.: 'A Short History of Trengganu', *JRASMB*, vol. xxii, pt. 3, 1949.

Song Ong Siang: *One Hundred Years of the Chinese in Singapore.* 1923.

Straits Settlements, Report on the Progress of, from 1859–60 to 1866–67. Singapore, 1867.

——, *Tabular Statements of the Commerce and Shipping of, for the years 1853–58, 1862–66.* 3 vols. Calcutta, 1855–67.

Straits Settlements, the, or How to Govern a Colony, by a Singapore Merchant. 1869.

Swettenham, Sir F. A.: *British Malaya, an account of the Origin and Progress of British influence in Malaya.* 1906 (1st ed.)

——: *Footprints in Malaya.* 1942.

——: 'The Independent Native States of the Peninsula', *JRASSB*, 1880.

——: Perak Journals, 1874–76. *See* Cowan, C. D. (Ed.)

Treaties and Conventions (Commercial). *See* Hertslett.

Vetch, R. H.: *Life of Lieut.-General Sir A. Clarke.* 1905.

Wilkinson, R. J.: *A History of the Peninsular Malays, with Chapters on Perak and Selangor.* Singapore, 1923, (3rd Ed.).

——: 'Sungai Ujong', *JRASSB*, no. 83, 1921.

——: *See also* Winstedt and Wilkinson.

Winstedt, Sir R. O.: 'A History of Malaya', *JRASMB*, vol. xiii, pt. 1, 1935.

——: 'Notes on the History of Kedah', *JRASMB*, vol. xiv, pt. 3, 1936.

——: 'A History of Johore,' *JRASMB*, vol. x, pt. 3, 1932.

——: 'A History of Selangor', *JRASMB*, vol. xii, pt. 3, 1934.

——: 'Negri Sembilan, the History, Polity and Beliefs of the Nine States', *JRASMB*, vol. xii, pt. 3, 1934.

Winstedt and Wilkinson: 'A History of Perak', *JRASMB*, vol. xii, pt. 1, 1934.

Wright and Reid: *The Malay Peninsula, a Record of British Progress in the Middle East.* London, 1912.

INDEX

Set in Great Britain by
Spottiswoode, Ballantyne and Co. Ltd.,
and reprinted lithographically
by Halstan and Co., Ltd., Amersham.